Ball Tales

Ball Tales

*A Study of Baseball,
Basketball and Football
Fiction of the 1930s through 1960s*

MICHELLE NOLAN

McFarland & Company, Inc., Publishers
Jefferson, North Carolina, and London

LIBRARY OF CONGRESS CATALOGUING-IN-PUBLICATION DATA

Nolan, Michelle, 1948–
Ball tales : a study of baseball, basketball and football fiction
of the 1930s through 1960s / Michelle Nolan.
p.   cm.
Includes bibliographical references and index.

ISBN 978-0-7864-3985-0
softcover: 50# alkaline paper ∞

1. Sports stories, American — History and criticism.
2. Sports in literature.   I. Title.
PS374.S76N65   2010
813'.5093579 — dc22   2009051813

British Library cataloguing data are available

Cover images ©2009 Shutterstock

Manufactured in the United States of America

McFarland & Company, Inc., Publishers
Box 611, Jefferson, North Carolina 28640
www.mcfarlandpub.com

To my sports-loving son and inspiration, Ray Nolan; his wife, Nikol; and their daughter, Logan Grace, with all my love and respect. Ray's academic dedication and athletic skills, plus his consistent sportsmanship, never-quit nature and leadership in four team sports, make him my very own Chip Hilton. Thanks, Ray, for 16 inspiring years, 17 championships, 1,200 games and countless thrills, from your first Little League game through college baseball.

Table of Contents

Preface

When I first decided to write a comprehensive book about sports fiction, I realized I first had to determine just how comprehensive I wanted to be. I concluded that the most efficient way was to write primarily about sports fiction that had never been widely covered in books—or not covered well enough—and to focus on an area few writers have paid attention to: the pop cultural aspects of the baseball, football and basketball fiction of the 1930s through the 1960s.

I quickly realized that the academic and sociological aspects of sports fiction have been well covered in a handful of books, especially in three invaluable volumes by Michael Oriard, and in dozens of journals. I also realized that sports fiction in film has been thoroughly covered in several books, so my treatment of films is primarily an overview to whet your appetite. As for modern adult novels, plenty has been written about Bernard Malamud, Mark Harris, Peter Gent, Dan Jenkins and the handful of other noteworthy literary authors who emerged in the 1950s, 1960s and 1970s. That is why I have touched only lightly on these areas. I do try to provide a solid look at Frank Merriwell and what came before the 1930s, but I leave post–1970 books and films for someone more enthusiastic about them. (I do, however, love sports mysteries and films such as *Bull Durham* and *Hoosiers*, among many others.)

I also realized I wanted to confine this book almost entirely to the team sports I care about the most: baseball, football and basketball, along with girls' basketball and softball, although a good track, hockey, golf or tennis story can be fun, too. While some of the most compelling of all sports stories and films have dealt with boxing, I have no interest in that activity, so I leave it for someone else to examine.

I believe this is the most complete overview of the pop cultural aspects of baseball, football and basketball fiction ever presented, but I also realize I could easily have written twice as much. Some of my writing involves purely personal choices. I feel Clair Bee's Chip Hilton books are far more interesting than Wilfred McCormick's Bronc Burnett series, yet McCormick's numerous novels of Coach Rocky McCune are wonderful and highly evocative of a bygone era. In my opinion, John Tunis and Duane Decker wrote many of the best young-adult sports novels—unique, often innovative stories that many adult collectors still savor and read today. So I paid special attention to Tunis and Decker.

I recommend the vast majority of books in my bibliography. Oriard's books proved invaluable, although he writes from a different academic viewpoint. *Ball Tales* would be nowhere near as complete without the invaluable help of Andy McCue's *Baseball by the Books*, along with the monumental *A Collector's Guide to Hardcover Boys' Series Books* by E. Christian Mattson and Thomas B. Davis. John Axe's *All About Collecting Boys' Series Books* was also useful.

1

I owe more thanks than I can adequately express for the support and endless encouragement of book lovers Patty and Bob Lundquist, Bob and Karen Carter, and Russell and Noriko Ciochon, none of whom know anything about sports but all of whom know how to nurture an author. The fabulous bibliophiles Bud Plant and Anne Hutchison always helped keep my spirits up, and so did two personable collectors, readers and baseball fans, Dan Stevenson and Eric Moothart. You folks all score touchdowns and hit home runs in my book!

Introduction

For more than a century, untold thousands of baseball, football and basketball stories have been told in multiple formats, yet the story of these tales has never been covered in any comprehensive book. Enthusiasts have had to refer to a wide variety of seldom-seen original resources, ranging from rare dime novels to scarce pulp magazines and comic books, and from long-unseen movies to hard-to-find hardback novels originally sold mostly to libraries. The limited available information on sports fiction tends to focus on one topic, such as films, pulp magazines or academic aspects of the stories, or to include a tiny fraction of sports fiction as part of indices or price guides to young adult series books.

It would be impossible to locate and catalog every story, long and short, involving the heroes and antiheroes who cavorted on the diamonds and gridirons and in the gymnasiums of old. I've been collecting and reading sports fiction since the 1960s and I'm still making new discoveries every year in obscure publications. In every medium — books, pulps, film, comics— sports fiction is less than 1 or 2 percent of the total output.

The major heroes, beginning with Frank and Dick Merriwell in the Gilded Age nickel novels of the late 1890s, have been cataloged. Twentieth century baseball novels, in particular, have been reasonably well annotated. (There were only a handful of sports stories of any kind written until Gilbert Patten's Frank Merriwell debuted in 1896.) Film titles and descriptions of most plots are available, of course, even if many of the films aren't. In recent years, collectors have banded together to assist this writer with intense research into exactly what was published involving sports. Since collector interest has never been intense — sports pulps are collected mostly for their nostalgic covers— information from many years remained sketchy. I've been fortunate enough to have access to the files and collections of most of the nation's pulp authorities, so only a handful of "mysteries" remain to be solved, almost all involving the lesser-known Columbia and Red Circle/Marvel publications.

I have a collection of 750 of the 1,103 published sports issues produced in addition to *Sport Story* magazine's long run of 429 issues. Thus, I have been able to make meaningful surveys of the magazines, though discoveries doubtless remain to be made, both from the standpoints of well-known authors or their pseudonyms and the confirmation of the very existence of some heretofore unseen issues. When a publisher typically used three, four or six issues to a volume, or published with a certain frequency, one can logically assume the existence of certain unseen issues, much as astronomers extrapolate the existence of planets based on gravitational perturbations and other scientific evidence. Even so, I'm still trying to confirm the existence and contents of every sports magazine, not to mention adding to my collection. Other collectors have helped me fill in volume numbers and dates of issues I am still missing.

Nobody could possibly know about all the sports-related stories to be found in the thousands of pulp and slick magazines published from the 1920s through the 1950s (along with numerous stories both before and after that Golden Age of magazine fiction). And it wasn't just the sports pulp magazine: not a few stories with a sports angle appeared in the love and detective pulps. And what about the countless sports stories in the many magazines aimed at the youth market in the era before television? A few hundred pre–1970 sports stories have been anthologized, mostly not long after they originally appeared; yet many thousands more of those tales have been totally forgotten.

My collection is nowhere near complete, nor is anyone else's I've ever heard about during my more than four decades as an enthusiast. Many collectors have long sought these items in relative anonymity, since their value has seldom been enough to generate widespread enthusiasm, although that has slowly changed in recent years. There's a good reason that twentieth century science fiction and detective stories in the magazines have virtually all been indexed, and an equally understandable reason sports and romance sagas have gone largely unreported. Sports and romance stories have been the rag-tag relations of their far better known genre cousins.

The sports story market, with regard to both novels and short stories, tended to be dominated by a few dozen highly prolific authors, although distinguished genre writers such as John D. MacDonald and Louis L'Amour also penned a few tales on athletics. Writers who knew little or nothing about sports often could come up with an endless source of conflict-ridden plots. That is exactly what virtually all sports stories were about — conflict. The most compelling sports fiction, however, revealed the developing character of the protagonists rather than merely related their heroics in the games. Many stories could be frustrating; authors often made no effort to explain why the hero refused to tell the coach or his girlfriend about his troubles. "Strong silent types" were the bane of many a sports reader, not to mention their mythical coaches, parents, educators and girlfriends. Even more frustrating were the gangsters and lowlifes involved in so many sports stories; indeed, one might get the impression that "fixes" were attempted in seemingly every other "Big Game." Then, too, sports journalists were perhaps more often than not depicted as sleazy and unethical, when in reality the majority of sportswriters were just trying to make a living, usually in a fair-minded manner.

That, however, just makes the better sports stories and novels, involving complex plots and intriguing characters, that much more rewarding. Unlike other genre characters in days gone by, who were largely supermen and superwomen regardless of their fictional milieu, many of the on-field successes of sports heroes have been duplicated in real life. Few lawyers are remotely as successful or as interesting as Perry Mason, but many athletes are every bit as physically talented as Chip Hilton, if rarely as selfless.

That's why effective sports stories invariably needed (and still need) an "angle" to be intriguing, just as the best journalists look for the story behind the star athlete or the game-winning home run. What reader wouldn't feel more satisfied to learn that the rival quarterback was really "Our Hero's" brother, or a rival for the affections of "The Girl" instead of just reading about how our hero threw the winning touchdown pass? Just as the best real-life sportswriters today try to emphasize the human aspects of talented athletes in magazines and newspapers, so do the best storytellers try to stress motivation and character. What goes on in the minds of athletes can be every bit as fascinating, and often more so, as what the super detectives, space travelers or cowboys think.

Of course, you could survey 1,000 college football players, and only a handful could offer a story more dramatic than merely using exercise and practice to hone their natural skills for success. Coaches often don't like to acknowledge this fact: most athletic stars are genetic freaks, albeit also usually the products of hard work. And even athletes with dramatic backstories are more likely to have dealt with drugs, ill health or misdeeds than with nefarious gangsters, cruel coaches or scheming rivals. When was the last time you heard of a college or high school football hero being kidnapped?

Yet that opens the door to the real drama of sports: for most participants in real life, athletic success is relatively limited and failure is something to be dealt with all too often. Indeed, how athletes deal with failure often determines whether they will enjoy at least a modicum of success. The vast majority of high school, college or professional athletes eventually "max out" at a given level, and spend plenty of time on the bench or in frustrating situations involving more losses than victories. Even the finest quarterbacks see more than one-third of their passes fall incomplete; the best pitchers win only two-thirds of their games over their careers. The vast majority of athletes deal with quiet desperation and frequent frustration regardless of their level of success. Thus, the pulp story of the bench-warmer who finally gets the chance to make one game-winning play—even if he or she fails—is invariably more compelling than a tale of a "natural" who seldom loses.

Unlike most other genre fiction, sports has real-life counterparts with even more compelling and almost unbelievable stories. Fabulous movies or novels could have been written about Ken Griffey father and son, who hit consecutive home runs in 1990 for the Seattle Mariners, or U.S. Olympic goalkeeper Hope Solo, who heroically won a women's soccer gold medal in 2008 less than a year after being removed from the national team for making negative comments about her coach. Every year, at least one or two college football or basketball heroes emerge after they didn't make the cut in high school, or big-time pro performers develop who were college lesser lights. As television began to spread athletes' fame beginning in the 1950s, and as cable networks like ESPN made sports highlights a daily affair, most of the old sports fiction doesn't seem as compelling as sports fact.

A few highly literate writers, such as Mike Lupica and Carl Deuker, have kept sports fiction alive for young readers today—indeed, their novels are invariably far better than those written a half-century or more earlier—but athletic epics are now a minuscule fraction of young adult literature. Since the 1980s, more mystery novels with sports themes, many of them delightful, have been published than any other type of adult sports fiction, although the general sports genre began to come of age with a few sterling efforts in the 1950s and 1960s. I have several dozen wonderfully human sports novels written from the 1970s on.

As someone who has long been a journalist, with more than 10,000 published newspaper and magazine articles over 44 years, and as the fortunate parent of a successful athlete who participated in more than 1,200 games in four sports and won 17 championships as well as being a participant and coach, I have been involved in well over 7,000 games in team sports spanning more than half a century. Even so, as a collector of sports fiction, some of my most rewarding "athletic moments" continue to involve reading about athletes who never were, yet who surely were people I would love to have had the chance to cheer and get to know.

ONE

What Came Before: There Was Never Another Hero Like Frank Merriwell

In one respect, baseball, basketball and football fiction was never more iconic than the era shortly before and after the turn of the 20th century. The prolific author Gilbert Patten's highly moral sports superguy, Frank Merriwell, written as by Burt L. Standish, became far more famous in his era than any successor in the 1930s through the 1960s and beyond.

For boys (and many girls, too), Frank Merriwell was to juvenile sports stories what Sherlock Holmes was to adult detective tales—the unquestioned icon of his era. But while Holmes has had several iconic mystery story successors, such as Miss Marple, Nero Wolfe and Perry Mason, no one with the cultural impact of Merriwell and his family has ever appeared again. As popular as famed basketball coach Clair Bee's hero, Chip Hilton, became from the late 1940s to the mid 1960s, his adventures were published in only 23 books (with a 24th following posthumously many years later).

It's likely that almost all of the authors of sports novels through the 1960s and of sports stories in the pulp magazines, which ended in the 1950s, grew up reading the Merriwell stories in either paperback or hardcover format. Virtually all adult males in the first half of the 20th century knew just what sportswriters meant when they said some real-life sports hero "pulled a Merriwell"—a dramatic game winning performance. To paraphrase a thousand newspaper accounts of heroics, "Seldom even in the pages of Frank Merriwell would such a situation have seemed likely."

What definitely would seem unlikely to young adult readers today, however, would be the concept of reading a 20,000-word story each week throughout much of their school days. That, however, is just what many young readers did from 1896 to 1912, when the original epics starring the Merriwell brothers, Frank and Dick, appeared in 850 issues of *Tip Top Weekly* (known as *Tip Top Library* for the first 45 issues). Patten wrote the vast majority of those stories. The 32-page magazine, featuring full-color covers but no interior art except for logos, sold for a nickel, even though *Tip Top* was part of the "dime novel" era (one of the first of the early comic books was titled "Tip Top Comics" when it began in 1936, though it had nothing to do with either the Merriwells or Street & Smith). Throughout much of its run, *Tip Top Weekly* praised itself as "An Ideal Publication for the American Youth" and bannered "Largest Weekly Circulation in America" above the larger logo, which early comic books later imitated in style.

Many of the stories, which began with the April 18, 1896, issue, did not involve sports. Many told of travels, outdoor adventures, mysteries and the like involving Merriwell, who was first the prep hero of Fardale and later the college nonesuch at Yale University. All of these stories were published with two titles in the manner of the day, such as the fifth Frank Merriwell story in 1896: "Frank Merriwell's Fault, or, False Steps and Foul Snares." Each of the first 284 stories began with Frank Merriwell's name. Issue #285 featured his younger brother in "Dick Merriwell enters Fardale, or Following His Brother's Footsteps"—10 issues after Dick's debut in #275 in 1901. Thereafter, the title starred one or the other of the brothers, and sometimes both.

The exotic realm of the Merriwells

When *Tip Top Weekly* began in 1896, sports as we know it today was an exotic realm for many youth, limited largely to prep school and college students. Frank Merriwell's adventures kicked off seven years before the first World Series. Professional baseball was less than three decades old; the National Football League was well in the future. Indeed, the concept of basketball itself was invented a mere five years before the first Merriwell epic.

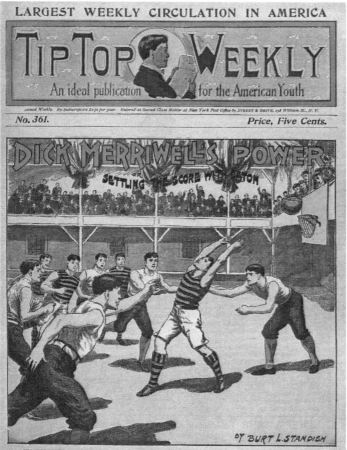

Tip Top Weekly #361, March 14, 1903 (copyright Street & Smith). This is one of the earliest illustrations of a fictional basketball game; the game had been invented only 12 years earlier. Dick Merriwell makes an outrageous behind-the-back shot into a peach basket.

Tip Top Weekly ended with #850 (July 27, 1912), "Dick Merriwell's Marathon or How the Last Olympic Mile Brought Victory." One week later, *New Tip Top Weekly* began, starring Frank Merriwell Junior, who was the titular hero of the first 76 issues. Other characters sometimes starred, including older versions of Frank and Dick, until the title ended with #136 in 1915 and was succeeded by *Tip Top Semi-Monthly* #1 (March 10, 1915). After 18 issues covering three volumes of that magazine, the title changed to the pulp *Wide Awake* magazine with Volume 4, #1, starring the last chapter of the serial "Dick Merriwell in Alaska, Part IV." Merriwell stories continued through *Wide Awake* Volume 5 #3 (#27), dated April 10, 1916. At that point, exactly 20 years after the Merriwell saga began, the heroic family's original run of more than

1,000 consecutive stories ended, though more were to appear in pulps of the late 1920s and early 1930s (see chapter two).

In "Frank Merriwell's Father" (1964), Patten's posthumously published (and long awaited) autobiography edited by Harriet Hinsdale with assistance from Tony London, Hinsdale notes the staggering statistical impact of the Merriwell series in her introduction. She notes that publisher Street & Smith had estimated the printing of more than 500 million copies of the various Merriwell publications, presumably including reprints. Well over 200,000 copies of many issues were sold, at a time America's pre–World War I population was less than one-third of today's—and when most elementary school students did not go on to graduate from high school.

Merriwell, in fact, made such an impact that the eminent literary critic and editor George Jean Nathan, in an essay in the September 1925 issue of *American Mercury*, called for a "biography, or better still an autobiography, if he is still living, of the man known as Burt L. Standish." Nathan estimated that more than 15,000 Merriwell stories were published. He can be forgiven the wildly excessive guestimate—there have never been 15,000 Merriwell stories or of any fictional character—as such was the overwhelming impact of the Merriwells. "For week after week and year after year, he poured forth in gaudy-covered brochures the trials and conquests, the adventures and amours, the deeds of derring-do and hair's-breadth escapes of the eminent and well-remembered Francois, hero and idol of perhaps half the kids in the Republic when Cleveland, Harrison and McKinley held the throne," Nathan wrote. "I doubt, in all seriousness, if there was an American writer of twenty-three and thirty years ago who was so widely known and so widely read by the boys of the time." (Benjamin Harrison's presidential term ended in 1893, but errors of recollection are common among nostalgic writers, however accomplished.)

In *The Fiction Factory* (1955), a history of Street & Smith by Quentin Reynolds, a copy of the letter from Street & Smith dated January 3, 1896, is reproduced, acknowledging receipt of Patten's first manuscript. The letter was addressed to "Gilbert Patton, Esq."—a misspelling of the name of the author who was to become one of history's most prolific writers.

Patten explains how he named his hero

Explaining how he came to invent the name Frank Merriwell, Patten wrote, "The name was symbolic of the chief characteristics I desired my hero to have—Frank for frankness, merry for a happy disposition, well for health and abounding vitality.... [O]f course, as I pictured him, he was too perfect to have been a boy of flesh and blood. There was little of such perfection in my own nature, but I knew I would have chosen to be like Frank had fate made it possible, and I believed all respectable, clean-minded boys felt the same. And so I depicted Frank as an ideal to emulate, and in doing so I may have made him sometimes seem slightly priggish."

The original Frank Merriwell saga was not destined to end in 1916, thanks to the increasing popularity of pulp-paper fiction magazines, which began with *Argosy* in 1896. The *Wide Awake* pulp itself lasted only 13 issues, merging in 1916 with *Top Notch* magazine, which since 1910 had been publishing some of the earliest sports fiction read by adults and youth alike among a wide variety of general-interest fiction of all types. *Top Notch* was supposedly edited by Burt L. Standish, which Street & Smith had appropriated as a house name and was used by several authors other than Patten, much to Patten's distaste.

The first all-sports pulp magazine, Street & Smith's *Sport Story* magazine, was aimed at both adults and youth when it began in 1923. Other than a few boxing publications, *Sport Story* was the only all-sports pulp magazine for a full decade while dozens of pulp magazines devoted to other genres sprang up around it. In fact, more issues of the twice-a-month *Sport Story* magazine appeared through the 1920s (152) than were ever to appear from any other sports pulp publisher. *Sport Story* ran 429 issues through 1943; the next-longest run was the 85 issues of *Sports Novels*, produced by Popular Publications from 1937 to 1952. Despite its financial success, however, *Sport Story* magazine was accorded little respect in *The Fiction Factory*, which devoted all of seven lines to the magazine, noting a circulation of 150,000 in the 1920s. Indeed, *Sport Story* was a minor-league venture compared to the immense success of the like of Street & Smith's *Detective Story* magazine, *Western Story* magazine, *Love Story* magazine and *The Shadow* (see chapter two). *Sport Story*, in fact, became a victim of World War II paper shortages, along with numerous other sports pulps.

Frank Merriwell reappeared with seven two-part serials in *Sport Story* magazine during 1927 and 1928, followed by five novelettes in the short-lived Fame and Fortune Magazine in 1928–1929 (the fifth appeared in the July 19, 1929, issue after the financial fiction-oriented magazine became *Fortune Story* magazine). The last of the Merriwell sports epics were the 12 Merriwell novelettes, novels and serials published in *Top Notch* magazine in 1929 and 1930. In the Fame and Fortune series, ironically appearing in the months shortly before the stock market's crash began the Great Depression, Frank became a financial wizard in "Frank Merriwell Tackles Real Estate," "Frank Merriwell and the Wall Street Wizard," "Frank Merriwell in the Curb Market," "Frank Merriwell's Lucky Dollar" and "Frank Merriwell's Crooked Tip." *Fame and Fortune/Fortune Story* ran a combined 17 issues and the five Merriwell stories are among the hardest to find for collectors, listed as "rare" in *The Ultimate Guide to the Pulps* by Tim Cottrill.

Tip Top Weekly #378, July 11, 1903 (copyright Street & Smith). Frank Merriwell tries to score by leaping over the catcher—a move that would not be allowed today.

The original Merriwell

"dime novels" were eagerly collected in the 1930s and 1940s. There was a Frank Merriwell comic strip in the 1930s, a Frank Merriwell Big Little Book in the mid–1930s and even a Frank Merriwell movie serial from Universal in 1936, starring an otherwise unknown actor named Don Briggs (see chapter three). The female lead, Jean Rogers, was to become far more famous that same year as Dale Arden in the first Flash Gordon serial.

Alas, the stories are badly dated

The original Merriwell stories don't hold up well at all today. Here is dialog from "Dick Merriwell's Sand or Winning by Pure Grit," a baseball story in *Tip Top Weekly* #417 (April 9, 1904) in which Dick talks with foil Chester Arlington about physical fitness and how it affects studying:

"I won't bother you but for a moment, Capt. Merriwell, " said Arlington, with an air of deference, which he assumed with no small difficulty. "I see you're studying,"

"Have to," smiled Dick. "Don't get all the time at it that I should. When I can snatch a little more time to bone, I do so."

"Some of the fellows here think you never study," returned Chet. "They regard you as a wizard. They imagine you keep up with your class without studying. In fact, old man, I don't see how you do it. You have so much on your shoulders."

"Well, it's a hard pull," admitted Dick, "but I have found a fellow can do a lot if he improves every moment possible. I waste little time. When I play, I play in earnest; and when I study, I simply drive at it like a wood-chopper. It's the only way I can get along. If I doodled and wasted my spare moments I'd soon be in a bad muss. The fellow in school who takes a deep interest in athletics should be careful not to let his sports get on his mind so he cannot study."

"Lots of them do," said Chester.

"I know it," nodded Dick. "That's where they make a big mistake. Healthy exercise and outdoor sports should put a fellow in better condition to study. They provide work and training for the body, making it strong and healthy; and a chap with a strong and healthy body should be able to study much better than one who is physically weak. This is my brother's theory, and I have found it true. I am always sorry when I see a fellow permitting athletics or sports to carry him away so that he neglects his studies. Such fellows provide apparent proof for those who argue that athletics and sports are harmful to students. At the same time the fact that the boys who are physically best fitted for sports almost always take the deepest interest in them, while chaps who are not properly developed get discouraged, seldom show themselves in the gym, or on the field unless compelled to do so, is another strong argument to the list of reasons put forward by the opponents of athletics. The boys who most need physical training are frequently the ones who get little of it. It is their own fault. They should work harder than the others who are stronger and better developed, but few of them do it. Once in a while, you hear of some chap who is physically weak and who sets about deliberately and methodically and with good judgment to build himself up. And in many instances such a fellow becomes the marvel of his school or college. Have you ever noticed, Arlington, that most always the famous strong man of any college has developed himself from an unusually frail boy?"

"I don't know that I have noticed it in particular," confessed Chet.

"Well, it's a fact," nodded Dick, "and it proves the correctness of the argument that physical culture is a great thing. The shame is that more fellows who need it do not go in for it earnestly. We have plenty of examples of this thing right here in our own school. I can pick out a score of fellows who need special training, but who get no more training of that sort than they are obliged to take. Not all of these chaps are lazy; some of them are genuine grinds. They study hard, but they have no love for physical culture, and such work as they are compelled to do in that line they do in a heartless manner. Now I have found out a strange thing: the weak chap who develops himself has to put his mind into his work just as much as his body. It does little good if he goes at it with a feeling of repulsion and distaste. If he wishes to develop certain muscles or parts of his body, he must take proper exercise, and while he is doing so he must fix his mind on the object he wishes to attain. If his shoulders and back are weak and he is working to strengthen them, the very fact that while he works his mind is fixed intently on the object he desires of accomplishing aids him greatly. The fellow who goes at physical culture and yanks away carelessly at the chest weights, the rowing machine or gesticulates needlessly with the dumbbells and Indian clubs, rarely ever accomplishes as much as he might."

"Well, I suppose you're right about that [Arlington says]. Say, by Jove! You will develop into a professional instructor and lecturer in physical culture if you don't look out."

Merriwell smiled. "Not that," he retorted, shaking his head, "but I shall always try to help anyone I can by such hints or suggestions as I believe beneficial. Not all of these ideas are mine, Arlington. By no means. I don't pretend to take credit for them. Some originated with my brother; but the great mass of principles have been discovered by different persons and simply adopted by him. He has discovered that many things in the teachings of physical culture instructors are false, and these things he has abandoned."

It's difficult to imagine high school boys speaking this way or at such great length in 1904, much less more than one hundred years later! The mind boggles, but this was Patten speaking to his readers, almost all of whom were young and impressionable. In the same issue is a long letters column entitled "Applause," in which readers passionately discuss the merits and demerits of the various characters and stories. That is followed by two pages on physical culture.

The uncredited color covers of *Tip Top Weekly* are often charmingly fascinating period pieces, making them collector's items today. For example, "Dick Merriwell's Power, or Settling the Score with Eaton" in #361 (March 14, 1903), shows Dick shooting a basketball into a peach basket! James Naismith had invented the game only a dozen years earlier, so there weren't too many basketball covers compared to the plethora of football and baseball scenes.

In his autobiography, Patten explained why he "used so much space for character delineation.... Maybe today [the early 1940s] modern up-to-the-minute juvenile stories depending as much on character delineation as upon impossible hair-raising action, would be 'comic books,' but I believe that is a misfortune for the youngsters. And I am proud of the fact that no Merriwell story written by me gave its readers a harmfully distorted view of life." That is a most rational viewpoint, by an author who meant well.

At one time, Patten estimated that "it's probable that fully twenty-five percent of the readers [of the Merriwells] were girls." No one will ever know if that figure is accurate, but not a few letters published in the Merriwell letter columns had female names.

Not many competitors

The Merriwells had a few competitors, most of them short-lived, such as the 58-issue run of *Boys' Best Weekly* in 1909–1910 starring Jack Standfast, credited to Horace Paine. *Boys' Best* made shameless and sometimes illogical boasts about their quality, such as this one from #55 (June 3, 1910): "The Boys' Best Weekly is the most popular boys' publication in America because it deserves to be the most popular."

Jack Standfast is introduced this way before each story: "A boy who has his way to make in the world, and who starts right by endeavoring to overcome his own faults, and building up his body so that he may take his place in school as an athlete. Because of his firm determination to succeed, and abiding faith in his own ability to accomplish things, Jack usually 'gets there,' and when he fails, has only to examine himself, learn the reason, and avoiding all pitfalls, try again until success rewards his efforts. Jack is a natural leader, and while he has devoted friends, he, of course, makes bitter enemies as well."

The then-famed dime novel collector/dealer/historian Charles Bragin, in *Dime Novels Bibliography 1860–1928*, published in 1938 out of his home in Brooklyn, N.Y., talked about the appeal of dime novels, sounding very much like many of today's collectors of old comic books while answering frequently asked questions:

[Q] How can I get dime novels cheaply?

[A] By searching for them personally—in old attics, barns, bookstores, etc. When a "cache" is found, the novels can be bought for one tenth the prices mentioned herein. Which is not the last interesting aspect of the hobby. The main cost of dime novels is the expense of finding them. The writer maintains a staff of book buying scouts all over the country. Hundreds of other collectors also are active searchers—no other type of book is so widely tracked down.

[Q] Will dime novels increase in value?

[A] Decidedly so. Even during the depression years, when most rare books slumped in value, dime novels increased over 100% in price. The supply is constantly diminishing, while demand increases with entry of new collectors in the field.

Bragin's catalog shows that none of Merriwell's rivals lasted long other than the often non-sports oriented Fred Fearnot and his 733-issue run in *Work and Win*, which began in 1896 and continued with hundreds of reprints through #1,382 in 1924. Then there were the 32 issues of *Young Athlete's Weekly* in 1905, followed by the 32 issues of *Frank Manley Weekly* in 1906, along with 56 issues of the *All Sports Library* in 1905–06. The 60 issues of *Three Chums* in 1899–1900 and the 65 issues of *Do and Dare* in 1900–1901 tried but largely failed to capitalize on Frank Merriwell's early success.

Much of the fun for the few remaining collectors of these nickel novels is the titles of the stories. For example, the title of the first Dick Merriwell story in *Tip Top Weekly* #275 in 1901 is "Frank Merriwell's Brother or Training a Wild Spirit." Dick was really a half-brother, of course, and he proved just as wildly popular as Frank. He entered Yale with #550 (October 27, 1906) in "Dick Merriwell, Freshman, or First Days at

Tip Top Weekly #394, October 31, 1903 (copyright Street & Smith). Still in prep school, Dick Merriwell gets off a punt for Fardale under heavy pressure.

Yale." The Merriwells at one time or another took part in almost every sport, including what is probably the first of very few water polo stories: "Dick Merriwell in the Tank or Rushing the Regulars at Water Polo" in #561 in 1907. Then there was "Dick Merriwell's Flyer or The Champions of the Ice" about sledding in #673 in 1909. Three months later, he even became a marathon man in "Dick Merriwell in the Marathon or The Sensation of the Great Run" in #686. Week after week, there were endless fascinations in those pre-comic book days.

Frank Merriwell became a coach in such stories as "Frank Merriwell's Pupil or The Boy with the Wizard Wing," about tutoring pitching skills in #682. As the original series wound up in 1912, Dick Merriwell became a track and field star at the Stockholm Olympics in the final four issues, #847–850, through July 27, 1912. Street and Smith, though, didn't miss a trick (or a week) when the firm began *New Tip Top Weekly* with #1 (August 3, 1912) in the story, "Frank Merriwell, Jr., or The Camp on Wind River." By that time, however, Patten had left the series to write novels.

In fact, after 76 Merriwell Junior stories, Street and Smith decided to change gears and used "Owen Clancey, Motor Wizard" as the hero in #77 through #94 before the three Merriwell family heroes returned for #95 through #136. The nickel novels then morphed into *Tip Top Semi-Monthly* for 18 issues and *Wide Awake* magazine for nine more issues through April 10, 1916, with "Dick Merriwell's Ruse," the last original story in the original 20-year run of the Merriwells.

Books, books and more books about sports

As if the more than 1,000 dime novels covering the adventures of the Merriwells weren't enough sports fiction for young readers, hardcover juvenile sports novels began to boom shortly after the turn of the century, with at least 42 by Gilbert Patten himself, most of them after he had left the Merriwells behind. In all, more than 500 sports novels appeared before the 1930s, most of them in a series format and almost all of them directed at young (and young at heart) readers.

Frank Merriwell himself appeared in 28 hardbound reprints, originally published by the David McKay Company from 1898 through 1911 and usually sold for 75 cents each (easily the equal of $15 today). Each book reprinted several Merriwell dime novels. Street & Smith also published at least 245 paperback reprints of the Merriwell family saga, first appearing around the turn of the century and running into the Great Depression and collecting several dime novels in each.

Even though no series characters ever came remotely close in popularity to the Merriwells until they were ultimately passed in sheer bulk many years later by comic book icons such as Superman, Batman and Spider-Man, the youngsters in pre–Depression America often could count on seeing their favorite sports heroes more than once.

Patten, under his Burt L. Standish byline, wrote the 16-book Big League Series from 1914 to 1928, starring the likes of star pitcher Lefty O' the Bush, the title of the first book. The Big League Series and Edward Stratemeyer's concurrent Baseball Joe Series were the earliest books to feature professional athletes in boys' series books. Lefty went by the name of Tom "Lefty" Locke, but his real name was Philip Hazleton. The series included several other big league protagonists, including catcher Brick King, who was the star of *Brick King Backstop* (1914); the characters for the series included Pebble Stone (!), Bob Courtney, Jack

Keeper, Rick Armstrong, Matt Schuyler, Ken Tapland, Lego Lamb, Chesty Blake, Hobe Bolt, Pop Doyle, Tighe Rawson and others. The Big League Series was done far better, and with much more character consistency, by Duane Decker with his Blue Sox Series from 1947 to 1964.

Patten also penned the Clif Sterling series (five books, 1910–1916), the College Life Series (six books, 1914–1915) and the Rockspur Series (three books, 1900–1901) under his own name. He used pen names for the Rex Kingdom Series (six books, 1914–1917, as by Gordon Braddock) and the Oakdale Series (six books, 1911–1913, as by Morgan Scott). Patten (1866–1945) was 62 when he penned his final sports novel, the 16th in the Big League Series, though his work remained in print for quite a while longer.

Ralph Henry Barbour, second only to Patten when it came to prolific production of sports novels, wrote nearly 100 over a period of nearly five decades, beginning shortly before the turn of the century and continuing into the first half of the 1940s. He created 18 series, with a total of 70 books in all, and the vast majority of his work involved baseball or football, most often in prep school settings. He wrote numerous one-and-done novels, along with a plethora of shorts.

Considering how prolific Barbour was, much of his work is surprisingly difficult to find now, albeit not usually highly sought after. Were it not for the monumental *A Collectors Guide to Hardcover Boys' Series Books* (1997) by E. Christian Mattson and Thomas B. Davis, many of these books would be totally forgotten, along with numerous other series types of the pre–1930 era. This invaluable book lists hundreds of series and thousands of volumes printed from 1872 to 1993, many of them sought by only the most hard-core series book collectors.

Unlike Patten, Barbour never wrote many books about the same characters. Some of the titles of his series—*Ferry Hill, Yardley Hall, Grafton, Wyndham, Cheltham*—provide the flavor. All but two of the series ran at least three books but none ran longer than 11 volumes. The latter was the appropriately titled *Football Eleven Series* from 1914 to 1925, detailing the triumphs and travails of players at each offensive position. The Mattson/Davis index also lists 73 non-series Barbour books, many of them non-sports stories, which means this literate, articulate author wrote at least 143 full-length novels (and a few nonfiction books) over slightly less than half a century. Yet today, his work is largely forgotten, since it was reprinted primarily during the early years of the 20th century and was seldom seen in the post–World War II era.

Other than Frank Merriwell, the best-remembered character of the pre–1930 era is Baseball Joe, the star of the 14-book Baseball Joe Series as by house name Lester Chadwick from the Stratemeyer Syndicate. Edward Stratemeyer—whose syndicate produced hundreds of series books, most notably the Hardy Boys and Nancy Drew—purportedly wrote some of the Baseball Joe novels himself, though famed children's author Howard Garis is also credited with producing several. "Baseball Joe" Matson, who was 15 when the series began, encounters all manner of improbable circumstances on and off the diamond as a player who could both pitch and hit with otherworldy skill. The exploits of a real pitcher/slugger—Babe Ruth—began at about the same time and doubtless contributed to the popularity of the series in the Golden Age of Sports before the Great Depression.

Hall of Fame pitcher Christy Mathewson lent his name to six highly collectible titles, together called the Baseball Series and sometimes the Matty Books and ghostwritten by sportswriter John Neville Wheeler from 1910 to 1917. They are still avidly sought after today, especially in their original editions (they were frequently reprinted). The titles are *Won in the Ninth* (1910, perhaps written by sportswriter Bozeman Bulger), *Pitching in a Pinch*, or *Baseball from the Inside* (1912, nonfiction), *Pitcher Pollack* (1914), *Catcher Craig* (1915), *First Baseball Faulkner* (1916) and *Second Base Sloan* (1917). Mathewson's World War I duty and resulting health problems, and then his premature death in 1925, prevented further volumes. Wheeler wrote a seventh, *Third Base Thatcher*, in 1923 as by Hall of Fame shortstop Everett Scott.

The immortal Walter Camp, who created and popularized the concept of college football All-America honors, wrote two series from 1908 to 1915 — the six-book School and College Series and the six-book Frank Armstrong series, as by Matthew Colton.

The Stratemeyer Syndicate also produced the six-book College Sports Series from 1910 to 1913, the five-book Fred Fenton Series from 1913 to 1915, plus two highly popular series as by Elmer Dawson — the 10-volume Gary Grayson football stories from 1926 to 1932 and the five-volume Buck and Larry Baseball Series in 1930–31. The Gary Grayson books were highly popular well into the 1940s and bridged the gap between the popularity of Baseball Joe in the 1920s and Chip Hilton and Bronc Burnett beginning in the late 1940s. In fact, almost every used-book store of any depth has at least one or two Gary Grayson stories, most likely reprints, lingering on the shelves.

The prolific Harold M. Sherman and William Heyliger both wrote more than 30 sports novels, Heyliger from 1911 to 1937 and Sherman from 1926 to 1937 (see chapter two). Most of them were one-and-done volumes, and many were reprinted endlessly in cheap editions, selling well into the 1940s. Like the Gary Grayson stories, many Sherman and Heyliger books still languish in used-book stores, unlike the far more collectible and sought-after Christy Mathewson, Baseball Joe and Lefty O' the Bush tales.

There were about four dozen other short-lived pre–1930 series, all detailed in the Mattson-Davis book, including the Belle Haven Series by George Barton, the Bert Wilson Series by John Duffield, the College Years Series by Frank Ralph Paine, and the Jack Lorimer Series by Winn Standish. There are enthusiasts who enjoy plucking one or two volumes of each series, especially the ones devoted to baseball, football or basketball. Almost all of the books were issued with either dust jackets or colorful picture covers, often both. Many of the pre–1930 dust jackets are considered quite scarce and some have seldom if ever been seen, although some authors— most notably Sherman — still show up with jackets far more often than others.

By far the most famous name to contribute to this early glut of juvenile sports novels was the western novelist Zane Grey. Grey, a former baseball player, was most famously known for *The Short-stop* in 1909, followed by *The Young Pitcher* in 1911 and *The Redheaded Outfield and Other Baseball Stories* in 1915. The latter is a collection of 11 baseball tales. These books were reprinted endlessly, including 1940s versions from Grosset and Dunlap, to take advantage of the Zane Grey name. The A.C. McClurg Company, which published the first hardcover Tarzan novels, was the first publisher of *The Short-stop*, which used the spelling of the era.

The athletic interests of girls (see chapter twelve) were almost entirely ignored during the pre–1930 period except for two series: The Girls of Central High by Gertrude W. Morrison, a seven-book series from 1914 to 1921, and Jane Allen by Edith Bancroft, a five-book series from 1917 to 1922. Both were reprinted several times, so they must have been at least moderately popular. Only two of the Central High books specifically addressed sports: *The Girls of Central High at Basketball* (1914), which seems likely to have been the first novel about girls' basketball, and *The Girls of Central High at Track and Field* (1914).

Some dust jackets of the Jane Allen series feature striking illustrations of a confident-looking girl in full basketball regalia and thus must have been considered groundbreaking oddities in their day, especially in an era long before most American high schools offered interscholastic girls' basketball. The titles are *Jane Allen of the Sub Team* (1917), *Jane Allen, Right Guard* (1918), *Jane Allen, Center* (1920), *Jane Allen, Junior* (1921) and *Jane Allen, Senior* (1922). Since these first appeared less than three decades after the game's invention, they surely had a unique appeal.

A staggering amount of sports fiction

From the first Frank Merriwell dime novel in 1896 to the second December 1929 issue of Street & Smith's *Sport Story* magazine, the vast majority of sports fiction was aimed at readers of high school age and younger. The early years of *Sport Story* magazine provided sports fiction primarily directed at readers of high school age and older. Merriwell had little competition, either in dime novels or hardbound series books, until the 1899–1901 period, which was well before the sports pulp magazine era and long before the sound films, radio shows and comic books of the 1930s and 1940s.

Fred Fearnot, created for the Tousey line of dime novels in competition with Street & Smith, appeared in more than 700 original dime novels as the primary rival of the Merriwells, though Fred is not nearly so well remembered. Fearnot's first baseball story was "Fred Fearnot's Base Ball Club" in *Work and Win Weekly* for May 19, 1899. According to the invaluable *Baseball by the Books* (1991) by Andy McCue, Fearnot appeared in 65 baseball-themed stories through 1912 (there were later reprints), so his was not a primary sports presence.

Nonetheless, Fearnot's baseball tales and other sports adventures were part of well over 2,500 publications featuring baseball, football and basketball and in the first three decades of the 20th century, including the more than 1,000 Merriwells. The total number of sports stories, in fact, probably exceeded 3,000, as many of them appeared in the numerous children's magazines of the era. Even though athletics was a significant part of printed popular culture throughout the rest of the 20th century, it's certain the three decades through 1929 exceeded any similar period of sheer athletic bulk—and bunk, in many cases!—available to young readers.

The total examples of sports fiction over the 1930s, 1940s and 1950s—primarily pulp magazines and hardcover books, along with dozens of stories in slick magazines such as the *Saturday Evening Post* and *Collier's*—may have come close to the 3,000-plus of the previous three decades. But the vast majority of this post–1930 fiction was aimed at readers of what today is called the "the young adult" field, in contrast to the majority of pre–1930 stories.

By 1930, all the nickel novels (though not all of their reprint versions) had vanished from the cultural landscape, soon to be replaced in the hearts of youngsters by comic books. Slightly less than 1,400 pulp magazines devoted entirely to sports appeared exclusively in the 1930–1957 period—following the pioneer *Sport Story* magazine's domination of the 1920s—before pulps in general vanished from the newsstands. (Including the 1923–29 *Sport Story* magazine issues, the total sports pulp count is 1,530, give or take a couple of issues). But the pulps' only significant competition for athletics-oriented readers came from hardcover books, most of them directed to the young adult market. Likewise, the pulps were not aimed at pre–high school age readers, as indicated by the fact that pulp stories almost never featured high school or prep school athletics, in contrast to the feats of teen athletes featured in hundreds of hardcover books—both pre–and post–1930—along with the dime novels.

The coming of the baseball film

In the years before the silent film era gradually ended over 1927 to 1929, baseball fiction was featured in at least 25 full-length films, ranging from *Little Sunset* and *Right Off the Bat* in 1915 to *Fast Company*, of which both sound and silent versions were produced, in 1929. Football emerged strong on the college scene in the post–World War I era, yet was still considered in the minds of many sportsmen to be a relatively minor sport compared with baseball, boxing and horse racing. Yet, in the Roaring Twenties, football had become popular enough to have 31 films circulated in the 1921–1928 silent-film period, as listed by Michael Oriard in an appendix to *King Football* (2000). This is the most accurate and complete listing I have found. Interest in the college game exploded during Great Depression years and continued until after World War II, as reflected by Oriard's listing of 82 football films from 1929 to 1953, plus six biographies.

The incomparable resource *The Baseball Filmography 1915 through 2001* by Hal Erickson (McFarland) provides more information than ever available before on the development of silent baseball films, which focused entirely on fiction, in contrast to the growth of the biographical movies to the 1940s and 1950s and the concurrent decline in baseball fiction in the films. This is not surprising, considering that baseball's growth as a major league sport did not really begin until the formation of the American League in 1901 and the creation of the World Series, in 1903, which matched the American League champion against the pennant winner of the so-called senior-circuit, the National League. The creation of the Baseball Hall of Fame in 1936, following the beginning of the Major League Baseball All-Star Game in 1933, also did much to interest the public in the sport's history.

In his entry on *Little Sunset*, Erickson notes that, at four reels, the film "was the longest dramatic baseball movie made up to 1914, and since it secured better States Rights' bookings on the basis of its length than it would have as a short subject, the picture can be regarded as the very first baseball feature film." Erickson notes that the film was based on a 1912 short story by Charles Emmett Van Loan, "who in his time was the foremost writer of baseball fiction in America." This was undeniably true, even though Van Loan wrote only short stories and novellas for the pre-pulp era magazines and never penned a baseball novel. Baseball novels for adults, in fact, were seldom seen before the 1930s. Van Loan's stories appear in four scarce collections published between 1911 and 1919: *The Big League, The $10,000 Arm and Other Stories of the Big League, The Lucky Seventh* and *Score by Innings*. As mature as Van Loan's stories were in contrast to the likes of Frank Merriwell, Fred Fearnot and almost all of the hardcover books of their era, his tales are, regrettably, forgotten today.

An amusing and informative source of information on silent baseball and football films, especially those produced at the dawn of the movie era from 1894 to 1919, is Robert Cantwell's essay, "Sport Was Box-Office Poison," in the September 15, 1969, issue of *Sports Illustrated*. This piece, which primarily concerned the silent era, appeared when a good number of people were still alive who had seen these films in their youth.

The baseball, football and basketball fiction published in the 1930s and 1940s during the pulp magazine era, however, along with the growth of hardcover fiction, has been far from forgotten.

TWO

The Great Pulp Sports Rally
During the Depression

For slightly more than a full decade, Street & Smith's *Sport Story* magazine had the general-interest pulp sports field entirely to itself from 1923 to 1933, other than the occasional sports stories in the anthology men's adventure pulps such as Frank Munsey's weekly *Argosy* and Dell's monthly *Five Novels*.

Street & Smith, of course, was by far the best-capitalized pulp publisher, both before and during the Great Depression. The company's pulps were apparently immensely profitable until the 1940s, when several titles were abandoned in 1943 (when World War II paper restrictions took serious hold) and at the point the venerable firm gave up entirely on both pulp-sized magazines and all of its comic books in 1949 to focus on slick nonfiction magazines.

This helps explain the thorough dominance of the field by *Sport Story* magazine, which had sales consistently reported at well over 150,000 throughout most of its 429-issue run from 1923 to 1943. Since *Sport Story* appeared biweekly for a full 16 years—from September 1923 through August 1939—the magazine was also one of the few sports pulps to publish full-length serials, giving readers serious motivation to buy each issue.

A few issues of *Sport Story* are frequently offered for sale at conventions of pulp collectors, although to amass a complete file would be a most challenging and daunting task, especially since the 1920s issues are far less often seen than later issues. Even more difficult, however, is chasing down the rest of the sports pulp field of the 1933–1957 era, since these have been among the least-valuable of the classic pulps, not far above the romance pulps, which are almost always at the bottom of the collectors' desirability scale. Dealers and enthusiasts thus have not been especially motivated to make space for sports and romance pulps on their crammed tables and in their paper-packed booths. For every sports pulp collector, there are dozens who seek the hero pulps, the horror/terror publications, the detective tales and the science fiction epics, not to mention the forever popular obscure titles such as *Civil War Stories*. The one-shot *Basketball Stories* (Winter 1937–1938) from Fiction House is every bit as scarce as most short-run pulps but nowhere near as valuable as the likes of *The Scorpion* or *Zeppelin Stories*.

Sport Story magazine scores big

Sport Story magazine was, in fact, very much the most dominant of all sports publications, including books, throughout much of its two-decade run, except for the likes of the nonfiction weekly baseball "bible," *The Sporting News*. By the time the Wall Street crash of 1929 precipitated the Great Depression, the five-cent Merriwell publications were but a fond memory of now-grown readers, and the intense three-decade popularity of new hardcover sports series books for youth was on the wane. Boys (and a few girls, too) turned to detective heroes like the Hardy Boys (which debuted in 1927), flying stories, jungle epics and so on, along with the girls' mystery and adventure icons such as Nancy Drew (begun in 1930) and Judy Bolton (1932), among many others. Although a handful of early sports series books continued to be reprinted into the 1930s, no major new series character or characters appeared again until the postwar 1940s. A few long-time standbys—Ralph Henry Barbour, William Heyliger, Harold M. Sherman—produced a handful of short-run series, but none are well-remembered and they are seldom seen today. Only the most hard-core collectors pursue the 1930s like of Barbour's Cheltham, Cooper Lake, Franklin High, Glendale and Hillfield series, all of which appeared from 1930 to 1940, or Heyliger's Stan Kent or Buddy Books series. The Hillfield stories (1931–1934) were the only fresh series books to reach as many as six volumes during the 1930s (more about this shortly).

Well over 200 pulp titles of all genres had come — and, more often than not, gone — by the time *All-America Sports* magazine appeared in December 1933, as the first challenger for the dimes of *Sport Story*'s readers (other books that talk about other late 1920s and 1930–1932 sports pulps are incorrect, except for boxing pulps).

Like most issues of *Sport Story*, *All-America Sports* magazine actually cost 15 cents during the Great Depression, the equal of about $3 today. Nat Fleischer, who achieved fame as the longtime editor of the iconic boxing magazine the *Ring*, edited *All-America Sports* magazine for the Phelps Publishing Company, which always prominently advertised *Ring* in *All-America*. The *Ring* began in 1922 and quickly became fabulously successful and remained so for decades, chronicling boxers and wrestlers during a period when they were especially in America's sport spotlight. The *All-America Sports* magazine specialized in short stories— running almost nothing but — and seldom ran "name" authors such as Jackson Scholz, whose earliest market was Street & Smith. *All-America* ran 45 known issues through September 1938, mostly on a monthly basis, and they are not highly sought after today.

By the time the *All-America Sports* magazine expired, several other successful general-interest sports pulps had begun, perhaps convincing Phelps the market was saturated. (Fiction House's popular *Fight Stories* began in 1928, but it specialized in boxing.) In all, 26 sports pulp titles followed the *All-America* on the crowded stands from 1935 to 1939, beginning with *Dime Sports* from the prolific and powerful Popular Publications in July 1935.

Dime Sports was a natural for Popular, which also produced *Dime Detective*, *Dime Mystery* and *Dime Western* for many years, among dozens of titles over more than two decades and more than 4,000 issues through the mid–1950s. "Dime" of course, was prominently featured in the title to lure Depression readers, for many of whom a dime was not easy to part with.

Since *Sport Story* magazine appeared twice a month and the *All-America* ran on a monthly basis when Dime Sports debuted, Popular Publications decided on monthly publication, too. It was apparently a smart move, since sports-oriented readers—including many teachers— did not have a large number of reading options dealing with athletics.

A flood of 1936–1939 sports pulps

Soon, however, more sports pulps began to appear than the typical reader could handle — if, indeed, the typical reader could afford all of them, which was probably not the case. Through 1939, six prominent pulp publishers — Popular, Thrilling/Better, Columbia/Double Action, Fiction House, Martin Goodman/Red Circle, and Ace — produced those 26 titles, including Street & Smith's nine-issue run of *Athlete* in 1939–1940.

Six of the new pulps were strictly seasonal (as were all pulps with baseball, football and basketball in the title). Other titles did not make it out of the 1930s. Here's the complete chronological list of the rivals for Street & Smith's *Story* magazine, with the first month of publication and the publisher:

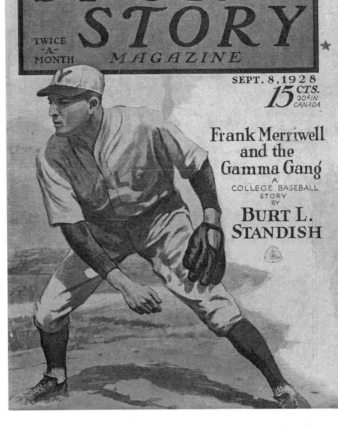

1935 — *Dime Sports* (July, Popular).

1936 — *Ace Sports* (January, Ace); *Thrilling Sports* (September, Standard); *Star Sports* (October, Red Circle).

1937 — *Best Sports* (January, Red Circle/Goodman); *Sports*

Sport Story, September 8, 1928 (copyright Street & Smith). This features the first of the two-part "Frank Merriwell and the Gamma Gang," one of several pulp Merriwell stories as by Burt L. Standish in the late 1920s and early 1930s, long after the end of the original dime novel series.

Winners (February, Columbia); *Sports Fiction* (April, Columbia); *Baseball Stories* (Spring, Fiction House); *Super Sports* (September, Columbia); *Variety Sports* (September, Ace, becomes *Twelve Sports Aces* with the second issue in December); *All-American Football* (Fall, Fiction House); *Bulls-Eye Sports* (Winter 1937-1938, Fiction House).

1938 — *Real Sports* (January, Red Circle/Goodman); *Sports Winners* (February, Columbia); *Sports Fiction* (April, Columbia); *Baseball Stories* (Spring, Fiction House); *Super Sports* (September, Columbia); *All-American Football* (Fall, Fiction House); *Bulls-Eye Sports* (Winter 1938-1939, Fiction House).

1939 — *Athlete* (August, Street & Smith); *All Sports* (October, Columbia); *Football Action* (Fall, Fiction House); *Thrilling Football* (Fall, Standard).

Counting issues appearing only through 1939, the most successful titles were *Dime Sports* (46 issues); *Thrilling Sports* (22 issues); *Popular Sports* (16 issues); *Sports Novels* (16 issues); and *Ten Story Sports* (either 12 or 13 issues). Not counting *Sport Story* magazine, the total number of other general-interest sports pulps, plus those that specialized in baseball, football and basketball, from December 1933 (*All-America Sports* #1) through 1939, was 303 issues, give or take one or two issues of uncertain existence. In huge contrast, *Sport Story* magazine appeared 140 times from 1934 to 1939 (in other words, from the point it first had any competition) and published 388 issues in all from 1923 to 1939. *Sport Story* was the unquestioned king of the field.

Pulps from most major publishers have been well accounted for by historians and indexers, but a handful of questions remain about definite number counts for the Columbia/Double Action and Red Circle/Martin Goodman publications. That means number counts for those publishers are still being discovered, although this author and other historians have nailed it down to within one or two issues in every case. Complicating the situation were bookkeeping indicia errors, leading to the likes of a pair of Volume 4 #2, issues with different dates in a handful of cases. All such known errors are listed in *Ball Tales* in the appendix of sports pulps. However, since publishers almost always had a set number of issues in each volume—for example, three for Thrilling/Standard, four for Popular and Ace, six for Columbia and Red Circle—it makes the probable counts more accurate. Numbering errors still provide some puzzles.

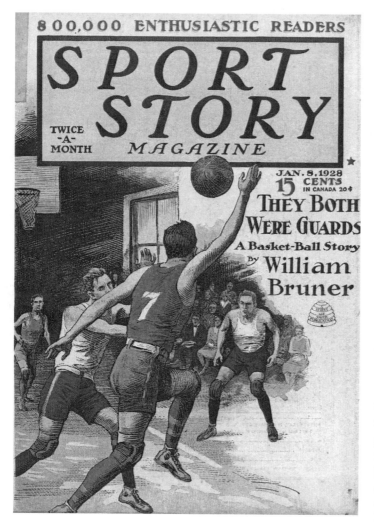

Sport Story, January 8, 1928 (copyright Street & Smith). Basketball (as the magazine spelled it then) in undershirts! The boast of "800,000 enthusiastic readers" included pass-along readership, since circulation was generally reported at about 150,000 for *Sport Story*, the first sports pulp.

Pulps provided more bang for the buck

Considering that the total number of all sports pulp issues from 1923 to 1957 was 1,530, give or take a few, the fact that nearly 700 issues appeared before 1940 is significant. Early, experimental television had not yet begun to cut into reading time, although talking films surely had done just that. Yet pulps gave the reader far more bang for the buck than most hardcover novels. The typical pulp contained well over 50,000 words and some ran to more than 100,000. Pulps were not, for the most part, publications that could be read in a single sitting.

As the 1930s wore on, sports pulps often had an increasingly difficult time competing for space on crowded newsstands with their pulp brethren, not to mention the influence of the modern comic books, a creation of the mid–1930s. The ten-cent comics began to multiply like rabbits in the late 1930s and 1940s, and pulps often suffered as a result.

Ever since pulps had achieved mass popularity in the 1920s in the wake of the demise of the dime and nickel novels, they were often fragile in circulation potential as well as paper quality. In fact, because of Street & Smith's overall financial success, *Sport Story* magazine was one of only 12 pulp titles to appear throughout *Sport Story*'s entire run from 1923 to 1943. It's telling that three others were Street and Smith publications—*Detective Story* magazine (1915 debut), *Western Story* magazine (1919) and *Love Story* magazine (1921), all fabulously successful.

Of the other 8 pulps to publish from 1923 (or before) to 1943 (or later), no publisher produced more than one title, and several titles had multiple publishers. These were *Action Stories* (which had only one issue in 1933 during a Depression-caused financial hiccup for Fiction House), *Adventure, Argosy, Black Mask, Blue Book, Ranch Romances* (which started in 1924 but belongs with this elite company), *Short Stories* and *Weird Tales*.

In fact, so difficult was it for pulps to survive the financial crucible of the early 1930s that only nine other titles that started in the 1920s appeared throughout the 1930s, as listed in *The Adventure House Guide to the Pulps*. These were *All Story Love Tales, Amazing Stories, Clues, Detective Fiction Weekly, Five Novels Monthly, Flying Aces, Lariat Story* magazine, *Sweetheart Stories* and *Western Trails*. A handful of other titles started early in the Depression and refused to wilt—*Astounding Stories* (1930), *Dime Detective* (1931) and *The Shadow* (1931).

Every one of the two dozen titles in the above three paragraphs stands as a major financial and artistic pulp success story, yet only Street & Smith's *Sport Story* magazine represented athletics. That speaks volumes about the small place of sport in the literature of the 1930s. Athletic stories took a serious backseat to love, detective and western epics. Even so, there were 389 known issues of sports pulps on the stands from July 1935 through 1939, including *Sport Story*—an average of seven issues per month. No other four-year period could claim that distinction.

Even so, of the 22 general-interest, nonseasonal sports pulps on the stands at any time in the 1930s, only Standard publisher Ned Pines' *Thrilling Sports* and *Popular Sports* continued uninterrupted through World War II, after beginning in 1936 and 1937, respectively. Even those two titles, which were among the longest-running sports successes in the pulp industry, were reduced to quarterly publication throughout most of the war. That says a lot about both wartime paper restrictions and a lack of stateside male readers. Several titles, such as *Sports Novels* and *Ace Sports*, picked up after the war for a few years following significant interruptions.

Sport Story magazine and the unrelated *All-America Sports* magazine both fairly often featured athletic activities such as track and field, skiing, tennis, and swimming on their covers, although baseball, football and boxing predominated (in those days, basketball was a distant fourth in public interest). Their rivals, however, seldom published a cover that did not feature baseball or football, with boxing and basketball, boxing and football and boxing and basketball occasionally prominent (see chapter five).

Sport Story magazine and variety

In Quentin Reynolds' *The Fiction Factory* (1955), a history of Street & Smith, *Sport Story* magazine was dismissed with only a few lines, so the best information available about this formidable publication comes from John Dinan's *Sports in the Pulp Magazines* (1998). Dinan's book devotes a fascinating chapter to the eclectic and pioneering *Sport Story*, including a count of all the different types of stories in the 429-issue run from 1923 to 1943.

Dinan counted a four-part baseball serial as four baseball stories because "a count of this kind gives a true picture of the sports-types balance both in individual issues and in the totals." I agree, and thus find the count a fascinating reflection both on the popularity of boxing and the decision of the editors to spotlight track and field, which was featured far less often by other publishers when the sports pulp boom began in the mid–1930s.

Dinan's research found 478 baseball stories in *Sport Story* magazine, or an average of more than one per issue. There were 363 boxing stories, which is not surprising considering that the likes of Jack Dempsey, Gene Tunney and Joe Louis created a golden age of boxing during the two decades *Sport Story* dominated the field. I was surprised, however, to see track and field rated third in total stories, with 281, just ahead of football's 259. The drama of football dominated the vast majority of other sports pulps, with an emphasis on college football. Also surprisingly, there were actually more hockey stories (164) than basketball tales (156) in *Sport Story*. Hockey, however, fell far behind in the 1940s and 1950s sports pulps.

In one sense, it's understandable that there were so many track and field stories, since 1924 Olympic champion (200 meters) Jackson Scholz worked primarily for Street & Smith in his pulp days, although he also contributed stories to other publishers before he began his prolific

Argosy, October 9, 1937 (copyright Frank A. Munsey Company). Uncle Sam, as rendered by V.E. Pyles, throws out the first pitch at the World Series.

novel-writing days (see chapter eleven). Scholz debuted in *Sport Story* in the second October 1924, issue, the same year he was a toast of the track and field world. He published a collection of ten of his track and field stories, *Split Seconds*, in 1927. This may have been the first collection of track tales.

Dinan notes that baseball stories led the totals for every year except 1930, 1931 and 1938, when boxing was number one. One of the most intriguing facts is how Frank Merriwell's creator, Gilbert Patten, was paid $620 for "The Rockspur Athletic Club" that appeared in the May 8, 1926, issue. If that figure is correct, Patten was paid the equivalent of well over $10,000 in today's dollars. Two other pieces in that issue were $100, Dinan notes, meaning well over $1,500 in today's dollars. The simple fact is that writers were paid much better in the 1920s than they are today; a single short story or novelette was more than enough to make house or rent payments!

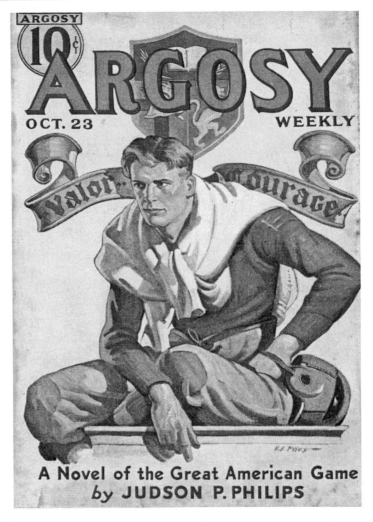

A Novel of the Great American Game by JUDSON P. PHILIPS

Argosy, October 23, 1937 (copyright Frank A. Munsey Company). V.E. Pyles portrays the hero at rest, the Big Game having been won.

One of the highlights of the information in this chapter is the listing of the so-called missing Merriwell story, since "Frank Merriwell and the Mystery Ship" by J. Irving Crump as by John Samson appeared in the two October 1929 issues. However, the story is not included on other lists of Merriwell's stories, including what I previously thought was a complete list in my reference collection. I have referred to that list for 40 years. Frank Merriwell — his exploits sometimes written by authors other than Patten but always appearing as by Burt L. Standish — was featured in four two-part serials in 1927 and three two-parters in 1928 in *Sport Story*. "The Mystery Ship" was Merriwell's final appearance in *Sport Story*. My list shows that during 1929 and 1930, stories of Merriwell by Patten frequently appeared in Street & Smith's *Top-Notch* magazine — four novelettes, four complete novels, one two-part serial and three three-part serials. *Fame and Fortune* magazine and its successor, *Fortune Story* magazine, featured five Merriwell novelettes in 1928 and 1929.

In 1932, *Sport Story* magazine ran Max Brand's only football story, "Thunderbolt," in three parts in October and November. Dozens of western stories and novels by Brand, whose real name was Felix Faust, have been reprinted following their original publication in Street & Smith's *Western Story* magazine, but I've never seen a reprint of "Thunderbolt." Michael Oriard, in his superb *King Football*, writes that this unique Brand piece "tells the story of Joe Cochrane ... a magnificent physical specimen with speed, brains and strength but not the most important quality of all — 'grit.' Joe Cochrane seems 'yellow' on the field, but one day the narrator of the story, the team's line coach (Lew Marvin), overhears a group of striking teamsters planning to beat up Cochrane, and learns that Joe works five or six hours a day as a drayman, around sleep, studies and caring for his younger brother.... While pondering this mystery, Lew rushes to assist Joe against the strikers, only to see him transformed into a 'madman,' emitting 'a whining sound of horrible joy' as he mangles the men who ambushed him. Afterward, Joe sees Lew at home with his kid brother, Tommy, who pleads with him to say he has not hurt anyone. And the next day at football practice, Joe asks Lew to forget what he saw last night. Lew is left baffled as the first installment ends, wondering why Joe 'seemed to have everything that should be in a man, except too little gameness on a football field, and too much of it in a fist fight.'"

Oriard reveals that the story later tells of Joe's father killing a man with his fists in a prizefight, and later being shot and killed in a brawl. Joe is afraid to use his hands, so the line coach switches him to the offensive line, where the use of hands is proscribed. That was only one of the pulpish plot devices Brand used. As Oriard puts it, "in its atavistic fascination with brute instincts and magnificent bodies, 'Thunderbolt' might seem close to Edgar Rice Burroughs's Tarzan novels and Robert E. Howard's Conan stories of the same period than to formulaic football fiction, but pulp football stories were in fact loaded with such stuff. Joe Cochrane's challenge was less to prove to others he was not 'yellow' — the more typical plot — than to prove to himself that he was civilized, but the obsession with physical toughness and fighting spirit, and the fascination with the 'magnificent' male body, were elements in dozens of stories."

Although no Merriwell pulp stories appeared after 1930 except for one in *Super Sports* in 1947 (see chapter nine), the Burt L. Standish pen name continued to appear on many stories from several different writers throughout the 1930s. Dinan notes 15 Standish stories in 1937 alone. *Sport Story* magazine often carried nonfiction, and Dinan notes nonfiction pieces outnumbered fiction in 1938! No other pulp sports magazine ever approached that distinction.

Dinan's notes on authors and trends in *Sport Story* magazine are the best information available on this publication. This admirable chapter, moreover, seems to be generally accurate and on point. Dinan's book, however, reminds researchers that it's difficult to write a comprehensive volume about any subject without at least a few errors. For example, in talking about the writer Doc McGee's predictions for the 1954 baseball season in the spring 1954 issue of Fiction House's *Baseball Stories* — the last issue — Dinan points out how McGee picked the Yankees and Dodgers to meet in the World Series. Dinan then says the Dodgers actually wound up sweeping the Cleveland Indians. It was not the Dodgers, of course, but the Willie Mays–sparked New York Giants who swept the Indians in four 1954 World Series games.

In talking about the relationship between the pulps and comic books in the 1930s (in chapter two), Dinan says, "[T]he pulp Adventure, for example, evolved into Adventure Comics, which in turn became Action Comics and later became Detective Comics." Nothing could be further from the truth, of course. Adventure was picked up by pulp titan Popular Publications beginning in 1934, continued into the 1950s and never had anything to do with comic books. National Periodical Publications (later DC Comics) began New Comics in December 1935, then changed the title to New Adventure with #12 (January 1937) and to Adventure Comics with #32 (November 1938). Meanwhile, Detective Comics began with #1 (March 1937) and Action started with #1 (June 1938).

In talking about the origins of the sports pulps in chapter three, Dinan talks about eleven long-running pulps "first published in the late 1920s or early 1930s." In reality, other than a few boxing pulps, there were no sports pulps to rival *Sport Story* magazine in the late 1920s and early 1930s until *All-America Sports* magazine appeared in 1933 and the next sports pulps debuted late in 1935 and in 1936, as detailed earlier in this chapter. Notwithstanding errors, I recommend Dinan's book to the reader interested in the sports pulps.

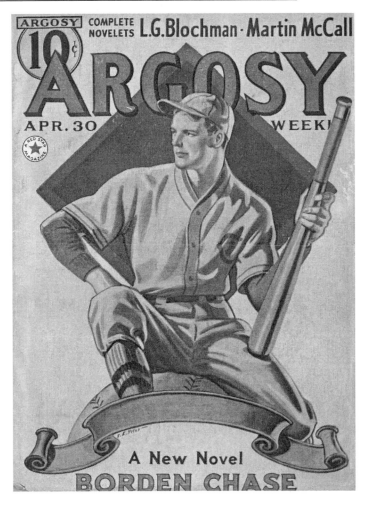

Argosy, April 30, 1938 (copyright Frank A. Munsey Company). Contrast this symbolic baseball hero with Pyles' football warrior.

Sports novels diminished in the 1930s

It's fortunate for readers who loved sports stories during the Great Depression of the 1930s that sports bloomed in the pulps, and that football movies were frequently seen, too (see chapter three). New hardcover sports novels for young adults (which adults read, too) were fairly infrequently published except for about 50 football, baseball and basketball books by those three old standbys from the pre–Depression era — Ralph Henry Barbour, William Heyliger and, later, Harold M. Sherman (several of Sherman's books are story collections, not novels, even though they seem to have been marketed by the title of the primary novelette).

That prolific threesome also contributed to the early sports pulps, especially Sherman, but they became best known for their novels. The three authors combined for no fewer than half of all new sports novels produced in the 1930–39 era, from the full first year of the depression to the beginning of World War II in Europe. While Barbour, Heyliger and Sherman combined to contribute those 50 Great Depression books near the end of their careers as sports novelists, only another 50 or so other football, basketball and baseball novels appeared in that decade, along with a handful of books dealing with other sports, such as John R. Tunis' two Iron Duke novels in 1938 and 1939 dealing with school life and running.

This total of about 100 books—not even one new sports novel a month on average during the 1930s—contrasts greatly with what came before and with 1940–1969, when there were about 650 (plus more about other sports). In part, this helps explain why so many old Sherman and Heyliger books still can be found in used-book stores, albeit far more often

All-America Sports, May-June 1938 (copyright All-America Periodicals, Inc.). This is the next-to-last issue of the second general-interest sports pulp, published from 1933 to 1938. "5c Each" reads the stamp below the title, evidence that the 15-cent magazine wound up in a second-hand book store.

without dust jackets than with them. There simply weren't many other sports novels available. Barbour's 1930s and 1940s books, written near the tail end of a novel-writing career that spanned nearly half a century, were not generally available in inexpensive reprints, in contrast to those by Sherman and Heyliger, and thus Barbour's books are much less often seen today.

During the 1930s, Barbour wrote six short series totaling 17 books about school and college life, football, baseball and basketball. Heyliger composed two stories, totaling eight volumes: the Stan Kent college football series and the Buddy Books. None of these are well remembered today. Sherman's books often were billed as part of a publisher's series, but they were almost all either collections or of the one-and-done story variety.

The Stratemeyer Syndicate was stunned by the death of founder Edward Stratemeyer in 1930, yet it carried over into 1930 to 1932 the final three books of the well-loved 10-volume Gary Grayson football series from Grosset & Dunlap, written as by Elmer Dawson, a Stratemeyer house name. The same pen name was applied to Dawson's five-book Buck and Larry series from 1930 to 1932 from Grosset, which was primarily a reprint or children's book firm, yet published many more first editions than even many veteran book dealers realize. (First editions, yes: fine literature, almost never.) The little-remembered Buck and Larry novels were all about baseball and sandlots, during summers and in prep school.

Andy McCue's incisive and vast compendium *Baseball by the Books* (1991) — the most comprehensive list of diamond fiction — shows just what a paucity of baseball novels there was in the 1930s. Other than Ring Lardner's last adult baseball book, *Lose with a Smile* (1933), and the classic adult mystery *Death on the Diamond* (1934) by Cortland Fitzsimmons, McCue lists a grand total of 29 baseball books, including the five Buck and Larry stories. (McCue is admirably comprehensive; I have not been able to find any other 1930s baseball novels or collections.)

Francis Wallace wrote

Street & Smith's *Love Story* magazine, November 9, 1935 (copyright Street & Smith). Modest Stein, one of the firm's most accomplished cover artists, portrays the glories of autumn love between a stylish coed and her leather-helmeted warrior.

seven football novels in the 1930s. Noel Sainsbury, writing under both his name and as by Charles Lawton, contributed five baseball/football novels for Cupples and Leon's briefly popular Champion Sports Stories series. Donal Haines wrote *The Southpaw* in 1931 and also had five other novels, primarily about football, during the decade. The total number of 1930s sports book authors, including the grand standby "Big Three" mentioned above, was no more than two dozen! Two of them, Elsie Wright and B.J. Chute, wrote what seemed to have been the first full-length hardcover sports novels by women writing for the young adult market (see chapter twelve). Thus, Wright produced *On the Forty Yard Line* as by Jack Wright (1923) and Chute came up with *Blocking Back* (1938, nicely revised in 1966). One can only guess what the reaction in 1932 would have been if a boy had picked up a football novel written by Elsie Wright! Wright also produced the hockey story *Champions on Ice* (1940), and both of her sports novels were reprinted in World Publishing's late 1940s six-book Falcon Sports Series, again presented as by Jack Wright, of course.

The famed, prolific and exceptionally versatile author Stephen Meader — a favorite of librarians for several decades — published an early collection of his sports stories from the young-adult magazines, titled *The Will to Win* (1936). The groundbreaking anthology *American Boy Sport Stories* appeared in 1929, but my research hasn't turned up any sports anthologies outside collections in the 1930s (see chapter thirteen).

Sports and glory in *Argosy*

It should be noted that *Argosy*, one of the best-selling anthology pulps, carried several serialized sports novels in the 1930s among the famed magazine's glorious potpourri of adventures all over the world (and other worlds, too). *Argosy* also occasionally offered dramatic and often idealized sports cover illustrations, especially those involving football and baseball. Few, if any, of these serials were ever reprinted as hardcover novels, but they surely entertained millions of adult readers and older teenagers. The October 9, 1937, issue of *Argosy* shows Uncle Sam throwing out the first ball at the World Series, amid a circled background of excited fans. Alas, there was no story of baseball or any other sport in that issue.

The heralded mystery author Judson P. Philips (1903–1989), who wrote numerous mystery novels as by Hugh Pentecost, penned his multitude of sports stories for several publishers under his real name. Philips headlines *Argosy*'s November 4, 1939, issue with the first chapter of the three-part pro football novel *Touchdown Broadway!* complete with a leather-helmeted football hero "carrying the mail" and about to employ a heroic straight-arm, with a huge football image in the background. Billed as "a fine new novel of racketeers in the pigskin," the story featured this enticing title-page blurb "From whistle-stop colleges to Times Square, from deans to gunsels, from cheerleaders to chiselers, the Slickers come to carry the ball for Dear Old Shylock."

Philips published what was billed "the football novel of the year" in *Argosy* with the five-part *Tiger on Parade*, beginning October 23, 1937. It's a story of Ivy League ball at Princeton, complete with another symbolic cover of a footballer with the scrolled coat-of-arms labeled "valor" and "courage" in the background. The cover is by the often underappreciated V.E. Pyles, who later did the above-mentioned Uncle Sam cover and many others for *Argosy*, several with sports themes.

Argosy would sometimes run the football "novel" complete in one issue, such as Philips' 34-page college story *Pigskin Pirate* in the October 13, 1934, issue. He contributed the novelette *Baseball Bandit* in the October 5, 1935, issue, which was billed this way: "Mike Havens, the tramp pitcher called himself — but that wasn't his name, and his past was to play a vital part in a Big League championship." In this unusual 24-page tale, the pitcher left the team following his heroics to begin a five-year prison sentence! "The Wingless Wonder," yet another Philips sports story, features a handsome Rudolph Belarski cover, with the pitcher appearing to throw at the reader while the hitter and catcher stand ready behind him. Who could resist a story with this title-page blurb: "So Tex Dillon, the veteran of a thousand tight pinches, took the long walk for the last time — finished. And maybe he was a little dumb, because he didn't know he'd pitched his greatest game with an arm that was as useless as a cripple's."

Richard Sale (1911–1993), like Philips, was usually at his best as an author of hardboiled stories of mystery and suspense; but Sale would occasionally tackle sports, too. His unusual *Argosy* baseball short story, "Screwball," in the May 22, 1937, issue, is narrated in the first person by a journalist named Pat — Patty, that is, and she married the hero! Pyles does a nice cover to illustrate it, but there's no female reporter in sight, just a pitcher releasing a very odd two-fingered fastball.

Aviation writer George Bruce's pulp novel *Navy Blue and Gold* (1936) was reprinted in hardback as one of the best sports stories of the 1930s — and one of the few made into a successful movie through the 1950s. Bruce (1894–1974) also wrote baseball novels, such as the tongue-in-cheek *The Speed King*, a four-part serial that began in the Aug. 29, 1936, issue. It's the entertaining tale of Lancefield Lee, a hillbilly pitcher/slugger in the Babe Ruth mold with dazzling minor league statistics. He is counted on to rejuvenate a struggling major league team, but finds it's tough to cope with modern society.

Cover artist Pyles drew a symbolic baseball cover for the *Argosy* of April 30, 1938, with a distinctly noble hitter, bat firmly in hand, portrayed atop a giant baseball, with a green

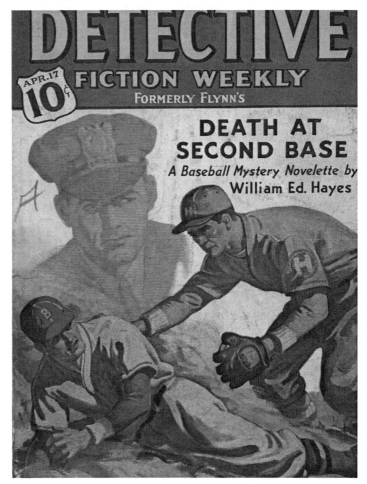

Detective Fiction Weekly, April 17, 1937 (copyright 1937, Red Star News Company). Sports mysteries first appeared in pulp magazines in the 1920s and occasionally pushed detectives off the cover. Note, though, the faint image of a police officer in the background.

diamond in the background. This one is a true gem of Americana. The name Martin McCall is given cover billing for the 16-page baseball romance "Rubber Arm," a novelette billed this way: "Crack of the swinging ash against leather [actually, horsehide], a hoarse roar from the bleachers, and a glove lifted high in the sunlit field ... that's the game of millions — and Bullet Jo Denning's life." The game wasn't his whole life, however — he and his intended head for their marriage license after he also proves himself a pitcher, not just a mindless thrower — complete with guts, cleverness and the help of his wily catcher.

Other general-interest pulp magazines, such as Dell's *Five Novels Monthly*, sometimes carried sports stories, but *Argosy* carried the most, though they were not even close to being in every issue. One of the joys for a sports fiction collector is searching through piles of *Argosy* issues, hoping to find an unexpected sports gem. The same can be said of the likes of slick magazines that regularly carried lots of fiction, such as the *Saturday Evening Post,* *Collier's* and *Liberty*. In an appendix in *King Football,* Michael Oriard lists 133 football stories in the *Post* and *Collier's* from 1920 to 1960, and 48 of them appeared in the 1930s. It's likely that hundreds of unexpected sports stories remain to be unearthed. Even though there were few hardbound sports novels in the 1930s, Oriard's list indicates that the slick general-interest magazines— and probably the general-interest pulps, as well — most likely carried more sports stories during that decade than any before or since. The Great Depression was a time for cheap literature.

THREE

When College Football
Was King on Film

The coming of sound to motion pictures in the late 1920s, the popularity of college football, and the explosion of escapist entertainment during the Great Depression gave football themes a huge edge over baseball in the 1930s. In that era, the color and pageantry of college football was a natural for sound films. Pro football was still of relatively minimal interest, and then only in the Midwest and Northeast. Baseball, both fiction and biographies, meanwhile, almost disappeared entirely from films until the 1940s. Unlike football, college baseball was virtually of no interest to moviemakers; and Major League Baseball was also too slow and colorless for the brand of fast-moving films audiences quickly came to love during the first 15 years or so of the "talkies," as so many people called them. The only other sport taken seriously by moviemakers of the time was boxing, which then ranked with baseball, football and horse racing as the "big four" of 1920s and 1930s sports, in the worlds of both fact and fiction.

Even college football, however, was considered little more than a lightweight topic in Hollywood at the time. Michael Oriard's comprehensive listing in an appendix of *King Football* shows 67 football films, including the first nonfictionalized biopic, released in the 1929–1941 period before the start of World War II. No fewer than 34 of these football films have heavy doses of comedy, musical themes and farce — almost all dealing with the zany antics of college heroes and coeds— including films Oriard labels "comedy-drama." There are, of course, "serious" dramas about football, in the sense that almost all of the plots came straight out of pulp magazines, if not the earlier Merriwell family epics, along with several films adapted from solid dramatic stories by the prolific slick magazine contributor Francis Wallace.

Football films were generally bottom-of-the-bill fare, judging from their plots and lengths, as detailed in the invaluable reference *Sports Movies* (1989), edited by Jeffrey H. Wallenfeldt and the staff at Cine Books. Of the "straight" football movies in the 1929–1941 period, perhaps the longest was *Huddle* (1932), a 103-minute Metro-Goldwyn-Mayer film based on Wallace's novel of the same name, followed by *Navy Blue and Gold* (1937), a 94-minute adaptation of famed aviation writer George Bruce's only hardbound sports novel, itself originally a pulp story.

Salute (1929), an early 20th Century–Fox talkie in which John Wayne and Ward Bond had small roles as football players, ran 83 minutes; *The Band Played On* (1934) from MGM ran 87. The comedy *So This Is College* (93 minutes, 1941) also could be considered a feature presentation, along with a few others. One of the difficulties, however, of looking back at the various books dealing with films of sport is determining just what should be called a "sports film."

The vast majority of those 67 football films in the 1930s ran less than 80 minutes in black and white, and are thus almost entirely forgotten today except by genre enthusiasts. Most of them were seldom, if ever, shown on television, and so virtually no sports fans today have seen these films, unlike the memorable likes of famed biopics about Knute Rockne (1940) and Jim Thorpe (1951).

During the same 1929–1941 period, moviemakers almost entirely ignored anything serious about baseball. The inimitable Joe E. Brown starred, along with the baseball, in the wonderful Warner Brothers comedies *Elmer the Great* (1933) and *Alibi Ike* (1935)— drawn from the remarkable fiction of Ring Lardner — and clearly loved the sport. Brown was the ideal man to star in diamond comedies (and many other memorable comedies as well. Who could forget Brown's performance in the 1959 *Some Like It Hot?*). *Elmer the Great* was a remake of the early talkie *Fast Company* (1929), which was the first screen version of the Lardner/George M. Cohan stage play about slugger Elmer Kane, otherwise known as Elmer the Great.

The few 1930s baseball films

While football was making frequent appearances on the screen, albeit often in less-than-memorable quickies, the only other 1929–1941 baseball film fictions were *Death on the Diamond* (1934), *Girls Can Play* (1937), *Swell Head* (1935), *Hot Curves* (1930) and *They Learned About Women* (1930). The latter two films are thoroughly forgettable comedies, while *Death on the Diamond* is a good-of-its-kind whodunit featuring a baseball detective story, and *Girls Can Play* is a long-forgotten softball mystery.

Death on the Diamond, published in 1934 by Cortland Fitzsimmons, was the first widely distributed adult baseball mystery. It was not marketed for young adults, nor were the author's football whodunit, *Seventy Thousand Witnesses* (1931) and his seldom-seen hockey mystery, *Crimson Ice* (1935). The baseball and football mysteries were made into entertaining movies with the same titles, although the baseball film, released in 1934, emerged as far more successful and better remembered than the football movie, released in 1932.

Death on the Diamond, a 69-minute release from MGM, stars Robert Young, still two decades removed from television fame in *Father Knows Best*. Young, then 27 years old and three years into his movie career, plays energetic rookie pitcher Larry Kelly. The pitcher and the ever present 1930s spunky sports reporter, in this case a journalistic dynamo named Jimmie Downey played by 35-year-old Paul Kelly, witness the murders of several St. Louis Cardinals. The killer is revealed to be a deranged groundskeeper, which makes sense, when you think about it. *Death on the Diamond*, despite serious technical flaws that make it seem severely dated, remains an entertaining mystery and a nice period piece. Film critic Hal Erickson, in his *Baseball Filmography* (2002), says the film "works as a fast-paced, satisfying whodunit," but *Sports Movies* calls it a "strikeout." I agree with Erickson; the film is still worth seeing.

Even the most enthusiastic annotator of sports films hasn't heard of them all, much less seen every one of them; and so it was that Erickson's remarkable *Baseball Filmography* introduced me to *Girls Can Play*. It is, I believe, the first movie about softball, based on the story "Miss Casey At Bat" written for the studio by Albert DeMond. It's a 59-minute quickie, directed by Lambert Hillyer for Columbia in 1937, one year after he directed *Dracula's Daughter* (1936), which was Universal's sequel to *Dracula*. Hillyer, who directed an untold number of "B" films in the 1930s and 1940s, achieved notoriety among pop-culture fans with his direction of the unintentionally hilarious first Batman serial for Columbia in 1943. That serial was "rediscovered" in January 1966 and played in theaters during the early run of the sensationally popular Batman television show, during an era when sports fiction in the films and on television was almost nonexistent.

Rita Hayworth swings a bat

Girls Can Play is such an obscure sports mystery that it isn't listed in *Sports Movies*, which was the best available compendium at the time it was published in 1989. Just as in *Death on the Diamond*, the softball team's ace pitcher and a star reporter discover the murderer, who turns out to be the team's owner, also a drugstore owner. The ace pitcher, Casey, is played by Jacqueline Wells, who went on to achieve fame as Julie Bishop, and the reporter is portrayed by Charles Quigley, whose roles in many B films included a lead in the outstanding 1939 Republic serial *Daredevils of the Red Circle*. What has made *Girls Can Play* of interest to historians, however, is the appearance of Rita Hayworth, who was then a stunning 19-year-old. Aside from a couple of roles as a child, Hayworth's film career began in 1935 as Rita Cansino, and she was still billed as Cansino—her real name—in three of the eight films in which she appeared in 1937. In *Girls Can Play*, she plays Sue Collins, who falls victim to poison on her catcher's mitt.

One of the earliest adult baseball fiction books, the short-story collection *Hearts and the Diamond* (1921) by Gerald Beaumont, provided the source material for an earlier and even more obscure Columbia quickie. This was the 62-minute quickie *Swell Head*, but Erickson Calls' story involves a conceited power hitter who temporarily goes blind when he is beaned, but is redeemed by his girlfriend and her kid brother.

One can easily see why Erickson, whose comprehensive and entertaining book is a must-read for anyone interested in baseball films from any period, is surely correct when he calls Joe E. Brown's star vehicle, *Alibi Ike*, "also the best baseball picture made during the 1930s. It is jam-packed with comedy, ranging from situational humor to farce to out-and-out slapstick, and its ballpark scenes, particularly the climactic night game, are first-rate. The biggest advantage 'Alibi Ike' has over the handful of other baseball films of its era is that its star unabashedly adored the game, and this love permeates the movie's every frame." Erickson's praise is 100 percent warranted; *Alibi Ike* is one of the best of all Warner Brothers comedies, and a fabulous baseball film. It remains eminently watchable today.

Ring Lardner's "Alibi Ike," first published in the *Saturday Evening Post* in 1915, provides endless excuses for Joe E. Brown's marvelously rendered version of rookie pitching star Francis X. Farrell, who earned his nickname for making the most creative excuses in baseball history. If you haven't viewed this 72-minute tale of romance, gangsters and baseball heroics, make every effort to see it. As Erickson points out in his perceptive essay on *Alibi Ike*— one of the best pieces of baseball filmography ever — the picture brings in numerous real major leaguers, and Brown did his own baseball stunts. The real-life wackiness of Dizzy Dean, then a national pitching hero with the "Gashouse Gang" of the St. Louis Cardinals, unintentionally gave the film a significant lift. Olivia de Havilland, then 19 and just beginning her distinguished career, played Brown's love interest in the same year she achieved greater renown with Errol Flynn in *Captain Blood*.

Erickson reports that Brown's favorite baseball role was that of Elmer in *Elmer the Great*, the 72-minute 1933 Warner Brothers comedy in which the Chicago Cubs win the World Series over the New York Yankees, one year after the reverse situation occurred. Like *Alibi Ike*, this earlier film is well worth seeing. So is the 67-minute *Fireman Save My Child* (1932), although Erickson points out that the short film is "hampered by a script that can't make up its mind whether it wants to be a baseball story, a firefighting farce, a 'crazy inventions' yarn or romantic comedy, and as a result, it falls short in all its potential categories." Fans are directed to Erickson's work for in-depth information.

Judy Garland's feature debut in *Pigskin Parade*

Of the pre–World War II football films—there were virtually none yet devoted to basketball—one of the most memorable is the 95-minute *Pigskin Parade* (1936), a thoroughly enjoyable send-up of the conventions of college football fiction in all media. Here Judy Garland, at 14, made her feature film debut, outside of group appearances with her sisters. Robert Cantwell, in his groundbreaking essay "Sport Was Box-Office Poison" in *Sports Illustrated* for September 15, 1969—one of the first pieces ever written about sports film as genre—dwelled primarily on silent films. But Cantwell was spot-on when he wrote this about *Pigskin Parade*: "It was [director David] Butler who gave sports movies a sudden boost in 1936—after they were thought to be hopelessly outdated—when he put together 'Pigskin Parade,' a musical about a small Texas college that received, by mistake, an invitation to play Yale and hastily assembled a football team built around a cantaloupe tosser from the farmlands. The movie was quickly and inexpensively made, with Stuart Erwin and Betty Grable starring, and was an enormous financial success, in part because of the singing 14-year-old girl, Judy Garland, and in part because it expertly ridiculed the innumerable tedious college football movies of the past."

Erwin earned an Academy Award nomination for his truly funny role as the country football bumpkin. Grable was only 20, a long way from her own glory days as the iconic World War II pinup queen. Patsy Kelly and Jack Haley were wonderful. If you haven't seen *Pigskin Parade*, make every effort to do so. As for football films of the pre–World War II era there weren't many, unless, of course, you want to count the Marx Brothers classic *Horsefeathers* (1932), which really belongs in another category. There were some intriguing titles—*Spirit of Notre Dame* (1931), *Gridiron Flash* (1935), *The Big Game* (1936), *Navy Blue and Gold* (1937), *Saturday's Heroes* (1937), *$1,000 a Touchdown* (1939)—but these films are almost totally forgotten. Cantwell put it this way: "[T]he shows were by and large entertaining when they were comedies—or melodramas—and disasters when they were tragic or sentimental. The movie colony was simply too knowing about sports to shed an honest tear over a horse race or football game."

One year after Nelson Eddy made his unforgettable *Rose Marie* (1936), he became a battling baritone as a West Point football hero wooing Eleanor Powell in *Rosalie* (1937). Eddy, though, was about 35 years old!

The Misadventures in *The Adventures of Frank Merriwell*

Frank Merriwell, whose multi-sport dime novel and pulp heroics won more games than any fictional character in American history, was the first fictitious sports "name" to be featured in the movies. It might seem odd that Frank did not "break into" films until 1936, two decades after the 20-year run of the original Merriwell Family dime novels ended. But the syndicated Merriwell radio show and comic strip, along with the endless Merriwell book reprints, may have inspired Universal to produce "The Adventures of Frank Merriwell" in 1935. The 12-chapter serial was released in January 1936, three months before the iconic serial that was to make Universal many millions: *Flash Gordon* (1936). The "Ace of Space" made Universal many, many more big bucks when additional Flash Gordon serials followed in 1938 and 1940, sandwiched around a Buck Rogers serial in 1939, with 1932 Olympic swimming gold medalist Larry "Buster" Crabbe playing the classic comic-strip space adventurer in all four epics.

There is heavy irony involving fictional fame and Universal's serial fortunes. When the *Flash Gordon* serial was released, the character was only two years old, having been introduced on January 7, 1934, as a Sunday comic strip drawn by Alex

Under the Basket by Harold M. Sherman, 1932 (jacket copyright Goldsmith Publishing). Although basketball was almost never seen in 1930s films and was then seldom the theme of pulp fiction, young adult stories such as this collection of seven tales by Harold M. Sherman kept the game in the public consciousness.

Raymond, who also achieved great fame with Jungle Jim and Secret Agent X-9. When "The Adventures of Frank Merriwell" debuted on the screen in 1936, Gilbert Patten's character was 40 years old and Frank (and his brother and son) had appeared in more than 1,000 stories (see chapter one). In 1936, infinitely more Americans were familiar with Frank Merriwell than with Flash Gordon.

Yet word of mouth and the exotic nature of Flash's adventures fighting Ming the Merciless on the planet Mongo ultimately made his serial the best known in the history of chapter plays. The very nature of Frank Merriwell's adventures—in athletics and a variety of battles against bad guys in exotic locales—were a staple of many media. In contrast, Flash

Gordon was the first "space opera" ever filmed, long before the likes of *Destination Moon* in 1950 and *The Day the Earth Stood Still* in 1951 set the tone for a multitude of 1950s and 1960s science fiction epics. The few genuine science fiction movies until 1936, such as *Metropolis* and *Things to Come*, were high-concept films and were anything but space opera, a genre many buffs have described as "shoot-em ups in space" and "horse operas with ray guns."

Universal had been producing "talkie" cliff-hangers (as the serials were affectionately called) since the first such were made in 1929, two years after the introduction of sound, but *The Adventures of Frank Merriwell* looked creaky throughout for 1936. Many serial historians have never seen it and there are many misconceptions about this chapter play (for example, one respected film historian has Frank scoring the winning run in baseball, not the winning point in football), but I have been fortunate to obtain a copy. The year 1936 was basically the "dividing line" between old-style production values and far better special effects (albeit badly dated today). By 1936, the smaller studios had either merged with larger outfits or had given up on serials. Except for four forgotten serials in 1936 and *Blake of Scotland Yard* from Victory Productions in 1937, only Republic, Columbia and Universal would produce serials over the next two decades, or until television killed them for good in 1956.

The Adventures of Frank Merriwell looks and sounds like something that belonged, if not in the silent era, then with the primitive 1929–1932 introductions of serials, when 31 cliff-hangers were released. The only one of those chapter plays seriously involving sports was the 1931 *The Galloping Ghost*, starring Red Grange, the real Galloping Ghost of Fighting Illini fame. He was six years removed from college glory but still the most famous name in his sport, along with Notre Dame coach Knute Rockne and the fabulous Jim Thorpe. In Grange's serial, released by long-forgotten Poverty Row studio Mascot, Grange battles criminals to clear his name and resume his college football career in a plot that even then was hackneyed.

There were no more sports-related serials until *The Adventures of Frank Merriwell*, which may have convinced the powers-that-were at Universal that the chapter play would seem original to the kids. But poor production values and a cast of unknowns doomed Frank to a one-and-out film "career" and there was no other fictional sports hero featured in the 231 sound serials released from 1929 to 1956, though Flash Gordon, of course, had been a polo player.

The only performer in the Frank Merriwell serial to eventually become the least bit successful was Jean Rogers, who was 19 and indeed looked like a college student when she played Elsie Belwood, one of Frank's two love interests in the dime novels. (The only other name lifted from the dime novels for this serial was, indeed, Frank Merriwell!) Bart Hodge, Frank's talented sidekick, became Bruce Browning in the film, played by the unknown John King. The equally unknown Don Briggs played Frank with an earnest, energetic style but not much acting ability. The gorgeous Rogers went on to make an immediate impression as Dale Arden in the first two Flash Gordon serials, and she enjoyed a successful career in several "A" films in the 1940s before retiring in 1951. Carla Laemmle, of the famed Universal executive family, played Elsie's sidekick and did some dancing, but she became no better known than Briggs or King.

Many of Frank Merriwell's dime novel adventures involved adventurous settings off the athletic fields, so in that sense the serial was not off-base. Only the first two and last two chapters involved college sports activity — baseball, track and football in that order — although boxing and crew played small roles in other chapters. Frank and his entourage —

he always had an entourage!—battled some truly nasty villains throughout as Frank sought to help his father find a treasure. Ironically, the chapters that did not involve sports were a whole lot more convincing than those that did.

In the serial's preview, the epic was billed primarily as a sports serial and as "the super serial of the year." On the title card of every chapter, Frank was called "The Hero of a Thousand College Sports Stories," which was accurate only if you counted Dick and Frank Junior, too. Patten was credited with being "The Original Burt L. Standish," no doubt because Patten never liked the fact that Street & Smith let others use the pen name.

In chapter one, "College Hero," Frank arrives late at Fardale's crucial baseball game against Calford. That's right, Fardale is a college instead of a prep school in the serial, and the story is set on the West Coast instead of at Yale, which everyone knew was Frank's real alma mater. This was doubtless because Universal did not want to move shooting to the East Coast. In fact, at the very time the serial was being shown in theaters, the only Frank Merriwell Big Little Book was on sale; it was entitled *Frank Merriwell at Yale*. Who knows how many kids *that* baffled! Frank doesn't appear until the ninth inning because he had to take a boy's hit-and-run victim dog to the "hospital," thereby telling the kids in the audience that here, indeed, was a good guy par excellence. When a police officer chases a speeding Frank and Elsie, who are trying to get to the game, Frank first outruns and finally ditches the motorcycle officer and nothing more is ever said about it! When he finally arrives at the game, without so much as one minute of a warmup, he pinch hits a grand slam when he takes over with two strikes on the hitter and Fardale one out away from defeat. Then he takes over the mound and sets Calford down in order, striking out the final hitter on three pitches, and is carried off amid boola-boola celebrations.

After surviving a train crash at the end of chapter one, Frank wins the 220-yard dash at a track meet in chapter two, "The Death Plunge," then fills in for a missing pole vaulter and prevails with a 14-foot leap. In 1935, the Olympic record was 14 feet, and three-quarter inches! Indeed, when Frank and his rival both clear 13 feet, the bar is immediately raised to 14 feet—an unheard of situation in the real world of track and field. The baseball game was improbable; the track and field meet was impossible!

Football doesn't enter the picture until chapter eleven, when Frank has returned to Fardale to become a "Merriwell Sensation!" as huge headlines put it, superimposed over action scenes in the manner of movies of that era. When he is held out of the game against Tech—the reason is never stated—the coach calls him into action in the fourth quarter and he helps beat Tech 21–0 with a 95-yard interception return for a touchdown and a long punt return for a score. Frank survives a car crash at the end of the chapter, then arrives late in the fourth quarter of Fardale's showdown against Calford. He runs for a touchdown and kicks the conversion, then catches a long touchdown pass after the gun sounds and kicks the game-winning goal (as extra points were then known), giving Fardale a 20–19 victory. Frank immediately receives a telegram telling him his father has prevailed over the gangsters, then hears "Three Cheers for Frank Merriwell" from his teammates and entourage as he hugs Elsie and the film fades out.

Whew! Frank, though, was never again on the screen. Nor was there ever to be another serial based on a sports hero, although *Daredevils of the Red Circle* from Republic in 1939 featured three circus acrobats, including famed stuntman Dave Sharpe and Herman Brix, the Olympic shot putter and football star from the University of Washington. In 1941, following Slingin' Sammy Baugh's fourth season of National Football League stardom in 1940 as a quarterback, defensive back and punter, Baugh played a heroic, two-fisted lawman in

King of Texas Rangers from Republic. His fictional ranger was, like Baugh himself, a college star from Texas and there were football scenes in the first chapter. This was Baugh's only significant fling with films.

In 1946, Universal abandoned serials, leaving the genre to Republic and Columbia for its final decade. Columbia released a Jack Armstrong serial in 1947, starring John Hart as Jack. But athletics plays no role in this adventure pitting Jack and his entourage — he always had one, too — against enemy agents and a mad scientist (there was rarely any other kind in the serials).

FOUR

A Smattering
of Adult Sports Fiction

In the fall of 1950, a little more than a decade into the readers' revolution that 25-cent paperback books produced, then-fledgling Canadian paperback firm Harlequin Books used a telling blurb on the back of an obscure hockey-centered novel, *Rink Rat*, by Don MacMillan. This blurb for *Rink Rat*, which was published in hardback by the Canadian branch of the British film company J.M. Dent & Sons, said much about the state of sports fiction for adults: "Against the background of the fastest game on earth is laid an ADULT story dealing with the timeless search of man for a meaning in life.... Men will enjoy the inside story of the game, women the hero's romantic adventures." What makes this blurb so significant is the capitalization of ADULT. Until the 1950s, sports fiction was almost entirely the province of the young-adult or juvenile market, aside from the pulp magazines ostensibly directed at adult readers but also often read by teenagers. The Harlequin folks surely knew this; an ADULT paperback novel dealing with sports was, indeed, something different. The author never had another paperback published.

In 1950, Harlequin was 15 years away from the beginning of its romance-novel empire. The firm published a wide variety of paperback books, but did not produce another sports fiction book until Harlequin reprinted Frank O'Rourke's *The Football Gravy Train* (1951) in 1957, the same year the firm republished *Rink Rat*. The lack of Harlequin sports fiction was typical: fewer than two dozen adult baseball, football or basketball novels—originals or reprints—appeared through the 1950s and not many in the 1960s, coinciding with the almost total absence of movies about team sports during that decade (see chapter fourteen).

Sports-related mysteries, which proliferated beginning in the 1980s and now number in the dozens, were almost unheard of through the 1950s outside stories in the pulp magazines, plus Cortland Fitzsimmons' groundbreaking football, baseball and hockey hardbound mysteries of the 1930s and the much better known mystery writer Marc Stein's baseball whodunit, *Twin Killing*, in 1947 as by George Bagby, which appeared in both hardbound and pulp magazine format.

Even high-concept "literary" sports series—tales that few teenagers or pulp action fans would have found satisfying—were almost totally unseen until the 1950s. Millard Lampell, not normally a sports novelist, produced in 1949 for Julian Messner the football novel *The Hero*, which was reprinted in slightly abridged form by paperback giant Popular Library in September 1950. The story, on which the film *Saturday's Hero* (1951) was based, was plugged on the paperback cover as *He Loved Another Man's Woman* and on the title page as *A Football Romance*. The romance angle had been used a decade earlier in an obscure adult baseball novel entitled *Dust in the Afternoon* (1940) by Holmes Alexander. A female author wrote her only sports novel in 1950, also with a theme of romance, although set in the 19th century: Lucy Kennedy's little-known *The Sunlit Field*.

The noted novelist Robert Wilder published the downbeat college football novel *Autumn Thunder* in 1952, which was reprinted by Bantam in 1954 as one of at least 13 Wilder novels reprinted by that leading paperback firm, including his much better known *Written on the Wind* in 1952. Neither Lampell nor Wilder would have been thought of as a sports story teller by the general public, nor would Bernard Malamud, whose densely written *The Natural* (1952) for Harcourt, Brace was quickly reprinted in July 1953 in an edition of 255,000 copies by yet another paperback giant, Dell. Yet by the time *The Natural*, which was Malamud's first book, became a hugely popular Robert Redford film fantasy in 1984, the book had been largely forgotten by all but Malamud devotees, first edition collectors, and dedicated sports fiction enthusiasts. (A fine first edition of *The Natural* today is worth several thousand dollars and is the most valuable sports fiction novel.) Likewise, Mark Harris was not well known when he came forth with his Henry Wiggin baseball trilogy, *The Southpaw* (1953), *Bang the Drum Slowly* (1956) and the short novel *Ticket for a Seamstitch* (1956). Harris' books were not sought by paperback publishers during their original era; only "The Southpaw" was reprinted, and then by the little-known Perma firm in 1954. These three novels were followed much later by the morose *It Looked Like Forever* (1979), which told the tale of the colorful pitcher's inevitable final days after a long, successful career. The Harris books were not published in paperback for many years, but they received a huge boost when the tragic comedy *Bang the Drum Slowly* hit the screen in 1973 as a thoroughly "A" production featuring Robert De Niro and Michael Moriarty.

Ring Lardner's stories of a generation earlier surely influenced writers of 1950s sports fiction, especially Harris' creation of the bizarre Henry Wiggin. Jackie Robinson's historic promotion to the Brooklyn Dodgers in 1947 influenced the little-known, 80-page book *Behold Thy Brother* by the non-baseball author Edmunds Murrell from the obscure Beechhurst Press in 1950. This bizarre story might as well be classified as an alternate-world piece, since it takes place in 1945! Andy McCue, in *Baseball by the Books*, describes the story this way: "Team with a failing pitching staff late in the 1945 pennant race has a black pitcher thrust on them by the owner's liberal son. The manager tries to avoid using him, but eventually must. He wins the pennant clincher."

It's fascinating to note the more than 125 baseball, basketball and football novels listed in the bibliography included with the academic volume *The Achievement of American Sports Literature* (1991) edited by Wiley Lee Umphlett. Of the baseball and softball fiction, aside from a note about Ring Lardner's works, the only pre–1960 novels listed are Eliot Asinof's *Man on Spikes* (1955), the three 1950s Harris books and Malamud's story. Of basketball and football, there is only the obscure football tale *The Homecoming Game* (1957) by Howard Nemerov, on which the stage play and basketball film *Tall Story* (1960) was based, along with the obscure football-related *Professor Fodorski* (1950) by Robert Taylor.

The 1955 *Man on Spikes*, Asinof's first book, is literature, not pulp fiction in any way, yet it is probably the first truly "pure baseball" adult novel to appear in hardback. In other words, it's a story that would appeal to the same reader who enjoyed young-adult novels or pulp fiction, but told on an adult level. The same could be said of two paperback originals by the famed journalist/mystery novelist/baseball biographer Charles Einstein: the well-regarded *The Only Game in Town* (1955) and the obscure but nicely done short novel *Win — Or Else!* (1954), written as by D.J. Michael. A fourth original novel to emerge from this era of paperback sports scarcity was pulp mystery writer Fletcher Flora's *The Hot-Shot* (1956), a genuine curiosity from Avon, which along with Dell, Popular Library, Bantam, Ballantine, Ace and Gold Medal was a paperback publishing goliath in the 1950s.

In the exploitive, pulpish cover-art manner of the 1950s era, *The Hot-Shot*, *The Natural* and *The Hero* all featured the athletic protagonist in the company of a full-figured woman with plenty of cleavage exposed and, in each case, a come-hither expression. Women were major figures in Einstein's two baseball paperback originals, but were not shown on the covers. *The Hot-Shot*, of which there is more to come, has easily the most outrageous cover theme of any sports paperback of the pre–1970 period. A studly basketball player is shown peering out of the corner of his eye at the overly ample charms of the young woman draped all over him. With cigarette hanging from his mouth and an illegal payoff in his hands, the three-inch headline "The Big Fix" stands out at the top of the *Daily Star*. This is the kind of cover that often appeared on the likes of exploitive paperbacks of all genres, but almost never on the pulp magazines outside of the titles generally sold under the counter.

From the late 1940s through the 1960s, there were also a couple of dozen young-adult novels by the likes of Jackson Scholz, Joe Archibald and John Carson reprinted from hardbound editions by the "young adult" branches of large paperback houses, such as the three Frank Merriwell Junior novels from Award Books in the 1960s and three 1960s novels for the American Sports Library, ostensibly cowritten by no less than Willie Mays, Yogi Berra and Whitey Ford!

Yet, among the more than 14,000 paperbacks published from 1939 to 1959, there were fewer than a dozen devoted to adult novels of team sports! Only a handful followed in the 1960s. The paucity is similar to the distinct scarcity of fictional team sports themes in the films and comic books of the period, in stark contrast to the availability of numerous pulp magazines (through the early 1950s) and young-adult/juvenile books. Apparently, not only were sports "box office poison," as *Sports Illustrated*'s Robert Cantwell once famously said in 1969 of films, but paperback impresarios had little use for team sports themes either.

Most paperback publishers in the 1940s reprinted hardback originals during the industry's first decade of existence. Yet paperback originals became predominant or frequent from several publishers in the 1950s, but the vast majority involved themes of exploitation, mystery, western, science fiction and juvenile delinquency (some paperback enthusiasts prefer to place Flora's *The Hot-Shot* in mystery or juvenile delinquency categories). Paperback publishing has been thoroughly catalogued by several price guides, and the only 1940s or 1950s sports team originals to be found are Flora's basketball novel and Einstein's two baseball novels, all prized by collectors.

Einstein's *The Only Game in Town*

Former New York and San Francisco newspaperman Charles Einstein's second baseball novel, *The Only Game in Town* (1955), was his second book in the Dell First Edition Series, sandwiched around his novel *Win — Or Else!* (1954) written as by D.J. Michael for Lion Books, one of the lesser paperback publishers.

The absorbing *The Only Game in Town* followed *The Bloody Spur*, a tense 1953 newspaper mystery and among the best of its era. RKO adapted *The Bloody Spur* for a 1956 movie thriller, *While the City Sleeps*, directed by Fritz Lang and starring Dana Andrews, Ida Lupino and George Sanders. Somewhat deceivingly, Dell reissued *The Bloody Spur* in its First

Edition series in 1956 under the title of the movie, although the publisher did list the original title in small type. *The Only Game in Town* was just as well written, if not better, as *The Bloody Spur*, but this splendid baseball story was neither reprinted nor filmed. Einstein went on to concentrate on three award-winning *Fireside* anthologies of baseball fact and fiction, the first of which appeared in 1956, along with such outstanding baseball accounts as *A Flag for San Francisco* (1962)—written the season before the Giants actually won the 1962 pennant in a memorable playoff with the Los Angeles Dodgers—and *Willie Mays: My Life In and Out of Baseball* (1966), and *Willie's Time* (1979), a memoir that was Einstein's 29th book.

Einstein, of course, knew longtime big league manager Leo Durocher well, and thus this blurb from Durocher appeared at the top of *The Only Game in Town: From Class C to the Majors — This is Baseball!* That alone, probably sold a good many books, since no one had ever seen a Durocher endorsement on a baseball novel before! As the book states on the copyright page, "A shorter version of this book appeared in Collier's," which by the 1950s was among the few remaining adult magazines that occasionally published sports fiction. For the paperback cover, Einstein used part of Fletcher Martin's painting *Out at Home*, the full version of which was used for the front endpaper in the first Fireside anthology.

The protagonist of *The Only Game in Town* had one of the great fictional baseball names of all time, Stat Hunter. His real name was Andrew and it was with some disappointment, though no surprise, that readers learned he acquired his nickname, short for "Statutory," from other players when he dated the 17-year-old daughter of an umpire. That tells you a lot about Einstein's skill as a writer; not many other novelists could come up with a typically sardonic baseball nickname and yet make it a clever double entendre.

Stat, as the story opens, is a sore-armed former major league outfielder, a veteran of 16 seasons in the Big Time (as they called it in the days before it became The Show). Stat, not quite 37 years old, is managing the Conway Bears in the Class C Empire League in upstate New York (in the days when baseball's organized minor leagues had numerous ratings, ranging from Triple-A to Class D). Stat is thoroughly adult, cynical, and hardheaded; yet, in many ways, he seems to be a decent, grown-up Frank Merriwell sort, hopelessly in love with baseball. He has divorced his wife, Marian, in large part because of his devotion to baseball, and she has custody of their 8-year-old daughter, Janet, whom, it is always made clear, he cares for responsibly and loves with all his heart.

The other primary characters are a selfish, egotistical, unethical but undeniably talented young second baseman, Joe Whittier; the self-defeating baseball floozy Jo Ann; and Walt Corio, a talented veteran power-hitter who was banned from baseball for life for participation in a gambling ring in 1946 under his real name, Carsi. He didn't throw games, but he bet on them, much as the Pete Rose situation developed many years later. Organized Ball (as the professional game reverently was known) was (and still is) unforgiving of anything to do with gambling. Gamblers have appeared in hundreds of baseball stories on all levels, but Einstein made them seem weak-willed, seriously flawed humans, not the cartoonish villains of so many pulp magazine stories and baseball books. Einstein takes all the pulp conventions to heart—the baseball lifer, the gamblers, the women who wait and hunger, the game's dramatics, the improbable promotions and developments—and turns them on their heads, making them seem like a logical part of a heart-warming story. A real-life tale like Stat's would have been improbable, yet any particular character and any particular circumstance was very much part of reality, then and now.

Corio, seeking a ball-playing situation he can take advantage of both on and off the field, lasts through nearly half the story before Stat discovers his secret. Stat hands him a serious pounding for several reasons—described fearfully well by the hardboiled mystery writer Einstein sometimes was—and throws him off the Conway team. Two-thirds of the way through the book, the parent club, Philadelphia Bears, mired in sixth place in an eight-team league, give their managerial job to Stat, who also places himself on the active roster during a period when a few player-managers still existed. Meanwhile, Boston acquires hot prospect Whittier in a trade and soon brings him to the big time, where his fate and Stat's soon become intertwined.

Although Einstein uses cities, not team nicknames, he has Stat engage in a delightful mental digression about the quality of baseball players, from the year he first came up to his present time. Einstein mentions dozens of names and has fun with the reader. From a remove of more than 50 years, it's easy to see why he capped this exercise in fun for fans with this: "[A]nd [the current game] had the most exciting center fielder Stat had ever watched: Willie Mays."

Occasionally, Einstein jars the reader with cynical baseball reality: "The Bears had culled [aging black pitcher] Moses Jones out of the obscurity of a touring, clowning team which at that time was in Salem, Oregon, in a patent effort to bolster the gate by bringing in colored fans, but Moses had saved games [for the Bears] and his presence on the team called for an immediate exercise of sports-writing ingenuity in a drive to dress him with a suitable nickname ... and, as finally formulated by a columnist for an afternoon paper ... they all called him Ol' Man Mose." Stat, moreover, is no bigot; he immediately gives Jones a significant role commensurate with his true ability.

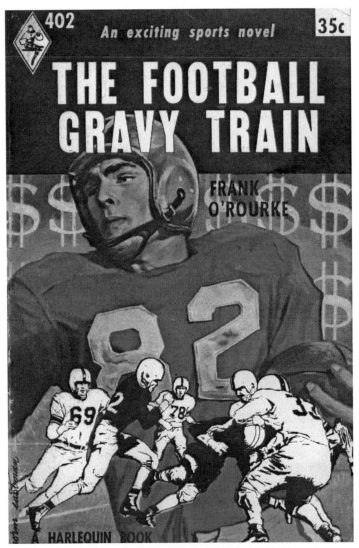

The Football Gravy Train by Frank O'Rourke, 1957 Harlequin paperback reprint of the 1951 Barnes novel (copyright Harlequin Books). This was the only football novel by O'Rourke, who wrote numerous baseball novels, novelettes and short stories.

Einstein did not update his story; his unnamed league included New York, Chicago, Boston, St. Louis and Philadelphia. All those cities were in the American League in 1953, but the St. Louis Browns moved to Baltimore following the 1953 season and the Philadelphia Athletics shifted to Kansas City after the 1954 campaign. Stat manages the Bears well, surging from sixth place to third going to the final two games of the season, and has obviously earned a chance to return as manager. Meanwhile, he has taken time out to find his daughter, who becomes lost in a cave in Nebraska after she sets out to find a way to visit him in St. Louis. It's pretty obvious this will result in the family being reunited. What isn't obvious is how Stat and Whittier, who engage in a vicious on-field fight late in the story, conclude their nasty enmity.

Einstein uses a few artifices, such as having a timely injury sideline Philadelphia's center fielder, thus putting Stat in his own lineup, sore arm and all. It is not strange to see Stat pinch hit a single in his first at-bat upon returning to the Major Leagues, nor is it odd to see him hitting a home run later on. But it is thoroughly unrealistic to see Stat batting third in the order — hardly a spot for a 37-year-old retread, drama or no drama. At any rate, heading into the final two games, Stat's Bears have a chance to spoil the pennant hopes of Whittier's Red Sox, while Stat realizes his bad arm means he is playing the final games of his career (though he is already assured of returning as manager). The finish couldn't be more wonderful, unexpected or creative: Whittier has told his Boston teammates to run on Stat's weak arm at every opportunity (even though he once throws out Whittier at third base).

The Only Game in Town is satisfying from first page to last. It's pulp story writ large and with vastly more originality, a grown-up version of a Chip Hilton or Frank Merriwell story. Baseball fiction collectors often treasure this little paperback, because, in many respects, it's the best "pure baseball" story written to the point it was published. However, *Man on Spikes* by Eliot Asinof, published later in the same year, would come to claim that distinction in the minds of some readers.

How did *The Only Game in Town* get its title? Einstein's clever answer is to have Margolies, the world-weary but decent small-town sportswriter who exposed Corio's scam, tell Stat this story about why Stat never quits on himself: "Fellow gets taken in a crap game and a guy says to him, 'Didn't you know the game was crooked?' and the first fellow says, 'Sure, but it's the only game in town.'"

Einstein's *Win—Or Else!*

In Andy McCue's exhaustive compilation of baseball fiction, one of the few books the editor left undescribed in *Baseball by the Books* (1991) was Einstein's second novel and first baseball book. This was the highly unusual 124-page *Win—Or Else!* written as by D. J. Michael for the Lion paperback firm in 1954. The baseball novel, divided into 34 short vignette-like chapters while describing one game and the immediate pregame period, was like nothing else that had ever appeared on the sports fiction scene. It's a study in irony and how life is often unfair. Ironically, Lion was part of the large company that produced Marvel Comics and created characters such as Captain America and Spider-Man, but Lion was a minor-league paperback publisher in contrast to the half-dozen or so giants that dominated the 25-cent book field in the 1950s. The scarce *Win—Or Else!* is seldom seen; most copies are locked up by collectors of sports fiction or completists of obscure paperback novels.

Einstein foresaw the arrival of major league baseball on the West Coast with his Ocean City Stars, who replaced a minor league team in much the same way the San Francisco Giants supplanted the Triple-A San Francisco Seals four years after the novel was published in April 1954. The primary protagonist, Stars manager Roy McIlvaine, gets off to a 1–10 start, with a nine-game losing streak. Although he doesn't know it, he must beat the New York Yankees in their first visit to Ocean City, or the club owner — an arrogant, powerful businessman who knows nothing about baseball but everything "about making decisions"— will fire him, against the advice of his top two club officials, who do understand the game.

Politicians and journalists, all with their distinct anti–McIlvaine agendas or personal axes to grind, get involved in the one-day stew, along with weak-willed baseball fan Stanley Jones, a small-town habitué who has his wallet stolen by a prostitute named Edna the night before the game. The wallet winds up in the hands of rookie Darrell Blakely, who has been sleeping with Edna, not realizing her "real" game until he finds the wallet just before the fateful matchup for McIlvaine. Blakely, a less-than-admirable sort, badly wants to beat out veteran first baseman Fred Lazar, who is a much more sympathetic character.

It all ends in the ninth inning, when Blakely pinch-hits for the pitcher and hits a game-winning two-run homer, then rounds the bases with Jones' wallet in his back pocket, not knowing Jones is watching from the stands. Other than the assumption the reader can make that McIlvaine is temporarily safe, nothing is resolved and no one is either benefited or punished.

Einstein's last lines, however, about the transient nature of both heroics and troubles, are nothing short of genius in the wake of the excitement of the Stars, their manager and their fans over the drama created by the home run: "Indeed, in all Ocean City, only the Yankees realized [one thing] and they gave it no more than a passing thought, because it was part of their business. The fact, the simple fact, was that there would be another baseball game tomorrow." It was Einstein's way of saying easy come, easy go, and who knows who will be the next person to be arrested, get fired, be released, or hit a game-winning home run?

For anyone who knows much about journalistic banalities, one of the high spots of *Win — Or Else!* was the brilliant satire on pregame interviews Einstein produced between TV announcer Ace Ludlow and right fielder Chet Jazwinski:

> "Well, how do you feel today, boy?" Ludlow began the interview. "I guess I feel pretty good, Ace." He [Jazwinski] never had met Ace Ludlow, the announcer, prior to five minutes before going on the air with him today.
> "Going to win that one today?" "Gonna try." "[It would] feel pretty good to break that losing streak, wouldn't it?" "Guess that's right."

The interview went on like that for two more pages, with Ludlow sweating it out to answers like "You'd have to ask the manager that," and "Pretty good" and "Well, I don't know anything about that" and "Well, we're gonna try." Finally, after Chet twice says of a teammate, "Well, he's a good pitcher," the befuddled announcer gives the bemused player a new razor and blades to go with it, then says, "And good luck to you Chet Jazwinski!"

The Hot-Shot

Many collectors of sports fiction classify Fletcher Flora's seldom seen 1956 Avon paperback original *The Hot-Shot* (as it is titled on the cover) and *The Hotshot* (as it's spelled on the title page) as a hard-boiled crime or juvenile delinquency novel rather than a basketball story, and for understandable reasons. However, if this isn't the first bawdy, cynical and sardonic takeoff on the sleazy side of amateur sports, it's close. It was the third book by Flora, who broke in as a writer with pulp detective stories in the dying days of the magazines, and it was his only seriously sports-related novel. In some ways, this story of enmity between player and parents, player and coaches, player and teammates and player and girlfriends is absolutely brilliant, a sort of Chip Hilton meets *Catcher in the Rye*, with elements of Mickey Spillane and the fabulous mixture of satire, sarcasm and character development that *Sports Illustrated* writer Dan Jenkins was then on his way to developing as a future sports novelist.

If you have strong feelings about the eventual triumph of goodness and fair play, *The Hot-Shot* isn't for you. The college teammate who regrets shaving points in a basketball game and goes straight suffers a terrible beating. None of the malefactors or lowlifes are ever punished, and the antihero and narrator of the piece, the brilliantly named Skimmer Scaggs, not only escapes punishment, but goes on to win a national championship followed by riches and success in pro basketball. What makes it so superbly written is that Flora makes it all seem so logical. The reader isn't the least bit surprised the story ends this way.

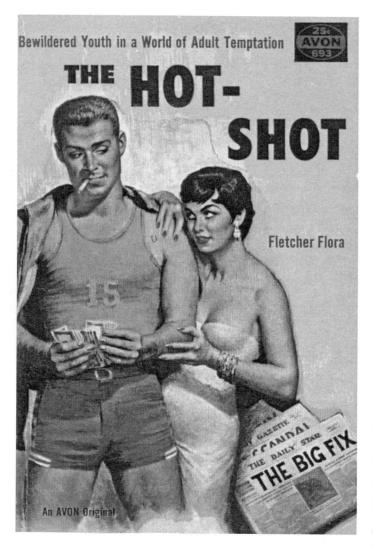

This is a basketball story that never names an opponent or a town, never uses a team nickname, never includes a score, never talks about tactics in any but the most rudimentary way, and yet tells all when it comes to the raw and true-to-life reality of a physically and psychologically abused and abusive athlete who is out only for himself. Skimmer Scaggs is surely one of the least likeable characters ever to be featured in a sports novel, forcing the reader to wish he would get his comeuppance — yet realizing

The Hot Shot by Fletcher Flora, 1956 Avon paperback original (copyright Avon Publications). Flora was a prolific mystery writer whose rare coming-of-age novel was wildly exploited by Avon with an outrageous cover.

full well why he doesn't. Skimmer is just smart enough to avoid hurting himself, except for one incident in which he takes a severe beating from gangsters. In short, for the cynical, this is the ultimate sports story.

When a buddy named Bugs taunts him into turning out for the team, Skimmer becomes a player by accident as a senior at a never-named high school in the chapter titled "Dear Old High." This may be the most unrealistic aspect of the story, because any player as good as Skimmer turns out to be — the state high school scoring leader, the nation's best player on the nation's best college team — is hardly likely to have ignored basketball until his senior year. But then, maybe the opening line explains it, because it tells the reader that Skimmer Scaggs is a man to be reckoned with: "My old man was a bum, and my old lady was a slob, and chances are I'd be a bum and a slob if it wasn't for this [profanity] crazy game."

While telling the story entirely in retrospect, Skimmer never sees anyone or anything else — including the girls he beds in the story, his coaches, his teammates and basketball itself — except as a means to an end. Here's how Skimmer describes basketball practice and his coach early in the story:

> Old Mulloy drew diagrams of plays and stuff on a blackboard with a piece of chalk, To tell the truth, I couldn't see much sense to it, because once we got the ball in the game, we hardly ever used any of the plays but just ran like hell and banged the damn ball at the basket, but I guess it made old Mulloy feel important go through all that bull just the same. He'd be talking about something, and all of a sudden he'd point his damn finger at someone like he was ready to pull the trigger, and he'd say real fast, "What would you do in these circumstances?" and then he'd go on to tell the circumstances, and whoever he pointed at had damn well better know what he was supposed to do or get chewed. You could see from the way the bastard acted that it made him feel important as all hell, a real hot-shot coach and all that, but like I said, we hardly ever went in for any of that fancy crap in a game, and what's more, he didn't seem to care whether we did or not, and all he'd do then was jump up and down on the [profanity] bench and yell, "Run, run, run!" until you wanted to poke him right in the stinking mouth.

Near the end of his championship high school season, Skimmer says it all: "Well, we played our first game that evening, and we won going away, and there's not a hell lot of use going into it anymore than that, or any other games in our bracket, either, except to say we won all of them, and I was high man in every damn one." Skimmer goes on to score 40 points — an extraordinary total in 1956 for a high school player, when many entire teams often did not then score that many points — and his team wins the state title by one point. Skimmer then gets recruited by the only school named in the novel, the pun of all puns: Pipskill U. He takes all the graft and gifts he can get — $100 a month, $50 a week, which were pretty pennies at the time — and eventually wins the national title as a junior for the bald but otherwise overly hairy coach Barker Umplett, a tyrannical, mean-spirited grown-up version of Skimmer, sans the association with criminals.

When Skimmer skips a practice as a sophomore in his first season on the varsity — freshmen then were not eligible for varsity teams — Flora makes Umplett sound like the most realistic character in the book, with a speech it's not hard to imagine a coach then or now making:

> Well, Mr. Scaggs, I'm sure an important fellow like you just has a lot of things to do that might interfere with basketball practice, so I think I'd better tell you how I feel about it. To put it bluntly, Mr. Scaggs, if your [profanity] grandmother dropped dead at your feet at five minute to three, I'd expect you to be at practice at three sharp as usual. Is that clear? While I'm at it, I might say that I've been in this business more years than I can count, and I've had my head on the chopping block

more times than I care to remember, and I've learned a hell of a lot of things a man has to know to stay hooked on the contract, and one of the things that I've learned is the smell of a sharp little opportunist like you. By God, you're just barely dry behind the ears, and you're making a business out of what was once meant to be fun. So it's a business. It's business with you, and it's a business with me, and there's no [profanity] fun left in it. You're getting paid to play basketball, and so you'll [profanity] well play basketball. You'll come to practice after this on time and every time, and you'll run and you'll sweat and you'll hate my guts, and the more you hate them the better I'll like it, and don't ever expect me to treat you like anything but the hired sharpshooter you are. You're paid to win games, and that's exactly what I expect of you and nothing more, and God help you if you don't. Is all this perfectly clear, Mr. Scaggs?

And when Skimmer tells the coach he's leaving after they've won the national championship in his junior season, the coach's reaction is perfect:

So, you're running out. Well, I've been expecting it, and I'm not surprised, and it's God's own wonder that you stuck around as long as you did. But you made us national champs. It was mainly you, and I'll hand it to you, and you're welcome. I made you, and you made us, and we're even and quits to hell with it. Go, and God go with you, Mr. Scaggs. I'll follow your career with interest, and I have no doubt at all that you'll be a shining star in the professional world, and God himself knows the satisfaction it will be to my soul to remember the part I had in the making of you.

The Hot-Shot, of course, is as wildly improbable, in its own way, as any Merriwell tale was a half a century earlier, although almost any given scene in *The Hot-Shot* is not improbable at all. Chances are, there were more than a few athletes, and coaches for that matter, in the Merriwell world, not to mention 1956 or 2010, with Skimmer's sense of himself, but those feelings could never, and would never, have been put down on paper. Such an author would have been damned even by people who secretly admired such emotional honesty. Chances are, most athletes, coaches and sports fans who read *The Hot-Shot*—although there probably weren't too many, displayed as it was among hundreds of competitors—would have been afraid to confront the naked truth that they sometimes used people, and used the game, much the same way others tried to use them. In short, *The Hot-Shot* is so vivid in its crude, lewd, rude view of the world that readers could not handle this type of story very often. Thankfully, most people aren't like the characters in *The Hot-Shot*—or at least they are seldom like these loathsome people — or it would be a dark and dismal sports world, indeed. To read of Skimmer Scaggs is to be thankful that one's own soul is seldom dark, even in the worst moments of the inevitable greed that even the best of us all succumb to, at one scattered and, hopefully, brief moment or another.

Arnold Hano's innovative *The Big Out*

New York sportswriter, magazine contributor and baseball biographer Arnold Hano was in his late 20s and in the early stages of his productive career when he wrote his only sports novel, the highly unusual *The Big Out*, in 1951 for Barnes to accompany two other well-known East Coast baseball writers, Ed Fitzgerald and Frank O'Rourke.

Unlike Hano's classic *A Day in the Bleachers* (1955), about the author's experiences during the first game of the 1954 World Series at the Polo Grounds in New York, *The Big Out* is seldom seen on used-book store shelves. *A Day in the Bleachers*, which was reprinted in 1982, with an introduction by Roger Kahn, is mistakenly found on some lists of baseball fiction.

It's difficult to describe *The Big Out* without making it seem like a pulp novel, but that's unfair. It is true that the story would not have been out of place had it been serialized in *Argosy* or some such, but by the time, *The Big Out* appeared, sports fiction in the pulps was largely confined to shorter works, and there no longer were serial-style markets for it, the way there would have been had the story been written two decades earlier.

"The Big Out" refers to the big plays a catcher must make to win games, although some readers were led to believe the title referred to how the character, Brick Palmer, was unfairly banned from Organized Baseball (a confederation of big league and minor league teams). Hano's dedication—"To Shoeless Joe Jackson, who batted .375 in the 1919 World Series"—relates to the unfairness of a player banned simply for not reporting a gambling plot of which he supposedly had knowledge. Jackson—whose .356 lifetime batting average otherwise would have qualified him for the Baseball Hall of Fame—did not die until December 5, 1951, a little over three decades after being banned from baseball as part of the 1919 "Black Sox" scandal (the eight banned players performed through 1920 before decisions involving the scandal were made).

Brick Palmer—what a wonderful baseball name!—is a grizzled 38-year-old all-star catcher. Having caught 344 consecutive games—unheard of at his demanding position—he is caught up in the foolish gambling escapades of his much younger brother. Brick cannot betray his brother Johnny, even to clear himself of suspicion, after an overly ambitious sportswriter hears snatches of a conversation about gambling debts and assumes Brick is involved in something nefarious. Circumstantial evidence condemns Brick, who smashes and disfigures the face of a punk who is acting as a middleman in offering gambling bribes.

Brick, though, can't quit playing and receives the love and support of his remarkably understanding wife, Cathy, who had looked forward to the day her husband would accept an offer to become a college coach and they could have children. Brick ultimately finds a Canadian team known as the Outlaws—for good reason—that plays minor-level ball in a cross-border conference. Very much like a man who molests children is received in prison, the now-infamous Brick finds he not only has to battle self-righteous fans, vicious opponents and biased umpires, but also the members of his own team. That is the essence of an absorbing story, full of "inside baseball" and loaded with descriptions of physical and mental pain seldom seen in a sports novel mid-century.

In the end, the thug Brick had smashed finds a way not only to try to blackmail Brick's brother, but also hires two other thugs to beat Brick so severely that he ostensibly could not play in the final two games of the Outlaws' season, which will decide the league title. Or so the three thugs thought—Brick, with help from his wife, his manager and his brother, does play. He endures the pain and somehow comes up with the game-winning hit, not realizing that his brother has cleared his conscience by spilling all and thus clearing Brick's name. The reader realizes Brick has played his last game anywhere, however, although a coaching career is now possible after all. Hano threw in a painful dose of "life isn't always fair" when the three thugs are not yet caught as the story ends, although there are strong hints that the primary punk has a fatal illness.

There is much inside baseball in *The Big Out*. For example, in what became Brick's last major league game, he signals his manager that his pitcher has nothing left, without the pitcher realizing it. Then there is this paragraph about the morning Brick is called to the owner's suite after the story has broken: "But outside Malcolm Stutz's office on the sixth floor stood another group of newspapermen, trained to be where all good reporters should be, face to face with the accused. 'Brick,' yelled one, who had never before addressed Palmer before in his life, 'Brick,' look over here,' and a flashbulb went off. 'Over here,' yowled another, and another, and the timeless call of the photographers, look over here so we can hang you properly."

One photographer, however, is silent, Timmons, of the *Herald*, and Timmons steadfastly continues to believe in Brick and helps as he can. When Brick proclaims he is innocent but can't explain why to his team's owner, the owner tells him, "[Y]ou cheap crook, I'll crucify you." The owner tells Brick the commissioner of baseball is really under his thumb, and here Hano has the owner saying how he made sure he got his lapdog appointed to the post instead of other men. He gives examples of the others, including the name Frick, referring to Ford Frick, then president of the National League and, ironically, a future commissioner in real life. (It was Frick who famously declared that Roger Maris' record 61 home runs in 1961 would have an asterisk, since he played a schedule eight games longer than Babe Ruth did.)

Cathy is touchingly devoted to Brick. When he tells her he must find a place to play out the season, if only to restore his sanity, she tells him, "Where? With you. When? Any time. For how much? For peanuts and love. What difference does it make?" There is no sex, only tender affection, in "The Big Out," but this is one of the most erotic statements ever written into a baseball novel.

When Brick finds a team that wants him, the Osage Outlaws, the manager, Addison, later tells him his name is phony and that he himself was banned from baseball as a member of the Black Sox! This, of course, is incredibly pulpy, but the reader just has to accept it. It's not hard to accept the idea that the other players all have disciplinary crosses to bear—hence the team's nickname—but to find a member of the Black Sox managing an outlaw team three decades later was quite a stretch.

Thus informed, Brick realizes there is a lot more than his gratification at stake. Before the start of the pennant-deciding series, Hano describes Brick's feelings: "There would be no bow today, no mocking gesture. Too long, Brick knew, he had been all gesture.... The bow that first day, the strong man act in the locker room when he had chinned by one arm, the words he threw into his teammates' faces when they had tested him with the epithet on his locker door, all these were for the show, and the show was over. There were ten thousand fans in the stands, but he wasn't playing for the fans today. He was playing for nobody, one man alone against the absolute standards of honor and truth, and only he would know whether Brick Palmer had played well or not."

He tumbles into the dugout to grab a foul fly for a game-ending catch, moving his team ahead one game over the opponent, meaning the Outlaws need to win only one of the final two games. It is that night, however, that the thugs move in to bash Brick senseless when he refuses to go along with an attempt to blackmail his brother. They tell Brick he must find ways to throw the final two games. As he is a catcher, the man who controls so much of every game, that would have very much been possible for him to do, unlike the situation an outfielder would face.

Brick's brother, summoned to aid him in the way only a doctor could following the beating, tells Brick, "I want you to play, Brick. I'm selfish that way. I want you to play for me.... So I can feel I've done some good. So I can feel good, that's what I mean. I haven't felt good since, since—the whole business began a month ago. Clean, that's how I want to feel. You know what I mean?" And Brick, indeed, tells him he knows.

Hano writes powerfully of Brick's feelings late in what he realizes is his last game:

What had happened to the yesterday Brick Palmer, the Brick Palmer who had felt once more the full power of his body, the great strength hidden in his arms and legs? In one day, that man had been wiped out, reduced to the alien flesh of baseball's old age. He knew, now, more than he had ever known before, how Marty Marion must feel when he bends for the grass cutter in the hole, how DiMag must feel now that his great legs are dying and his arm is an empty shell.... He knew it, now, Brick Palmer, old and beaten, and there paraded before his eyes the old-timers he had seen in their glory. And where were they, Gehringer, Mize and Paul Waner, where were they, Frisch, Terry Moore and Marion? Ah, no, they were not still around, not even Mize and Marion, they had gone, long ago, over the hill and into the shadows, though men who resembled them still played, and sometimes out of the shadows they'd come, ghosts of their old glory, great ghosts, perhaps, but ghosts.

This was a story for the true baseball fan, the fan who keeps up with everything. As Hano wrote this in 1951, Joe DiMaggio was playing his final season for the Yankees. St. Louis Cardinals shortstop Marty Marion did not play in 1951 in his first year as manager, only to return to shortstop as a .247-hitting part-timer in 1952 as player-manager of the St. Louis Browns. Hall of Fame first baseman Mize, once one of the fiercest of sluggers, was a weak .259 batter in part-time action in 1951 with the Yankees, then served them primarily as a pinch-hitter before retiring at the end of the 1953 season.

Eliot Asinof's brilliant *Man on Spikes*

With the passage of more than half a century since Eliot Asinof wrote his first book, *Man on Spikes*, and the increasing historical acceptance of just how brutally unfair Major League Baseball's reserve clause truly was, this unique novel has grown in stature. First published in 1955 by McGraw-Hill, the original book had only one printing and was read by very few until the Southern Illinois University Press published a paperback reprint in 1998 as part of its admirable Writing Baseball series of classic reprints.

It's the constantly painful story of a minor league outfielder's 16-year obsession with reaching the major leagues, and how he is helped (a little) and hindered (a lot) along the way before he ultimately fails in his only major league game. The world's foremost expert on the sociology of sports fiction, Michael Oriard, calls the novel "uninspired" in his ground-breaking *Dreaming of Heroes: American Sports Fiction, 1868–1980*. As much as I respect Oriard's unparalleled scholarship, I politely disagree. *Man on Spikes* may be too extreme, sometimes far too unlikely and even a bit too pulpy for those who prefer *The Natural* (1952) and *The Southpaw* (1953) as the beginning of the literary sports-themed novel with adult sensibilities.

However, with all due respect to those treasures by a pair of wordsmiths, I far prefer the raw, emotional cruelty of *Man on Spikes*. The story is unlikely, but the emotions couldn't be more genuinely conveyed. Asinof—a former minor league baseball player best known for his Black Sox scandal history *Eight Men Out* (1963)—wonderfully captures gut-wrenching agony in *Man on Spikes*. It's the well-told tale that any skilled, dedicated person in any walk of life could relate to—anyone who has unfairly been denied the true opportunity to achieve the professional standing they have earned through sheer, dogged hard work. The novel speaks to me intensely on that level. *Man on Spikes* is, indeed, one of the ultimate examples of the "life isn't fair" school of writing, and it is especially painful to read for anyone who has been affected intensely and unfairly by life's endless multitudes of negative vicissitudes.

Yet for anyone who has come to grips with unfairness—for anyone who realizes that while life isn't always fair it can still ultimately be filled with joy and self-respect—*Man on*

Spikes has the most satisfying of all possible endings. The protagonist, Mike Kutner, fails in his only major league game, but realizes that he and his loving wife, Laura, have much to look forward to. He is only 35, old only in athletics. The last line of the book — "For a while, they were unable to control the wonderful laughter that poured out of them" — leaves any reader appreciating the best about life, not the worst.

One of the common misconceptions about *Man on Spikes* has been conveyed by several authors: that Mike Kutner had only one major league at-bat and struck out. Since *Man on Spikes* is one of the most valuable of all sports books in its original edition, this mistake is understandable for writers who may not have seen either the original or the reprint. The strikeout actually comes in Kutner's fourth plate appearance, with the potential winning run on base and two outs in the ninth inning, after he has played the entire game following his emergency call up to the Chicago Lions. His first three at-bats are a sacrifice bunt, a walk, and a well-hit flyball out.

With two strikes in his last at-bat, he hits a ball into the stands, barely foul, thus showing just how irrational the owner's response to Kutner's performance really was. In the proverbial baseball "game of inches," anyone who really knows the sport must evaluate an athlete on his potential, not an accident of inches. Had Kutner hit the ball inches fair instead of inches foul, his entire world might have been different.

In the 1998 reprint, Asinof — by then nearly 80 years old — for the first time reveals the inspiration for Mike Kutner. He was a former college league teammate, Mickey Rutner, whose major league career consisted of 12 games, with 12 hits and one home run in 48 at-bats for a .250 average, with the Philadelphia Athletics at the end of the 1947 season. Asinof notes that Rutner had spent four years in the minors and three in World War II military service before reaching the majors, then went back to the minors for six more seasons and never played another big league game. Asinof's final observation is eloquent: "In my 1969 edition of *MacMillian's Baseball Encyclopedia*, the stats of George Herman Ruth's record has thirty-three lines. Below, Mickey Rutner's has one single line. But they're on the same page, by God. This book is dedicated to Mickey."

It was with that passion that Asinof wrote his first novel. He can be forgiven his excesses. There have been numerous players who had the chance to play only one game in the major leagues. But on even one of those occasions did that single game come 16 years after the player's career began in the minor leagues? Yet, I would agree with famed baseball players' union leader Marvin Miller in his assessment in his foreword to the new edition, contending that *Man on Spikes* "is infinitely more true than the vast bulk of nonfictional books that have been published." Later, Miller says the book "marks Mr. Asinof as one of the few writers [about sports] who was ahead of his time. His depiction of players' real problems: the nature of the relationship between player, owner, media, club and league officials; the similarity of the baseball commissioner to the Wizard of Oz; and many other insights was not unusual eleven years before major league players formed the first legitimate union in established free agency rights for major league players, and thirty-nine years before the club owners revealed publicly their belief that a baseball commissioner served no useful purpose. Mr. Asinof's work demonstrates that he has been a prophet — with honor."

In a style never seen in a sports novel until *Man on Spikes*, Asinof tells Mike Kutner's story in chapters about "the scout, father, manager, old ballplayer, clown, sergeant, reporter, Negro, sister, commissioner, wife, junior executive, and mother" until he finally writes from Kutner's own viewpoint in the final chapter, "The Rookie." All of these chapters could almost be read as complete short stories in their own right; indeed, with a little rewriting, such an effect could be obtained. The scout tries to help Kutner; the commissioner realizes he can't, since his power is contingent upon the owner's vote to keep him in office. The clown, a talented but lazy outfielder who enjoys a long major league career even though his attitude is the opposite of Kutner's intensity, reflects the author's theme: life isn't always fair. The Negro is on the way to the major leagues because the owner wants someone of his race to integrate his team and he is good enough, albeit not as skilled as Kutner.

Pain is piled upon pain until the reader is frequently forced to put the book down, even though the narrative is compelling. I could not read more than two or three chapters at a time, so difficult is it to navigate the sheer venality of so many, many people in Mike Kutner's way. While some might see his obsession with reaching the major leagues as unhealthy, such was not the case. Kutner clearly deserved to play in the majors, in the same style of many singles-hitting outfielders with solid careers, then and now. Perhaps he would have been a journeyman at best, but he is clearly skilled enough, and other teams would have given him a chance had the ownership of his own organization not unethically blocked his progress. Today, with the advent of free agency after a designated period of original ownership of a player, the likes of Mike Kutner could not be portrayed as Asinof portrays him. In 1955, however, real-life Kutners toiled in baseball's minor leagues, held there for many of the same reasons as Kutner is.

It's agonizing to read early on about Kutner's father heaving his childhood baseball glove into a furnace; about a manager's unreasoning prejudice against players with glasses; about how Kutner's $2,000 bonus (equal to well over $30,000 today) is illegally whittled to $250. In the chapter about "The Old Ballplayer," a 38-year-old Class D player, the career minor-league Herman Cruller, is contrasted with the hard-driving young Kutner. Today, all the old Class A, B, C and D teams have long since been lumped into the A classification for commercial reasons, but no 38-year-old would be allowed to hang on at the lowest level of a major league club's farm team. (There were many more minor league teams in the late 1930s, and for a few years following World War II, than there are today, although some of the flamboyant modern independent leagues have signed former major leaguers in their 40s for gate appeal.)

When Kutner's first minor league manager, the venal and trashy catcher Lou Phipps, later finds himself playing against Kutner, Phipps basically assaults him during a tag and then illegally gets away with interfering with his swing. When Kutner despairs, Cruller tells him, "You gotta show the sonofabitch that you're here to stay, that you can't be pushed around! You gotta teach him that yourself, like you gotta teach every sonofabitch in every league you play in. The ump ain't gonna help you, you gotta do it yourself! Mike, you do it any way that ain't assault to a cop and ain't illegal to an umpire. You hear me? Any way!" Kutner soon collides with Phipps at home plate, knocking out one of the catcher's teeth and severely injuring him while scoring the winning run. Kutner, of course, makes an enemy who haunts him.

There is an astonishing scene during chapter 8, "The Negro," in which young outfielder Ben Franks is taunted by a noose held by a fan! Perhaps this scene had its counterpart in a real-life ballpark scenario, though it's difficult to imagine, even in the late 1940s when blacks were integrating major league baseball (and the minor leagues, too).

In chapter 10, "The Commissioner"—one of the most powerful portrayals in the story—the commissioner follows up Kutner's agonized request to investigate the venal Chicago team owner Jim Mellon's refusal to let Kutner go to another major league organization. "Sure, you buy up talent to win pennants to make big money to buy more players to win more pennants," the commissioner tells the owner, to which the owner replies, "That's bad?" The owner, like any number of real-life capitalists of his rich man's ilk, has no feeling for anyone but himself. Of all the characters in the book, the owner may be the most accurately drawn — not because all baseball owners were like him, but because a good many rich men were in numerous similar pursuits across the American capitalist system. It's not even hard to make the leap from Jim Mellon to some of the real-life executives at Enron a half-century later.

In chapter 11, "The Wife," the first sexual encounter between Mike and Laura — on the outfield grass of a ballpark — serves as metaphor for his obsessive desire to make good in baseball. Likewise, Mike's failed attempt to win a minor league batting championship when his father is on his deathbed serves as a similar metaphor, especially since Mike is denied the opportunity both father and son badly needed to make amends before the father's death. For anyone who has been frustrated by unfairly blocked ambition, Mike is a sympathetic character. Indeed, in "The Negro" chapter, the inherent decency of both Ben and Mike is vividly conveyed. But the two metaphor scenes are weak and pulpish, especially the sex scene.

However, when Laura and Clark Mellon, Jim's nephew and second in command on the major league club, get drunk together and Laura follows Clark into his room, this scene is very real indeed, especially since the two are too drunk to do anything but fall asleep. Those who consider sex holy will find this scene distasteful, but it's actually among the most realistic aspects of the story. Laura loves Mike so much that she's willing to give a club executive her body in order to fulfill her husband's great passion. It's simply a quid pro quo, no doubt the kind made in many areas of American life. How many people, given the opportunity to achieve great fame by resorting to the casting couch, would not trade a sexual experience for a lifetime of riches and ego gratification?

Asinof provides much-needed closure when Durkin Fain, the scout who signed Mike, appears on the scene of his only major league game. "Don't compare me with the kid you went out on a limb for," Asinof has Kutner thinking. "You're looking at an aging athlete, tired, almost old, as old in his profession as you are in yours." (Fain, having been fired shortly after signing Kutner, recently has decided he is too old to continue his long college coaching career.) The inherent goodness of the old scout — a man who deep in his gut believes in the meritocracy of baseball — provides some balm for the intense pain the reader feels in the story. On the other hand, the fact that Charlie Caulfield, "the only full-fledged clown on spikes," has spent seven years in the major leagues, albeit as a less-than-stellar journeyman, is just as painful for the reader as it is for Kutner. Who hasn't seen someone thoroughly undeserving get more opportunities at the top than someone who has actually earned them?

Mike Kutner's one game in the major leagues happily frees him from his obsession. One hopes not only that he and Laura can enjoy children and family life, but also that Kutner, somehow, finds a way to enjoy the rest of whatever life this intensely obsessed man pursues.

Millard Lampell's remarkable *The Hero*

Publisher Ned Pines' Popular Library, one of the leading paperback firms of the 1940s and 1950s, took the unusual step for this genre-oriented outfit of reprinting a little-known literary coming-of-age novel that combined a search for self-identity with football. There isn't much on-field football in Millard Lampell's *The Hero* (1949), but there's a world of angst caused by the negative aspects of college football commercialization following World War II.

In the end, the reader has no idea whether the hero of the piece, once-brilliant halfback Steve Novak, will ever "get the girl," and it's made clear he is too severely injured to play the game effectively again. This humble son of New Jersey blue-collar roots does, however, emerge with his self-respect and the desire to become a legitimate college student with an engineering career in mind.

The cover blurbs—"He loved another man's woman" and "Steve was made for football ... Melissa was made for love"—are deceptive. Those blurbs and an attractive cover by famed pulp cover artist Earle Bergey effectively disguise that this remarkable novel has an important message; it's nothing like the exploitation-themed stories that so many paperback publishers

The Hero by Millard Lampell, 1950 Popular Library reprint (copyright Popular Library). The paperback publisher tried to sex up a literary novel with a minimum of football action.

had begun to produce and would publish with increasing frequency in the 1950s and 1960s. Popular Library, however, had a policy for a few years of using a combination of big breasts and leg art, cleavage and dramatic circumstances to sell its 25 cent books.

The only two games extensively described in the novel involve severe pain and injury—to a teammate who tries to defend Novak from dirty play, then later to Novak himself. Novak tries to play with a serious shoulder injury and suffers career-ending physical problems in his junior season, a season when he had been ballyhooed for All-American honors at Virginia's Jackson University. Novak, "a Polack from a small mill town," as he is described, is the best of a group of stars recruited to give a once-woeful football program the best team money could buy.

The villain of the piece is not the head coach but T.C. McCabe, a wealthy, football-crazed alumnus who today would be described as a "control freak." McCabe is Novak's benefactor — part of a system that avoided scholarship limitations — and Melissa is the girl he calls "Lovecat," not his mistress yet a girl he tries to control emotionally. When Novak finally goes back home and Melissa stays behind because of McCabe's influence, it's uncertain whether they will ever wind up together.

Near the end, Steve, shaken by a distraught teammate's suicide and by the crass commercial nature of college football, by a $150 bounty on him, and by a rival coach's attempt to steal him away from Jackson, retreats to a conference with Megroth, his favorite professor and a decent man who has gradually made Steve aware that life and college are so much more than football. The author often speaks through Megroth, and the professor's final conversation with Steve — though the professor urges him to keep in touch — is one of the most striking in the pre–1970 history of sports fiction:

> Of all the nations on earth, it seems to me that America is peculiarly a country fed on myths. Work and Win. You Too Can Be President. Bootblack to Banker. The Spirit of the Old School. We've developed a whole culture designed to send young men chasing after a thousand glistening and empty goals. You too, Novak. You believe the legend. Like the rest of us, you dreamed up your image of The Hero — the man you want to be. You've distilled him, out of a thousand movies and magazine stories, second-rate novels and photographs in the advertisements. The Hero. The tall, lean, manly, modest, clean-cut, middle-class, Anglo-Saxon All American Boy, athletic and confident in his perfectly cut tweeds, with his passport from Yale or Princeton or Jackson, with his beautiful and well-bred girl. The dream, the dream — To be accepted and secure; to be free of the humiliations of adolescence, the embarrassment of being Polish or poor, or Italian, or Jewish, or the son of a weary, bewildered father, a mother who is nervous and shouts, a grandfather who comes over from the old country. The subtle snobbery infects us all, Novak. It is thrust upon us from a thousand sides, long before we're old enough to resist.

Lampell's description of Steve at that point in Megroth's talk is remarkable: "Steve listened to Megroth's words with an odd sense of recognition, hearing coherently for the first time an echo of a thousand fragmentary secret doubts." Megroth continues:

> And it is the world of amateur athletics, that is particularly the realm of the Great American Myth. Athletics beckons with the illusion of release. It is the chance for success and acclaim most easily within reach. For some — boys from mill towns and coal camps — it is almost the only chance. It is a profound social comment that there were so many Polish, Italian and Jewish and Negro athletes. Because athletics offers one of the few ways out of the tenements and the company houses. More than that — it fills some deep psychological need for a ritual of belonging, of being part of a group. [Lampell describes Steve's reaction:] It was uncanny — Megroth had caught it exactly. The hunger to belong, to participate — dressing in the locker room, playing together — the intimate, intense comradeship — how hungrily he had sought it, welcomed it, felt at last fulfilled by it.

Megroth concludes:

> There are good emotional and social reasons why sports have become the religious festivals of Americans. Especially when sports are linked with college, with a calm and isolated and romantic world, with Youth and Honor, with Fair Play, with a hundred alluring traditions. The Myth lies in this: that what is sold as amateurism is really industry. Athletics is in fact not an escape from the world, but a reflection of it. I'd have to be deaf, dumb and blind to be on campus and not know that football is a profitable business. A major industry. Yet it maintains the illusion of purity. The industrial aspects operate underground. Players are bribed, bargained for, cajoled, paid. And paid less than a cotton-mill hand. The prospect of an education is dangled before you. An education for which athletes rarely find time. I don't blame you. Lord knows, I don't blame you.
>
> You have to recognize the myth, Novak. You have to learn what is the illusion and what is the reality. That is when you will cease being hurt, baffled and disillusioned by a place like this. You won't learn it from me. You won't learn it from a lecture, or a conversation over teacups. But you'll have to learn.

That must suffice for the "happy ending"—that Steve, in fact, has learned. This isn't the first sports story to condemn the excesses of college football, but it's one of the strongest and most effective condemnations, and one of the earliest to express condemnation in such strong terms.

As football practice begins during Novak's freshman season, tackle Gene Hausler, a party-loving, hard-drinking, 26-year-old veteran of World War II and the son of a West Virginia coal miner, expresses indignation when he finds out Steve hasn't arranged to be paid off. Steve tells him he's playing for "a free education." Hausler tells him he can get "sixty a month, easy." (Sixty dollars then would be more than $500 in buying power now.)

When Steve insists, "I told you I came here for an education," Hausler erupts with indignation: "Crap. Get the dough. Don't be a sucker. Do they let people come to see the games for free? It's a racket, it's all a racket." To which Steve responds: " I don't think everything's cheap and crooked. I think a place like this is more than a racket. I think it's a good place, something I never had, something I've wanted all my life. I respect it.... They put me through college, and I play. But that doesn't make it a racket. That doesn't make it something dirty." Hausler has the last word in this encounter: "I'm a little older than you, Novak. I got a philosophy, you can have it free. It's a racket, see, life, everything, a con game, a deck full of jokers. Everything's fixed by the house. Poor slobs like you and me, we got the play and the angles, we got to play it smart. Or else we wind up in the alley, eating out of garbage cans."

Learning that he's capable of greatness on the field, Novak eagerly seeks out his press notices. "He was quiet and modest, a little embarrassed — no one was ever aware that he had bought the paper as soon as it reached the stands, avidly reading it a dozen times," Lampell writes. Eddie Abrams, a friendly sportswriter who has counseled Steve in New Jersey, takes a job in public relations at the university, knowing he has one of the nation's true greats to publicize. When Steve and Eddie are treated by a local restaurant owner after one of Steve's great games during an unbeaten sophomore season, the old writer, spotting Steve's reaction to praise, tells him,

> You love it. Don't apologize.... Who doesn't love to be told he's good? You're human ... yes, you're human. Sixty thousand people out there. They came from hundreds of miles away. Most of them never saw you before in their lives. And they sat there screaming your name. They went crazy....
>
> Most of them have never been near a college in their lives. And they cheer. Why? ... Who are they? Insurance men and housewives, butchers and stenographers. What kind of life have they got? Nothing. Get up, work, go to bed. They go to the movies and life is wonderful, exciting as hell, and they keep expecting it to be that way for them. Only it isn't. So they look for a way out. That's the whole damn country — you can feel it, you can smell it on the street corners, everybody looking for a way out. They go to the movies, they read True Story, they take an aspirin. That's why we're hero-happy. Because if you can find some guy who's young and strong and exciting, you can read about him or watch him and you're him for a while. Heroes, you've to have heroes.... Somebody you can pay two bucks admission to see, and you can be him for a while.

But Steve doesn't yet believe Eddie, and that is the rest of the story.

The early sports mysteries

Although a strong element of mystery had been present in some sports stories from the early times of Frank Merriwell, the modern concept of the "baseball mystery" and "football mystery," as they were labeled on the title pages, emerged with mystery novelist Cortland Fitzsimmons early in the Great Depression. Two adult sports whodunits—*70,000 Witnesses* (1931) and *Death on the Diamond* (1934)—were reprinted for the mass market by Grosset & Dunlap and provided the basis for films after first appearing with small print runs from Stokes. An even smaller publisher, McBride, produced his rare hockey mystery *Crimson Ice* (1935).

Detective Jack Kethridge was the primary protagonist in the football mystery *70,000 Witnesses*, which was pretty much a police procedural with football strictly at the margins. The only genuine football action takes place in the 22-page opening chapter, which consists entirely of the radio broadcaster's description of the Big Game between undefeated University and State, although what university and what state are never revealed. Since mainstream commercial sports radio broadcasts were less than a decade old, this was one of the first such fictional descriptions of a game and somewhat innovative at the time.

Death on the Diamond by Cortland Fitzsimmons, 1934 (jacket copyright Grosset & Dunlap). For Grosset's reprint of one of the earliest baseball mysteries, the publisher came up with this nifty but uncredited art-deco style dust jacket.

The rest of the story is almost entirely conversation as Kethridge tries to determine how and why Walter Demuth, State's star halfback, dies during a game-deciding 8-yard touchdown run. Later, when Kethridge orders a "replay" of the fateful period, the player who portrays Demuth also dies, along with a third teammate in the locker room. Although team manager Randy Buchan, who is in love with Demuth's sister Dorothy, is suspected at first and stands to benefit financially from the star's death, the demises of the second and third athletes clear him. Kethridge eventually coaxes referee Harry Collins to confess to using a chemical compound that led to Demuth's demise. Collins, in gambling difficulties, merely wanted to slow him down, but found himself caught in a web of murder. Ironically, Kethridge uses his skills as a potential forger — skills he realizes he must not use for ill-gotten gain — to trap Collins. Unfortunately, the referee is pretty much the obvious suspect, and the story is not especially strong.

Death on the Diamond is much better, written at a breakneck pace with far more variety and pace that

70,000 Witnesses. The hero, the clever star reporter Terry Burke, eventually solves the crime and saves the baseball star; Larry Doyle is in love with an opposing manager's daughter; and there is even a hint that manager, daughter and Doyle will soon be on the same side as the story ends. Burke, having survived several perils, finally solves a plot by a fellow reporter and the scribe's baseball-playing brother. *Death on the Diamond*, however unlikely, is bursting with baseball and crime scenes and is much more fun than *70,000 Witnesses*.

Fitzsimmons' three sports novels were an isolated phenomenon in the 1930s from the standpoint of the novel market, although pulp magazine stories made frequent use of the mystery motif. It wasn't until the 1970s and 1980s that the genuine sports mystery novel began to flourish, with on-field action by active athletes, managers, and journalists.

The literary lists of Grant Burns

Grant Burns ignored sports mysteries in his useful and innovative 1987 volume from Scarecrow Press, *The Sports Pages: A Critical Bibliography of Twentieth-Century American Novels and Stories Featuring Baseball, Basketball, Football and Other Athletic Pursuits.* Burns uncovered many long-forgotten and little-known literary sports novels and stories and was the first to assess many of them. He was indeed on a literary mission; however, he entirely ignored the thousands of stories in the pulp magazines, not to mention the well over 1,000 young adult and juvenile novels available. Their absence, in turn, helped to inspire *Ball Tales*.

Burns' commendable book, which stressed post–1960 works with regard to novels, critiqued 166 baseball entries that included 40 novels, 26 basketball pieces with 9 novels, and 76 football tales with 25 novels, among 631 entries covering numerous other sports. That's a total of only 74 novels (including a handful of short-story collections) among 268 baseball, basketball and football tales. And of those 74 novels, only 21 appeared before 1960, showing what a genuine paucity of literary adult sports fiction existed during the first six decades of the 20th century, in contrast to the thousands of sources for pulp, young adult and juvenile sports fiction.

Even though the sources are distinctly obscure with regard to some of Burns' selections, they are more readily available through library resources, and nowhere near as difficult to locate as many of the sports pulps, which have been preserved primarily by a handful of enthusiasts, along with tough-to-find dime novels, 1920s and 1930s magazines for youth, and a surprising number of scarce young adult novels. Burns also vividly shows just how many publications, ranging from mass-market slicks to college magazines, carried sports fiction. The largest number of American sports stories, however, was carried in the sports pulps, the vast majority of which appeared in the two-decade span of 1935–1955.

FIVE

The Man Who Beat Merriwell

One of the oddest stories in the history of pop culture did not receive so much as a cover mention when it surprisingly appeared at the time sports pulp magazines were about to enjoy a brief burst of post–World War II popularity. Before we look at sports pulps in the 1940s and 1950s, let's examine this little known, offbeat tale.

The Man Who Beat Merriwell, a novelette by the prolific pulp western and sports story writer Roe Richmond in the September 1947 issue of Columbia's then-quarterly *Super Sports* pulp, must have been an eyebrow-raiser for more than a few readers of middle age and older. Virtually all of those longtime readers would have remembered Frank and Dick Merriwell, the heroic dime novel brother act about whom more stories were written than any sports characters (see chapter one).

"This is an old story," Richmond began his unique tale, using the voice of protagonist Mike Rocklin, sans a few commas that would have provided welcome clarity:

> Old-timers will not believe it, and the younger generation will not remember the Merriwell brothers anyway. For the benefit of the latter I can say that the Merriwells once held the place Superman holds today. Those that remember will know the Merriwells always won, but they haven't heard this story either. So while it is about old times it is still new. I was in it for the money and not the glory, and I didn't mind having it suppressed. I didn't need publicity, and I didn't want to hurt the Merriwells because they were good boys. Over-rated maybe, but plenty good.

At the time, Richmond's comparison of Merriwell and Superman was a significant understatement, not giving the Merriwells nearly enough credit. The Merriwell family, including Frank Junior (who appeared late in the original run and was not part of Richmond's story), appeared in well over 1,000 original adventures from 1896 to 1916, plus a handful of original stories in Street & Smith pulp magazines from 1927 to 1931, not to mention selling millions of reprint books. In contrast, Superman was nine years old in 1947, having debuted in Action Comics #1 (June 1938) from National Periodical Publications, which eventually became DC Comics. In 1947, Superman was also appearing in a widely syndicated Sunday newspaper strip, plus single 12-page stories in the monthly Action Comics and the bimonthly World's Finest Comics. His adventures as a teenager also were appearing monthly in Adventure Comics. All four titles were best sellers in the four-color world. The Man of Steel, as he was constantly called even though his super powers stemmed from being born on the exotic planet Krypton and had nothing to do with any metals, had appeared in less that 250 issues of comic books when *The Man Who Beat Merriwell* appeared. He had yet to appear on television (which was just getting started commercially) or in the movies, except as a short-lived series of cartoons, and his greatest exposure came via national radio broadcasts, which began in 1940. It is also likely that many, if not most, young readers were quite familiar with the Merriwell name in 1947. *The Adventures of Frank Merriwell*, a half-hour NBC Saturday morning radio serial, enjoyed a three-year run from 1946 to 1949, as documented by radio historian/mystery novelist/bookseller John Dunning.

All of this does nothing to explain why *Super Sports* editor Robert W. Lowndes, best known in pop culture for his science fiction work, did not banner the story on the cover. Instead, he preferred to plug *Swing, Ya Bum, Swing* by the remarkably prolific T.W. Ford, along with a story by workhorse Arthur Mann, both then better known than Roe Richmond. Even so, one would think that the Merriwell name would have warranted more publicity. But then, the Merriwell name was still owned by the publishing goliath Street & Smith, and for Merriwell to appear in a story from a rival pulp publisher was unexpected, indeed. Since the story was apparently intended as a one-shot appearance of the Merriwells, perhaps Columbia did not want to call attention to this unique story, as John Dinan speculates in his book *Sports in the Pulp Magazines*, from McFarland, in 1998.

The story was set in the era (circa 1910) when Dick Merriwell was still cavorting to great applause on diamond, gridirons and hardwoods for dear old Yale in the years following Frank's graduation. (The original Merriwell stories actually appeared, more or less, in real time.) Richmond included several of Frank Merriwell's old dime-novel teammates, notably the fabulously talented Bart Hodge; but Frank's girlfriends Inza Burrage and Elsie Bellwood were nowhere to be found. Instead, much of the *Super Sports* story theme involved the machinations and dreams of Kay Van Allyn, Frank Merriwell's wealthy heartthrob, and also well-to-do Ginger Grace, the melodiously named woman Rocklin chased.

As the story opened, Rocklin, a hard-drinking mercenary sort, explained he had just been "sent down from the Big Time baseball circuit." "They said I was hitting the bottle harder than the ball, but that wasn't the truth," he told the reader. Putting together a team for a charity baseball game — although Rocklin was playing for pay — he pitched against the Merriwells and their friends. Rocklin's collision with Dick Merriwell after Rocklin's fourth-inning bunt forced sore-armed Frank Merriwell to the mound, but not before Frank muttered, "Rocklin, that was dirty — and unnecessary" in his reserved but forceful dime-novel style.

In the final inning of a wild contest, Rocklin tells the reader,

> I could always murder lefties and I was feeling good, but Frank Merriwell must have heard about it. He shifted gloves again and starting working on me with his right arm (Merriwell was an ambidextrous pitcher). But his fast one no longer exploded in your face, and his curve no longer did dizzy tricks. I got one I liked and I cut at it with every ounce. It rang like a bell and it felt like a home run, but it was a ground drive straight at Dick Merriwell in the short-field. Cursing I headed for first, and then my heart went up like a sky-rocket. The ball had taken a freak bounce over young Merry's head and on toward the fence. There was plenty of power behind it, and it carried between the fielders. Both runs scored and it was our ball game, 8–7. Of course they called it a fluke hit and a lucky victory, but I know that ball was really hit. Even in the unusual role of loser Frank Merriwell was the big hero, and young Dick was the runner-up.

Shortly before the ensuing football game, Kay Van Allyn visits Rocklin and acknowledges she wants Frank to lose! "Did you ever think how it would be to live with someone who was always right, who always won and never lost, who was the symbol of invincibility?" she asks Rocklin, explaining her rooting interest in Rocklin.

Rocklin, as the story title indicates, also beats the Merriwells in football, following a couple thousand words to describe the wild action, including Rocklin's punch-out of one

Dodo Dodd. It turned out dumb Dodo was trying to throw the game for gamblers! (The dime novels involved a countless number of gamblers.) Rocklin scores a touchdown on the final play as he and would-be tackler Frank Merriwell both tumble together over the goal line, capping a trick-play backfield reverse. Rocklin had beaten the Merriwells 19–16.

Frank, though, emerged as the ultimate winner, frustrating Kay during a postgame party at the Van Allyn estate. Yet Frank did not act in dime-novel character. Finding Rocklin talking with Kay in "the perfumed dimness of the garden," Merriwell calls him a cad. "Yes, that's the word he used," Rocklin says. When Frank slaps his face, Rocklin feels called to respond:

> But I was in no mood for fighting. I threw a couple of light punches. Frank Merriwell glided in at me swinging. There were two blinding explosions and I was down on the gravel walk. When my head cleared Merry was gone and Kay Van Allyn stood there looking down at me.
> "Oh, Mike, that spoils everything, everything," she said, and then she went away, too. I got up and bathed my face in the fountain and wondered at the ways of women. Well, that's my story and you can believe it or not. I beat the Merriwells twice, and I would have whipped Frank with my fists if I hadn't come to like the guy. But it didn't do my any good to beat the Merriwells. In fact it ruined my career. I married Ginger Grace and grew soft helping her spend all that money, and I never did anything more worth mentioning in athletics. Still, I beat the Merriwells in baseball and football, and nobody else ever did that. Ginger still says I was lucky but I know better. It took more than luck to lick those boys.

Thus ended the final print appearance of the original Frank Merriwell in American pop culture. How many readers must have been left hoping that somehow, with Kay unsatisfied at the outcome, that Frank would have instead wound up with the far more deserving Inza.

In his account in *Sports in the Pulp Magazines*, Dinan concludes as follows: "It's bad enough that the Merriwells lose a baseball and a football game in their last ever appearance but at game's end Frank proves to be that sport's anathema of a bad sport, venting his ire by slapping Rocklin's face." This incomplete observation, however, unfairly tarnishes Frank's reputation, since his slap of Rocklin and the ensuing fight occurred long after the game, at the party, and then only after Frank finds Kay in Rocklin's company (it is only implied they might have been kissing).

Ironically, *Super Sports* itself became the last surviving pulp sports magazine, expiring with its undated 1957 issue (the last three issues were annuals). The magazine, apparently timed to appear during baseball season, featured a reprint cover of a batter's broken bat exploding between the legs of a pitcher. One could only hope the batter was Frank Merriwell and the pitcher was Mike Rocklin.

Conflict, conflict and more conflict

The pulps, regardless of genre, were about all manner of conflict between the characters, in the case of sports both on and off the field or court. Sports pulps fit that formula well with the most "true to life" stories of any genre represented in the pulpwoods. The most breathless, unlikely on-field heroics, of course, were duplicated somewhere in the nation pretty much every month. That's why the sports pulps—unlike the science fiction and mystery digests that survived in the 1950s, 1960s and beyond—could not overcome television's influence. Readers could see heroic home runs, baskets and touchdowns in real life with far more frequency on television than they ever could when they actually had to be at the games, many of which were more or less routine.

The off-the-field conflicts, of course, weren't revealed on the broadcasts and telecasts, although reporters did their best to uncover whatever potential conflict they could with ever-increasing behind-the-scenes work. Reporters who covered the three-time World Series champion Oakland A's of 1972–1974 were kept constantly on the alert by players who sometimes battled each other as well as their irascible pinch-penny owner, Charles O. Finley, as Bill Libby's amazing 1975 book, *Charlie O. and the Angry A's*, so well detailed. That book reads like a pulp novel come to life, well after sports pulps were left to molder on the shelves of second-hand book stores until pop culture scholars like me began to realize they needed to be preserved from extinction. And what went on behind the scenes when Brooklyn's Jackie Robinson broke Major League Baseball's color line in 1947 was a lot more intriguing than any pulp story.

The wonderful aspect of sports pulps, however, is that the off-the-field conflict could come from anywhere. Current teammates fought each other, former teammates did the same, old coaches battled their rival coaches, former players, current players and would-be players. There were battles galore with reporters, who often came across as less realistic in the pulps than some of the golden boys they covered. And, of course, there was never ending inner conflict as players constantly sought to prove they weren't "yellow," and that they had "what it takes in the clutch." The conflicts of players against themselves were never ending in their variety. Then there were, of course, the ladies, shady and otherwise, to contend with, and the ever-present gamblers, alcoholics, lowlifes and other ne'er-do-wells. Lots of pulp stories ended with revelations — the opponents/teammates who hated each other were really brothers; the coach was really the star's father! — and others just tried to show that "a winner never quits, and a quitter never wins," as untold thousands of coaches have told athletes.

The best of the sports novels, and the pulp stories, too, use on-field action to reveal character — the brash rookie, the greedy quarterback, the selfless teammate — rather than to pad the story to a word length that paid better or filled out a thin novel. Of all genre fiction, sports has always been the easiest to pad, with endless word pictures of game developments. It's true that many of the pulp stories were weak and forgettable at best, yet every now and then, pulp sports tales would sparkle with an inspirational morality and an athlete who really does win out because he never quits.

The Golden Age of Sports Pulps in the 1940s and early 1950s

Sports fiction was never a major genre in the pulp magazines, yet the exploits of athletic heroes were not insignificant in the pulpwoods. Of the slightly more than 40,000 pulp magazines of all types listed in *The Adventure House Guide to the Pulps* and *Bookery's Guide to the Pulps*, the vast majority were published in the four decades from 1920 to 1960. As the 1,530 issues of general-interest sports pulps — give or take a handful that may or may not exist — were all published from 1923 to 1957, sports consisted of less than 4 percent of the pulp fiction market. Even so, pretty much the only consistent outlet for adults in sports fiction from the 1920s through the 1950s was in the pages of the pulp magazines, though they were also avidly read by many teenagers. Very few adult sports novels were published during the pulp period. The *Saturday Evening Post*, *Collier's* and *Liberty*, among others, would publish the occasional football or baseball story or serial, but nowhere near as many as the well over 12,000 sports stories that appeared over a 34-year period in the sports pulps, with baseball, boxing, football and basketball by far the most dominant subjects.

Nonetheless, sports may indeed have been enjoyed less than 4 percent of pulp circulation, considering that sports was unquestionably last among the major genres (and, today, only romance pulps trail sports in general collector interest and value). Western stories and love stories were by far the best-selling genres, of interest primarily to men and women, respectively — although nearly 2,000 issues combined the two big genres with the likes of the best-selling *Ranch Romances*, *Thrilling Ranch Stories* and *Rodeo Romances*, among many others. It says a lot about popular tastes that there were more western romance pulp issues than sports pulps.

Also well ahead of sports in reader interest were the detective pulps and their exotic first cousins, the super heroic epics such as The Shadow, The Spider and Doc Savage, along with the science fiction magazines. Aviation and war pulps — bolstered by memories of World War I and an ever-increasing interest in flying and World War II — also outnumbered and outsold the sports pulps until almost all the aviation pulps quickly vanished in

Baseball Stories, Spring 1946 (copyright Flying Stories, Inc.). George Gross nicely portrays the emotion of catcher and manager in a furious argument with the plate umpire, while the batter in the on-deck circle grins.

the postwar period. And the long-running pulps devoted to a wide variety of manly adventure of all sorts — notably *Argosy*, *Adventure*, *Blue Book* and *Short Stories* — vastly outnumbered the sports pulps, although these worthwhile and often well-written anthology pulps would not infrequently include a sports story or serialized novel and occasionally even featured a sports cover.

Nearly one-third of all sports pulps were represented by the 429-issue run of Street & Smith's *Sport Story* magazine from 1923 to 1943. But this venerable, high-caliber magazine, which had no competition in its genre during its first decade, was clearly on the downside as 1940 began. *Sport Story* was published twice-monthly for 16 years until going to monthly publication in September 1939. The magazine remained monthly until the last two issues were published in May and July 1943, skipping April and June with a not-so-subtle hint of declining circulation (along with World War II paper restrictions).

During the 1943–45 period, most pulp magazines of all types either decreased publication frequency, suspended publication or expired, although those that remained inevitably urged readers to forward the magazine to a serviceman. Of the 830 or so sports pulp issues published from 1940 to 1957, only 55 were produced in 1944 and 1945 combined — slightly more than a mere two per month. Only Better Publications' *Popular Sports* published as many as seven issues; sisters *Thrilling Sports* and *Exciting Sports* appeared six times each. All were listed as quarterlies, having shrunk to 80 pages, with often eye-straining type. Of the other companies still publishing sports pulps during World War II, Popular, Columbia and Ace suspended all of their sports titles in the later stages of the war. Martin Goodman's Red Circle/Marvel line also put all of its sports pulps on hiatus (and most other pulp types) to focus on its increasingly profitable comic book line.

Other than pulp, paperback and comic book impresario Ned Pines' Standard Publications, the only other company not to suspend its sports pulps was Fiction House. Fiction House had been publishing a wide variety of pulps since its first in 1921 and by the 1940s had become a large comic book publisher as well. But then, Fiction House never really published anything but seasonal sports types, except for its long-running *Fight Stories* (which is outside the range of this book) and its three-issue *Bulls-Eye Sports* in 1939, one of the firm's few outright failures. Fiction House, which killed *Basketball Stories* after one issue in winter 1937-38, continued to publish two in-season issues of *All-American Football* magazine, *Football Action*, *Football Stories* and *Baseball Stories* each year during World War II.

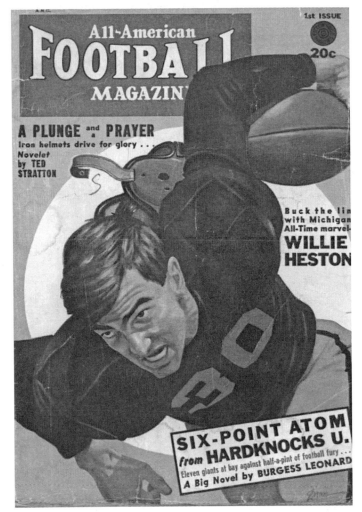

All-American Football, first (Fall 1949) issue (copyright 1949, Love Romances Publishing Co.). George Gross consistently gave Fiction House some of the most emotionally intense pulp covers on the newsstands.

Sports pulps experienced a significant, albeit short, resurgence in the postwar era, pretty much in conjunction with the temporary growth of minor-league baseball plus the return of the war-weary stars to the big leagues, and the steady growth of both pro football and pro basketball. But the real-life drama of televised sports — and television in general — played a major role in killing the sports pulps in the mid 1950s, along with a plethora of sports novels intended for the young-adult market. Indeed, the twin-pronged explosion of television and 25-cent and 35-cent paperback books steadily turned Americans away from pulps until the pulps slowly staggered to their death by 1960, although *Ranch Romances* hung on until 1971.

It was no surprise that the only genre of fiction that thrived in magazine format in the 1960s, albeit in digest-size publication, was science fiction (although a few detective digests prospered, too). Most science fiction pulps morphed into digests during the 1950s after *Astounding Science Fiction* started the trend in 1943. It was no coincidence that science fiction was the only genre television could not convincingly, frequently and inexpensively provide for adults in the pre–computer chip early 1950s, although the print genre became increasingly more mature, given the scientific realities of space exploration. Western and detective heroes abounded on TV in the 1950s and 1960s. Meanwhile, real-life events took care of the sports thrills for former pulp readers of all ages.

Baseball Stories, Spring 1953 (copyright Flying Stories, Inc.). George Gross symbolically portrays "The Slugger from Heaven," although this cover is actually a reprint.

Sports pulps steadily declined in the early 1950s. Standard Publications abandoned its three anthology titles in 1951 and Popular Publication quit in 1951 and 1952. Marvel's Goodman tried starting or reviving ten sports pulp titles in the 1947–1948 period, only to kill them all quickly except for *Best Sports*, which staggered into 1951, and *Complete Sports*, which somehow made it into 1955 as by far the firm's most successful sports pulp. Fiction House's last sports pulp was the 33rd issue of *Baseball Stories* (Volume 3, #9) in spring 1954. A year later, the company was out of business with the final issue of *Planet Stories*.

Columbia, which consistently published the worst pulps from the standpoint of both story and cover quality and reportedly paid the lowest rates, abandoned its ultrageneric *Sports Fiction* title in 1951. Columbia then converted *Sports Winners* in 1952 to a second run of *Ten Story Sports*, which lasted until January 1957 and was the last regularly published sports pulp. *Super Sports*, Columbia's most successful sports title, ran through 1954 and then published annuals in 1955, 1956, and 1957. The 1957 issue of *Super Sports*, featuring a baseball cover, was the last sports pulp.

To the best of my knowledge, none of the 1940–57 sports pulps carried any continuing characters with the exception of several seasonal Lew Young baseball stores by Arthur Mann in Street & Smith's *Sport Story*, beginning with the April 1940 issue. Mann would later serve the Brooklyn Dodgers in a variety of front-office capacities and wrote the entertaining books *The Jackie Robinson Story* (1950) and *Baseball Confidential* (1951), along with numerous newspaper and magazine stories both before and after his pulp story days.

In the decade following World War II, there were only 20 general-interest, nonseasonal sports pulp titles, making it easy for readers to follow them all, so there must not have been an expansive market.

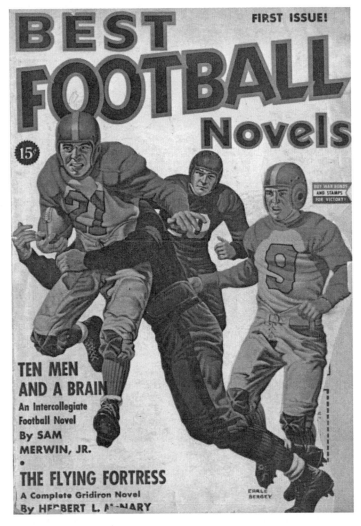

Best Football Novels, December 1942 one-shot (copyright Nedor Publishing Co.). Earle Bergey vividly portrays a breakaway back on the cover of one of the scarcest sports pulps. World War II paper restrictions may have halted publication, since Standard soon downsized its pulps, both from the standpoint of size and publishing frequency.

Marvel had eight, most of them unsuccessful, Columbia had five, Standard and Popular had three, and Ace had one, *Ace Sports*, which expired in 1949 with the rest of the company's pulp titles. Standard, also known as Thrilling, even went so far as to discontinue its decade-long run of *Exciting Sports*, converting the title into *Five Sports Classics* for the final four (quarterly) issues so the company could unashamedly use novella-length reprints. In 1951, though, none of the Standard/Thrilling reprints could be more than 14 or 15 years old, so they did not seem dated, the way stories from the 1920s surely would have seemed.

Of the seasonal titles in the 1940–57 period — all from Standard, Goodman or Fiction House — eight were football issues and six were devoted to baseball. It's a measure of basketball's relative lack of influence in those days that, in the wake of the 1938 one-issue failure of Fiction House's *Basketball Stories*, the only all-basketball pulp to appear later was the one-shot *All Basketball Stories* from Goodman in winter 1947–48.

The few sports pulp publishers

After the demise of *All-American Sports* in 1938, and of Street & Smith's *Sport Story* in 1943, only six pulp publishers remained who were willing to take a flyer on sports stories, other than those that appeared in anthology magazines. All six invested significantly but far from overwhelmingly in the market. Indeed, the 429 issues of *Sport Story* magazine from 1923 to 1943 were about twice as many as the entire sports output of Popular Publications (230 issues, give or take a couple, from 1937 to 1952). The other publishers were Martin Goodman's Red Circle/Marvel (146 issues, give or take a couple, from 1936 to 1955), Ace Magazines (111 issues from 1937 to 1949) and Fiction House (109 issues from 1937 to 1954).

It's interesting to note that many fly-by-night pulp publishers— and even some large, well-capitalized firms, such as Dell, Ziff-Davis and Fawcett — never published general-interest sports pulps. Apparently publishers felt either there was a profitable market or no market at all. Of course, circumstances during the Great Depression often imposed limitations in the 1930s, followed by the publishing complications created by World War II. And when the war was over, only the hardiest pulp publishers remained, and most of those did invest in sports.

All six of the post–1943 sports pulp publishers used stories— almost always either novelettes or short stories— by authors who went on to become prolific novelists in every genre, but most notably in sports stories, westerns, mysteries and science fiction. In many cases, they wrote for both adults and young readers. And every publisher can claim to have at least a couple of writers who went on to become best-selling icons, such as Louis L'Amour and John D. MacDonald.

Popular Publications, which produced more than 4,000 issues of all types and lasted until the mid–1950s, focused entirely on the nonseasonal, general-interest pulp, with *Dime Sports* and its successor, *New Sports*, along with *Sports Novels* and *Fifteen Sports Stories*. (Popular also produced nine issues of *Knockout*, a boxing pulp, but those are outside the scope of this book.) Popular believed strictly in variety and used colorful cover artists such as the fabulous Norman Saunders and the competent Charles De Feo. Popular's covers simply exuded sweat and they were almost always of violent action scenes or intensely focused faces. They fairly cried to the reader, "Have we got drama for you!"

Most of the popular sports authors of the pulp period and the two ensuing decades worked for Popular, including William R. Cox, William Heuman, Jackson Scholz, Burgess Leonard, Robert Sidney Bowen, William Campbell Gault, Joe Archibald, Curtis Bishop, David Goodis, Duane Yarnell, C. Paul Jackson, Duane Decker, Les Etter, Nelson Hutto and Arthur Mann and his pseudonym, A.R. Thurmann. Another frequent contributor was Judson P. Philips, the real name of the man who went on to achieve fame as mystery novelist Hugh Pentecost. It's not coincidence there are no female names on the list as women rarely contributed to sports pulps, or they wrote under male names when they did. Since sports pulps were purchased primarily by men and teenage boys, it was thought that women's names would not sell them, just as most of the stories in the romance pulps were authored by women or by men who wrote under female names.

Before he became famous, beginning in the 1950s, as one of America's best and most prolific crime novelists, John D. MacDonald wrote numerous science fiction and sports stories as well as mystery tales. Most of MacDonald's sports fiction wound up in Popular pulps — well over a dozen stories in all. He wrote boxing, football, golf, baseball, basketball, tennis and even bullfighting, with the unique "Salute to Courage" in the April 1951 *Fifteen Sports Stories*.

MacDonald — or Popular's editors — used typically compelling titles for his stories, including these from *Fifteen Sports Stories*: "Hell's Belter" (February 1952); "Cloob from Glasgow" (October 1951); "Take the Bum Out!" (January 1949); "Money Green" (May 1950); "The Glory Punch" (July 1949) and "Six Points to Remember." The stories he wrote for *Sports Novels* include, among others, "Runaway Cleats" (September 1948), "Loser Take All" (August 1948), "Last-Chance Cleats" (March 1949) and "Glory Blaster" (November 1948). For *New Sports*, he penned "Fight, Scrub, Fight!" (February 1949); "Buzz-Saw Belter" (December 1948) and "The Plunder Five" (April 1950).

When *Dime Sports* debuted in July 1935, the only author of note on the contents page was baseball historian Fred Lieb, who contributed a nonfiction piece, just as so many famed sports journalists did for the pulps, including the likes of John Drebinger and Arthur Daley for *Dime Sports*. Soon, authors would appear in *Dime Sports* and then would go on to far better things in other genres: Steve Fisher ("Leather-Pusher USN" in May 1936); Frank Gruber ("Mat Menace" in August 1936) and Nelson Bond ("Touchdown Medicine" in August 1938).

Novelettes, not novels

Even Popular's long-running *Sports Novels* seldom ran stories longer than novelette length, since the publisher's hallmark in this title was versatility, although covers tended to follow the season. Titles were especially colorful when *Sports Novels* resumed publishing with the February 1946 issue following an 18-month break, perhaps caused by wartime paper rationing. Typical titles included "Blast 'Em, Busher!" by William R. Cox (July 1949); "Star Maker" by Burgess Leonard (April 1948); "The Ghost of Coffin Corner" by Curtis Bishop (December 1946); "Slaughter on the Sacks" by William Heuman (May 1950); "Last Chance Chucker " by Wallace Umphrey (May 1949); "Tearaway Terror" by Heuman (January 1950), and "High, Hard and Dynamite!" — the title of stories by both Nelson Hutto (April 1948) and Daniel Winters (August 1951).

Considering that more than 12,000 stories appeared in the 1,530 or so sports pulp issues from 1923 to 1957, title duplication was far from rare. It's likely that editors frankly did not care, since it's doubtful that readers would have cared, either. They just wanted good sports plots, and not a few titles might have been applied to almost any sport, although most of the time there was a hint. The insult "busher" — a reference to a minor league baseball player, or talent or attitude of minor league proportions — appeared in dozens of story titles, often followed by an exclamation point. "Busher" was about the worst thing a baseball player could be called, short of words that could not be printed in sports pulps.

Although some pseudonyms will never be discovered, it's my estimation that fewer than 1,000 different writers produced the pulp sports stories, and perhaps even fewer than 500. Many writers produced dozens of stories; a few authors, such as T.W. Ford, produced hundreds of tales. Ford was among several dozen prolific writers who wrote almost entirely for the pulps, regardless of the story length. Like the science fiction, mystery, western and romance pulps, however, the sports pulps featured a high percentage of authors who wrote both hardback and paperback novels along with pulp stories, although sometimes at different points in their careers.

Like Street & Smith, Popular liked publishing "as told to" stories with double bylines, such as the Arthur Mann/Frank Frisch collaboration in *Sports Novels* for December 1939 – January 1940. Frisch, a popular Hall of Famer known to every fan as "The Fordham Flash," retired as a player in 1937 but continued as a manager, so the wisdom of such a baseball figure was especially appealing to readers. In the pulps, fact-based stories tended to cover sports figures who had been in the public eye for a good many years, not the 20-something youngsters who appear so frequently today in the likes of *Sports Illustrated*.

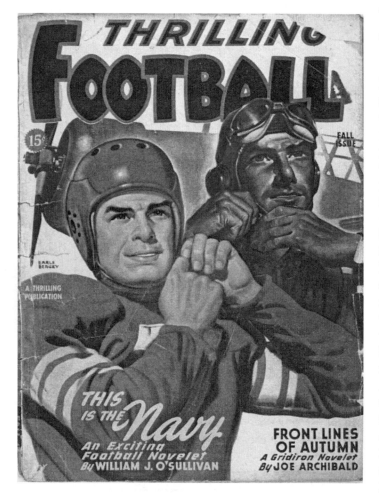

Thrilling Football, Fall 1945 (copyright Better Publications, Inc.). Earle Bergey shows how the football star and fighter pilot both gear for action by strapping on their head protection. The Ned Pines pulp factory frequently used patriotic covers during World War II, although this issue may have hit the stands after the war ended.

Thrilling, Exciting — and Popular

The entrepreneurial Ned Pines ultimately became the most prolific publisher of popular fiction during the 1930s, 1940s and 1950s, when that 30-year period is considered as a whole. No one else during that period was as deeply invested in a newsstand flood of pulps (beginning in 1931), comic books (1939) and paperback books (1943), along with a handful of other publications such as astrology and men's magazines. His firm continued beyond 1960, primarily with its Popular Library paperbacks, after giving up on pulps in 1958 (except for *Ranch Romances*, which lingered through 1971) and comic books in 1959 (after selling its successful Dennis the Menace and Mighty Mouse titles to other franchises). The total count of Pines' pulps, paperbacks, comics and magazines produced through 1959 exceeds 6,000.

Throughout most of their history, Pines' pulps carried the

logo "A Thrilling Publication." Indeed, Pines made a point of using "Thrilling," "Exciting" and "Popular" in the title of pulps involving every genre, not to mention the use of "Startling" for a long-running science-fiction magazine and a popular superhero comic book. Newsstand customers were thus probably not surprised to see *Thrilling Sports* debut in 1936, followed by *Popular Sports* in 1937 and *Exciting Sports* in 1940. Pines was the only successful publisher of both general-interest pulps and seasonal pulps. His editors — the most famous of whom was Leo Margulies, who worked for Pines from 1931 to 1950 — used "Thrilling," "Popular" and "Exciting" on both football and baseball pulps. The most successful was the 14-issue run of *Thrilling Football* stories from 1939 to 1951.

The Thrilling folks stressed the use of versatile current and future novelists in their sports pulps, which were both a wonderful market and a marvelous training ground. Many of Thrilling's sports authors became much better known in

Exciting Sports, April 1948 (copyright Better Publications, Inc.). An uncredited artist nicely portrays the grim intensity of preparing for a clutch baseball situation.

other genres, including the iconic western novelist Louis L'Amour, the fantasy and science fiction writers Nelson Bond, Sam Merwyn, Jr., Ray Cummings and Oscar Friend, the mystery novelists William Campbell Gault, Richard Sale, Stewart Sterling, Robert S. Bellem and David Goodis, and the western writers Giles A. Lutz and Richard Brister, not to mention Johnston McCulley, the creator of Zorro and many lesser-known series characters, and the famed aviation writer George Bruce. John D. MacDonald, in the period before he became a best-selling crime novelist, produced a considerable amount of science fiction for Pines' publications but sold most of his mystery and sports stories to Popular. William J. O'Sullivan, who played major roles in producing many of Republic Studios' best serials, also was a frequent sports contributor. The house name Jackson Cole, best known for western epics, also appeared on sports stories.

The above names, and doubtless others, are what make looking at the contents page of a Pines sports pulp so much fun. However, Pines also used most of the big names in sports fiction, including Gault (who later became famed for both adult mystery and young-adult sports fiction), Joe Archibald (an editor on Pines' comic line in the early 1950s), T.W. Ford, Robert Sidney Bowen, Jackson Scholz, C. Paul Jackson, Arthur Mann, William R. Cox, William Heuman, R.G. Emery, Nelson A. Hutto and Burgess Leonard.

Like many sports pulps in the 1930s, Pines aimed for variety on Standard's covers, including those on early issues of *Thrilling Sports* including hurdling (September 1936), sprinting (May 1937), pole vaulting (September 1937) and hockey (March 1937). *Popular Sports* had covers celebrating horse racing (August 1939 and Summer 1940) and hockey (February 1938) and also featured sports celebrities such as baseball's Dizzy Dean (June 1937) and Bob Feller (October 1938), basketball's Hank Luisetti (February 1939) and boxing's James J. Braddock (August 1937).

Pines, however, soon turned to featuring almost nothing but baseball, football, basketball and boxing on the covers of its general-interest pulps before they expired in 1951, obviously feeling that they appealed to the most modern readers. This writer's survey of 149 of the 178 issues of *Thrilling Sports*, *Popular Sports* and *Exciting Sports* (plus its four-issue successor, *Five Sports Classics*) showed 134 covers featuring the big three team sports along with 11 boxing covers.

Many of the Pines sports pulp covers were luminescent beauties by Earle Bergey, who achieved fame in the science fiction pulps and honed his craft while (earlier) working for Street & Smith's *Sport Story* magazine. Fans of college football in the 1940s and 1950s were frequently treated to a heroic Bergey image on their game programs. There were also a few Pines sports pulp covers by Rudolph Belarski, best known for his work in the mystery and adventure pulps. Those two illustrators — who combined realistic art with a sometimes surrealistic or symbolic approach — are among the best-loved among pulp enthusiasts, and their compelling art doubtless sold untold millions of pulps.

It's fascinating to note that Louis L'Amour's contribution to *Thrilling Football* stories for Winter 1949, "Moran of the Tigers," was not cover-featured — but the names of six other authors were! He also wrote the football short "Backfield Battering Ram" for *Popular Football* in the Winter 1947 issue, along with a number of boxing stories before he began his career as a western novelist in the early 1950s. L'Amour wrote more than two hundred stories for the pulps, almost all of them much later reprinted in his personally updated format in a series of anthologies.

Standard stopped publishing sports pulps in 1951 — the first major genre to be abandoned by the Pines people — except for the inexplicable Spring 1953 issue of *Exciting Baseball*. Ironically, the lead story was "Nice Guys Don't Win Pennants" by Giles A. Lutz — shades of then–New York Giants manager Leo Durocher! Robert Sidney Bowen — already five years into his two-decade career as a prolific sports novelist for young adult readers—contributed the unique "Pennant for a Lady." In this story, female ownership of a major league baseball franchise is anticipated — although, of course, the woman of the piece wound up marrying the star player!

Sports drama from Fiction House

The venerable firm Fiction House, one of the original pulp publishers, celebrated its 30th anniversary in 1951. But the company would survive only four more years, and several of its final issues were in the sports category. Of the large pulp sports publishers, Fiction House was the only one that specialized in nothing but seasonal pulps, following the failure of its three-issue quarterly run of *Bulls-Eye Sports* in 1939. Although the company's longest-running sports pulp was *Baseball Stories* (33 issues from 1938 to 1954), Fiction House heavily favored football with *Football Stories* (25 issues from 1937 to 1953), *Football Action and All-American Football* magazine). The first issue of *Basketball Stories* (Winter 1937-38) failed to generate enough interest for even a second issue.

Fiction House published one noteworthy nonfiction publication — *The Illustrated Football Annual*, which began in 1930 and provided a much-heralded "Coast to Coast Preview" of college football, which then far exceeded pro football in popularity and publicity. This was one of the first magazines of its type and gave Fiction House's editors access to many of the nation's big-name sportswriters; most of them frequently supplemented their newspaper incomes with freelance work. Accordingly, Fiction House's sports pulps featured fact-based articles by the likes of Jimmy Powers, John Drebinger, Tim Cohane, Dan Parker and a young Edwin Pope.

Like the sports publications from Popular and Pines, a reader never knew who might show up in a Fiction House sports pulp content page. Who would have guessed that Michael Avallone would go on to become one of the most prolific of all mystery novelists when his "Aw, Let the Kid Hit" appeared in the Summer 1950 *Baseball Stories* when he was 25 years old — his first published fiction. Likewise, venerable sports novelists William Heyliger and Harold M. Sherman, who between them wrote more than 60 sports novels, contributed some of their final sports fiction to Fiction House, including Heyliger's "Sand-Lot Champion" in the first issue of *Baseball Stories* (1938). Famed San Francisco newspaper reporter and columnist Dick Friendlich, who wrote 18 literate and realistic young adult sports novels over two decades beginning in 1949, got his fictional start in the pulps with work in *All-American Football* magazine (First Fall 1948) and *Baseball Stories* (spring 1953), among other short stories.

One of the best of all sports pulp cover artists, George Gross, did much of his finest creative work for Fiction House, featuring athletes sweating at all sorts of angles and poses. Collectors have long loved his work. Fiction House, however, frequently reprinted its best covers, so collectors have always had to refer to lists, not memory, since other companies did this far less frequently, if at all (although the Pines people used many of their best pulp covers on paperback books published only a few years later). For example, *Baseball Stories* used the same covers on Spring 1942/Spring 1951, Spring 1939/Spring 1945, Spring 1938/Spring 1944 and Spring 1944/Spring 1953, on the theory that few readers would remember them.

There were even odder reprint practices. For example, there were reprint covers for *Football Stories* First Fall 1944/First Fall 1951 and Fiction House titles both lead stories "The Pigskin Privateer" by Ted Roemer (1944) and Burgess Leonard (1951). These were separate stories! And in *Football Stories* for Fall 1949, the reprinted cover features a story entitled "Revolt of the Red Vikings" by William R. Cox. That story, along with the cover, first appeared in the Fall 1943 issue, but did not appear in the 1949 issue, despite the cover plug. However, a different Cox story, "Hobo at Fullback," did appear in the latter issue.

All-American Football for First Fall 1944 and Fall 1952 featured exactly the same cover except for the price — it had changed from 20 cents to 25 cents, showing how slowly inflation moved in those days. It's also interesting to note that two most prolific nonseries sports novelists of the postwar era, Joe Archibald and Jackson Scholz, both appeared in the First

Fall 1943 issue, while the first issue in 1938 featured one of William R. Cox's earliest stories and among the last to appear from Heyliger and Sherman.

The gritty Fiction House style

The down-and-dirty grittiness of the Fiction House sports pulps distinguished them from almost all of their competition, which was usually suited for readers of all ages. But then, that was Fiction House; during World War II, the company sold millions of comic books to soldiers because Fiction House stressed a "guns and gams" formula on the covers and in suggestive stories of extreme, exotic violence.

The sports pulps, stressing intense emotion in the faces on the covers, fit right in with the likes of Burgess Leonard's "The Rhubarb Kid" in *Baseball Stories* for Summer 1952 and Leonard's "Six-Point Atom from Hardknocks U" in the First Fall 1949 issue of *All-American Football*. Blurbs tended to make sense only if you read them two or three times: "To the sputtering 16-cylinder Gold Sox came Lew Warden — the aging mechanic with the gas-house spark" was the cover introduction for "The Rhubarb Kid." For "Six-Point Atom," the editor came up with "Eleven giants at bay against half-a-pint of football fury." The prolific pulpster Leonard is the kind of author who makes researching and reading the pulps so much fun. The crackling, no-holds-barred conversational style of his sports characters sounds like something out of the hard-boiled detective pulps. His clubhouses, dugouts and fields were filled with caustic, angst-ridden comments; feelings were never spared.

In "The Rhubarb Kid," fiery Lew Warden — the divorced father of two — is fired by the greedy owner of his club, the Wolves, even though Warden is named his league's manager of the year and is still good enough to be known as "Mr. Shortstop." He joins the Gold Sox as a player but not as a manager. Realizing the field manager is emotionally weak, Lew finds a way to "blackmail" him — sans financial payment — because of something in the manager's past, so that Lew can take over as decision-maker. His behind-the-scenes moves drive the Gold Sox to the pennant with the final shreds of his playing ability, earning him a chance to manage the third team, the Clippers. There are dozens of nasty comments along the way; and the dirty man who took his place with the Wolves, Teddy Grundy, even deliberately slashes Lew in the face with his shoe spikes when Lew knocks the shoe off during a hard tag at second base. Before that incident, Lew tells the team prima donna, right fielder "Prince Hal" Royall, "If I see you dog it on one ground ball, I'm going to take myself a walk into right field and kick my initials onto your backside. And unless you want a knot tied into that long nose right now, shut your big yap."

In "Six-Point Atom," 138-pound orphan Monk Jones, denied varsity opportunity at State College, goes to the rival school and plays offense, defense, special teams and as a kicker! He's an incredibly intense little guy, with a chip on his shoulder bigger than he is; and he ultimately learns that his new coach, the erstwhile alcoholic Rummy Roberts, is really his father. After he helps to win the Big Game over the coach who spurned him — with 13 pages of no-holds-barred game action described — the coach tells him point blank, "You still couldn't play State football, kid. And that's not taking a thing away from you. I never low-rated you; you're the toughest man to beat I ever saw; always were. But I string along with size. One time in a thousand it beats me. You played yourself a football game today."

Some of Fiction House's colorful titles defy explanation, such as the novel-length "The Galloping Ghost" by Curtis Bishop in the Fall 1940 issue of *All-American Football* magazine. This story has nothing to do with Red Grange, football's original "Galloping Ghost" of the Golden Age of Sport in the 1920s. Perhaps the editor thought the title would be evocative, since it's difficult to imagine the editor of a 1940 sports pulp who had never heard of Red Grange!

"The Forward Flash," a basketball story by Harold M. Sherman in the first issue of *Bulls-Eye Sports* (Winter 1938-1939), appeared after the last of the author's more than 30 young-adult sports books appeared in 1937. No other publisher used alliteration more often than Fiction House, including the likes of "The Dipsy-Doo Dazzler!" by Stewart Sterling in the Second Fall 1947 *Football Action*, "West Point Whirlwind" by Bishop in the Second Fall 1945 issue, and "Pass Their Pants Off" by William Heuman in 1943. Well-known novelists wrote all six stories for the final issue of *Football Action* (Fall 1953), showing how tight the pulp market had become and how hard it was for neophytes to break in. In *Baseball Stories*, there were the likes of "Horsehide Magician of the Graveyard Nine" by Curtis Bishop (Summer 1948) and "Fan That Fence Buster!" by William Heuman (Spring 1944).

Many of the popular sports novelists who appeared in Popular and Pines publications also wrote for Fiction House, including Jackson V. Scholz, Joe Archibald, Curtis Bishop, William Heuman, Duane Yarnell, Les Etter, C. Paul Jackson, Nelson A. Hutto, Arthur Mann and William R. Cox. Gene Olson, who wrote at least six young-adult sports novels from the mid–1950s to the mid–1960s, appeared in the Summer 1953 *Baseball Stories* — yet another of the many sports novelists who began (or ended) in the pulps.

Ace Sports gave up early

Ace Publications, soon to become famous for paperback books for more than three decades, gave up its pulp publications in 1949, the same year Street & Smith decided pulps were no longer profitable and abandoned them. *Ace Sports* (1936–43, 1947–49) ran 68 issues as one of the most successful of all sports pulps, featuring many covers by the prolific and exceptionally talented Norman Saunders and the under-rated Rafael de Soto. But the company's other sports pulps all debuted earlier: *Champion Sports* (13 issues, 1937–39) and *Twelve Sports Aces* (30 issues from 1938 to 1943, including a first issue entitled Variety Sports).

Saunders did dozens of covers in a variety of genres for Ace. In fact, he did so many that he received credit on the title page of *Ace Sports* for January 1949, the last issue, when in fact the cover was a reprint of de Soto's most outstanding basketball cover for December 1936!

Ace was a good market for young writers. One of Louis L'Amour's first pulp stories, a boxing short entitled "Fighter's Fiasco," appeared in the January 1938 *Ace Sports* when he was 29 years old and more than a dozen years away from writing his first novel. William Campbell Gault, at age 27, had one of his earliest stories in the December 1937 issue, an auto racing yarn that presaged the many racing novels he would write beginning in the 1950s. Frank Gruber's "Vault of Victory" in the May 1936 issue was heralded on the title page as a "pole jump" story by an editor who apparently didn't know the correct term was "pole vault." Mystery novelist-to-be Hal Masur produced, at age 32, a tennis tale entitled "Net Nemesis" for the October 1941 issue. The wonderfully titled "Hits, Runs and Terrors" by prolific pulpster Duane Yarnell appeared in August 1942.

Like Pines' *Popular Sports* in the late 1930s, Ace's *Champion Sports* featured some cover celebrities' portraits, including de Soto's take on baseball pitching great Carl Hubbell in May 1937 and tennis star Ellsworth Vines in September 1939. Real-life celebrities, however, were by far the exception during the sports pulp era.

Goodman's Marvel mysteries

Martin Goodman's publishing firm, so famous for creating the Marvel Age of Comics in the 1960s with icons-to-be such as The Amazing Spider-Man, The Fantastic Four, The Incredible Hulk and Iron Man, among others, was never a major pulp publisher. The firm's titles, primarily in the western and sports genres, came and went and sometimes came back. Although there are probably a few discoveries to be made, I've found 88 of the firm's 146 known sports pulps (the true count is doubtless very close to 146).

The best things about the Goodman sports pulps—published under imprints such as Red Circle and Marvel and produced by a number of indicia imprints for tax purposes— were often highly dramatic covers by Norman Saunders and J.W. Scott. The most surprising aspect of the stories, at least from the standpoint of pulp enthusiasts, was how many science fiction and fantasy writers contributed sports stories to Marvel, including the likes of James Blish, Milton Lesser (Stephen Marlowe), Philip St. John (Lester del Rey), Gardner F. Fox, Arthur K. Barnes, Damon Knight, Nelson Bond and Paul Fairman, among others.

Some of the novelists who worked for most of the pulp publishers also worked for Marvel; but on many title pages, the author's name of almost every story draws a blank. Some of the well-known authors include Duane Decker, C. Paul Jackson, Burgess Leonard, William Heuman, Charles Coombs, William R. Cox, Arthur Mann, Curtis Bishop and Arnold Hano.

Only one Marvel sports pulp was successful. *Complete Sports* (some 62 issues from 1937 to 1955) pretty much covered the company's entire pulp history, although the title took a three-year break between April 1943 (Vol. 4 #5) and March 1946 (Vol. 4 #6). The firm's first sports pulp, *Star Sports*, ran only 10 issues from 1936 to 1938. Two other pulps, *Sports Action* and *Best Sports*, started in 1937 and ran 11 issues and 17 issues, respectively, in their original runs, and *Real Sports* ran six issues in 1938-39. Marvel discontinued almost all of its pulps during the latter stages of World War II to focus on its more profitable comic book line.

The return of *Complete Sports* in 1946 was the harbinger of a sports pulp binge by the Goodman publishing empire, which ultimately went on to far more profitable ventures in the 1950s with its line of "men's sweat" magazines, commonly seen as the successor to the pulps (and often with covers even more garish and suggestive).

During the 1947–49 era, no publisher tried harder than Goodman to make sports pulps a commercial success. In addition to the ongoing *Complete Sports*, there were fully a dozen other sports titles attempted. This included three seasonal one-shots, *All Baseball*, *All Basketball* and *All Football*, plus three issues of *Big Baseball Stories*. There were also seven short-lived general interest titles, none of which ran more than six issues. These included *Big Book Sports* (two issues), *Sports Leaders* (three), *Big Sports* (four), *Sports Short Stories* (four), the second run of *Best Sports* (four), the second run of *Sports Action* (five) and the second run of *Real Sports* (six).

By 1950, all the sports titles were gone except for *Complete Sports*, perhaps in part because the comic book division suffered a major, albeit temporary, financial setback late in 1949 and early 1950. Inexplicably, *Best Sports* resumed with vol. 2, #5 (February 1950) after last previously appearing with vol. 2, #4 (September 1948), but *Best Sports* ran only six issues in 1950-1951 before expiring for good. The third time definitely was not a charm for *Best Sports*, which does have one distinction: a baseball column by famed sports journalist Grantland Rice in the third issue (June 1937). There may have been others, since Rice's work appeared in an untold number of publications during his long career, but few names as august as his seldom appeared in the pulps.

Before and during the early run of Duane Decker's 13-book Blue Sox series (see chapter eight), the famous baseball novelist did most of his pulp work for Goodman. Most of his short stories were not directly related to the Blue Sox, although familiar names would occasionally pop up, but at least two of his pulp stories were shortened versions of his first two books. "Home Runs Don't Count" in the first issue of *Big Baseball Stories* (May 1948), the tale of singles-hitting third baseman Johnny Madigan, appeared after "Good Field, No Hit" (1947), which was Madigan's story and the first book in the Blue Sox series. Decker's "Last Chance Chucker," the story of how Eddie Lasky converted from an injured shortstop to a standout pitcher, appeared in Popular Publications' *Sports Novels* for November 1948. The novel devoted to Lasky, "Starting Pitcher," was the second book in the Blue Sox series and appeared in 1948.

By the time Decker's unrelated "Miracle at the Plate" appeared in the November 1952 *Complete Sports*, Goodman's editors were heralding Decker with "a hilarious feature-length horsehide yarn by a best-selling novelist!" The boast was not an exaggeration, since by then he had produced six Blue Sox books in his memorable series — by far the best of all baseball series.

More often than not, however, Goodman's sports pulps did not present memorable fiction, and they were clearly a cut below Popular, Pines and Fiction House, if only because fewer well-known authors wrote for Goodman. But the surprise element of the contents page makes each issue worth taking a look at, and many of the covers are well above average, especially the action-packed, anatomically accurate efforts from the remarkable Norman Saunders.

Columbia's overlooked sports pulps

By far the least-studied major pulp publisher is Columbia, also known as the Double-Action Group. Columbia produced pulps of all types from the mid–1930s to 1960 and was part of the company that began publishing Archie in the comics, on a fairly limited basis from 1941 to 1947 and then with a flood of Archie titles beginning in the late 1940s and continuing today.

Columbia, though, was the last pulp publisher standing — unless you want to count Pines' *Ranch Romances*, which had no sister pulp publications for nearly 14 years, from the point early in 1958 when the firm's other remaining pulps ceased publication until *Ranch Romances* expired with its November 1971 issue. Columbia published numerous magazines in both pulp and digest format until 1960, covering the western, romance, detective and science fiction genres. Columbia last produced a sports pulp in 1957 — two decades after its first — with the *Super Sports* annual referred to early in this chapter.

Columbia paid some of the lowest rates and often had erratic publishing schedules, complicated by the Great Depression, World War II paper shortages, distribution problems and a printing process that often produced muddy, unattractive covers. The company had no famous, long-running single-character titles, as Street & Smith had with The Shadow and Doc Savage, Popular with The Spider, and Pines with The Phantom Detective and a raft of others. Even so, Columbia produced well over 1,500 pulps and digests over a little more than a quarter century, including 222 sports pulps. That is the estimate of this author, who has amassed 113 Columbia sports pulps and data on many more. However, since the company often skipped publication dates and was not always consistent with volume numbers, the number 222 may be subject to minor revision for years.

Columbia's complications did not prevent the firm from attracting the occasional bright writer, albeit fewer than other companies, and the steadily shrinking pulp market in the 1950s worked in Columbia's favor, since on many newsstands it was Columbia and almost nothing else by the mid–1950s, other than digest format mystery and science fiction magazines. Two of Columbia's titles had limited runs, with *Blue Ribbon Sports* (probable 13 issues from 1937 to 1940) and *All American Sports* (2 issues, 1940-41). The other five titles had split runs, thanks to the publisher's hiatus during World War II to focus on comics, much as Martin Goodman's Marvel firm did. And, like the Goodman pulps, second-banana Columbia was a frequent market for young science fiction and fantasy writers who moonlighted in the sports genre, including Lester del Rey and his pseudonym Philip St. John, James Blish, William Tenn and George O. Smith, along with Robert Silverberg and his pseudonym Calvin Knox, plus Hunt Collins, who was born S.A. Lombino and later achieved fame as Evan Hunter and Ed McBain, who used the pen name Hunt Collins primarily for science fiction.

Super Sports ran a probable 58 issues from 1938 to 1944 and from 1946 to 1957. *Super Sports* was unquestionably Columbia's flagship title and was one of only eight sports pulp titles to run as many as 50 issues. *Ten Sports Stories* ran an estimated 37 issues, pretty much split between 1937–1941 and 1952–1957 after taking over for *Sports Winners*. *Ten Sports Stories*, which appeared quarterly throughout its second incarnation, was the only regularly published pulp to appear in 1956 and finished with the January 1957 issue.

All Sports ran an estimated 38 issues from 1939 to 1945 and from 1948 to 1951. *Sports Fiction* lasted an estimated 44 issues from 1938 to 1944 and from 1947 to 1951. *Sports Winners* published 31 issues from 1938 to 1944 and from 1950 to 1952, finishing with April 1952 (Vol. 6 #1) and handing off to *Ten Sports Stories* July 1952 (Vol. 6 #2).

Every now and then, an examination of a previously unseen issue of *Super Sports* results in a significant surprise, in between the endless features by T.W. Ford. These pleasant surprises include a polo story by mystery author Robert Leslie Bellem (March 1940), work by David Goodis on swimming (July 1940) and track (October 1941), and a variety of humorous stories by the prolific pulpster Thomas Thursday, and the Hunt Collins story "Fury on First" (December 1951). *Fury on First*, a baseball novel, was published before Evan Hunter's first book and five years before the first Ed McBain 87th Precinct police procedural. Irwin Hasen, who famously worked on the Dondi comic strip beginning in 1955 and earlier on the Golden Age Green Lantern, did sports cartoons for Columbia pulps in 1940, early in his distinguished career.

In *Super Sports* for December 1947, John D. MacDonald pops up with a boxing story with an African American protagonist, "Big John Fights Again," as first detailed in John Dinan's *Sports in the Pulp Magazines* in 1998. One can only wonder whether this groundbreaking story was rejected by larger pulp publishers, since most of MacDonald's pulp mystery, science fiction and sports stories were published by either Popular Publications or Ned Pines. Throughout the sports pulp era — and, for that matter, the young-adult series books and comic books into the 1960s — fictional black heroes were rare indeed. MacDonald also had a nifty golf short, "So Sorry," in the July 1948 *Sports Fiction*.

In the 1956 *Super Sports* annual — the 1955, 1956 and 1957 issues were annuals — Robert Silverberg, Milton Lesser and Michael Avallone all contributed stories, yet the authors cover featured are the little-known Bill Erin and Richard Brister. The 1955 issue had no "names" at all but the 1957 volume featured Avallone, Silverberg and another Silverberg piece as by Knox. Silverberg, in fact, appears at age 20 in the final four issues of *Ten Sports Stories*.

Columbia wasn't known for catchy titles, à la Fiction House and Popular Publications, but every now and then it would come up with a honey, such as "Hoosegow Halfback" by Joe Blair in *All-American Sports* for December 1940. Columbia also had occasional pieces by the likes of novelists Jackson Scholz, William Heuman, Robert Sidney Bowen, C. Paul Jackson and Arthur Mann, but the majority of Columbia's sports stories were done by names that seldom appeared in other publishers' pulps.

Nothing but white faces on postwar pulps

Given the fact that Jackie Robinson broke Major League Baseball's modern color barrier in 1947 with the Brooklyn Dodgers — the year after African Americans began to play modern professional football — it has always surprised me that I have seen nothing but white faces on postwar sports pulps.

Seeking a way to quantify this, I came up with a list of the 415 sports pulps published from 1947 to 1957, give or take a couple of statistically insignificant issues from Columbia and Goodman that may or may not exist. Of the 415 issues, I was able to examine 333 in my collection, or slightly more than 80 percent (81 of 92 from Pines, 96 of 104 from Popular, 43 of 45 from Fiction House, 56 of 76 from Marvel, 53 of 90 from Columbia and 4 of 8 from Ace).

The vast majority of these pulps have football, baseball, basketball or boxing covers, a trend that began earlier in the 1940s, as noted in this chapter. I could not find a single African-American athlete (or any other black people) on any of these covers, not even in the backgrounds. There may have been a few, since I could not survey every single sports pulp, but it was a precious few if there were any at all.

On the cover of the first issue of Red Circle/Marvel's short-lived *Star Sports* (October 1936), a boxer who appears to be the African American Joe Louis falls back following a punch from a boxer who appears to be the German Max Schmeling, who beat Louis in their first bout but lost in the rematch. This may have been the first use of an African American on a cover, unless the Olympic star Jesse Owens also appeared on a cover following the four gold medals he won in the 1936 Berlin "Nazi Olympics." At the time, Louis and Owens were among the few African American athletes who would have been considered as cover subjects for a fiction magazine of national circulation.

Comic books beat the pulps to the use of African American athletes on covers from 1947 to 1954 on sports titles from Fawcett, *Parents* magazine and Eastern Color. These included the likes of Louis and Robinson along with early black baseball stars such as Don Newcombe, Larry Doby, Roy Campanella and Willie Mays. These, however, were all biographical titles. Historically famous blacks also occasionally appeared on the "true life" comics from several publishers in the 1940s and 1950s. The only African Americans I can recall on the covers of fictional comics during the final years of the sports pulp era from 1947 to 1957 were used on Fawcett's *Negro Romances* (#1–3) in 1950 and Charlton's #4 in 1955 (a reprint of #2).

There may have been a few black faces used on titles issued by religious publishers, but blacks in all varieties of fiction — except stories set in Africa, where black images were often blatantly racist — were clearly considered a commercial liability in the 1940s and 1950s. This is vividly shown by their absence in both pulps and comics for stories set in America, not to mention the vast majority of sports novels intended for juveniles and young adults. Other than on the covers of jungle stories, blacks almost never appeared on pulp covers in the genres of romance and mystery, not to mention their unlikely use in science fiction and western stories.

The Margulies method

During the decades through 1950 that Leo Margulies supervised one of the industry's largest lines of pulp magazines for paperback, pulp and comic book impresario Ned Pines, the editor frequently wrote detailed and entertaining "what-we-want" articles for magazines such as *Writer*, *Writer's Digest*, *Writers' Journal*, and *Author & Journalist*.

Even though the Pines pulps, today best known as Standard or Thrilling Publications, were prominent among sports magazine publishers, Margulies seldom wrote extensively about what he needed in the way of sports stories. Considering Thrilling's known total of 230 sports issues over 1936–1953 constituted a tiny fraction of the more than 3,500 issues the firm produced from 1931 to 1958 (only *Ranch Romances* survived beyond that date), he probably had more sports stories submitted to him than he knew what to do with, especially from prolific sports specialists such as Joe Archibald and T.W. Ford.

For example, in "The Millions of Words Market," an article of nearly 1,000 words in *Writer* for April 1947, the entire extent of his sports commentary occurred in the penultimate paragraph: "Finally there are the sports magazines, stories in which the characters play baseball, football, hockey, lacrosse, handball or checkers. These stories have a plot within a plot — the game itself plus the dramatic circumstances surrounding it. Here, too, specialization is needed; you have to know the game quite well to invent plays and situations and avoid boners." Not very helpful, is it?

Nearly a decade earlier, Margulies was far more helpful to would-be contributors, though his essay of more than 5,000 words did not appear until the June 1943 issue of *Writer*. He makes reference to dates in the late 1930s and to magazines that had been discontinued well before the article appeared, but the reason for the delay is not known. People familiar with his pulp line when they read this article in 1943 must have wondered about his references to *Strange Stories*, which last appeared in February 1941, and *Lone Eagle*, which became *American Eagle* with the August 1941 issue.

He wrote:

> The wide field of sports is covered by our magazines *Thrilling Sports* and *Popular Sports* [the only Pines sports pulps early in 1939], which alternate monthly. *Popular Sports* uses a fifteen thousand word novel [the word novelette should have been used]. Both use short stories of up to six thousand words, and novelettes from seven to ten thousand. Every branch amateur, professional and collegiate athletics is covered; mature and vigorous stories, with real people and a hero facing

a realistic problem. Human interest and woman interest are both desirable — for the stories should be slices of life. Solid story structure must bolster any sport angle. No sport story should ever be so nearly plotless as to read like a newspaper report of a game. Naturally, sport scenes must not be ignored in order to build up plot, but the plot should be forwarded by them, should grow out of the sport conflict, whether the story is told from the point of view of the hero, the trainer, the coach or an observing friend.

Certain trite situations are not wanted. The crooked angle, the "yellow" complex; the mental hazard-fear complication, the wishy-washy rivalry-over-girl theme. There are always exceptions to any rule, however, but a story breaking those taboos has to be a wow to click. Two further points I would like to stress: Be meticulously careful about the authenticity of sport material. Keep the story adult! American readers are essentially sport-minded. They are eager for good sport stories, whether about baseball, football, swimming, horse racing, motorboat racing, water polo, golf, tennis, rowing, track, boxing, or any other sports that keep young and old Americans out in the open rooting for their favorite exponents of their favorite game.

"Keep the story adult!" did not apply a few years later, when Margulies became the only editor (to this day) ever to compile two anthologies of pulp sports stories. His *Baseball Stories* (1948) and *All-American Football Stories* (1949), both put together for noted children's publisher Cupples & Leon, were marketed to boys 10 to 14 years old! It is true he did not select complex or overly long stories for those anthologies, and that many of the sports stories in his pulps would have been far too challenging for most 10- or 12-year-old readers, though 14-year-olds should have been able to read them.

In both of these blurbs, Margulies left out basketball. That says a lot about where the game — then a little less than half a century old and not yet established on the professional level beyond a rudimentary structure — stood in the minds of American sports fans at the time. It's also probably no coincidence that Margulies produced three titles apiece devoted to football and baseball, but never one entirely about basketball. He did however, use the occasional basketball cover on *Thrilling Sports*, *Popular Sports* and *Exciting Sports*. It's also interesting to note that even though this article appeared in 1943, *Exciting Sports* (begun in 1940) is not mentioned.

In his introduction, Margulies summarized why the article should be of interest to potential contributors: "Every month a golden stream of checks bearing the flourish of Ned Pines' signature flows steadily from the inner sanctum of the story-hungry editorial offices of Standard Magazines, Inc. Every month good money is exchanged for a million good words. Why? Because every month that many words, and more, are required to make a complete whole of each of the twenty-five monthly and bimonthly publications that pour from the printing press hoppers that turn manuscripts into magazines."

Oddly, even though World War II paper restrictions had forced Margulies to cut the frequency of many pulps, he was ironically conservative for 1943 readers from his vantage point in 1938 or 1939 (whenever he actually wrote this piece). No fewer than 39 titles published at least one issue in 1943 — for a total of 180 issues, or an average of 15 per month — and almost all of them appeared from four to six times that year (some bimonthlies became quarterlies). The only monthlies, however, were two of his original three flagship titles in 1932 — *Thrilling Detective* and *Thrilling Love* (the other, *Thrilling Adventures*, was discontinued at the end of 1943). By 1943, the three anthology sports pulps were dropped to quarterly status, and the three football pulps appeared once each year, making sports a tough market to crack. But, indeed, with an average of 15 issues per month, surely close to one million words per month were purchased. At Standard's rates, this probably represented an outlay of about $20,000 per year, or well over $200,000 in today's dollars, spread among fewer than 400 or so writers, at most, since a few writers appeared eight or more times each year. Standard's pulps in 1943 shrunk to 80 pages that year, but the type size shrunk to the point of being difficult for many people to read, so the word count remained at well over 50,000 per issue.

Near the end of his extensive 1943 article, Margulies talked of what he called "amusing and interesting experiences":

> Last Winter, when I was in Miami, Jack Kofoed, our interviewer of sports celebrities, suggested we interview Dizzy Dean, since I had expressed the opinion that he'd make a grand feature to run in the first issue of the new *Popular Sports* magazine, which we were then planning to publish as soon as I returned to New York. [The first issue of *Popular Sports* was dated June 1937, so Margulies may have begun this article well before 1939.] So we set out for Dean's home in Bradenton. We drove across the Tamiani Trail, and at the edge of Bradenton asked a motorcycle policeman the way to Dizzy Dean's house. He jerked a thumb.

> "Follow me," he said. We did, but how I will never be able to explain. Kofoed said he only made sixty during that crazy ride, but from the way my hair stood on end, it certainly was ninety, if I know how to count. Right through town we roared and into the suburbs. We drew up in front of Dizzy's house with a flourish and a cloud of dust, but the hurler wouldn't even talk to us. He was too busy scowling at the man on the motorcycle. We finally managed to elicit the information that Babe Ruth had called on Diz that morning, and had been arrested by the same policeman—for making thirty miles an hour! It seems to make a difference in Florida who is doing the speeding, or whether you chase a cop or are being chased.

> The Babe got such a mad-on, he swore he would never go back to Bradenton—and never has. And old Diz was so hot under the collar that it was like pulling elephant teeth to get our interview.

So ended Margulies's adventure with "Old Diz."

In the winter of 1936-37, Dizzy Dean indeed would have been a great feature interview, considering his flamboyant and highly successful role as ace pitcher of the famed St. Louis Cardinals' "Gas House

Thrilling Love, December 1941 (copyright Standard Magazines). Earle Bergey combines his skill with sports and romance covers to come up with this creative image of a postgame kiss in the mud.

Gang." By that time, he had won 120 games and lost only 63 in his first five full seasons. However, an injury in the 1937 All-Star Game ultimately caused the finish of his Major League career, which ended in 1941 after a single appearance that season with the Chicago Cubs, to whom he was traded before the 1938 season. (His appearance at age 36 in one game in 1947 for the St. Louis Browns was a stunt, although he gave up no runs in four innings and slammed a hit in his only time at bat.)

In the last year of his long tenure at Standard Magazines, Margulies listed story requirements by genre for the *Writers' Journal* of April 1950. His six-paragraph entry primarily concerned titles and word counts, though he did say that "the 'odd' angle, or the lesser known sports, will receive a warm welcome in Thrilling Sports." By that time, however, the vast majority of the sports stories in the Standard Publications were about football, baseball and basketball or boxing.

Popular Love, January 1941 (copyright Better Publications). A football hero and a majorette celebrate victory in this Earle Bergey image.

Sports mixed with love

More than 7,000 romance pulps were published from the 1920s through the 1950s, trailing only the 9,000-plus output of western pulps as the most popular genre among readers. Today, though, the romance pulps are all but forgotten except among a small cadre of collectors, most of whom collect them for their often attractive and nostalgic covers. At the major conventions of pulp enthusiasts, romance pulps are often the last priority, considering that precious few of them make much money for the dealers in nostalgia. They are unquestionably the cheapest genre to collect, and have been since pulp collectors began to seek out old issues of superhero, mystery and science fiction in the 1960s, seeking to relive part of their youth or read the type of stories no longer available. Thus, love in the pulps has not been researched or indexed the way most other genres have. In fact, romance and sports are by far the least-researched genres. There is no issue-by-issue information available on the long-running romance pulps, but I did a survey to provide a hint of the frequency of sports-themed stories in the romance pulps.

Standard's line of long-running romance pulps—*Thrilling Love, Popular Love* and *Exciting Love*—produced 370 issues from 1936 (the year *Popular Love* joined *Thrilling Love*) to 1958 (the year *Exciting Love* expired, having become a combination of the three in 1955 after the other two expired). *Thrilling Love* was one of Standard's first three pulps, all of which hit the stands late in 1931, but sports covers weren't often seen until Standard's line of sports pulps began with *Thrilling Sports* in 1936. By sheer coincidence, I was able to survey 185 — half the total — of those 370 romance issues for sports covers. There were only a dozen: nine football and three baseball. There was the occasional golf or tennis cover, too, but nary a basketball cover, just as there were only two one-shot basketball-specific pulp sports titles, both one-shots, in contrast to the goodly number of pulps devoted to football, baseball and boxing. Of course, the other 185 Standard romance issues of the 1936–1958 period — the magazines I did not have on hand to survey — surely produced a few more sports-themed covers, but I think my survey provided a pretty good idea of the tiny frequency of sports covers on the love machines.

Thrilling Love, **December 1947 (copyright Standard Magazines). Earle Bergey creatively turns the autograph convention on its head with the girlfriend signing the ball for the hero, who celebrates his hard-won victory with torn jersey.**

In those 12 romance issues with sports covers, only three stories involved sports— all football — so the cover was somewhat deceiving, although romance pulps often ran covers unrelated to any story in that issue. In most sports pulps, the female angle wasn't heavily used, but Standard occasionally had a female protagonist in its sports pulps. It's understandable why football was used so much more than any other sport for the few athletics-oriented covers, since college football and coed romance was a natural, especially since the vast majority of love pulps told stories of 20-something women.

"Block That Blonde!" by Jean Francis Webb, a novelette in *Thrilling Love* for December 1947, tells the story of Colleen Tyler, the secretary of Senator Millard Bates. Colleen returns for alumni weekend at Carter College, from which she graduated a year earlier. Colleen unexpectedly encounters her college heart-throb, former star lineman Daly "Day" Leland, who is in his first season as the university's line coach, in hopes of gaining the top job when the elderly head coach, Dad Jenkins, retires. Day, a paragon of young coaching idealism, had spent the previous year coaching football at "a jerkwater high school out West" before returning to Carter College as an assistant coach. Colleen, herself an idealistic sort who hoped to serve society through politics, saw that passion cause her to break up with Day because he stubbornly insisted women didn't belong in the political arena. On the rebound, Colleen had eloped with the senator's son, Garner Bates; but before they could be married, he died in a car crash which she survived. Complicating the situation, Teresa "Tizzy" Bates, the senator's daughter, now seeks handsome Day Leland's attention, while Rich Craig, a political associate of the senator, seeks Colleen's hand. (Who said pulp stories were simple?)

During alumni weekend, Colleen confesses to Day that she changed her mind about marriage to Garner Bates almost immediately after they eloped, but Garner was going to force her hand — or something much worse! — until his reckless driving killed him and injured her. She had withheld the secret from Garner's father, the ethical senator for whom she worked, because she didn't want him to know his son was a cad. And when Day tells Colleen that Tizzy means nothing to him, she responds this way: "Colleen's breath caught in her throat until it ached. 'You mean — no other girl has broken through your heart for a touchdown, Coach?'" Can you imagine a girl asking a football man that in the 1940s, much less today? That kind of verbal silliness is what makes pulps fun, but also makes them less than literature!

Day tells Colleen, "Look at it this way, Collie. [Football is] pretty much the same thing to me that you've always been after for you. It's my chance to help people find something better in life. Your idea was to do it through laws and bills and clean-ups in government. Mine is to do it through football.... Football's always seemed more than a game to me. And it's not a big business, either, or a matter of running up gate receipts on nine autumn Saturdays so the college ledgers will be yanked out of the red.... It's fun, first of all. And it's clean fighting and self-discipline. It's law and order in action. Kids who really catch the spirit of the game never turn into anti-social problems later in life. You never read of an All-American gangster. Why, if I knew I could turn out a fresh batch of youngsters with that idea every year for the rest of my life — hey, I'm making a speech!"

Colleen worries that her reputation and Tizzy's plotting will doom Day's chance to become head coach, since she fears her father would not approve of Day if Tizzy were to object. The author writes of Colleen's thought process: "Clearly, Day didn't even suspect that his pretty bond [sic] admirer was uncapped dynamite. But then, men like Daly Leland never did understand the Teresa Bates tribe in real life. They were too fine, too direct, too honest themselves, to have any conception of what might lie behind a smile." Colleen decides that Day's future as coach means so much to his happiness that she fakes a kiss with Craig, hoping to convince Day she doesn't love him. But, in the end, nobody is fooled — neither the senator nor Day, who hide in the backseat of a car as Craig coaxes Colleen's true feelings out. She gasps when she realizes they have overheard her, but they tell her they haven't been fooled by Tizzy and they knew all the time what a cad Garner was.

Realizing how much Colleen loves him, Day relents and acknowledges that both she and her political ambitions have a place in his life if she'll be his wife. The corny but fun ending was pure 1940s pulp, outrageous metaphor and all: "The arms which held her tightened and his head bent closer. Colleen swayed to meet his kiss with a bright light in her eyes that the racing stars overhead might have well envied. And Heaven made a touchdown in her pounding heart."

Thrilling Love for December 1941 featured "Lucky Girl, a Football Romance" by Nina Kaye, a short story in which gorgeous coed Damaris Allen finds herself forced to fend off the advances of an unethical pro football scout. The scout is punched out by State University star Hank Braley, the football hero of this silly piece, even though it means he may be blackballed from the pro ranks by the scout. Damaris, it turns out, wanted her man to pursue aeronautics, not football, since engineering was a more stable career. Perhaps punching out a wolf who scouts football players might have given Hank a bad reputation, but it's doubtful a man of his caliber would have been turned down by another pro team in need of a star running back. The entire story makes no sense at all. However, the cover of a lady's lovely legs in muddy shoes tiptoeing to kiss a muddy football player was one of Earle Bergey's most creative covers — and highly unusual for a love pulp.

"Cupid's Forward Pass" by Ruth Anderson in *Popular Love* for January 1941 tells the five-page story of a football player who has been unfairly barred from his team before the big game and the girl who tries to see that the situation is straightened out. When he is reinstated in this piffle, she tells him, "Win for me, darling! Cupid made a forward pass, and stole my heart — now you go out and grab that game!" These period pieces can be fun, but they are definitely not the stuff of anthologies, so the only way you can read them is to search out the original sources. Again, the Bergey cover is creative — a handsome hunk of a football player, leather helmet on his arm, apparently celebrating a victory with a band majorette in full costume.

Street & Smith's *Love Story* magazine would occasionally carry a sports-themed romance, especially football, such as "Football Honey" in the November 1939, issue and "Football Wife" in the November 9, 1935, number, both by Ruby la Verte Thomson. "Football Wife," a story of misunderstood lovers, ends happily with the hero scoring the winning touchdown at the final gun, then finding solace in the arms of the girl it turns out he truly loves. The description of the winning touchdown is written for women, not pulp sports fans: "It didn't seem possible that any human could keep on throwing himself at the other line, going down in a heap, getting up, dragging back into position, then doing it all over again. But Craig did. And, relentlessly, he pushed toward the goal. Then, just before the timer's gun ended the game, he summoned all his strength, all the fine courage in that vital body — and hit the line. It [the line, not his body!] bent, sagged farther — farther. Finally it broke, and Craig went through. Past the first backfield man, past the second; hunched his shoulders, and rammed straight into the safety. He staggered, but regained his feet, and plunged on, with the safety hanging on to him, then broke away — and was over the goal line! ...The game was won! For a moment, Sherry forgot her heartache in the wild surge of victory that seized her. Victory and pride." Thankfully for the reader who likes happy endings, Craig retains enough energy to chase down Sherry and tell her he loves her.

"Football Honey," like "Football Wife," features a cover by Modest Stein, one of Street & Smith's leading cover artists. The cover illustrating "Football Honey" features conflict, which is rare for a love pulp with a sports cover (or most other kinds of covers). A football player and girl laugh — actually, he looks as though he's a substitute who is just grateful for the attention. It's a lovely cover, but far different from the fierce images of the handful of 1930s *Love Story* issues when football was cover-featured.

Football or baseball themes are infrequent, even in season, on the covers of the vast majority of the hundreds of romance pulps I either own or have seen. But even when there was a football cover, such as the cute hero-hugging image on the cover of *All-Story Love* for November 1946, from Popular Publications, there was often no football-themed story inside. Such is the case with this issue, but that is not unusual with regard to topical themes of any sort. Romance pulp covers seldom were matched to any of the stories inside.

Death at Second Base

Crime in a sports setting would sometimes show up in the detective pulps, too, although with less frequency than in the romance pulps, except where boxing was involved. There were many mystery stories with boxing sidelights, a few involving football and baseball and almost none featuring basketball. Unlike the romance pulps, however, sports scenes did not appear on the covers of the mystery pulps unless they were meant to illustrate the featured stories. Indeed, sports covers were undoubtedly used to call attention that a given issue offered a different sort of crime story. Until George Bagby's baseball mystery *Twin Killing* appeared in 1948, perhaps the only hardbound sports murder mysteries were the three published by Cortland Fitzsimons from 1931 to 1935 (see chapter four).

One of the most frequently published and most popular of the mystery pulps of the Roaring Twenties and Great Depression eras, *Detective Fiction Weekly* (formerly *Flynn's*) from the Frank A. Munsey Company, came up with the 1930s stories like "Kill the Umpire" and "Death at Second Base," both with covers that might just as well have appeared on sports pulps were it not for law-enforcement people in the background. "Death at Second Base" by the little known William Edward Hayes appeared in the April 17, 1937, issue as the lead novelette and cover feature.

The murderer was far from obvious, but the problem with this story is that the murderer is also a minor character up to the point where he's unveiled as the villain! The yarn definitely cheats the reader in that respect. It's the story of infield rivals Jimmy Kane and Lee Blodgett, still feuding even after the likeable Kane's trade away from the New Orleans Birds to the Herdsman (city never stated). It turns out that Blodgett is a bully and a cheat, as he shows while tripping Kane as Kane races around second base trying to score an important run. Later, Kane accidentally spikes Blodgett while tagging him out and Blodgett soon dies in the locker room.

Naturally, the police suspect Kane, since it's well known the two middle infielders hated each other. Following a grilling, Kane returns to the ballpark and stumbles across the body of the night watchman. With the suspense growing, Kane is attacked in the dark of the dugout as he seeks a clue to the killing. Something is stuffed into his mouth, but he manages to spit it out and soon is rescued by a teammate, who trailed Kane back to the park and called the police. It turns out the killer is the acting manager of the Birds, Dutch Ludwig, who was being blackmailed by Blodgett, his bully of a second baseman. The murder weapon is tobacco chew laced with the deadly drug aconitine. The story is good of its kind, but it's strictly a period piece. Oddly, it's unclear whether the author intended this to be a mythical major league game or whether the story is set in the minor leagues.

Third-String Center

It's possible that the spate of young-adult sports novels that began to appear in the 1940s by a new set of prolific authors (see chapter ten) helped to keep the sports pulps going a few years longer than might have been expected in the early 1950s. Standard, Popular, and Columbia continued to publish several titles, along with three seasonal football pulps and single seasonal baseball pulp from Fiction House, plus a couple of surviving titles from Martin Goodman. In general, the quality of writing in the 1950s pulps is well above that of the 1930s issues, in part because with shrinking markets it was tougher for the less-talented "hack" writers to sell stories. In addition, with the demise of Street & Smith's *Sport Story* magazine in 1943 and the end of *Ace Sports* in 1949, plus the failure of most of Martin Goodman's late 1940s burst of sports titles, there were a good many weeks in the 1950–53 period when the true sports story buff could have easily read every sports pulp as it appeared on the newsstands—fewer than one per week on average.

Most sports pulp publishers in the early 1950s either could not acquire novels, since there was such a healthy hardback market for them, or preferred to present two or three novelettes along with four or five short stories. A look at Standard's *Popular Football* for Fall 1950, and *Thrilling Baseball* for Spring 1950, shows how the publishers followed this formula. Short stories were seldom bannered on any publisher's covers; the novelettes were the feature. They usually ran 8,000 to 12,000 words, short enough to be read in a single sitting.

Popular Football for Fall 1950 features *Third-String Center*, an entertaining melodrama by John Wilson, who was similar to T.W. Ford in that he was a prolific contributor to the pulps but not a hardcover novelist; *One Last Throw* by Robert Sidney Bowen, near the end of his long pulp career but just starting his long run as a hardback novelist; and *Gridiron Giant Killers* by little known Add Aretz (if this is not a pen name).

Third-String Center is first-rate entertainment, and reasonably plausible. The blurb is typical Standard drama: "Hod Duncan was rated low on the Wesleyan roster—but when he got his chance to shine he showed a lot of better players how the game should be played!" The earnest and modestly talented Duncan takes abuse from swellheaded teammates for his student job as a waiter, and dreams of playing enough in his senior season to earn a letter after being bench-bound the previous two years.

Wilson, who was consistently one of the most readable writers of pulp sports fiction, infuses Duncan with a charming idealism and an ethic of decency: "The monogram itself wasn't important in the sense that he could stick it on his chest and look pretty. But one day soon Hod was going to leave the college campus behind and there was a job open for him in the rural section where he lived. There he'd teach and coach. But how could he make the kids—the pluggers like himself and there were lots of them—believe that sheer hard work and determination could accomplish miracles? How to make them understand the willingness to put up a scrap was a big long stride toward any goal? A guy had to believe those things in his own heart and feel the confidence of real achievement. He himself in three seasons hadn't even come close to earning what many scrubs owned—the varsity squad monogram."

There is nothing unrealistic about those sentiments—coaches, teachers and administrators all over the country have stressed them for more than a century. Every now and then, a pulp story had something meaningful to say about life as it really is. It's also worth noting that while good coaches abound who were not good athletes, there is a certain something extra a coach—or an expert in any field—gains from having accomplished a job at a high level. Just as being a standout athlete can enhance a coach's resume—although such a reputation does not guarantee a good coach—a decorated fighter pilot enhances his credibility for any job in aviation.

Hod Duncan respects the first-string center, senior Moose Dohler, who has kept Hod securely on the bench for three seasons. Hod, however, feels the talented but selfish second-stringer Stan Steffin will hurt the team more than help — and Hod turns out to be right in the inevitable Big Game. Before the Big Game, however, he tells a fib to his coach about a selfish teammate's training violation, since Hod wants the coach to enjoy his long-sought unbeaten season and the teammate, Sal Jarvis, is a must-keep player. Hod gets his chance in the second half when Moose is knocked out of the game by his chronic shoulder injury and Steffin showboats once too often. During that big victory, Hod considers "what [football] did for a guy, whether All-American or scrub. What really counted was that he kept fighting and never quit [on] himself.... He could tell them [the athletes he would one day coach] with his heart that the real score was in the effort made." Hod's tip to the brilliant Jarvis helps win the game with a kickoff return for a touchdown. In the end, when the coach tells Hod he knew about Jarvis' infraction all along, the coach assures Hod he's "the third-string center with the All-American heart" and Hod wins his letter at last.

The Last Throw

Bowen's *The Last Throw* is typical Bowen, pure pulp and pure fun. The sore-armed hero, veteran star Johnny Sawyer, decides to run instead of pass in the game his team must win to preserve the coaching job for his best friend, Frank Cabot. But when he finds he has no choice but to make a final throw, Sawyer's clever play goes for a game-winning 91-yard touchdown with 1 minute and 30 seconds to play. Cabot keeps his job but the girl he would have liked to marry instead chooses Johnny. "It's — it's like football, Johnny. You can't win them all." Johnny himself admires the honest Betty Norris because she has "an absolute minimum of feminine wiles," which is about what you might expect from the male author of a thousand pulp stories like this one. Bowen also calls Standish, the unethical reporter of the piece, "a special kind of louse." Unlike *Third-String Center*, *The Last Throw* is all plot and no message, inspirational or otherwise, but it's still the good read typical of Standard sports pulps.

The clunker is *Gridiron Giant Killers* by Add Aretz. It's the tale of an avaricious college coach, Tod Richards, who slowly learns what it means to treat others with dignity instead of using them for self-aggrandizement, in part through the example of his humble assistant coach, Sully McMichaels. In this story, the coach deliberately keeps his best players on the bench for four consecutive games after they perform brilliantly in the opener, because there are only three really important and challenging games on Freemont College's schedule. This, of course, makes no sense whatsoever, then or now, and doubtless would have inspired a rebellious backlash. Richards also skips one of his team's games so he can scout one of the key opponents. Again, this wouldn't happen in any realistic scenario. The entire story is a great example of how poorly contrived fiction can be. It was the lead story in the issue, and yet it's pure junk.

In *Thrilling Baseball* for Spring 1950, the three novelettes were *The Platinum Bat* by Stewart Sterling, *Fifth Man in the Infield* by Richard Brister, and *Ride That Rookie* by Herbert L. McNary. Sterling, the pen name of Prentice Winchell, was among the most prolific writers of his era, primarily in the detective field, but he could also pen a rousing sports yarn as well. In *The Platinum Bat*, he came up with a highly entertaining tale of a girl whose hobby is learning about baseball catchers — her brother, a catcher, was killed in the war.

The blurb tells it all: "When Jerry Ostrom took over the backstop job on the Sox, he inherited a touch of girl trouble along with a slew of touchy diamond problems!" Ostrom's "platinum bat" tag developed out of resentment by teammates for the $80,000 the Sox paid to acquire him when they were desperate for catching. In the end, Ostrom wins both the first-string job and the girl after numerous complications. It is a bit startling to have his girl, Tina MacLane, tell Jerry, "You didn't help your pitcher on those low balls. This afternoon you were trying to make a lot of Lobo's bad shots look good by pulling them up behind the batter's knees. That gave the ump ideas. He gets to thinking maybe the close ones only look good because you made 'em look that way. It's all right to hold your glove in the strike area when you can, but trying to center every pitch"—at which point Jerry interrupts her; he thinks she's a "dizzy dame." But, in the end, he realizes her advice is sound when it comes to solving all his problems. Sterling was best known for his well-done novels about fire marshal Ben Pedley and hotel detective Gil Vine, plus department store detective Don Cadee in novels as by Spencer Dean.

Richard Brister's *Fifth Man in the Infield* tells the highly unlikely but amusing tale of Eddie Jacoby, who goes from sore-armed pitcher to shortstop to healthy pitcher to unwilling shortstop and back to pitcher, with lots of baseball psychology thrown in, along with descriptions of both minor league and major league managers who are half manager, half psychologist. Brister wrote many paperback westerns, but he did plenty of sports stories, as well, and often did them pretty well. He was typical of the many pulp sports authors who ventured into other genres, either before or after their pulp days.

Herbert L. McNary wrote only novelettes and short stories for pulps; he didn't have a single paperback novel published, nor perhaps any hardbacks. *Ride That Rookie* is the far-out story of how wealthy rookie Kim Turner wins over both the fans and a special girl when he finally gets wise to his own arrogance. In real life, such an arrogant rookie wouldn't have lasted as long, but it does make the story move along. Every now and then, though, a pulp writer shows how far away from reality he could get, such as when he has sportswriters asking Turner, "How about it, Turner? Are you really good? What do you tell your public? Are you better than Williams or DiMaggio?" To which Turner snaps, "Tell them any darn thing you please." Syd Jason, a sportswriter "who thrived on name-calling and starting controversies," tells Kim, "Oh, one of those prima-donna guys," to which Kim responds, "How would you like the back of my hand against that wide-open mouth of yours?" Jason, though, winds up as a perceptive, helpful journalist in the end. The story isn't bad, but that question about Williams and DiMaggio is nothing short of ludicrous. No sportswriter would ever ask a rookie such a question, and no rookie would ever answer it. And it was a serious question in this story! Utter nonsense.

Two imitation Merriwells

Occasionally, a pulp writer would revisit the "Merriwell miracles" that he, or his parents, may have read several decades earlier. These stories would sometimes show up in the general-interest anthology pulps, some of which clearly had weaker standards for sports manuscripts, instead of the sports pulps, the editors of which actually knew sports fairly well in most cases. Such was the case with Dell's *Five-Novels Monthly*, an anthology style pulp that enjoyed a 20-year run beginning in 1928, but became *Five-Novels* magazine when it went quarterly and then bimonthly beginning in 1943.

The five "novels" were really novelettes of less than 20,000 words, but, like the stories in *Argosy*, they took place all over the world. Unlike *Argosy*, they were usually written in the most purple prose imaginable. That also applied to some of the sports stories, notably those by the otherwise little known Ben Peter Freeman. In Freeman's "Hit That Hoop!" for February 1941 — one of the few anthology issues from any publisher with a basketball cover — Merriwell lives in the person of Douglas "Brandy" Brandon, a quick 160-pound sharp-shooter whose speed leads little Mountain Tech to a 6–0 record in the "national championship tournament." In the days before the National Basketball Association, "pro-fessional" basketball teams could be found in several locales of the United States. In one such fictional locale, the Western Industrial League, Brandy is abused by the disgusting bully Joe Rucker, a fading but still powerful star. Eventually, though, Brandy disposes of Rucker, defeats Nazi agents, forms a team of overlooked old-timers that beats another professional squad for the championship, wins the hearts of teammates who have spurned him, and, of course, gets the girl who had been Rucker's honey. Along the way, he makes shots from 40 and 35 feet during ordinary parts of the game — shots that nobody then or now ever takes except as last resorts at the buzzer. This story is fun, but it's really a dime novel in disguise. And all this takes place in 32 pages!

The same applies to Freeman's "Pigskin Poison" for November 1942, one of several fall football covers over the years in *Five-Novels*. This is the story of drop-kick specialist Dixie Bell, who yearns to do more than kick field goals and extra points for the Grange College Riveters. Bell, it turns out, is the right man not only to make dazzling plays, but also to defy tyrannical coach Fats Hamill, who tries to boot Bell off the team until it turns out that Bell's election as captain entitles him to run the team's lineup in games. All sorts of cor-ruption and skullduggery ensues, partly inspired by a student journalist, until Bell wins both the Big Game and the girl.

SIX

Sports Fiction Strikes Out
in the Comic Books

From the 1930s to the 1970s, comic book publishers produced thousands of issues in every major genre of fiction. The only time they struck out was with sports comics, especially fictional sports-themed titles. Indeed, these failed miserably.

Since youngsters of the period had far fewer distractions than they do today, most spent many hours involved in sports and the outdoors. Youth sports teams were seldom organized as they are today, but that didn't stop the kids from choosing sides on their own. Of all the genres in comic books, sports was the only that could closely approximate the youngsters' own experiences—or at least experiences they hoped to have when they were in high school and college. Readers might literally have found sports comics not fantastic enough. Other comic book genres were either outright fantasy—superheroes, horror, science fiction, jungle guys and girls, anthropomorphic animals—or were fantastically glamorized versions of stories dealing with the Old West, crime, war, romance or teen humor.

Two generations earlier, the fabulous success of the sports- and outdoor-themed Frank and Dick Merriwell dime novels in the late 19th and early 20th centuries reflected on a different way of life for Americans (see chapter one). Most of the population did not even complete high school, much less college. Athletic opportunities were far fewer for young people than for those who later grew up reading comic books. The only successful comic book genre that also was widespread and popular in the gilded age of the Merriwells was the dime-novel western of Deadwood Dick, Buffalo Bill and the like.

By the time the modern comic book came along in the 1930s, extending well into the 1970s, sports-themed books were among the volumes most popular with young readers, especially boys. On the other hand, what appeared in the comic books seldom appeared in hardcovers. Chances are, then, themes that youngsters loved in the comic books were what they couldn't find in their school and public libraries. When science fiction for young readers began to appear on school and public library shelves in the 1950s, that became the only genre concurrently popular in both hardbound books and the comics.

The total of comic books with sports fiction was fewer than 200, out of the more than 50,000 corporate comic books published from the 1930s through the 1960s. Even comics based on factual sports stories almost invariably failed. The only commercially successful such comic was Street & Smith's "True Sport Picture Stories," which ran 50 issues from 1940 to 1949 (the first four issues were entitled "Sports Comics").

Yet from 1940, when Dan Duffy, College Athlete, debuted in Standard's "Thrilling Comics," to 1967, when Coach Chat Chatfield appeared in one issue from Charlton, publishers never stopped trying to sell baseball, football or basketball themes, along with a handful of stories devoted to other sports.

Sports Action: a unique experiment in comics

Timely comics, also known as Marvel and Atlas, often responded to comic book trends by flooding the market with horror, romance, western and war titles in the late 1940s and the 1950s. But publisher Martin Goodman's company wasn't afraid to try something unique: a sports anthology title. "Sports Action" was a typical biographical sports comic, beginning as "Sports Stars" with #1 (November 1949) and continuing as "Sports Action" with #2 (February 1950). Beginning with #10 (January 1952), editor Stan Lee tried something never attempted in comic books: a genuine sports fiction anthology. It was a noteworthy attempt at a new concept in comics, but the experiment lasted only five issues, through #14 (September 1952).

The quality of the art and stories was above average, but "Sports Action" encountered the most crowded newsstands in the first half-century of comic book publishing. In 1952, more than 3,150 issues were published, and dozens of titles failed to make it into 1953. With the growing influence of television and increasing criticism over the influence of violent comics on youngsters, the market simply couldn't sustain that many issues.

The formula for each issue was the same: four stories, usually six pages, stressing human interest in the arena of the most popular sports of the time. There were seven baseball stories, three football stories and one basketball story, along with four devoted to boxing, two each to wrestling and auto racing, and one to the Olympics.

The first baseball story in "Sports Action," "Grandstand Player," nicely illustrated by Morris Weiss in #10, was a startling tale for a comic book. It's predictable in the first five pages, as cocky slugger Pete Adams is rejected by his minor league team for lack of teamwork, only to be picked up by an unspecified New York big league team. The final two pages are good writing, indeed: Adams insults and slugs a teammate after being sent to the showers, only to have the teammate inadvertently break the conceited rookie's back in a fight. Adams thinks his baseball career is over, only to receive an offer from his old minor league manager, who wants the crippled star to serve as a coach. "And that was twelve years ago," Adam says in the final panel. "I'm still with the Red Wings and love every minute of my job! Three of my youngsters have made the majors and they're going to stick! Know why? Because they've been taught teamwork! Take it from me ... it's the only way to play baseball!" Oddly, the uniforms of the New York team were drawn without a team name. This story was a revision of "The Story of Pete Sims, the Grandstand Player!" in "Sports Stars" #1. The debut issue also carried a fictional story entitled "They Called Him a Coward! The Saga of New York's Own Terry Barker." That story seems to have been designed to convince readers that Barker had actually existed. When "Sports Stars" became "Sports Action" with #2, the title abandoned fiction until #10.

The two baseball tales in #12 (May 1952), "Behind the Mask" and "Glory Hound!," were more typical, in which both protagonists learned moral lessons before achieving success in the major leagues. The twist in "Behind the Mask" was that a selfish pitcher and a team-oriented catcher were both in love with the same girl. The pitcher ultimately learns that he was must work with his catcher; the catcher surrenders his claim on the girl because she loves the pitcher. In "Glory Hound!" a young star convinces a sportswriter to pile on the publicity, but soon learns his plan produces so much pressure on him that he can't succeed. He returns to the minors, learns his lessons and comes back to the majors. There's no mention of the total lack of ethics on the part of the sportswriter. In addition, first baseman Tex Rondell is called to the majors because he is "hitting .422 and fielding .900." Any player, much less a first baseman, who is fielding only .900 in the minors would be suspect. A first baseman who can't field in the high .900s on any level would soon find himself on the bench. That kind of error helps spoil the story.

"Sports Action" #13 (July 1952) followed with "Home Run King ... or Heel?" and "Flash in the Pan!" In "Home Run King," brash rookie Lew Andrews tells reporters circa 1941, "I'm going to as good as Ruth, Gehrig, DiMaggio and Williams ... better even!" Jack Keller's effective art portrays the rookie's emotions well as teammates and fans sour on his personality even though Andrews' home run indeed wins the pennant for the Panthers. But it turns out Andrews has a good side; he enlists in the army and emerges as a hero in World War II. He returns to baseball with the same attitude, but he realizes the fans have learned they admire him and he becomes a complete player. "Flash in the Pan" is corny and contrived yet touching, telling the story of a player whose career was cut short by injury but who later guides his son to the major leagues. When the son executes an unassisted triple play in his first big league game, his father dies in the grandstand of a heart attack! The father's dying words to his son: "Just ... just ... do your best ... show 'em you're not a flash in the pan!" The son overcomes his ensuing loneliness and problems in the field thanks to a stinging lecture from his manager, who knew his father. In the final panel, his father looks down from above as his son gets a hit and seems on his way to stardom.

The two baseball stories

"Sports Action" #13, July 1952 (copyright Sports Action, Inc.). The last five issues of this Marvel title (#10–14) featured the only anthology-style sports fiction (without continuing characters) in comic book history through the 1960s.

in "Sports Action" #14 are both good enough to have made readers wish this wasn't the title's last issue. "The Rookie!" told the unlikely but compelling tale of a 21-year-old rookie pitcher who gains an enemy when he strikes out his team's 32-year-old slugger in an intrasquad game. Eventually, a sportswriter plays the hero when he learns that the veteran has lied to him about the unpopular rookie's opinions of his teammates. The writer reveals the truth, but the rookie, Ken Roper, has been waived and claimed by another team. When he strikes out the crusty veteran Joe Bascomb in a crucial late-season game, everyone knows he has arrived as a pro. Oddly, the cover indicates the rookie is a batter, not a pitcher! Inconsistencies like that have provided fodder for enthusiasts. In "The Goat!" an injured outfielder, Dinty Bradbury, feels he can't use his injury as an alibi, even though it has cost his team a World Series game. In the next game, he crashes into a wall and saves a victory — moments before his father had decided to tell the team the truth. He wins the respect of the fans and his teammates as his father says, "That's my boy!"

The best of the three football stories in "Sports Action" was "Letter for Lenny" in #12. Lenny Steele, trying to win the football letter at Arden College that eluded his father, is crushed when he realizes he's too light to earn playing time despite his speed. But the kindly football coach turns him over to the track coach and he quickly turns into a star good enough to earn his letter! There's one huge flaw in this story, however: the writer apparently did not realize that outdoor track meets are conducted in the spring, not during football season! Even so, the story is otherwise realistic and might genuinely have inspired a small athlete that football isn't the only sport in which to earn a varsity letter.

The first football story in "Sports Action," "Defeat!" in #10, had a twist typical of Atlas comics. Coach Ziff Gordon inexplicably uses a rookie running back whose mistakes ultimately cost him the big game. When called on the carpet by college officials, he tells them why he used the scrub: the boy is a son he never knew he had. His former wife sent him a telegram, explaining the boy had six months to live due to an illness and wanted to play for Eastern University more than anything else. College officials learn the coach once played under his real name before he was kicked out of the professional ranks, only to reinvent himself as a college coach. They decide his humanity warrants retention, and he stays at the university.

In "Yesterday's Hero" in #11 (March 1952), former college star Pack Leonard takes his protégé, Cass Healy, to "a small Midwest college" to play and continues to coach him with the agreement of the head coach. Healy turns into a star, but suffers a dangerous head injury. Pack wants him to keep playing, but the coach, who was Pack's college mentor, reminds Pack of a similar injury he suffered in his youth, and Pack relents. Ultimately, Cass recovers and turns in an outstanding game, now sure that he's in good hands.

It's instructive that all three football stories take place in college, not the pros, and that all seven baseball stories take place in the pros, not college or high school. In 1952, college football was still significantly bigger than the National Football League — and college football certainly was bigger when the writers of the stories grew up. College baseball, a significant college sport today, was not yet a major college sport in 1952; indeed, the vast majority of professional players often signed contracts right out of high school and never attended college.

The only basketball story in "Sports Action" is better than any of the baseball or football tales. In "The Man Who Failed," basketball-loving Clyde Bowen, too small and slow to play on his high school team, works hard both on and off the court while growing into a player tall enough to try out in college. But Calvin College coach Barney Hale has to break the bad news at tryouts in Clyde's freshman and sophomore years: Clyde simply isn't good enough to play. Clyde sticks around at Hale's invitation to be team manager but doesn't endear himself to the team's star, who thinks is undermining him with his suggestions to the coach. Hale, however, realizes Bowen is a budding tactical genius and makes him his assistant coach. Eventually, the star realizes that Bowen's only ambition is to make the entire team better. As the story ends, Hale has retired and Bowen is the head coach. He tells the reader, "I've seen the players come and go ... but I'm still in the game I love and always will be! I guess that is better than a few short years of playing!"

On the whole, the stories in "Sports Action," however contrived, were better than those in many comic books of the period. The lack of romantic themes—so common in the sports pulps read by older readers—spoke to the younger market Atlas was trying to reach.

The one-man superhero teams

Every now and then during the 1940s and 1950s, National Comics (later known as DC) and other publishers would throw their superheroes into a sports story, resulting in several of the most fantastic tales in history. One of the first such epics was "Nine Empty Uniforms" in National's "Flash Comics" #90 (December 1947). This anthology title was named for its lead feature, The Flash, usually referred to as "the fastest man alive." In an entertaining story, The Flash helps a team of bedraggled big league baseball players, the Bobtails, regain their confidence by assisting with seemingly super fielding and batting feats (there was no discussion of the ethics of a superhero giving one side a super advantage). When, in the worst sports fiction tradition of an earlier era, the entire team is kidnapped by gangsters, The Flash moves so fast he fills every uniform before they can collapse! But if that "game" sounds unlikely, consider that the ailing manager's daughter, Ginger Stanton, is the one calling the shots in place of her father! Ginger—an old slang term for pep, vim and vigor in sports—was the perfect name for that girl.

National Comics recycled this plot with amusing variations in "Superboy" #57 (June 1957) for "The One-Man Baseball Team." Superboy (Superman when he was a teenager), who can move with the same superhuman speed as The Flash, volunteers to donate $100,000 to charity. Superboy "runs" the basepaths underground, popping up in an amusing scene at home plate, and also hits balls around the world, defying not only the best pitching available but also the laws of physics. He even knocks a large hole in the outfield fence with a line drive when his X-ray vision spots a group of youngsters who haven't been able to get into the park. When it's his turn in the field, a fan asks how to mark a double play: "Superboy to Superboy to Superboy—what else?" his neighbor tells him. But, disguised as Clark Kent so he can greet Lana Lang, he makes a mistake when he throws a ball out of the stadium. He solves that problem by convincing his friendly nemesis—who was always trying to prove Clark and Superboy one and the same—that what she really saw was a throw by Superboy in low-earth orbit. He ends the story with this message to the reader: "Whew! Maybe I was all right as a baseball player—but in this little 'game' with Lana, I nearly made the worst error of my career!"

National even guest-starred a real baseball hero, Hall of Fame pitcher Bob Feller of the Cleveland Indians, in "Boy Commandos" #30 (November-December 1948). The Boy Commandos, created as a wartime group, rescued Feller from kidnappers. In turn, the pitching star saved their leader, Captain Rip Carter, from assassination at the ballpark when he unleashed what seemed like the wildest of wild pitches in order to knock out a gunman in the stands. This story was circulated well before Feller helped the Indians win the 1948 World Series.

During the early years of the Space Race, National even tried a five-issue science fictional sports series in 1963 entitled "Strange Sports Stories," with tales such as "The Gorilla Wonders of the Diamond." The series ran in a "tryout" title, "Brave & the Bold," in #45–49, but sales apparently didn't warrant continuation. Ten years later, DC tried again with a six-issue series under the title "Strange Sports Stories," but it failed to catch on.

Dan Duffy, the triple threat of "Thrilling Comics"

In the dozens of anthology titles that dominated comic books during the Golden Age of the 1940s, only a tiny fraction of the characters were sports heroes, just as sports titles represented less than 2 percent of the immense pulp magazine market.

One of the longest-running sports strips was "Dan Duffy, College Athlete," who appeared as a back-of-the-book feature from 1940 to 1942 in "Thrilling Comics," the flagship title from Better Publications. Duffy was the classic triple threat—football, baseball and basketball—for dear old Carson University, but the majority of his stories dealt with football. In the 1920s, '30s and '40s, no college sport came even remotely close to matching football in its appeal. The college game was far bigger than pro football in those days. College baseball was played largely by players not good enough to sign professionally, and college basketball was a relatively slow second-generation sport created in the 1890s and at the time still played below the rim.

In Dan Duffy's 21 adventures in "Thrilling," #8 (September 1940) through #29 (August 1942)—he failed to appear only in #26—nary a minority character was to be found, except occasionally in the role of villain. In real life African Americans were still seldom seen on most college teams during Dan Duffy's day. Other than that, nothing speaks to the remarkable period-piece atmosphere of these little jock epics than the picture that often accompanied the logo. There, in all this glory, was a pipe-smoking Dan Duffy! And this wasn't funny smoke.

Dan Duffy was very much a knockoff of Frank Merriwell. Ironically, Duffy enjoyed a longer comic book career than Merriwell, who was owned by Street & Smith. In Golden Age comics, Merriwell appeared only in "Shadow Comics" #1–4 in 1940 (his four odd mid–1950s issues from Charlton are another story).

Doubtless the creators of Dan Duffy grew up on the heroics of Merriwell, who was forever solving problems on and off the field of friendly strife. Likewise, much of the detail in Duffy's adventures involved criminals, fifth columnists, spies, Nazi agents and the like. Dan Duffy was an original comic book creation, unlike many of the pulp-inspired characters presented in Standard's early comics. Standard—often known as Thrilling Publications for its dozens of pulp titles—led the field in 1940s sports pulps, with bimonthly and quarterly *Thrilling Sports*, *Popular Sports* and *Exciting Sports* along with less frequently published titles devoted exclusively to football and baseball.

The name Dan Duffy sounds like the archetypical college jock. Later on, the same company produced a few postwar adventures of Bart Bradley, Teen Athlete. Alliteration paid, on and off the playing field. Dan Duffy's adventures almost always involved his buddy, bespectacled football waterboy "Blink" Gordon, and gorgeous Marcia Lee. Duffy could be a bit of a hothead in his early adventures. In "Thrilling" #10, for example, he meets Fred Thomas, a star transfer from Yale. It takes only five panels for Thomas to score the winning touchdown, to win praise that he — not Duffy — is now Carson's real star, for a new trainer to taunt Duffy over his rival, and for Thomas to move in on Marcia.

"So now you're butting in on my dates! Can't I ever get rid of you?" Duffy exclaims, to which Thomas replies, "Looks like I'm taking the play away from you with our girl, too, eh, Duffy?" This is followed by Duffy's attempt to land a roundhouse right on his new rival as Marcia breaks up the melee. But Thomas quickly proves to be a good guy as he helps prevent the crooked trainer from framing Duffy for a crime and Duffy rewards the team by drop-kicking (!) a "miraculous 60-yard field goal." Miraculous, indeed! Duffy was also on good terms with every science professor on the Carson faculty, giving the wonder boy frequent chances to foil the theft of inventions by a motley conglomeration of criminals and spies.

In one of Duffy's relatively few baseball adventures, in "Thrilling" #18 (July 1941), he foils the plot of a crooked umpire to feed "dead" baseballs to the opposing pitcher when Duffy's team is at bat. Having grabbed the plate umpire by the neck and convinced the base umpire to play with the same ball for both teams, Duffy wins the game 3–2 with a three-run homer in the ninth. Then he rejects a pro contract so he can "stick to Carson!"

At the end of that story follows a grammatical doozy: "Dan Duffy carries his alma mater to new heights in our next issue!" One cannot, of course, have an alma mater without graduating! That's almost as bad as the error so frequently seen on newspaper sports pages: "former graduate Joe Blow." How many athletes have had their diplomas revoked in this manner?

Alas, America's entry into World War II ended Dan Duffy's athletic exploits forever. He was replaced in "Thrilling" #30 (October 1942) by the timely appearance of Lucky Lawrence, Leatherneck.

Bart Bradley, Teen Athlete

The same company that created "Dan Duffy, College Athlete" came up with the short-lived "Bart Bradley, Teen Athlete" for "Wonder Comics" #8 (Oct. 1946) through #10 (February 1947) and "America's Best Comics" #30 (April 1949) and #31 (July 1949), the last two issues. Bart Bradley was in uncommon company in the superhero-dominated "Wonder Comics" and "America's Best," because comic books of the 1940s and 50s featured almost everything but sports heroes, who may have seemed a bit too close to reality. Superheroes, magicians, jungle men and women, aviators, reporters, detectives, cowboys, all manner of military heroes — the list of fantastic figures, or mere mortals who consistently accomplished the fantastic, ran into the untold thousands.

Standard Comics introduced Bart Bradley in "Wonder Comics" #8 this way: "He's new! He's different! He's wonderful! Meet Bart Bradley, folks, and watch a crack college athlete go to town, using flying fists and heels against the challenge of a sinister plot!" Although continuing to use The Grim Reaper, a violent superhero, and Wonderman on the covers of "Wonder Comics," Standard tried hard with Bart, giving him a 12-page lead story in his first appearance. Bart is an all-around college star who is planning to leave the track team in order to support his family because "his dad just went broke." Elinor Winters, the daughter of the dean, hooked him up with the editor of the local newspaper so Bart could support himself and stay in school. When the editor asks him to prove himself, Bart just happens to find a great story — when he foils gamblers who kidnap him. By 1946, that was already a tired theme.

Will Eisner's Rube Rooky

Comic book impresario Will Eisner, best known for his creation of The Spirit in 1940, came up with possibly the most charming of all sports characters in comic books: Rube Rooky. Rube was not destined to last past one issue, although a second issue was advertised, because Eisner's experiment in publishing his own comic books began and ended with two obscure titles in 1949: "Baseball Comics" and "The Kewpies."

Eisner's genius — his comic strips were like no others, especially when it came to combining satirical storytelling and comical yet compelling art — has long left baseball collectors wishing he had been able to produce more than one issue devoted to Rube Rooky. Alas, Rube Rooky joined so many other one-off baseball heroes, although historians of Eisner's immense body of work have kept his memory alive.

"Baseball Comics" #1 (Spring 1949) is unlike any other sports comic book ever done, featuring 24 pages of the adventures and misadventures of Rube Rooky, a pitcher literally found on an ice wagon. Like so many of the best comic book characters, such as Little Lulu and Uncle Scrooge, Rube can be read on several levels. It's a creative amalgamation: Ring Lardner meets Damon Runyon meets Walter Winchell meets The Spirit, all drawn and written in Eisner's inimitable style.

Ironically, the story opens with a fiction that eventually turned into reality a few decades late: The interference of the female owner of a major league team. The John McGraw-like manager Pop Flye — only Eisner could have invented Pop Flye — finds himself fired by Lana Lash, the new owner of the Jaguars. Pop's team is barnstorming, about to meet "a local iceman's nine," when Lana insists on saving the receipts by having Rube, the ice wagon driver, pitch.

Pop Flye is boggled when Rube Rooky no-hits his club, but Lana Lash fires him with this salvo: "That does it! An eighth rate bush team beats us and our manager can't do anything but rave about their pitcher! A change is needed! Pop Flye, you're fired!" But this is only the beginning for Pop and Rube, who both soon wind up with the bedraggled New York Badgers. Baseball in 1949 was far more sophisticated than it had been during the Gilded Age when McGraw (and Pop) played, but that doesn't prevent Eisner from coming up with the likes of first baseman Slab Angler, third baseman Grapple Vance, shortstop Hinge McCoy and star slugger Cleat Biggers — all modeled on the baseball ne'er-do-wells of 50 years earlier.

The scheming Lana Lash tries to find ways to foil the fantastic Rube Rooky, but he's only temporarily in the doghouse. Ultimately, he clinches the game the Badgers need to get into the World Series by bunting and turning the play into a "home run" in the ninth inning. Shades of Little League! Rube also wins the heart of his girl, Sunny, who fell in love with the pitcher when she served him in a "hash wagon."

The plug on the bottom of page 24 reads: "Don't miss the next issue of Baseball Comics as Rube Rooky faces his first World Series!" Alas, the courageous iceman never "pitched" again.

Charlton's short-lived Frank Merriwell

Imagine, if you will, Batman pretty much vanishing from the pop cultural landscape for more than a generation, them popping up in a short-lived comic book series before abruptly disappearing. That much pretty sums up the iconic oddity that was Charlton's four-issue "Frank Merriwell at Yale" experiment 50 years ago.

Half a century ago, the vast majority of young comic book readers—and even not-so-young readers—had heard little if anything of Frank Merriwell, unless they talked with older relatives about their childhood heroes. The consummate clean-cut athletic hero had been immensely popular during the youth of their parents and grandparents. In fact, it's difficult to overstate the phenomenal cultural impact of the character.

"Frank Merriwell at Yale" #1, June 1955 (copyright Charlton Comics Group). Frank returned out of the blue for a four-issue run. Cover is by Dick Giordano, who later became a famed editor at DC Comics.

In biographical material about creator Gilbert Patten, it often has been stated that Merriwell's dime novels and book reprints combined to sell more than 500 million copies! This occurred at a time when the population of the United States was about a third of what it is now. Merriwell was created for Street & Smith by the unbelievably prolific Patten, who used the pen name Burt L. Standish for dime-novel tales of Frank Merriwell, younger brother Dick Merriwell, and Frank Merriwell Junior. For a full 20 years, from 1896 to 1916, Street & Smith produced a weekly story of some 20,000 words about the Merriwell clan's adventures both on and off playing fields. Patten wrote more than a million words during most of that period, although others wrote many of the post–1910 tales.

The Merriwell epics appeared in 850 issues of *Tip Top Weekly* and 136 issues of New *Tip Top Weekly*, both old-fashioned dime novels with colorful covers but no interior illustrations (see chapter one).

In 1915–16, their scene shifted from 27 issues to the early pulp magazines *Tip Top Semi-Weekly* and its short-lived successor, *Wide Awake* magazine. Many original Merriwell stories under the Standish byline, though not all by Patten, also appeared in the 1927–31 Street & Smith pulps *Sport Story*, *Top Notch*, and *Fame and Fortune.*

Well into the 1930s, Street & Smith also reprinted the Merriwell epics in more than 200 softcover books, along with 28 hardcovers from Street & Smith, Federal Book Company and David McKay. All told, Merriwell was a household name for more than three decades. But after that, Merriwell's history is curiously spotty for an icon. Charlton, of all comic book publishers, was a small part of that history.

Universal released a Merriwell movie serial in 1936 costarring Jean Rogers, the year she achieved fame playing Dale Arden in the first Flash Gordon chapter play (see chapter three). The only Big Little Book starring Merriwell appeared in 1935, years after a seldom-remembered newspaper strip adaptation. Five-page Merriwell stories appeared in "Shadow Comics" #1 through 4 in 1940. But the erstwhile icon disappeared in the comics until popping up again as part of Charlton's frequent and generally unsuccessful comic book experiments in the mid–1950s.

When "Frank Merriwell at Yale" #1 (June 1955) appeared, it marked the return of a character who at that point had starred in more stories than any character in the annals of American fiction. Yet it can safely be assumed that the vast majority of the readers who spotted that colorful Charlton baseball cover by Dick Giordano had never heard of Merriwell. One can only speculate how many fathers and grandfathers might have been startled to see youngsters reading a Merriwell comic book.

Charlton's four issues, with three short Merriwell stories in each, focus entirely on Merriwell's freshman days at Yale. He competes in baseball, football and track, and also boxes and plays polo. Basketball, though, was nowhere to be seen. There were also the usual quota of jealous upperclassmen and shady gamblers. Giordano and Vince Alascia, who did most of the stories, produced some of the most effective art to appear in Charlton comics of the era.

The first issue features the top cover and contents. In the initial story — the best of the 12 — Frank earns the respect of an older pitcher who was pressed into managing the freshman team. In the other stories, he turns the tables on hazers and overcomes criminals during a fire. Football was huge in the Merriwell dime novels, but he cavorts on the gridiron in only one story in the Charlton series, since only #4 (Jan. 1956) hit the stands during football season. The first three issues all appeared during spring and summer.

Even though Merriwell lasted only four issues, he was to appear in paperback form a decade later in three curious 1965 novels from the tiny Award Books: "Frank Merriwell Returns," "Frank Merriwell at the Wheel" (auto racing, of all things!) and "Frank Merriwell, Quarterback." The hero in these novels was revealed to be Merriwell Junior, even though there already had been a Merriwell Junior 50 years earlier!

Written in a style young adults could easily understand, by Mike Frederic, these three books were a genuine curiosity, since most of the Award lineup was definitely adult-oriented. A handful of reprints of the Merriwell dime novels also appeared in 1972 from Street & Smith and in 1975 from Zebra Books, all marketed as a cultural curiosity. Then Frank Merriwell seems to have disappeared, perhaps forever.

Swat Malone and Old Faithful

Swat Malone starred in one issue of an outrageously silly comic book and was modestly billed as "America's Home Run King" at the top of the cover of a truly bizarre one-shot dated September 1955. It was the height of irony, in fact, that Swat Malone was a one-shot issue, for this shameless steal from Bernard Malamud's 1952 novel, *The Natural,* always took only one swing at hitting a home run — and never failed! Swat always let two strikes go by before taking his cut. The proverbial "Kid Who Batted 1.000" had nothing on Swat Malone!

This supposedly bimonthly comic book had perhaps the most optimistic indicia in history, listing the publisher as "Swat Malone Enterprises, Inc.," and offering yearly subscriptions for 60 cents "plus 15 cents postage." The art on the first story was signed Hy Fleishman. The issue was approved by the Comics Code Authority, which should have turned it down on the basis of stories more genuinely fantastic than any tales that featured superheroes, vampires or jungle girls.

In the first of Swat's three impossible adventures, we meet the wonderfully named scout Birddog Bush, who is about to save his job with the struggling Blue Jays by finding a phenomenal minor leaguer named Swat Malone, who never strikes out and shows promise of being the world's greatest home run hitter. The real Blue Jays, the Toronto variety, weren't created until 1977, but these Blue Jays of 1955 were 30 games behind when they called Swat from the minor leagues. He and his bat, "Old Faithful" — a shameless steal from "Wonder Boy" in *The Natural*— arrived in time for Swat to swat a game-winning, ninth-inning, pinch-hit homer.

Swat's fielding apparently wasn't in the same league, for he was limited to pinch hitting in all three stories (the designated hitter innovation was 18 years in the future). But what a pinch-hitter. Old Faithful was good for a two-strike home run every time!

As the first story continues, Swat discovers a plot by the notorious rival team executive, "Wrong-Way Ellison," to douse the park lights just as the ball is heading toward our hero. Swat still hits one out of the park, however, after taping a magnesium flare to his wonder bat! This was a real comic book; it actually exists. In fact, there were nine full-page advertisements. What was it P.T. Barnum said? Yet this plot wasn't even close to the home run hysterics of the next two tales.

In the second story, Swat finds a personal batboy when he befriends a youngster named "Little Eager" — baseball's version of Red Ryder's Little Beaver, of course. And how does Swat meet Little Eager? Swat tacks a nail and a note to Old Faithful, then hits a foul so exactly that the ball arrives, along with the note nailed to it, in the lap of Little Eager! Many fans have heard the story of the day Ted Williams swatted one foul after another toward an aggravating fan, but not even the "Splendid Splinter" was a match for the eagle eye of Swat Malone.

At the end of the second story, Swat embeds Old Faithful with razors— no pine tar for this guy!— so that he can cut the string off the fearsome, albeit illegal, "lasso ball" invented by Wrong-Way Ellison. Why, not even Gaylord Perry ever thought of such a wicked pitch.

In Swat's last adventure, college beauty Hedda Hopps III, daughter of the Blue Jays' owner, steals his heart on the opening day of the World Series. "So you always make two strikes ... and then you hit a home run every time!" she asks Swat during the warm-ups. "I do, but I guess I've been lucky, Miss Hopps!" is Swat's response. Shades of "aw shucks!" and "gee willikers!"

Meanwhile, Wrong-Way Ellison is at it again, plotting to buzz the field with a jet plane, so he can knock Swat's inevitable mighty swat back onto the field and save the game for the Brooklyn Rogers! They are referred to as the Brooklyn Giants in two bubbles, but "Giants" is erased in favor of "Rogers" in the captions. Apparently the writer did not realize that Brooklyn already had the Dodgers, who were the hated rival of the New York Giants! (The two teams did not begin to play on the West Coast until 1958.)

Swat had promised Hedda Hopps III that he would hit the longest home run in history. He explained how he accomplished the feat when he stroked the ball toward Wrong-Way Ellison's jet: "I put a thick layer of a strong glue and Mexican jumping beans on 'Old Faithful.' When I hit it, the ball got coated with the stuff, so when it got near the plane, it took a jump! Wrong-Way couldn't reach it, and it stuck to the tail of the plane! Say, that plane is still going! I guess it was the longest home run ever hit! I did it for you and Hedda Hopps, gang, and I hope you all like me a little bit for it!"

"Swat Malone," September 1955 one-shot (copyright Swat Malone Enterprises). Ironically, not long after the most famed sports hero of all briefly returned in "Frank Merriwell at Yale" #1, a character nobody had ever heard of, Swat Malone, made a single appearance with his bat, Old Faithful. Hy Fleischman did the cover and interior art.

There were to be no further cheers for this comic book Casey, however, in a cartoon version of Mudville. Mighty Swat had finally struck out — with his readers!

Dick Cole, Wonder Boy

Dick Cole, a Golden Age hero, survived into the early 1950s in 10 issues of his own title and the ensuing five issues of "Sport Thrills" #11–15 from renowned cover artist L.B. Cole's new company, Star Comics. Cole was an ultra-athletic, square-jawed, teenage military cadet.

Dick Cole, also known as the Wonder Boy in the first three years of his feature in Novelty Press's "Blue Bolt Comics," began as a non-costumed character with supernormal powers. He quickly morphed into a supreme all-around athlete, outdoorsman and student. He seems to have been somewhat modeled on Street & Smith's dime novel athlete/adventurer Frank Merriwell. Dick Cole's adventures, originally bylined Bob Davis and often drawn in old-school style by Jim Wilcox, ran for all 101 issues of the Novelty Press run of "Blue Bolt Comics" (June 1940 through vol. 10, #2, September-October 1949) and in the first 31 issues of "Four Most" (Winter 1941/42 through vol. 7, #6, November-December 1948). The strapping athlete, complete with a large coterie of featured buddies and rivals along with his fetching if often jealous girlfriend, Laura Bradly, must have been popular with his readers. He was cover featured on many issues of both titles, both in traditional sports scenes and in military academy adventures.

Cole's publisher, variously known as Novelty Press, Premium and Curtis, sold out to Star Comics when the latter firm began publishing comics late in 1949. Nearly a year before that, the Premium Group of Comics, as Cole's publisher was then known, gave Cole his own bimonthly title the same month he left "Four Most" and not long before he stopped appearing in "Blue Bolt." Dick Cole #1 (December 1948-January 1949) featured a gorgeous cover by L.B. Cole, who numbered Premium among his varied clients before his own Star Comics existed. Amid a military school backdrop and Cole's handsome looks, he was shown in football, baseball, track and swimming poses on #1. Probably all of the Dick Cole stories were reprints in his own title, but team sports inexplicably figured in only two of the 20 Cole stories in #1–10.

Dick Cole may have been given his own title because of the renewed postwar popularity of series books. The first three titles in famed basketball coach Clair Bee's Chip Hilton series sold extremely well in 1948 and prolific sports author Wilfred McCormick produced his first two Bronc Burnett books the same year. Unlike team sports stars Hilton and Burnett, Dick Cole participated in virtually every sport.

Without any break in the publication schedule, Star assumed publication of "Dick Cole" with #6 (October-November 1949), which was among Star's first few comics. The only football cover among the 10 issues was on #8 (February-March 1950), when no other comics were producing "serious" sports fiction, and the only baseball cover was on #10 (June-July 1950). The marvelous basketball cover on "Dick Cole" #9 was actually a scene devoted to the obscure hoop strip "Rip Rory," who appeared in five-page stories in #9 and #10, billed as "Four-Letter Man at State College." (The correct term should have been "Four-Sport Letter Man" because freshmen weren't allowed to play varsity sports in those long-gone college days and thus three varsity letters were the maximum possible in the same sport.) Cole's handsome baseball cover for #10, showing an attempted steal of home, oddly portrays the batter in a set position that probably would have resulted in a ruling of interference.

When Star converted "Dick Cole" into the quarterly "Sport Thrills," issue #11 (November 1950) appeared after a significant hiatus. (The title is sometimes listed incorrectly, albeit with better grammar, as "Sports Thrills.") One Dick Cole reprint appeared in each issue, but this time all five stories featured strong sports angles, until the boy wonder disappeared forever with #15 (November 1951). If only because both reproduction and interior art standards were so poor, "Sport Thrills" seems to have had little chance to succeed.

By this time, Dick Cole seemed antiquated, especially in contrast to the up-to-date sports portrayals of Chip Hilton and Bronc Burnett in the series books. Star's production values suffered hugely in comparison with the far more polished work from the likes of National, Quality and Fawcett. It would have been intriguing to see those large firms try a fictional sports hero such as Dick Cole, but they never did. Fawcett's nicely done biographical sports comics of the same era provide a hint of how well that firm might have handled sports fiction.

Dick Cole's non-sport stories were often much more probable than his athletic exploits. The earliest reprint — the winter sports story in "Dick Cole" #7 — came from "Blue Bolt" Vol. 2 #10 (March 1942, whole #22). In one respect, Dick Cole's last appearance — the reprint in "Sport Thrills" #15 — hinged on one of the most improbable scenes ever to appear in a baseball story. During the middle of a championship game, a jealous Laura learns that Dick has begged female sportswriter Alice Grant — then a rarity in the job market — to write team-oriented stories instead of glorifying Cole. Laura also discovers that Grant is engaged and not interested in Cole. Laura proceeds to drag Grant onto the field (!), where Grant tells the team that Cole is not a glory seeker, leading the other players to apologize to Cole and regain faith in him. Cole, unable to pitch because his hand was spiked in the previous game, ends the game by playing second base. He makes a leaping bare-handed grab of a line drive — "Aow! That hurt!" — and turns the catch into an unassisted double play.

Comic book stories dealing with "real life" were not always accurate, either. In "Sport Thrills" #11, an inadequate four-page story dealing with how Ted Williams' early career developed says he had five hits in his last game of the 1941 season to wind up hitting .404. Actually, he went 6 for 8 in a doubleheader and finished at .406 after entering the twinbill batting .39955. (If he had played by today's rules, which count run-scoring fly balls as sacrifices and do not charge an official time at bat, it's estimated he would have been credited with an average of nearly .420.) As per custom, baseball statisticians would have rounded that .39955 to .400 — a figure exceeded several times before 1941 but never matched since. But .39955 would have forever remained an aggravating footnote for the incredibly devoted "Teddy Ballgame" if he had accepted an offer to sit out the last two games. He singled in his first at-bat of the day to raise his average to .401 but declined to call it a season.

Even Dick Cole never matched that type of real-life athletic courage.

Jack Armstrong, the All-American Boy

When old-timers recall their favorite radio heroes, Jack Armstrong, "The All-American Boy," often comes to mind. Hudson High's star student/athlete, however, enjoyed the vast majority of his hundreds of radio adventures away from athletics and emerged as a globe-trotting adventurer with a scientific bent. Fittingly, Jack Armstrong had only one adventure in the comic books involving team sports.

"Jack Armstrong" #1 (November 1947) was his first appearance in comic books. The issue came out near the end of his long radio career, but just in time to take advantage of his new newspaper comic strip and his only movie serial, released in 1947 by Columbia. Parents' Institute, Inc., published an oversized 13-issue Jack Armstrong series, ending in September 1949 when the firm went out of the comic book business. Jack could not have had a more appropriate publisher: Parents Institute, the publisher of *Parents* magazine, published a series of squeaky-clean comics such as "True Comics" and "Calling All Girls."

One of the oddest of all baseball stories was cover-featured on #7 (June 1948). "Jack Armstrong Solves the Mystery on the Diamond" was a refreshing change of pace, even though it did involve the seemingly ever-present threat of gamblers. Before Hudson "meets Brayton in a red-hot intercity rivalry," Jack is distracted by his uncle Jim. The scientist tells the young star that his "intro-ray" has been stolen. "The intro-ray is not deadly — it merely stuns the victim for a few seconds by interrupting the flow of brain-impulses to parts of the body." Uncle Jim explains the ray can be blocked at 50 yards or more by any non-conductor of electricity such as rubber. "I hope I can keep my mind on baseball — with that intro-ray set on the loose," Jack says.

With scouts on hand to see shortstop Jack's star double-play partner, second baseman Tommy Byrnes, it seems as though Byrnes can do nothing right. Playing a hunch late in the game, Jack tells his teammates to put on shower caps. They can't figure out his reasoning, but Tommy suddenly regains his form and comes up with the game-winning hit. The police seal the park and Jack leads them to crooks who have used the intro-ray to try to spoil Hudson's chances.

Jack Armstrong ran for 18 years on radio, beginning in 1933, and the comic book plugged the program. Issue #8 (August 1948), with a listing of American stations carrying the show, demonstrated that nearly 200 stations were still playing the half-hour daily adventures.

Vic Verity

A Jack Armstrong knockoff named "Vic Verity, High School Hero," appeared in seven issues of a comic book apparently published by Fawcett in 1945 and 1946, even though the Fawcett name was replaced by "Vic Verity Publications, Inc." in the indicia. C.C. Beck, famed for his Captain Marvel stories of the same period from Fawcett, contributed much of the art.

In the only cover-featured Vic Verity sports story, the pitcher/slugger provides "another smash hit" in a "thrilling championship baseball game" in #5 (June 1946). The humorous story, however, featured a game-winning catch by the feet (!) of a substitute catcher after the star catcher falls out of a car and injures himself too severely to play. It was not a high-water mark in the annals of baseball fiction, to put it mildly.

Iron Vic

A whimsical United Features Syndicate comic strip that has been almost entirely forgotten, Bernard Dibble's Iron Vic, featured impossible feats by a square-jawed adult hero who looked like a crude version of Dick Tracy on the baseball diamond. There was a non-sports cover issue of Iron Vic in the 1940 "UFS Single Series" (#22) followed seven years later by a baseball-themed cover on "Comics Revue" #3 (August 1947).

"Comics Revue" #3, one of the first issues to appear from the Archer St. John Company, carries a baseball story that seems positively primitive compared to other comic books of the era. Even so, it's fun in a suspend-your-belief way. The first story apparently consists of licensed newspaper strip reprints, even though no copyright notice appears in the indicia or on the strips. It tells the tale of an impossibly strong amnesia victim who discovers he can play baseball.

Seeking a major-league tryout with the Panthers, he finds himself pestered by players who think he is either a reporter or a joke or both. He winds up pitching both games of a doubleheader even though the first game went 15 innings; he hits improbably long home runs into apartment houses; and he turns an unassisted triple play by outrunning three players. As if that weren't enough, he pitches with his left arm after his right arm is injured by a line drive.

"Strange that he should take so to sport," says Dr. Degnan, his friend. "But then, I suppose no more strange than all else strange about the man!" Since this character appeared seemingly out of nowhere in this comic book world of 1947, the readers must also have considered Iron Vic pretty strange! "Comics Revue" was immediately discontinued and Iron Vic never appeared again in comic books. Like most sports heroes in comic books of the 1940s and '50s, Iron Vic was literally too good to be true. The art and reproduction was some of the worst in all comic books for that year.

Chuck White

Treasure Chest of Fun & Fact, published from 1946 to 1972 during the school year, was distributed almost entirely in Catholic schools, and thus many comic book readers never got a chance to see Chuck White, a Jack Armstrong type. He starred in dozens of continuing, relatively low-key adventures on and off athletic fields; for example, he had an airplane pilot's license in high school. *Treasure Chest* appeared every two weeks, so readers often were left hanging. Many of his stories dealt with adventures outside the sports world.

Since these comics were religious, unlike their secular counterparts, Chuck is often shown praying in addition to starring in baseball, basketball, football and track at St. John's, a Catholic secondary school. *Treasure Chest* sent Chuck White off to college in vol. 8 #1 (September 22, 1952). Rather than opting for Notre Dame, he chooses St. Mark's, a small Catholic college. When asked about military service, the clean-cut patriotic hero responds, "I'm going to sign up for the Marine Corps platoon leaders' course. [A]fter graduation, I'll be a second lieutenant and serve two years on active duty."

Chuck grew up during the strip's course and became a coach and a newspaper reporter, giving the writers endless opportunities to create a wide variety of plots and characters. Sensationalism and violence were consistently toned down in favor of characterization and plot devices, and the Chuck White series was always loaded with moral and religious overtones. There has never been much collector interest in this long-running character, especially since all of his stories were continued during each school year.

Speed Spaulding

"Speed Spaulding, Star Athlete" ran for 18 issues in the obscure Holyoke Publishing Co. title "Sparkling Stars," beginning with #2 (July 1944) and running through #21 (January 1947), missing on #7 and #20.

In the only two issues of the even more obscure "Cannonball Comics" (February and March 1945) appeared "Hardy of Hillsdale High," as little known as any sports character in history. Other than a few boxers such as Joe Palooka — licensed first by Columbia and later by Harvey — and Fiction House's Kayo Kirby, the list of sports figures is short, indeed, when compared with the untold thousands of comic book characters.

Gil Thorp, the first coach to headline a comic book

Shortly before the major league baseball season opened in 1963, a surprising comic book hit the newsstands: Dell's "Gil Thorp" #1, devoted to a full-length baseball story. The first issue, dated May–July, was listed as a quarterly, but it also was the last issue. Since sales reports of first issues usually didn't come in until after the second or third issues of any new title, it will forever remain a mystery why Milford High's legendary, longtime coach from the world of syndicated comic strips was given only one appearance in a comic book. But then, Charlton's "Chat Chatfield" one-shot in 1967 was the only comic ever headlined by a non-newspaper strip coach.

The Gil Thorp epic in #1 was unique: it was the only book-length fictional sports story in the history of Golden or Silver Age comics, a full 32 pages. Granted, only a handful of comics were devoted entirely to sports fiction from the 1940s through the 1970s, but it was nevertheless an intriguing experiment. The artist and writer were uncredited and the copyright for this authorized edition was claimed not by the Dell Publishing Co., but by the *Chicago Tribune* (and the *Tribune* Syndicate).

Dell had been involved in comics since the dawn of the industry in the mid–1930s, but until 1962 the firm's comic books were produced by Western Printing and Lithographing. Beginning late in 1962, Western released its work under the Gold Key logo. Dell itself, though, emerged fully involved as a significant comic book publisher in 1963. Since Gold Key retained most lucrative licensed characters such as Donald Duck and Little Lulu, Dell was forced to take on a large number of new projects. Gil Thorp was one such Dell license. ("Authorized edition" in the indicia was always an indication that the characters did not originate in comic books.)

Though the believability of what began as a solid story was spoiled by a melodramatic encounter with adult hoodlums late in the tale, "Gil Thorp" #1 remains perhaps the best attempt at sports fiction in the history of comics. It remains timely today. Gil Thorp, a handsome, crew-cut fellow seemingly not long out of college himself— or perhaps the Marines!— appears virtually out of nowhere in the opening blurb: "When the coach of Milford High's baseball team suddenly resigns, Gil Thorp is asked to take over. The assignment is a tough one." (Why not "It's a tough assignment"? One always wonders about such clumsy grammar.)

Gil is disturbed during early practices by the team's lack of hustle and by how the hitters try little but swinging for the fences. "Didn't any of you ever hear of placing the ball, hit and run, bunting?" he asks. "The big league scouts look for home run hitters. They're the boys who get the big bonuses," a player tells him, to which Gil responds, "I see. Well, you fellows better start thinking of teamwork and winning ball games for Milford High and less of major league bonuses. You will play the game my way or you'll be cut from the squad and replaced with boys who will!"

When Gil switches Bob Burwell, one of the team's stars, from shortstop to third base, the youngster rebels because he knows scouts look more closely at shortstops. (That's not always true, but it is true that most professional infield prospects begin as high school shortstops, since that's where the team's best athlete often plays.) Strenuous objections ensue from Burwell's father, himself a former shortstop and the archetype of the interfering parent, yet not an unrealistic character. As a member of the school board, Mr. Burwell threatens both Gil and the school principal. Bob Burwell himself makes deliberate mistakes, hoping it will convince Thorp to return him to shortstop. Along the way, Gil and the youngster's older sister, Kathy Burwell, develop a relationship.

Then follows a jarring and highly unrealistic interruption in the story. When Gil decides the team needs more speed, he recruits a sandlot baseball player who is the star sprinter on the track team. Now it was, and still is, true that a few smaller schools allow athletes to participate in both baseball and track in the spring, but most schools do not. In fact, virtually any track coach would strenuously object to one of his stars being recruited by a baseball coach. The sprinter, Tim Carter, immediately takes advantage of the opportunity to join the baseball team, implying that track and field is an inferior sport! There is no indication of any fair arrangement among Gil, Tim and the unnamed track coach — a total ethical absurdity, even in sports fiction.

At any rate, Tim Carter becomes a valuable baseball player. Meanwhile, Gil and Kathy, out on a date for dinner and dancing, sport Bob Burwell breaking training while doing the twist! "He's good, isn't he?" Kathy asks Gils and Gil replies, "At dancing yes. Not at obeying rules. There's a ten o'clock curfew for the team." But, since the team operates on the honor system, Gil gives Bob a chance to turn himself in. When he does not, Gil suspends him. When Bob's teammates threaten to quit the team, Bob acknowledges he did, indeed, break curfew and confesses that he earlier made errors on purpose. "I deserved everything I got. What matters is what you give to a team, not what you get from it!"

Gil lifts the suspension and Bob tells him, "I'll be a good third baseman if I have to knock balls down with my chest!" That, of course, is exactly what is expected of a good third baseman, hardly worthy of an exclamation point. Bob ultimately goes on to hit a three-run homer, with two outs in the ninth inning, to win the championship for Milford after receiving batting tips from Gil. It's contrived, yes, but not entirely improbable (although the story's author apparently did not realize that regulation high school games were seven innings, as they are now, in 1963, and Milford trails 2–0 into the ninth).

If that had been the extent of the story, it would have been reasonably believable. But after being reinstated to the team, a pulpish plot device from the 1920s suddenly plagues Bob: shadowy gamblers threaten to injure his sister if he doesn't accept their $5,000 offer (!) to throw the game. Their parting shot: "Think it over, kid.... Otherwise, we'll play baseball with yer pretty sister and she'll be the ball! And we hit hard!" Bob, though, turns out to be made of stern stuff and he tells Kathy and Gil, who work out a plan with Bob's father, the police and school authorities. Along with the police Gil punches out the not-so-smart crooks; Bob winds up with a crook's gun in his hand and Bob's father with the bag of the crook's money! As if all this isn't unlikely enough, it boggles the mind to realize that a $5,000 bribe in 1963 would be equal to more than $30,000 today!

The fine compilation of Gil Thorp strips, *The Gil Thorp Silver Anniversary Yearbook*, appeared in 1984, edited by Thorp fan Matt Shaughnessy and with an introduction by Jack Berrill, who created the strip in 1958 and wrote and drew it for many years. It's an intriguing comparison of stories devoted to football, basketball and baseball in 1958 and 1959 and those involving the three sports 25 years later. The book is recommended for the text perspectives provided by Shaughnessy and Berrill.

Berrill provided a fascinating take on how his viewpoint had changed: "When I first created my feature, Gil Thorp, I believed I had all the answers to the problems Gil faced. It was a less complicated era, and I felt little compunction about making judgments. But times changed and so did I! The metamorphosis was due, in no small measure, to the experience my wife, Veronica, and I had in raising seven children, some of them teenagers in the sixties and seventies. I was forced to see beyond the absolutes I had lived by. Now I am very careful about making judgments, and I have many more questions than answers. Hopefully, this attitude is reflected in Gil Thorp today. The problems I have dealt with recently — teenage pregnancy, divorce, homosexuality, alcoholism, mental retardation, to name a few — are more complicated and, in fact, could not have been addressed in the early years. But today's newspaper readers are more sophisticated, and so are the comics they read."

Gil Thorp, then, can surely lay claim to being the best of the comic strips devoted to the mainstream team sports. Milford High was not a small school, however, and even in the 1950s and 1960s very few schools of any size had the same varsity coach for football, basketball and baseball. It's possible that the best-selling Chip Hilton series, created by famed basketball coach Clair Bee in 1948 for Grosset and Dunlap (see chapter seven), may have been an influence, since Valley Falls High mentor Hank Rockwell coached the same three sports in the first eight of the 24-book series (the 24th was written in 1966 but not published until 2002).

Cotton Woods

Out of the thousands of comic books Dell produced, "Gil Thorp" was the third one-shot sports publication to appear from the company, all taken from newspaper strips. The first two were "Ozark Ike" in 1948 and "Cotton Woods" in 1957, both created by the famed sports cartoonist Ray Gotto as newspaper strips, but long forgotten today.

The Cotton Woods comic book, issued as #837 in Dell's "Four Color" line, was priced at 15 cents during an era when most comics were 10 cents, which may explain why Cotton Woods never again appeared in comic books. (Another reason is that the newspaper strip ended its three-year run in 1958.) Dell briefly experimented with a 15-cent price point on some of its more popular titles in the late 1950s, but to do so on a new character in comic books was not a prudent decision. The difference between 10 and 15 cents was significant for most youngsters 50 years ago, and that probably explains why Dell's single issue of Cotton Woods is seldom seen by comic book enthusiasts today.

In the comic book, Cotton Woods, "the Carolina Kid from Lonesome Gap," was a professional football and baseball star. Several athletes pulled off the two-sport combination before Woods was created in the 1950s and the feat was successfully pulled off much later by the like of Bo Jackson and Deion Sanders. However, the combination of Woods' demanding positions — quarterback and shortstop — is not seen beyond the college level, and now almost never in a major college. It's inconceivable today that a professional player at either position would be allowed to play a second major league sport (Jackson and Sanders were baseball outfielders). Oddly, a few years after the comic book appeared, a real two-sport Cotton appeared. Cotton Nash played both big-time basketball and baseball.

Cotton Woods wasn't played for laughs, but the uncredited Bay Gotto–like art on original 16-page baseball and football stories in "Four Color" #837 gives the issue a marvelously cartoonish feel. The stories are pure fun, and what few kids saw them must have loved them. The emotion-packed tales of the baseball Ducks and football Larks deal with Cotton's fantastic Frank Merriwell–like ability to shake off injuries to give his nefarious rivals their comeuppance.

In the baseball story, Cotton opens with a pennant-winning home run, while the nasty-tempered manager of the other league's pennant winner, Chuck Rovey, of the Bruins, scouts the game. When the boy who caught Cotton's homer takes it to him to be signed, the lad objects to Rovey's loudmouthed insults directed at Cotton outside the locker room. A gallant son of the south, Cotton responds with a devastating punch when Rovey harasses the boy. Cotton's heroics help the Ducks win the first game of the World Series, but Rovey orders his so-called Roughhouse Gang to take out Woods when he covers second base. Woods, left with a case of double vision, misses the rest of the World Series until he pinch hits with the championship at stake in the last inning of the championship game. After avoiding a bean-ball ordered by Rovey, he wins the World Series with a home run and Rovey is fired by the gentlemanly owner of his own team. Cotton's lady love, Candie Lane, is misspelled Candy in the comic book and does not play the large role she takes in the comic strip.

In the football tale, modest team player Cotton and outrageously boastful rookie Flash Grogan—"Old Flash in the flesh!" he calls himself—immediately tangle upon the rookie's arrival. Coach Brick Batz (!) soon realizes he must send the divisive Grogan packing and he winds up with the Larks' rival, the Apes. With the league lead at stake, Flash and Cotton are both injured in the same play. Cotton returns to the game but Flash fakes his way to the bench with a knee injury, only to see his coach realize the full situation. With the Larks in the lead by one point after Cotton returns, the coach orders Flash back into action. When Cotton tries to surprise the Apes with a long pass, Flash intercepts it, only to see Cotton tackle him a yard short of the goal line on the final play. The irony is that Flash really does suffer a serious knee injury on the play. "I'm really sorry Grogan got hurt, though," Cotton says sportingly. To which his coach responds, "That Grogan—a smart player. It's a shame he had to learn the hard way!"

More than three decades after the strip ended, Cotton Woods was introduced to many readers who had never heard of him when Kitchen Sink reprinted his 1955–58 baseball stories by the inimitable Gotto, who achieved great success as a sports cartoonist but also deserves high regard as a comic strip artist. Readers intrigued by Cotton Woods are directed to this book. Max Allan Collins points out how authors of comic strip histories invariably paid little or no attention to Gotto or his two athletic creations. Collins thus became probably the first writer to point out what an injustice this has been. "Cotton Woods is aglow with a kind of '50s art deco style; it's a streamlined, glossy strip, with surfaces that water would beat on," Collins writes. "Candie Lane's elaborately curvaceous figure is as '50s as a vintage Caddy's tailfins." (And that shows why Collins is often regarded as one of the finest modern wordsmiths.)

"The old timer, the underdog, the undersized athlete, represent a recurring theme in Gotto," Collins says. "Cotton Woods—like Gotto himself—is athletic yet diminutive.... Gotto admires those who try a comeback, but he understands the realities, the odds, against such courageous comebacks.... Gotto was a master at combining suspense and humor on the playing field—a pop-up will bounce off [buddy] Cy Clooney's head, players will collide, and yet the laughs don't detract from us wanting to know what will happen next."

General Features, the small syndicate that authorized Dell's "Cotton Woods" comic book, could not place "Cotton Woods" in enough papers and the strip ended abruptly on July 19, 1958. In Collins' essay, Gotto laments that General Features tried to sell strips by mail instead of calling on editors in person the way highly successful King Features did with "Ozark Ike."

Babe, Darling of the Hills

Boody Rogers was an old-style cartoonist best known for his Sparky Watts comic strip and comic books in the 1940s. He also produced 11 original issues of a sometimes outrageously funny Li'l Abner–inspired comic book covering the adventures and misadventures of Babe Boone, a gorgeous female hillbilly baseball player. Feature Publications, also known as Crestwood and Prize, produced these from #1 (June-July 1948) through #11 (April-May 1950).

Babe was variously known as "The Wonder Girl from Possum Holler," "The Amazon of the Ozarks" and "The Darling of the Hills." Feature Publications, which produced best-selling romance, crime and western comics, apparently couldn't make a success of Babe, although she was unique in the annals of comic books. Rogers' imagination produced a girl who could do anything in sports but often cared more about her off-the-field antics than athletics.

She would make statements like "Ah has nevah seen a real live ghost!" That came in

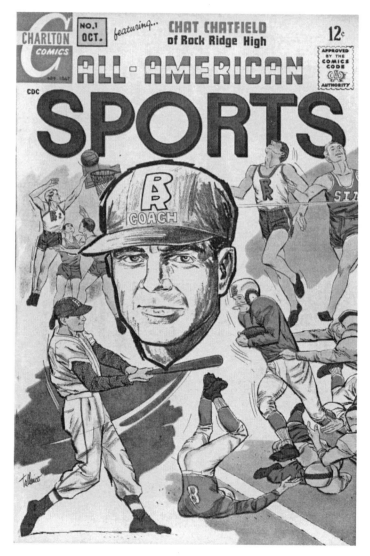

"All-American Sports," October 1967, one-shot (copyright Charlton Comics Group). Coach Chat Chatfield of Rock Ridge High stars in the last sports fiction feature of the 1960s. Tony Tallarico portrays the versatile coach and his athletes.

a hilarious 24-page story in which a cute Casper-like spook helps an injured Babe befuddle a bunch of the "New York Hanks" when she pitches for the "Brookdale Blue Sox" in the first game of the World Series. Rogers apparently had total editorial freedom and he could and did picture Babe involved in all manner of outrageous slapstick.

Comics historian Ron Goulart has called Sparky Watts, an amusing non-costumed character Rogers created in 1940 as the most powerful of all humans, "the foremost mock Superman in both comic strips and comic books." It would have been fun to see Sparky tangle with Babe Boone. Both are remembered by collectors of off-the-wall Golden Age comic books.

Ozark Ike, a hillbilly success story

Ozark Ike certainly did not strike out in comic books. In fact, by the astonishingly unsuccessful all-time standards of sports in the comics, the he-man hillbilly stroked a 450-foot grand slam. Famed sports cartoonist Ray Gotto's creation may be the most successful and beautifully drawn comic strip ever to be virtually ignored by most historians. No Ozark Ike reprint compilations exist, except in 16 largely ignored comic books from 1948 to 1952.

Indeed, the only comprehensive essay about the sensational yet naïve all-around athlete from Wildweed Run, Arkansas, was a perceptive piece by award-winning mystery novelist Max Allan Collins in the Cotton Woods comic strip anthology from Kitchen Sink in 1991. "Cotton Woods" ran from 1955 to 1958 as Gotto's second sports character after he left Ozark Ike to others.

As Collins correctly points out, Ozark Ike McBatt was easily the only successful fictional baseball and football character ever to appear in comic strips. At his height, Ozark Ike was syndicated to about 250 newspapers from King Features Syndicate. Collins is also right on the money when he says Ozark Ike is a variation of Li'l Abner, not an imitation.

Fortunately, the majority of Gotto's 1945–50 strips can be found reprinted in Ozark Ike #11–25 from Standard Comics, which followed the lone Ozark Ike appearance in the Dell *Four Color* series (#180, February 1948). These 16 issues reprint 438 pages of Gotto's daily strip art. Unfortunately, many of the issues can be hard to find.

No other fictional sports-themed comic book has ever run 15 issues, so from that standpoint Ozark Ike was a success. He must also have been something of a commercial triumph for Standard. Of the 13 comic book newspaper reprints for which Standard acquired licenses in 1947 and 1948, only Ozark Ike's title survived into 1952 on the crowded newsstands of the period. (Standard, of course, finally struck it rich in 1953 with the adaptation of a newspaper original, "Dennis the Menace," two years after his creation.)

"Ozark Ike" was a significant gamble and a departure from the norm for Standard, which in 1948 had never published anything like a sports comic, other than a handful of fact-based baseball stories in "Real Life Comics" and "It Really Happened Comics." Even though Standard published dozens of pulp magazines of every type in the 1940s, including several long-running sports titles, the firm's comic book line was almost entirely superheroes and funny animals until 1947.

Gotto played a significant role in the success of the series with original signed covers for #11–22 (he may have had a hand in the unsigned #23–24 as well, but #25 seems as though someone else drew it). The strip continuity is tied together by far less substantial splash-page art by other artists.

Most issues contain connected stories, but Standard broke them up into segments of at most four to eight pages, apparently feeling that would prove more reader-friendly with youngsters. Ironically, these issues of Ozark Ike surely were some of the most difficult-to-read comics for kids to come out of the era, since virtually all of the balloons featured hillbilly slang and often corrupted spelling. One can only imagine the horrified reaction of teachers and parents who saw these comics, unless they were fans of Li'l Abner.

Dizzy Dean, a real-life Ozark original, was a sensational pitching success for a few years in the 1930s with the St. Louis Cardinals until injuries did him in. He may have inspired Gotto to create Ozark Ike in 1945, although Ozark was usually a hitter, not a pitcher. Gotto's wonderful imagination came up with numerous costars, the most noteworthy of whom was voluptuous Dinah Fatfield. Ozark Ike and Dinah were the umpteenth knockoff of Romeo and Juliet; indeed, the Hatfields and the McCoys had nothing on the Fatfields and McBatts. Then there were Ozark Ike's baseball rivals Slag Slater and Spike Kleats, the appealing kid mascot Bugzy, and Skip Skelley, the ever-plagued manager of the Bugs, the only baseball team Ozark ever played for.

The annual Fatfield-McBatt "footbrawl" game and a boxing matchup were the focus of the single Dell issue's reprints, but Ozark Ike really hit his stride when Standard picked up the license. The first issue was mysteriously numbered #B11 (November 1948), possibly because it tied with Tim Tyler #11 as Standard's initial #11 first issue. Standard used #1 until newsstands became more crowded in 1947 and 1948, when the company often went with #5 or #10 to make titles seem better established (National Comics then often left #1 off its first issue covers entirely, such as "Superboy" in 1949).

Ozark Ike suffered a wide variety of calamities, usually caused by distractions such as Dinah's Fatfield family situation and her other suitors. In fact, the hillbilly hero seems to "lose" almost as many big games as he wins, or he loses money he had been loaned, and on and on. Trouble often followed Ozark's naiveté. One reason he had to play other sports was his constant need for big bucks. He didn't spend much time in Wildweed Run, so Dinah would tearfully cross out "Pop. 49" on the town sign and mark it "Pop. 48." Gotto's occasional hillbilly sequences were nicely rendered, but he focused most of his considerable creative and artistic energies on the sports stories.

There was, for example, the memorable time a missing Dinah returned in an airplane that buzzed the stadium, complete with skywriting. Ozark Ike was so excited he let a fly ball hit him on the head, losing the World Series! There was always a certain charm in Ozark Ike's travails; they made him seem, if anything, more human and more likeable. Gotto's action sequences are remarkably cinematic; you almost feel you're a few feet away from Ozark Ike's dust clouds as he slide in safely at home plate.

Dinah was often a major figure in the stories. In fact, she became the first female ballgirl with the Bugs (shades of the eccentric owner Charlie Finley and the Oakland A's in the 1970s).

Coach Chat Chatfield:
The last original sports hero in comic books

Charlton Comics, by 1967 one of only seven large comic book publishers remaining from the newsstand heyday of the early 1950s, could boast the occasional talented artist and writer. For the most part, though, Charlton was the low-rent district, paying the worst rates and often scooping up titles and characters from defunct comics publishers. Even so, historians and enthusiasts have long admired Charlton's willingness to experiment with virtually every type of character and genre. One such experiment was the one-shot "All-American Sports" #1 (October 1967), the last Silver Age corporate comic book to deal with mainstream sports fiction.

In the 1950s and 1960s, no publisher produced more short-run series than Charlton. Or, looking at it another way, no other publisher tried and failed as often as Charlton, although the company did have its share of long-running series, especially in the romance, war and western genres, where generic stories were more likely to succeed. Yet, other than Charlton's four-issue fling with the turn-of-the-century dime novel athletic icon Frank Merriwell in 1955 and 1956, the firm produced no sports fiction except the single issue of "All-American Sports," featuring Chat Chatfield of Rock Ridge High.

An attractive multi-scene cover by Tony Tallarico promised more than "All-American Sports" delivered. A gray, serious image of Chat Chatfield was centered around colorful basketball, track, baseball and football scenes, making him seem a middle-aged wizard of the high school coaching ranks—and a vastly overworked wizard, at that, since by 1967 few head coaches handled even three sports, much less four, at any but the smallest high schools.

This author remembers how odd this title seemed on the racks, since nothing else like it was available, from Charlton or anyone else. The indicia listed it as a quarterly, so the company intended a slow start at best for "All-American Sports."

The first story, "A Life and Death Decision," is a 9-page baseball tale right out of the most melodramatic pulps and films of the 1930s. Chat Chatfield is so concerned over his obviously worried star pitcher, Wally Craig, that he follows him to what the coach calls "a crummy dive." There, Chatfield listens outside a window to Ace Archer, a gambler who threatens Craig's girlfriend, Meg Ferris, if Craig won't throw the championship game—and the bad guy even gins up a photo to "prove" the pitcher was willing to take money. Rather than calling the police and possibly leaving lingering doubt about Craig's ethics, the coach concocts a plot to keep Meg safe. Craig throws a no-hitter, and both pitcher and coach leap into the stands seconds after the final out. Craig coldcocks the gambler with one punch, or "another beautiful one-hitter" as Chatfield puts it. In the final scenes, Craig puts off signing a pro contract to sign with nearby State University, giving him access to both the wisdom of Chatfield and the love of his girlfriend.

In the 9-page track and field story "The Downfall of Gregg Wallace," Chat Chatfield sees a potential Olympian slowed by his attraction to nightlife and a girl. Fellow Rock Ridge teacher Jeanne Evans, Chat's "one and only," approves when the girl, Lannie, drops Gregg so that he can focus on his sport again; but the plan almost backfires when Gregg loses his "do-or-die will to win" and looks dispirited in practice. On the day of the big meet, however, Jeanne takes Gregg aside to tell him that Lannie cares about him, after all, and he sees proof when Lannie arrives at the meet with a sign labeled "Win for Us Greg"—one can only assume Gregg didn't mind seeing his name misspelled! He proceeds to violate the rules of track and field while entering four individual events—one over the maximum allowed. He takes the 100-yard dash in 9.4 seconds, the 110-meter hurdles in 13.9 (meets did not combine meters and yards in those days), the pole vault at 16 feet, 2 inches, and the long jump at 22 feet (a mark that pales in comparison to the other three marks and should have been more than 24 feet). In the final panel, a grinning Chat tells the reader, "Well, Greg [*sic*] got his Lannie back, and I have a pretty sure thing for the Olympic decathlon [*sic*] this coming year."

In addition to the long jump being referred to as the "broad jump," the archaic former term for the event, the spelling mistakes were typical of Charlton, which generally had the lowest literary and production values of any major publisher.

By far the best story was the final tale, the 9-page football epic "Wise Guy Quarterback." When Chatfield's quarterback, Don Davis, combines poor sportsmanship with a negative attitude during a victory, the coach benches him for the next game. "Whatever you say, Coach!" the athlete tells him with a smirk. Jeanne Evans, though, assures Chat that Don Davis is not really a spoiled jerk, convincing Chat to call on his father. The coach introduces himself as Frank Chatfield—the only reference to his first name—and learns that the father seems more interested in his own business than in his own son.

At the end of the week's practices, Jeanne tells Chat that Don Davis has not been in school all week. "Not in school ... at all? I thought he didn't come to football practice because he was put out with me." The uncredited writer apparently had no idea that few, if any, coaches would allow a player—especially a quarterback—the option of skipping practice for a week after he had been benched. Chat tries to track down Don, who has run away, and accidentally finds him working at the diner. Convinced to return and come back to football, Don stars in the season's final game, knowing Chat had tried to find him with the help of a photo from Don's father's wallet. Don runs for six touchdowns and passes for two, not knowing father has finally shown up to watch him. "George Davis was so busy making good in the business world," Chat tells the reader, "that he almost missed his biggest deal, that of being a really interested father. And Don, he was a happy youngster from then on. I heard from him recently. He's All-American at State U. And guess who his biggest rooter is?" This was a decent attempt at a more realistic, human story, but it was the last line Chat Chatfield would deliver. It would have been nice to see this comic book continue and see if topics such as relationships, emotions and racial issues—rather than gamblers—could finally have produced a strong sports fiction comic.

SEVEN

The Longest-Running Heroes: Chip Hilton and Bronc Burnett

Well before the baby boom generation began to read juvenile and young-adult books in the mid–1950s, the two most successful fictional athletes of the postwar period began two decades of heroics.

Coinciding with a raft of sports novels by several prolific postwar authors (see chapter eleven), the Chip Hilton-Bronc Burnett series both began in 1948. They became the longest and most successful of all sports series except, of course, the Merriwell family dime novels, which were also reprinted endlessly in both paperback and hardback books (see chapter one).

The Chip Hilton Series, by Basketball Hall of Fame college coach Clair Bee, ran 23 books from 1948 to 1966, published by Grosset & Dunlap, plus a 24th published posthumously in 2002 in a special edition by Broadman and Holman, complete with a forward by no less than Bobby Knight, holder of the record for most college basketball victories. All 23 books were first editions from Grosset, in the manner of the Hardy Boys and Nancy Drew series from the same publisher. Grosset was primarily a reprint publisher, but it did produce its share of original books, especially for youth. From 1998 to 2002, the Christian publisher Broadman and Holman published the series in an updated, paperbound form produced by Bee's daughter, Cindy, and her husband, Randy Farley, although the nicely done series received nowhere near the nationwide distribution Grosset enjoyed. (It's also a little jarring to read about computer games and electronic communications in the revised Chip Hilton series.)

Seemingly every used-book store in America has a few of the original Chip Hilton volumes on the shelves, especially the early numbers. Total sales were in the millions. Sales, however, must have taken a drastic decline in the 1960s, since the last two volumes in the dust jackets, #18 and #19, are harder to find. The last four of the original series, #20–23, appeared only in pictorial cover format (as did reprints of the first 19) and those four volumes range from scarce to rare. The last book, *Hungry Hurler* (1966), is offered for hundreds of dollars by dealers in collectible books when it becomes available. One of the favorite stories told by the noted series book collector Eric Moothart of Kirkland, Washington, is how he found his copy of *Hungry Hurler* for $5. I found mine for $3!

Wilfred McCormick's Bronc Burnett series, 27 books from 1948 to 1967, is also well remembered, although probably not as well as the Chip Hilton books. Bronc Burnett had a much different publishing arc, since none of the original books were published by Grosset. G.P. Putnam's Sons published #1–11, followed by David McKay with #12–23 and Bobbs-

Merrill with #24–27. In the last three books, Bronc and coach Rocky McCune, of whom there is much more to come later in this chapter, appeared together in college stories.

Grosset reprinted the first 23 books, although with different dust jackets or pictorial covers. I have never seen Grosset reprints of the Bobbs-Merrill #24–27, which are considered scarce to rare and were probably purchased primarily by libraries. The higher-number Grosset books, especially #19–23, are also valuable and highly collectible.

Bronc Burnett's stories are confined to baseball and football (plus one about scouting), unlike "triple threat" Chip Hilton, who played football, basketball and baseball with equal enthusiasm and excellence in both high school and college. One of the Burnett/McCune stories involved basketball.

The fact that Chip Hilton was a three-sport college athlete probably hurt the credibility of the series in the 1960s, when such men were extremely unusual even in small colleges, especially in team sports (not that three-sport college athletes were ever common). However, Bronc Burnett's original editions frequently appeared on library shelves, in contrast to the Grosset Chip Hiltons. During the era that these two athletes cavorted with a raft of talented buddies, librarians far more often than not refused to purchase or display series books, which—for better or worse—they considered of little more literary value than comic books or pulp magazines. Many was the child of the 1950s who was told he or she should read "better books" along with the likes of Nancy Drew and Chip Hilton. I know; I was one of those children.

Although there were dozens of short-run character series about sports published in the first four decades of the 20th century (see chapter one), the longest ran only 14 books—the Baseball Joe series originally published from 1912 to 1928 and reprinted several times. Written by Edward Stratemeyer under his Lester Chadwick pseudonym, the books doubtless influenced future authors like McCormick (1903–1983) and Bee (1896–1983) in their youth.

The Baseball Joe books, published only by Cupples and Leon, sold for 50 cents, which was anywhere from half a day to a day's pay for some jobs in their era. There were far fewer copies published than the postwar Chip Hilton and Bronc Burnett series, which sold for 75 cents in the late 1940s, $1 for most of their run, and $1.25 or $1.50 toward the end. There's no question it was far easier for youngsters and their families to afford these, thus leading to more frequent publication, especially in the 1950s.

Neither Bee, who also wrote many technical books about basketball, nor McCormick, who produced 48 series novels in all covering four primary characters in only two decades, contributed much sports fact or fiction to the magazine market. So, as prolific as the authors were, they couldn't match either Jackson Scholz or Joe Archibald, who not only wrote more than 70 sports novels between them but also hundreds of sports pulp magazine stories each.

Bee took a chronological approach to high school and college athletics in Chip Hilton's career, while McCormick's novels primarily involved baseball tournaments and football all-star games. Neither athlete aged in real time, of course, and both authors were careful to leave out specific references to current events. Both Chip and Bronc, like so many sports heroes, came from small towns and lost their fathers before they became teenagers. Though specifying Chip's high school as Valley Falls and his college as State University, Bee took great pains to avoid regionalism in his stories. On the other hand, McCormick always made it clear that Bronc Burnett was the pride of tiny Sonora, New Mexico, and his tournament and all-star settings were always real places with numerous realistic details. When *Sports*

Illustrated presented its "Top 100 Sports Books" in 2002, Chip Hilton and Bronc Burnett received prominent mention in a small section for young readers.

Although Chip Hilton was involved with several coaches, the primary influence in his life was always kindly but often stern Henry "Hank" Rockwell, who, like Chip, had been an outstanding high school and college athlete. Likewise, Bronc Burnett had several coaches but his main mentor was Cap'n Al Carter, a former big-league catcher and one of the most detail-oriented coaches ever portrayed in fiction.

The Chip Hilton chronology

Other than one mysterious blip, Bee carefully kept the Chip Hilton chronology straight, so even the youngest reader had no trouble following Chip's career.

The first three volumes, all dated 1948, although some lists in other books are in error, were apparently released close together as a "breeder set." All the dust jackets I've seen — along with the three original-owner editions I purchased — list all three books. These are *Touchdown Pass*, *Championship Ball* and *Strike Three!* and they cover Chip's junior year at Valley Falls High, in which all three teams win state championships. It's noteworthy, however, that an injury forces him to serve as manager of the basketball team instead of playing, in a twist similar to what might have been expected from the noted author John R. Tunis (see chapter ten).

The fourth book, *Clutch Hitter!* (1949), concerned Chip's growth process in industrial league baseball in the summer before his senior year in high school. (Chip never plays American Legion baseball, which is odd considering the path of the concurrent Bronc Burnett series.) Oddly, the series skips to his senior basketball season for the fifth book, *Hoop Crazy* (1950), in which Valley Falls loses the state championship game.

Here is where the series goes temporarily awry, for the sixth book is *Pitchers' Duel* (1950), covering the heartbreak of Chip's senior baseball season, in which a repeat state championship eludes him. *Hoop Crazy* must have been written first, for one of the town's kindly sportswriters, Joe Kennedy, is part of the story, but he is missing (replaced by the unethical Muddy Waters) for both the football and baseball novels.

Hoop Crazy is the book advertised on the final page of the fourth book, in the correct book order if not the correct sport season order. At the end of *Hoop Crazy*, a football story entitled *Fourth Down Gamble* was advertised as the sixth book. It didn't happen that way, although the phrase "fourth down gamble" was prominent in the account of the big game at the end of *A Pass and a Prayer*. At the end of *Pitchers' Duel*, no book at all is advertised for the first time in the series. What made this blip so odd was that Hank Rockwell retires from Valley Falls at the end of *Pitchers' Duel*, instead heading for State University to coach Chip and his buddies on the freshman teams. But then, Rockwell is back for one more game in the reader's next calendar year!

At any rate, the series resumed correctly with #8, *Dugout Jinx* (1952), a story of Chip's experiences as an observer with a minor-league team. Books # 9, 10 and 11—*Freshman Quarterback* (1952), *Backboard Fever* (1953) and *Fence Busters* (1953)—cover Chip's freshman year at State University.

Chip's sophomore year is chronicled in #12 through #16, including the football stories *Ten Seconds to Play* (1955) and *Fourth Down Showdown* (1956), the basketball novels *Tournament Crisis* (1957) and *Hardcourt Upset* (1957) and the baseball story *Pay-Off Pitch* (1958).

Clutch Hitter! **Chip Hilton #4 by Clair Bee (jacket copyright 1949, Grosset & Dunlap). Artist Frank Vaughn portrays Bee's immortal three-sport star with his first cover as a hitter.**

One of the most remarkable books of the series was the summer baseball novel *No-Hitter* (1959), which appeared only 14 years after the end of World War II and talked of brotherhood between Americans and Japanese on Chip's trip to play in Japan. Written many years before Americans began paying attention to Japanese baseball, *No-Hitter*, the 17th book in the series, is remarkable for Bee's ability to predict Japanese diamond excellence and enthusiasm. If this wasn't the first such baseball novel about the Japanese game, it's close.

Bee followed with only one book about Chip's junior football season, *Triple Threat Trouble* (1960) but penned three novels about his junior basketball campaign: *Backcourt Ace* (1961), *Buzzer Basket* (1962) and *Comeback Cagers* (1963). Novel #22, *Home Run Feud* (1964), chronicled his junior baseball season. Alas, Chip's last basketball and baseball campaigns went untold, and we never find out about his pro baseball luck, either (readers were generally led to assume that pitching would be his pro sports pursuit).

Considering that Bee enjoyed great fame coaching basketball, although he knew plenty about coaching football and baseball as well, he achieved a nice balance with the Hilton series: nine books about baseball, eight covering basketball and seven about football, including the posthumous novel. When the stories were selling well in the 1950s and 1960s, three-sport high school athletes were still fairly common even in the larger schools. But now, the majority of high school athletes focus on only one or two sports, especially since being seen in select summer basketball or baseball settings has become increasingly important with regard to potential scholarships. The best basketball players now focus almost entirely on that sport year-round, simply because the competition for scholarship money is so fierce. (During the Chip Hilton era, African Americans were just getting started in college sports in the northerly parts of the country.)

Bronc Burnett's confusing career

Wilfred McCormick's 27-book Bronc Burnett series (including the scarce last three teaming with coach Rocky McCune) did not follow the logical order of the Chip Hilton books. In fact, Grosset & Dunlap juggled the order a bit for some of its 23 reprints, which are the books the vast majority of readers saw. The original volumes from Putnam and David McKay all had different pictorial dust jackets, several of the impressionistic variety, and they are hard to find today. The Grosset versions were so many times cheaper, beginning at either 75 cents or $1, that libraries were by far the primary purchasers of the more expensive first editions.

Of the 27 total Bronc Burnett books, 15 were about baseball and 10 about football, with one scouting story and one basketball book involving McCune and Burnett at Angor College. Bronc's Sonora team, including best friend "Fat" Crompton, his catcher, wins Sonora High's league title, the New Mexico State Legion championship and the regional four-state tournament in *Three-Two Pitch* (1948), and *Fielder's Choice* (1949), respectively, when Bronc is only 16 years old. Then they went on to win the sectional title in *Bases Loaded* (1950) and the national championship in the redundantly titled *Grand-Slam Homer* (1951).

The ensuing baseball books take Bronc and his teammates to Chicago, Mexico, Montreal, Vancouver, Alaska, Los Angeles and other venues. These books, full of solid "how-to" tips and accurate baseball lore, seem designed for younger readers than the Chip Hilton books, or at least they read that way. Whereas an adult can read a Chip Hilton book in much the same way Nancy Drew still can be entertaining, Bronc Burnett is more of a slog, in part because the plot lines— dealing with the likes of battles against the effects of superstitions, publicity and umpires— seem significantly simpler. Bee's bad guys were pretty bad, indeed, in Chip Hilton; McCormick's stories often center on self-esteem and self-awareness issues.

Bronc's first football story, *Flying Tackle* (1949), originally the fourth story for Putnam, finds him leading Sonora High to the conference title, followed by a state title in *Rambling Halfback* (1950), originally the sixth book. Oddly, the Grosset edition of *Flying Tackle* is #8 but refers to *Rambling Halfback* as next in the football series, even though Grosset already had published it fourth! In other words, Grosset published the wrong football book first. That must have confused a few readers. That was a hangover from the original, correct Putnam order of fourth and sixth, respectively, for *Flying Tackle* and *Rambling Halfback*.

Beginning with *Quick Kick* (1951), eighth in the Putnam series, Bronc and his buddies began to play in a series of special all-star games, in this case a charity game against Colorado all-stars. Bronc went on to play in New Orleans, San Francisco, Hawaii, New York's Yankee Stadium, Philadelphia and St. Louis.

Unlike the Chip Hilton books, which are best read in consecutive order, if possible, the Bronc Burnett series can be read in any order, especially after the first seven books in the original Putnam series. Oddly, *Flying Tackle* was chosen for Grosset's larger-size Famous Sports Story series in the mid–1950s, seemingly in direct conflict with the series-size volume still on the shelves. In addition to the 16-book Rocky McCune series, about which more follows in this chapter, McCormick also produced three books about pro athlete Roy Rolfe in the 1960s and two stories of college athlete Dyke Redman, the football story *First and Ten* (1952) and the baseball tale *The Starmaker* (1963). Collectors have discovered all five books are tough to find; they were not reprinted by Grosset, nor were the original 16 McCune stories. The Rolfe books, *The Pro Toughback* (1964) and *Touchdown for the Enemy* (1965) about football and *Rookie on First* (1967) about baseball, follow a 1960s trend of more novels about pro sports. Football and baseball big-time athletes such as Bo Jackson and Deion Sanders were yet to appear, so these books seem a bit prophetic, if somewhat disconnected from each other.

The best of Chip Hilton

Even though *Pitchers' Duel* (1950) was released out of sequence as the sixth Chip Hilton book instead of the seventh, the story was not weakened. This is perhaps the most emotional and intense of the 24 novels, since the fate of Hank Rockwell's coaching career hangs in the balance, right up to the final pages. Rockwell is seldom sentimental and always stubborn throughout the series, but his consistent sense of fair play shines for the readers and makes them admire such a coach.

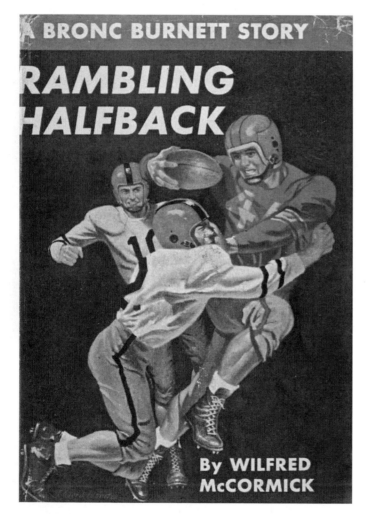

Rambling Halfback, Bronc Burnett #4 by Wilfred McCormick (jacket copyright 1950, Grosset & Dunlap). Burnett was the only real sports series book competition for Chip Hilton, but Burnett always appeared from other publishers first.

As a 65-year-old coach with 37 years of service as the story opens, Rockwell is the target of the town's political hacks and ambitious, jealous people who want him out as coach, including the clearly unethical sportswriter Muddy Waters. The verbal abuse of unsavory elements of a crowd — abuse that would not be allowed in most of America's high schools today — followed by a drink cleverly thrown into Rockwell's face present a situation too stressful for Chip and his buddies to bear. The principal of Valley Falls High suspends Chip on the spot after he and his buddies fight in the stands. It's a good lesson for a young reader, since Chip is clearly in the wrong, regardless of the nasty provocation.

The core members of the Hilton Athletic Club are forced to cope with Chip's absence for several games. Bee always carefully weaves introductions and background for the four key members throughout the series: peppery Soapy Smith, Chip's best friend and a three-sport athlete of limited but often useful versatility; brave Biggie Cohen, a

220-pound baseball and football star of monstrous strength who is every bit Chip's equal as an athlete; quick Speed Morris, a scrappy three-sport athlete at the skill positions; and reliable Red Schwartz, yet another three-sport athlete and always to be counted on when needed most. Their bantering seems natural in *Pitchers' Duel*. Soapy says, "I got an idea!" and Biggie tells him, "Treat it gently. It's in a strange place!"

Characters sometimes are allowed to behave in ways that wouldn't be tolerated in the real world, such as the way Muddy Waters ignores how Chip's triple puts him in position to score the winning run in a big game. No competent editor would have let such poor reporting go unchallenged, especially if he received a complaint. Bee, who was one of America's greatest basketball coaches, almost always writes with accuracy about any sport, although occasionally an error slips through, such as when he has Red Schwartz "lining a Texas League single" when, of course, that would be a bloop hit by definition, not a line drive.

Like John R. Tunis, Bee occasionally weaves philosophy into his stories, but he's almost never preachy about it, although he is occasionally

Pitchers' Duel, Chip Hilton #6 by Clair Bee (jacket copyright 1950, Grosset & Dunlap). Frank Vaughn employs an unusual cover angle.

more optimistic than real life might warrant. When Chip talks with an ethical baseball scout as he works out his difficulties in *Pitchers' Duel*, the scout tells him, "Everything will work out just the way you want it — if you want it badly enough! That's one of the wonderful things about this great country of ours — a fellow can do almost anything he sets out to do, providing it's honest, and he is honest in his desires and is willing to pay the price in study and work."

That's why the dust jacket blurb for the story quotes a teacher: "These Chip Hilton stories have the same quality that the John Tunis sports stories have — they teach good sportsmanship without the reader ever suspecting it. That's something that only a man who knows and likes boys could do!" Of course, girls read Chip Hilton, too; but in the 1950s, the pointed phrasing "boys and girls" was seldom seen in most literary situations.

Although Chip is clearly a paragon, Bee does not make him perfect. When a decent but erring sportswriter causes inadvertent trouble for Chip late in *Pitchers' Duel*, Bee writes: "For a brief second he almost hated Turk; felt like lashing out and driving his fists into the writer's face. But he remembered his mother's counsel and stifled the impulse."

The final game in *Pitchers' Duel* is pure Frank Merriwell — except for the ending, which is where Bee turns the then-50-year-old pulp convention on its head. As pitching ace Chip races to clear himself of a trumped-up charge of professionalism, Soapy Smith does his best pitching to keep Valley Falls in the championship game against Salem and even hits a grand slam to send it into extra innings. Chip arrives in time to strike out the opposition's final hitter in the bottom of the ninth — while wearing street clothes, a questionably allowable situation — then dons his uniform and pitches all the way through the 19th inning, striking out 14 batters. But the sportsmanlike opposing pitcher, Kip Parcels, pitches all 19 innings and wins the game, and the championship, with a fluke infield hit off Chip. That would never have happened in Merriwell, or in most pulp stories.

Rockwell, however, is forced to retire, since he is beyond the mandatory limits of 63 years of age and 35 years of service. True to the manly code of coaching, he doesn't say much to his boys, but they are distraught. "It's a dirty trick," Biggie says. "But you know the Rock! He's tough! He wouldn't let anyone know how he feels!" The coach's record is then summarized in a newspaper story: 37 years, 22 section championships in football, 19 in basketball and 14 in baseball; he has produced 55 title teams in 111 seasons of coaching! Chip's father, Big Chip, who died in an industrial accident when Chip was young, starred on several of those teams. The article concludes: "His personal interest, unswerving confidence, and loyalty to each boy who has played for him has built up in this community a love and respect which is a far greater tribute to the man than the hundreds of cups, trophies, medals and plaques which are on display in the Big Red's trophy room."

It's noteworthy that Chip, accompanied by his mother, Mary, at graduation, is with the mothers and fathers of all four of his closest friends, reflecting the family-centered era. Shortly after graduation, the boys score a victory, after all. Rock has decided to follow them to State University as freshman coach of football, basketball and baseball.

Rockwell had proved his worth, both as a tactical strategist and as a person. In the preceding fifth book, *Hoop Crazy* (1950), Rockwell demonstrates his courage by sending a black player, Clem Barnes, into action in a game on a special trip to Southern High, a place that had never allowed blacks to play. "The bedlam of yells and catcalls were too much for a sensitive youngster like Clem Barnes to take," and the youth takes himself out of the game. "I don't want to play against them if they don't want to play against me, Coach," he tells Rockwell. But the captain of Southern's team leads Barnes back onto the floor and he plays out the game, even though Valley Falls loses 41–35 (a score typical of the era). Bee writes:

> When the game was over, the first Negro boy ever to play against a white boy in the town of Southern never heard the deafening cheers which went up from the packed stands. And he never knew that many of those cheers were for him.... Some [of Southern's fans] even grudgingly admitted that the Negro boy was a good basketball player. But some were bitter and some were angry and some were ashamed. A few were proud, like the middle-aged man and his wife who made their way quietly toward the modest little home down near the river where a little name plate bearing the name of Berrien was tacked to the gatepost by the walk. And these two and many others could still see Southern's gallant young captain [Berrien] leading the Negro boy from Valley Falls out on to the floor. And most of these who walked out into the clean, cool night air after that great Southern victory somehow felt pride in the realization that the captain of the kids who represented their high school and their town was a courageous, bighearted boy who wasn't afraid to be a man.

In one of Chip's final high school games, Rockwell allows him a luxury: the opportunity to break Chip's father's school record of 39 points. Chip scores at the buzzer and is fouled, allowing him to score his 40th point, a mighty total indeed in a 1950 high school game and still close to many school records today. Mary Hilton, who is usually too nervous to attend most of Chip's games, closes her eyes and "was probably the only person in that building who did not see Chip drop a perfect toss through the basket to set a new Valley Falls High School scoring record of 40 points in thirty-two minutes of play" (as Bee writes).

It's strongly suggested in the seventh book, *A Pass and a Prayer* (1951), that Rockwell's enemies in town are out to see him retired by the school district, which makes it obvious even to the reader that this football story was printed out of sequence of Chip's senior year, which became basketball, baseball and then football in the fifth through seventh books. *A Pass and a Prayer* is unusually melodramatic for the Chip Hilton series, presenting a thor-

oughly detestable new football coach, Tom Bracken, who has been placed on the staff by the town's mayor without the permission of Rockwell or his long-time assistant, kindly Chet Stewart.

Bracken, actually playing in an intrasquad scrimmage in what would be considered grounds for a lawsuit today, injures a Valley Falls player early in the story. Yet when Rockwell falls seriously ill and can't coach, Bracken is placed in power and recruits a mouthy "ringer," Tug Rankin, to replace Chip. Bracken even twice drops Chip from the squad for fancied offenses. This story is sometimes painful to read, especially when Chip scores on what he improvises into a fake punt after he has been instructed to kick, then is cut from the team by an enraged Bracken.

With Chip still out but due back, thanks to protests, Bracken runs up the score behind Rankin in a 65–0 victory. But both Rankin and his father, who has moved to Valley Falls to take a much-needed job, soon are exposed, because Chip discovers Rankin already has played four seasons of high school football and is thus ineligible.

Before Rankin is exposed, however, there's a whirlwind of

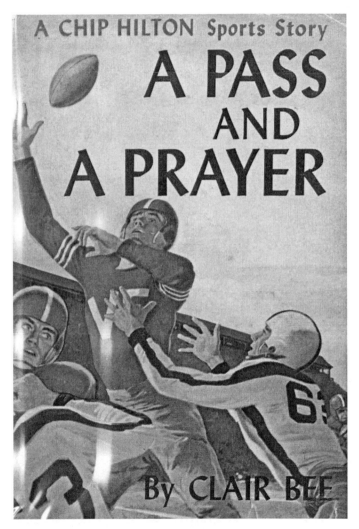

A Pass and a Prayer, **Chip Hilton #7 by Clair Bee (jacket copyright 1951, Grosset & Dunlap). Frank Vaughn puts a pulp feeling into this cover. This book actually should have been #5 and the real #5, *Hoop Crazy*, should have been #6. *Pitchers' Duel* should have been #7 instead of #6. It's the only time any Hilton books appeared out of the correct aging sequence of the 23 originals; there was also a 24th posthumous book.**

melodrama. In the penultimate game in *A Pass and a Prayer*, Chip fakes a field goal and passes to Red Schwartz for the winning touchdown, leading an enraged Bracken to drop Chip from the squad for the third time. Chip and Speed Morris then race to Illinois, bent on proving Bracken illegally recruited Tug Rankin. Meanwhile, sportswriter Pete Williams decks Muddy Waters in a fight while looking into the skullduggery. Rockwell, realizing what Bracken has been up to, leaves the hospital and tries to take over the team on the Monday before the big game, but Bracken loses all control and attacks the still weak, 63-year-old Rockwell in the locker room. Bracken also knocks out assistant coach Chet Stewart. To the rescue of both coaches comes mighty 220-pound lineman Biggie Cohen, one of Chip's lifelong friends. Cohen makes short work of Bracken and breaks his jaw, but Biggie is expelled by the school principal while Chip and Speed, having acquired the evidence they need, race back to Valley Falls.

The title of the last chapter tells it all: "Undefeated. Untied, Uncrowned." Valley Falls must forfeit all its victories when Chip exposes Rankin. Bracken is first humiliated, then fired. A repentant Rankin, however, is allowed to continue in school, because by this time he realizes what a foul fellow Bracken really is. But one vital aspect of the plot does not ring true: Bracken admits he fooled Rankin's father, John, into moving to Valley Falls for a desperately needed job, so John Rankin was not part of Bracken's scheme to bring in Tug Rankin. It's difficult to imagine any father not being aware that high school eligibility is limited to four seasons. But, of course, the entire story hinged on the otherwise-honest father's ignorance, and most readers probably didn't question this, especially the younger readers. Chip's field goal then wins the final game 3–0, giving the Big Reds an unbeaten season on the field. Oddly, with the two coaches sidelined because of their fight with Bracken, Bee allows Chip and Tug to coach the team! Of course, it's highly unlikely this would have been allowed in 1951 and certainly not today for reasons of liability. Bee should have mentioned that a faculty member from Valley Falls had technically been placed in charge. Even so, this is quite a story, isn't it? Such drama is one reason readers have never forgotten Chip Hilton, even 50 years later.

Chip becomes a social worker and college hero

Chip's first experiences in varsity football as a sophomore at State University — not to mention his remarkable conscience and sensitivity to other people — are detailed in two inspirational books, *Ten Seconds to Play* (1955) and *Fourth Down Showdown* (1956), the 12th and 13th books. Bee took a gamble of his own in *Ten Seconds to Play*, using more than half the story to detail Chip's experiences as a counselor at a state-of-the-art summer sports camp. It's there Chip meets an inspiring group of adults and tries to figure out another camp counselor, the supremely talented but arrogant athlete Philip Whittemore. The only football in the book occurs in the last third of the story, which is devoted to scrimmages and the first game, played on October 2. Even though the Chip Hilton stories remain eminently readable, such a late date for a college season opener stamps the story as antiquated, since workouts now begin in August and most teams open their seasons in late August or the first week of September. But then, big-time college football seasons have expanded from nine games in Chip Hilton's era to 12 or 13 today, even before the advent of bowl games.

The healthy philosophy that permeates the Chip Hilton series is expressed by one of the adult counselors early in the story in a conversation with Chip: "No two boys are alike,

Chip. Every youngster has a hidden spark and requires a lot of observation and study before anyone can really understand what makes him tick. Most people judge a youngster by his personality. But lots of boys— and girls too, for that matter — have little or no personality. The old saying 'You can't judge a book by its cover' just about expresses the point." Later, another counselor, while giving the boys a bit of a history lesson, tells them, "Well, boys, you know how much emphasis I place on athletics. But more important, much more important, is love of country."

Whittemore proves himself to be a coward in four separate situations, especially during a lightning storm, and Chip commits himself to helping him after Whittemore realizes how much Chip has put on the line while knocking out two hoodlums to rescue him. (Chip is a trained boxer by this point in the series.) Whittemore decides to join Chip at State University and by the end of the book has become a fast friend, much as Chip converted former rival Fireball Finley in his freshman season.

That's only part of the plot-packed story in *Ten Seconds to Play*. The last 90 pages of the 213-page story reveal how Chip and his sophomore buddies not only win places on the varsity, but also earn important starting roles over juniors and seniors with more experience. It's made clear that head coach Curly Ralston's philosophy is the same as Hank Rockwell's: to "play the best man" regardless of age or experience. That's a valuable lesson for teenage readers, who learn that a player must prove himself every season. As a coach/author, Bee constantly stresses ethics, and he makes it clear that there is nothing ethical about keeping a more talented sophomore on the bench and letting a less-talented senior play.

Chip wins the starting quarterback job over Tims Lansing (yes, Tims, not Tim), a two-year starter. When Lansing, an old friend of Whittemore, tells him he has lost his job at quarterback, Lansing's sportsmanship shines through: "Hilton's a better player," Lansing says. "A better runner, passer and kicker. Anyone who saw him yesterday against Western and stopped to think about it realizes it as well as I do. He's out of my class.... You've heard Ralston say a dozen times that the best man gets the job. Well, Hilton's the best man.... I'm going to block the daylights out of him [in practice] and tackle him and rough him up [Bee means hard but fair play] every time I get a chance, so he'll be even better than he is, and then when Saturday rolls around and I'm sitting on the bench I'm going to pull for [Chip] as if he were my own brother." And when the astonished Whittemore says, "You mean you're not going to quit?" Lansing replies, "Quit! You crazy? Football players never quit!" Such lines made Bee every bit as important as Tunis in helping young readers form concepts of dignity, determination and self-worth.

Chip eventually learns that Whittemore's cowardice stems from a day when he was 12 years old and could not bring himself to rescue a girl whom he thought was swept out to sea. Then Bee throws in a pulp plot device, having Chip accidentally discover who that girl was and enabling Whittemore to find out she's alive, after all. There's even an intimation, after Chip works up a double date that includes the girl, that she and Whittemore will eventually form a romantic connection. The story climaxes with Chip using trick strategy, the old "Statue of Liberty" play, on which Whittemore scores the winning touchdown. Whittemore becomes not only a hero but a good person, as Chip's head coach puts it, "all because of [Chip's] unswerving loyalty, courage and belief in another boy."

Fourth Down Showdown is just as revealing of Chip's decency off the field in a story dealing with the rest of his first varsity season. He battles juvenile delinquency — a major pop cultural theme in the books and films of 1956 — in his college town while playing football. In the end Chip's courage and boxing skills enable him to defeat the two thugs who have held the town's youth in fear, including brothers Eddie and Mark Redding, young teenagers Chip is mentoring. In a cathartic but patently illegal scene, Biggie Cohen and Fireball Finley hurl the two defeated thugs over a fence! That scenario, which in real life might well have killed the thugs, is similar to the endless fistfights in movie serials and western films.

During Chip's battle against the delinquents, one event results in Chip's and Soapy Smith's one-game suspension for breaking the coach's 11:00 P.M. curfew, and another situation causes the suspension of all six of Chip's sophomore buddies (the four from Valley Falls plus Finley and Whittemore). The reader admires how Chip and Soapy self-report themselves the first time, and how all the sophomores accept their suspension the second time. Yet the reader is also baffled by Chip's insistence on not telling his coaches why they have twice broken curfew. Chip explains it this way when his mother asks him why the coach wouldn't understand, since Chip was trying to help two youngsters: "You did just right," she tells him. "I'm proud of you. But couldn't you tell the coach what you've told me? Wouldn't he understand?" Chip's response is one of the least sensible statements in the entire series, considering the effect his actions have on the entire team: "He'd understand all right, Mother. But a fellow can't ask for sympathy or take credit for helping a friend. I just couldn't do it. It would sound like trying to be a hero or something like that. I don't care for myself, but it isn't right for the rest of the fellows to suffer just because they wanted to help me."

Such martyrdom doesn't ring true, especially after the boys and their parents successfully appeal the suspensions to the coaches. Chip and his teammates are reinstated on the day of the championship game. But having returned to Valley Falls, they race more than 200 miles to the stadium in time to play in the final quarter. Then Bee adds a sweet touch. To win the game on the final play, Chip calls a fake field goal on a play designed by Tims Lansings to take advantage of the fleet Speed Morris. Chip's buddy scores on the play and the always sportsmanlike Lansings— whose career had been ended by an injury early in the story when he fills in for Chip —can enjoy the satisfaction of a major role in the momentous victory.

Jack McCallum's historic rediscovery of Chip Hilton

Just as Jackson Scholz was the only Olympic star to become a prolific author of sports fiction, Clair Bee was Scholz's only famed counterpart in the college coaching ranks. It was with total fascination, then, that three decades ago I read a historic piece by Jack McCallum in *Sports Illustrated* about Bee, one of the greatest of all college basketball coaches, and his three-sport hero, Chip Hilton.

McCallum, who was 30 when he wrote "A Hero for All Times" in the January 7, 1980, issue of *Sports Illustrated*, went on to a distinguished career as an editor and writer at the magazine. But at the time I read this, I was only a couple of years older than McCallum. I thought it was odd that such a young writer would be nostalgic for fairly recent pop culture; it had been only 14 years since the last original Chip Hilton book, the now famously collectible *Hungry Hurler* (1966), the 23rd in the series. (At the time, no one knew that Bee's manuscript for a 24th book, *Fiery Fullback*, would be published in 2002.) As a writer about pop culture as well as various aspects of news and sports, in 1980 I was more intrigued by the 1930s and 1940s.

McCallum, though, not only spotlighted the remarkable Bee, who was then 83, but was surely the first writer to feature the series sports books of the 1940s, 1950s and 1960s in a national publication. McCallum pretty much did for Chip Hilton and Clair Bee what the famed cartoonist Jules Feiffer did for Golden Age superheroes of the late 1930s and early 1940s in his book *The Great Comic Book Heroes* (1965), since no doubt many more people read McCallum's article than Feiffer's groundbreaking pop-cultural tome. By 1980, numerous books had been written about the likes of comic books, pulp magazines, B westerns and movie serials, but the thousands of 1900–1970s series books remained a relatively still-fresh field for researchers and writers (the last original Hardy Boys and Nancy Drew hardcovers appeared in 1979, before both series went to paperback formats).

In no way, then, do I mean to be unfairly critical in the following observations, since McCallum did not have the reference sources, nor the massive collection of sports fiction, I used while writing this book. I have nothing but admiration for McCallum's social honesty, since in 1980 pop culture studies had not taken the strong hold they have today, and it may have been a bit risky to personally acknowledge such a love of a genre that McCallum himself acknowledged as dead in 1980. I greatly admired McCallum for the article, and still do.

McCallum revealed for the first time that Bee's model for Chip Hilton was the former Seton Hall athletic great Bob Davies, who competed against Bee's Long Island University basketball teams before Davies went on to a fine career in the National Basketball Association. Bee also revealed that he himself was the model for Chip's highly competitive, no-nonsense, yet wise and kind coach, Hank Rockwell. To no one's surprise, considering that both Bee and the mythical Frank Merriwell were born in 1896, Bee talked of his youthful love for the Merriwell epics. When McCallum told Bee he read his Hilton books with similar affection and enthusiasm, Bee responded "You don't say — Why, that makes me happy. Very happy."

McCallum also interviewed Davies, who was a four-sport high school star in Harrisburg, Pennsylvania, and earned Bee's admiration for his performance, poise and sportsmanship in college. It was fascinating to learn that Davies, like Bee a member of the Basketball Hall of Fame in Springfield, Massachusetts, never knew he was the inspiration for Chip Hilton until he visited Bee in 1957, nine years after the beginning of the series. At that time, the series had reached the 14th book, *Tournament Crisis* (1957), which was about Chip's sophomore basketball season at State University. "Clair was the smartest basketball mind that ever lived," Davies told McCallum, who noted that Bee's 82.7 percent career winning percentage was still the record for college basketball (John Wooden started relatively slowly at UCLA).

While accurately stating the seminal influence of the Merriwell family novels on millions of youthful readers, McCallum also noted that Chip Hilton's book series peer and rival for young readers' dollars, Bronc Burnett, was the last of the Merriwellian breed along with Chip himself. It's noteworthy that McCallum described the "11-volume Bronc Burnett series," since the series was really 24 volumes, plus three more in conjunction with Wilfred McCormick's other major sports creation, coach Rocky McCune. Grosset & Dunlap, Bee's first-edition publisher for Chip Hilton, also reprinted the 11 Putnam and 12 David McKay volumes of Bronc Burnett's football and baseball exploits, with Grosset beginning publication of both Chip and Bronc in 1948. I've always felt the Bronc Burnett books took a distinct backseat to Chip Hilton, and McCallum's 1980 article provides substantiation for this feeling.

"You can't get the Chip Hilton books anymore," said McCallum, who wrote that Bee "cranked them out in the 1940s and '50s," when in reality the 18th through 23rd volumes were published from 1960 to 1966. "The Strand Book Store in New York City, which specializes in out-of-print volumes, has none of the Hilton series on its shelves.... About the only place to find a Hilton book now is at a flea market, among old National Geographics."

That was McCallum's experience in 1979, when he wrote the article, but I have seen hundreds of copies of the Hilton books on store shelves during the past 30 years while building my collection of many thousands of books of various aspects of genre fiction by scouting through well over 500 book and antique stores in nearly as many cities in almost every state. Since the Hiltons, especially with dust jackets, are generally considered the most collectible by series book enthusiasts, dealers have eagerly sought to stock them for years. Dust jackets, of course, are usually well over 80 or 90 percent of the value of a series book, just as they are for first editions of the likes of John Steinbeck, Raymond Chandler and Robert Heinlein, with the value of any volume largely dependent on the condition of both the book and, especially, the dust jacket. The last Hilton in a dust jacket was the 19th book, *Backcourt Ace* (1961), and thus is the scarcest in jacket since there were few, if any, reprints of the book in jacket. The first 19 Hiltons were reprinted during the 1960s—still in hardcover but now with pictorial covers matching the original jackets—but the 20th through 23rd books appeared only in pictorial covers, sans jacket. In general, the higher the number, the more valuable a series book, and such is the case with Chip Hilton. And, though McCallum could not have foreseen eBay, the Internet makes Hilton stories more readily available than ever, at a wide variety of prices.

"This may be the last piece ever written about the Chip Hilton books," said McCallum. "It may also be the first, because Chip never spawned a cottage industry of nostalgic scholarship like that which grew out of the Merriwell stories." This book, of course, and several other pieces of pop cultural scholarship have happily proven McCallum wrong. Later McCallum wrote, "And the Hiltons still in circulation will never become collector's items of the class of, say, an original Merriwell. People like me, who wouldn't sell a Hilton for $500, are few and far between." The *Sports Illustrated* writer, however astute in most cases, could not have been more wrong about Hilton vs. Merriwell.

The Hilton books, especially the uncommon and scarce higher numbers, are hotly collected now, and I know several enthusiasts who have proudly amassed complete files. *Hungry Hurler* in fine condition would not be expensive at $500, though the earlier books are considerably less. But all of the Hiltons in fine dust jackets are worth more than the vast majority of the original 1896–1916 Merriwell nickel magazines, which are of only minimal interest now to most pop culture enthusiasts and can often be acquired for less than $10 each, even the ones with the sports covers. Not long ago, I purchased several of the Merriwell paperback reprints—the ones circa 1910 or 1920 that reprinted four or five of the stories together, with colorful covers—for only $2 each, and this at a major pop culture gathering, with hundreds of collectors who, mostly, thoroughly ignored the Merriwells. Dime novels that were worth $5 or $10 in 1940—figures now well over $50 to $100 in constant dollars—are difficult to sell for $5 or $10 in today's dollars. The original readers and the original collectors have passed on and few people remain to take an interest in them. (Not a few collectors have speculated that most 20th century pop culture will be of little interest beginning at about 2030 or maybe earlier.)

McCallum touched briefly on Bee's devastating heartbreak when the college basketball point-shaving scandals of the early 1950s touched one of his LIU stars during Bee's last season (1950–51). "He was still writing the Hilton series— specifically, the college books about the time [the scandals] broke, but never made the scandal part of his fiction," McCallum said. This was surely just as well, especially from a business and current-events standpoint, because Bee's first college story, *Freshman Quarterback*, wasn't published until 1952, and Bee's books about Chip's first college varsity basketball season didn't appear until 1957 and 1958. Given the public's reaction to the scandals, they were quickly snuffed, and scandals in the Hilton books would have made them seem woefully out of date. Score a 3-pointer (even though they didn't exist in those days) for Bee's authorial sense.

McCallum reported that Bee had "desperately wanted" to keep the price of the Chip Hilton books at $1 (the first three, at least, started at 75 cents, and I have the dust jackets to prove it). They were still $1 in 1960, as shown by my childhood copies of the beloved Nancy Drew and Rick Brant Grosset & Dunlap series and by the dust jacket of my first edition of Grosset's *Triple Threat Trouble*, the 18th Chip Hilton book, published in 1960. (Rick Brant was essentially a teen version of Doc Savage, the immortal pulp hero of the 1930s and 1940s.) When Grosset began publishing pictorial cover series books in hardcover in 1961 (and a year or two later for some characters), prices were not included on most of the books! It was thus left to the stores to price them, and this may have led to the problem of price increases. The comic book industry solved the price problem by cutting page counts from 64 interior pages in most 1934–1943 issues to 56 pages in 1943 and 1944, then soon to 48 (advertised as "a 52-page magazine," counting the covers, circa 1950), and finally to 32 (in some cases, as early as the 1940s). After Dell flirted with a 15-cent price point on some titles as early as 1957, comic book publishers late in 1961 all raised the price of the 32-page issues to at least 12 cents, to become 15 cents in 1969 and 20 or 25 cents soon thereafter. So the idea of keeping Chip Hilton at $1 was simply unrealistic. In fact, when the updated Chip Hilton series was begun in 1998 in paperback, the price was $5.99 — then more expensive than some originals sans jackets!

Ironically, Bee told McCallum, "Sure sales went down. There was also radio and television. And kids couldn't pay as much as they were asking. Why, the books weren't worth $2. Even in my mind today, I don't think they're worth $2." He went on: "I think about getting them out in paperback. You know, sell them cheap. I think they'd go good. I don't know, but I think they would." By 1979, however, when Bee said that, even mass-market paperbacks such as Bantam's Doc Savage reprints were $1.75, having risen from their original price point of 45 cents in 1964. In 1979, neither Chip Hilton nor any other hardback or paperback hero would ever again sell for $1 except in used-book stores (if then) and at flea markets and garage sales. By the mid–1980s, even 32-page comic books were $1, on the way to much higher prices.

If you want to read what still remains perhaps the best piece ever done on series books, find *A Hero for All Times* in the January 7, 1980, *Sports Illustrated*. If Chip Hilton's feats warm you, so will this piece by Jack McCallum. It still remains the tribute of all tributes for the best of all sports heroes.

The unique coach: Rocky McCune

During the two-decade run of 48 sports novels by Wilfred McCormick from 1948 to 1967, the prolific author experimented with a unique format: the continuing exploits of a high school coach. McCormick produced 16 Rocky McCune novels from 1955 to 1965, beginning the series well before the creation of the famed comic-strip coach Gil Thorp. McCormick also costarred McCune and Bronc Burnett in the final three Bronc Burnett books, # 25–27, from 1966 to 1968. Some enthusiasts have speculated that the three Roy Rolfe novels (1964–67) and the two Dyke Redman stories (1952 and 1963) were also part of the series, but those characters existed in a sports universe apart from McCune and Burnett.

Like the much older coach Hank Rockwell in the contemporary Chip Hilton series, McCune was a young, single-minded, straight arrow devoted to helping young men mature into productive citizens but not necessarily into college or professional athletes. In the two postwar decades when Chip, Bronc, and Rocky reigned supreme in the young-adult sports story league, far fewer students attended college for any reason, much less sports, than do today. In addition, in vivid contrast to the current college scene, the percentage of African American athletes on college teams during those years was miniscule. Blacks thus are rare in sports stories written before the 1970s, even though they began to make serious inroads in pro sports in the 1950s and 1960s after Jackie Robinson broke Major League Baseball's color barrier in 1947 with the Brooklyn Dodgers. Prior to the civil rights movement and legislation of the mid–1960s, few black students were encouraged — or allowed — to attend college.

The Rocky McCune stories still hold up fairly well today, although it seems quaint to see anyone handle the head coaching duties in varsity football, basketball and baseball at the same school, especially with minimal help. No doubt the original McCune readers would be astonished to see football coaching staffs of 10 to 12 men or even more, which is not that unusual at large high schools today. McCune, though, starred in those sports at Koulee High before returning as a coach following his college years. The McCune stories often tend to read like primers for potential coaches dealing with a variety of challenges coaches faced in those years. In two respects, however, they are badly dated: McCune rarely deals with the issues of college scholarships and college scouts, and he doesn't have to worry much about drugs.

McCormick wrote nine McCune baseball stories. *The Man on the Bench* (1955) began the overall 16-book series and *Wild on the Bases* (1965) ended the series, and both are baseball tales. The second book, *The Captive Coach* (1956), was a football story, as was *The Bigger Game* (1958), which is sometimes listed as the third McCune book but is really the fourth. *The Hot Corner* (1958), a baseball story, is actually the third book and lists *The Bigger Game* as forthcoming.

In 1959, McCormick produced both a McCune football novel, *Five Yards to Glory*, and a baseball tale, *The Proud Champions*. *Five Yards to Glory* is sometimes listed as the fifth book but it actually appeared after *The Proud Champions*, as certified in the first edition of *Five Yards*. Stories of football coaching, however, apparently didn't appeal as much to McCormick — or perhaps his patrons and readers — and he wrote no more McCune football stories until he met up with Bronc Burnett, who was a baseball and football player throughout his 27-book series. McCormick did, however, devote two of his three later Roy Rolfe novels to football.

There is a "phantom" McCune football story, *Fourth and Forty*, plugged as upcoming in both the baseball tale *The Automatic Strike* (1960), which is seventh in the series, and *Too Many Forwards* (1960), which is eighth in the series and the first of the four basketball novels. *Fourth and Forty*, however, never appeared, as confirmed in the complete list of

McCormick's sports oeuvre that appeared in the Roy Rolfe baseball story *Rookie on First* (1967). McCormick, though, was so prolific that it's doubtful readers were disappointed.

Rocky McCune did not gain anywhere near the exposure that Bronc Burnett enjoyed, since neither Grosset and Dunlap nor anyone else reprinted the McCune stories, which were published by the David McKay Company. Grosset and Dunlap reprinted the first 23 Burnett stories, so McCune apparently was not considered popular enough to reprint. With prices as high as three dollars for *The Bigger Game* in 1958 and *Too Many Forwards* in 1960, in contrast to the one dollar Grossets, it's likely that libraries purchased the vast majority of the McCunes. Indeed, it's extremely difficult to find McCunes in nice condition with dust jackets (or even to find ex-library copies), and they are valued significantly higher than most Burnetts. Three dollars was a very high price for a young-adult novel in 1960. Indeed, the handsomely produced Winston science fiction novels — a 36-book hardback series with beautiful dust jackets originally produced from 1952 to 1961 — sold for $2.50 in 1959.

Most librarians of the 1950s and 1960s did not buy original Grosset and Dunlap series characters, such as Nancy Drew and the Hardy Boys, despite their immense popularity, although they have long since backed down from that stance. Series books were often considered a higher-grade literary version of comic books. Yet librarians would buy the Burnetts from Putnam (#1–11), McKay (#12–23) and Bobbs-Merrill (#24–27) simply because they were produced by "good" publishers.

Basketball stories, a sorely lagging third behind baseball and football through the 1950s, became more popular in the 1960s and beyond, especially as professional basketball grew and the National College Athletic Association began promoting what became known as March Madness during its tournament. Powerhouses like Coach John Wooden's UCLA champions of the 1960s and 1970s captured the public's imagination. McCormick responded with three more Rocky McCune basketball stories: *The Play for One* (1961), *The Five Man Break* (1962), and *The Two-One-Two Attack* (1963).

McCune also appeared in five more baseball epics during this period, with one appearing each year during baseball season: *The Double Steal* (1961), *Home Run Harvest* (1962), *The Phantom Shortstop* (1963), *The Long Pitcher* (1964) and *Wild on the Bases* (1965).

Although Hank Rockwell continued to play a major role in the Chip Hilton high school and college stories, there was really nothing like McCormick's McCune stories on the market during the late 1950s and early 1960s. Several other prolific authors wrote tales with coaches as the primary protagonists, but they were one-off novels.

The McCune method

As McCune was portrayed as a former officer in the U.S. Army, official in the Boy Scouts of America, and president of the Crippled Children's Society, McCormick infused his Rocky McCune stories with frequent lessons on citizenship and moral obligations. There is no better example than his second McCune baseball story, *The Hot Corner* (1958), which is primarily (but not exclusively) concerned with salvaging the character of an orphaned scalawag named Red Bostic "from the tenement district of lower Chicago." Bostic, a pitcher and third baseman, is a twisted but highly personable and popular young genius, capable of throwing unhittable but illegal pitches along with picking both pockets and locks. McCune is appalled and dedicates himself to saving Bostic from a future in prison, if he can. McCune, of course, can and does accomplish the mission, and Bostic frequently returns to star in future books.

From the first page of *The Hot Corner*, McCormick leaves no doubt in the reader's mind that young Rocky is, in today's vernacular, a hard-ass, albeit a fair one. He throws one of his most dedicated players, Bert Winter, out of practice for clowning, then relents when Winter convinces his coach that Bostic is throwing something mighty strange during batting practice. "Go on to the showers," McCune tells Winter. "And be out here tomorrow ready to work!" Soon, though, the coach has second thoughts, and tells Winter, "Come on back, Bert! They say a wise man changes his mind, but a fool never does! I'm changing mine," to which Winter responds, "Gee, thanks, Coach!" McCune quickly detects that Bostic has been scratching baseballs with an emery board, resulting in illegal pitches, but the coach must move slowly. Bostic, who saved three people from a fire in which his parents died, is well liked in his new environs.

High school baseball, then seldom anywhere near as popular as football or basketball, is inexplicably big in Koulee. It's so big, in fact, that the school's "seventy-piece band" leads a parade through downtown before the first league game and the band plays at the contest. The vast majority of American regular-season high school games, of course, did not, and still don't, draw 70 fans, much less band members, so this sidelight is typical of how McCormick enhances the importance of his characters in the life of the town. For the next home game, for example, McCune must concern himself with selecting ticket printers and extensive police presence for crowd control! It's informative for readers to learn that a coach's duties often take place off the field, but McCormick goes somewhat over the top, to say the least, in describing the popularity of regular-season high school baseball games.

Oddly, McCormick thoroughly reveals McCune's character, and does an outstanding job with Bostic's quirky aspects, but the vast majority of his other players are pretty much just names. In *The Hot Corner*, there's very little description or characterization of other players, other than the girl trouble encountered by lovestruck pitcher Junior Nesbitt. The author includes the standings of the clubs, but he would have done better to also include a team roster, so the reader could better keep names and positions straight. On the other hand, McCormick does an outstanding job in discussing the mental and physical challenges of baseball, and often provides frequent playing and coaching tips. On balance, the McCune books are solid and accurate.

Even so, the finish of *The Hot Corner* relied too heavily on coincidence, since it takes an injury to the third baseman during the game to get Red Bostic into the championship contest and a second injury to the pitcher to put Bostic on the mound. Bostic displays his courage, ending the game with a fine fielding play after he has been injured by a line drive to his face, and one gets the distinct impression that his misbehavior is over, on and off the mound.

Football the McCune way

McCormick's first Rocky McCune football story, *The Captive Coach*, told how his Kouleans won the conference football championship, since Rocky himself played for Koulee High. His second football tale, *The Bigger Game*, is painful to read. It's a truly bizarre account of Koulee's reward: a trip to New York's Yankee Stadium to play a big-city powerhouse, DeWitt Clinton. What made this book so strange were the psychological tests and behavioral experiments conducted by the game's sponsor, the mythical Creager Educational Foundation. To his credit, Rocky often finds the experience distasteful; but his players want to play, so he goes along with the research conducted by professors affiliated with the foundation.

There's nothing overtly harmful — sending Koulee's players to a rundown practice facility isn't all that horrible, for example — but the story of the foundation's manipulations nonetheless creates a distasteful impression. But then, there wouldn't be a plot without those machinations. A weak opponent is deliberately chosen for Koulee's first scrimmage, with leaks to newspapers designed to test Koulee's mental adjustment. The second scrimmage involves college-age players; this would be considered horrifying today because of the injury potential. Rocky, to his credit, refuses to participate any more than necessary in the foundation's schemes.

One of the most astonishing aspects of this story is that McCune has no assistant coaches or adult chaperones! Or at least none are mentioned. His only "assistant" is his student-manager. Even more than 50 years ago, it would have been considered a ludicrous idea to travel to New York City without any other adult help to supervise a team of 33 youngsters (McCormick specifies the number).

Although calling football players "girls" was a common motivational stratagem more than half a century ago — and probably remains so in some locales — it's sad that Rocky falls into this sexist trap. During halftime of the big game, when he tries to point out "the profs" had sent a letter offering good advice to the team, the players still have their doubts, since they wonder if Rocky has really had their best interests at heart during the trip. Rocky ends the halftime meeting thusly: "My word is enough. I shouldn't have to prove anything to *men*. Come on, girls. Powder your faces and put on your bonnets — tea will be served in just two minutes!" Then, as the team is on the sideline, about to start the second half, he says, "You're playing a doubleheader here today. A big game, and a little game. The little game is against DeWitt Clinton. The big one is against yourselves. Apparently you girls need a pretty new hair ribbon, or some sort of prize to make you play. All right, I'll give you an incentive: Win these two games here today, and afterward — as *men* — you can duck me in the shower with my clothes on!"

Big running back Ralph Piers, the school's catcher in baseball, performs magic on the final play — a game-winning 99-yard touchdown pass. Early in the story, it's specified that he is the team's strongest passer; but since he's color blind, he can't differentiate uniform colors and thus can't be used as the regular quarterback. But the team devised a trick play, with the ball snapped directly to Piers, to be used in dire circumstances. This contrived finish is entertaining, if hardly likely, since the odds are highly against any strong defense allowing a 99-yard touchdown on the final play, regardless of who passes the ball. In contrast to the solid baseball tips covered in *The Hot Corner*, very little viable football knowledge is conveyed in *The Bigger Game*.

Oddly, and incorrectly, McCormick also has one of the foundation's professors make an astonishing statement about college students while discussing occupational aptitudes: "Nowadays no young man [!] is admitted to a reputable university until a series of tests has indicated his proper field." This clearly inaccurate statement, even coming from a fictional professor instead of narration by the author, pretty much caps an odd, less-than-pleasant story.

A better football story

The third and final Rocky McCune football novel, *Five Yards to Glory*, was a far stronger and more interesting story than *The Bigger Game*. The five yard reference is to the unique game-winning final play against previously unbeaten Charles City.

In this story, Red Bostic becomes Koulee's quarterback and displays plenty of talent. But because of his big-city tenement background and temper, Bostic finds himself under attack from booster club members who feel he's giving Koulee a bad image. Rocky, recalling how much Bostic matured in *The Hot Corner*, is convinced the boy is a worthwhile project and spends the story proving it.

McCune's verbal sparring with booster club members, plus an honest but erring Koulee newspaperman, holds up well today, with crackling tension and crisp dialog. This is a top-notch football story, with an unusual twist: Rocky has Red display his bruises for the booster club to see after Red has played hard but clean during a victory.

McCormick's penchant for fantastic finishes and contrived coincidences shows up again when Bostic's right (throwing) hand is stepped on in the final seconds of the championship game. Bostic fools his coach, his fans and the opponent when he bandages his hand and stays in the game, only to throw a winning pass left-handed on the final play!

A switch-blade knife, purportedly owned by Bostic, plays a major role in the story, typifying America's pop cultural fascination with juvenile delinquency in 1959. Early in the story, an unsportsmanlike opponent named Breeb Restor shows up briefly. Five years later, in the Roy Rolfe novel *The Pro Toughback*, the name reappears as Breeb Hendron.

Much space is devoted to unfair journalism early in the story. That's the weakest aspect of the tale; such writing would be rarely, if ever, allowed today, and it wasn't common even in small-town papers of the late 1950s.

A fourth McCune football novel dealing with a regional tournament, *Fourth and Forty*, was promised but never appeared.

Ed Fitzgerald's admirable Marty Ferris trilogy

One of the best short series of novels in the history of baseball fiction tells the tale of Marty Ferris, as told by Ed Fitzgerald, who served as editor of *Sport* magazine and became one of the best known sports journalists of the postwar era. All three books—*The Turning Point* (1948), *College Slugger* (1950) and *Yankee Rookie* (1952)—were originally printed by A.S. Barnes and Company, which called itself "The World's Largest Publisher of Books on Sport." Barnes, which produced both fact and fiction, produced many of Chip Hilton creator Clair Bee's technical books on basketball.

The series features colorful—and perfect—continuity as Fitzgerald takes young-adult readers, and probably a few adults as well, through Ferris' senior year of high school in White Plains, New York, his college days at Fordham University and part of his rookie season with the New York Yankees. These books are nowhere near as frequently found as the Chip Hilton and Bronc Burnett stories, particularly the scarce first volume, the oddly named *The Turning Point*, which has to be one of the strangest names of the period for a sports story. *The Turning Point* was published only by Barnes, but Grosset & Dunlap reprinted the other two books in its Famous Sports Stories series.

Ferris grew up not many miles from Yankee Stadium. As *The Turning Point* opens, he is a senior center fielder at White Plains High School. The book debuted in 1948, three years before Mickey Mantle joined the New York Yankees, who won 14 American League pennants from 1949 through 1964 in the most dominant such streak in baseball history. Mantle, who did not play college baseball, was still in the minors when *College Slugger* appeared in 1950. But Mantle's rookie year struggles in 1951, when he was briefly sent back to the minor leagues, may have influenced Fitzgerald's story in the final volume. *Yankee Rookie*, copyrighted 1952, definitely was concluded after the 1951 season, since Fitzgerald refers to Bobby Thomson's National League pennant-winning home run for the New York Giants in a playoff with the Brooklyn Dodgers.

Obviously written by a man who knew New York intimately, all three books are highly evocative of the New York baseball, media and celebrity scene of the late 1940s and early 1950s, when the Big Apple had three highly publicized major league teams and was unquestionably the hub of the baseball world as well as the book-publishing universe. There are no gangsters, no kidnappings, and no unlikely melodramatic circumstances in these stories, although there is a generous display of young Ferris' batting and fielding heroics. There is nothing, however, which could not have happened in real life — such as Marty's feat of hitting a home run in his first major league at-bat. Dozens of players have debuted with a homer.

The books focus primarily on Marty's ambitions and insecurities, along with his relationships with teammates, family members, the media and his girlfriend, Jean Turner. All three books are distinguished by realistic dialog among all concerned, and the bantering among players is some of the most realistic joshing seen in sports fiction of the mid–20th century. It's difficult to believe these three books appeared less than 40 years after the original Frank Merriwell dime novels, since Fitzgerald's writing is a quantum leap in sophistication. In fact, they still hold up extremely well today, despite period-piece elements, such as financial figures. Even the absence of African-America and Latin athletes on the Yankees' roster is understandable, since they were not integrated until the black catcher Elston Howard joined the team in 1955.

In an era when college baseball was nowhere near as important as it is today, when postwar minor league baseball was booming, and when less than 10 percent of the population earned college degrees, *The Turning Point* hinges on Marty's decision to turn down a Yankees baseball contract in favor of the college education his parents prefer. It's nothing less than one of the most literate, intelligent baseball stories ever produced up to the point it was released in 1948. In contrast to the Grosset & Dunlap and Couples & Leon series books of all types, however, *The Turning Point* was priced at $2.50 — an adult price in 1948 and two or three times what any series book cost. Chances are, then, that the vast majority of copies were purchased by libraries.

The only flaw in the series is that it ended at three books, making readers wish they could have known more about what happened to Marty Ferris, a character who is easy to empathize with. Fitzgerald wrote a lot of nonfiction, including two 1960s biographies of football immortal Johnny Unitas, but the only other baseball novel he wrote was *The Ballplayer*, an adult Barnes book published in 1957. But then, whether *The Turning Point* was actually intended as the first book in a series is hard to say. In fact, the blurb on the dust jacket doesn't even mention Marty by his first name. Oddly, as up-to-date as the story was, the dull, uncredited dust jacket illustration of Marty at bat looks as though it belonged on a book printed a generation or two earlier.

Fitzgerald consistently uses the names of real people, including both past and present major league players and managers in addition to several genuine media members, all of whom the author undoubtedly knew. His geography is also consistently accurate. Perhaps no author of fiction portrayed reality quite so well or so willingly. Of course, he does not have Marty meet any real current Yankees, except for his encounter with television personality Joe DiMaggio in the 1952 book, the year after the Hall of Famer last played for

New York. Ironically, the Yankees second baseman is named Bobby Richardson. The real second baseman of the same name, who played for the Yankees from 1955 to 1966, was a 13-year-old growing up in South Carolina when *The Turning Point* appeared!

One of the few aspects of *The Turning Point* that didn't seem to ring true was that Marty's parents made few efforts to attend his high school games. On the other hand, Marty is one of the few fictional series heroes of the era with a living father. But it seems odd when his mother asks him, "Are you playing today, Marty?" when he's already a major local media figure. But then, it is true that many parents took less interest in high school sports in an era when college was far less expensive and scholarships were not such a hotly sought prize.

Marty's high school coach, Vincent Xavier Riordan, is a no-nonsense leader with both a head and a heart. He is the epitome of the common-sense coach, stressing to Marty the value of a college education. Marty's teammates are typically lighthearted but competitive boys.

Fitzgerald's credentials as a first-rate sportswriter gave him an especially realistic outlook on the media, which so often serves as an unrealistic foil in other sports novels past and present. He writes in *The Turning Point*:

Yankee Rookie by Ed Fitzgerald (jacket copyright 1952, Grosset & Dunlap). This is the third in the famed editor's outstanding Marty Ferris trilogy.

> Publicity was a funny thing. When your name was splashed all over the paper, it made you feel embarrassed. Sort of as though you were getting false credit for the things the other guys were doing. You could always count on the fellows to ride you about it and you never were sure if they were just kidding or if they were serious. But if the paper ignored you, and you didn't get a break at all, you were sore. It's just that if you're going to get any where in the game you've got to have plenty of publicity, Marty decided. And then he laughed out loud. It was more than that, he had to admit. It was nice seeing your name in the headlines and your picture on the sports page. It was fun. It made a guy feel important. What was the use of tryin' to kid yourself?

Such honesty is common throughout all three books.

In the championship high school game, Marty hits a vital home run and throws out the potentially tying run at the plate to end the contest. Marty soon learns that it isn't the end of his season — he is chosen to compete with other star New York state seniors for a chance to take a road trip with one of the three New York teams. Marty wins and, of course, chooses the Yankees, whose scout Lazarus Dedrick has earlier offered him a minor league contract. Marty, though, is befriended by the affable journeyman outfielder Taffy Lewis. Lewis is frank enough to help convince Marty that a college education, followed by a pro career, is the way to go, since Taffy laments that he knows nothing but baseball and is not prepared for his post-baseball life. (Taffy is traded in the third book and achieves a modicum of success.)

Marty is invited to sit on the Yankees bench in uniform during the trip, though, of course, an as amateur he is not allowed to play. Marty is alert enough to anticipate a problem from the dugout and thus helps Taffy avoid being the victim of the "hidden ball" trick. This, too, is a realistic bit of heroics.

Marty, previously interested in tiny Ithaca College, receives help from the Yankees to attend Fordham University, in their own backyard. Fordham was far more influential in college sports in those days than the Rams are now. "When we get a fine prospect like you, we like to send him to a college of our choice," the Yankees farm director tells Marty. "A college where he can not only get a good education, but some excellent baseball training, too. Then, when he graduates, we expect him to join our organization."

This, of course, was well before baseball's free-agent draft began in the mid–1960s, because such a plan would not work today. Nor would the NCAA allow an athlete to receive up-front financial support from a professional team in the sport the athlete intends to play in college. (It is, on the other hand, permissible to play college football and minor league baseball, such as Stanford quarterback John Elway did for one season in an arrangement with the Yankees in 1982.) Such details remind the reader of the period-piece nature of old sports fiction.

Fast days at Fordham

College Slugger is one of the most intelligent and perceptive of all the vintage books about college baseball. The story skips over Marty Ferris' season on the freshman team and begins as he earns a starting spot in center field on the varsity as a sophomore. He doesn't make his first start until May 14, however, which even then was fairly late in the season, although college baseball teams — especially those in cold-weather climates — played fewer games in 1950. It doesn't take Marty too long to win veteran coach Al McBride's confidence and to attract the attention of Leo Hansen, the sleazy front-office official of a minor league team in Burlington, Vermont. Hansen tries to tempt Marty into playing for him under an assumed name — not an uncommon practice in pre–Internet days — but Marty rejects the offer, knowing it could lead to ineligibility for college ball.

Taffy Lewis, the journeyman major league outfielder who became Marty's mentor in the first book, introduces him to shortstop Johnny Metzger of the Red Sox. When Marty learns from Metzger how he lost his college eligibility for doing what Hansen offers, Marty is convinced he's on the right path. Marty refuses to buy into the cynicism of a fellow college player, who tells him after Marty objects to his dishonest approach, "But what did anybody ever get for being honest in this world? You have to look out for yourself, that's my motto. It's a cinch nobody else is going to do it for you."

Marty replies, "I don't know. Lots of people have helped me." That includes his stable, loving parents, who always remain concerned but seldom attend his games, even though they are within easy driving distance. Today, college baseball is a family affair and most parents make every effort to attend games, often traveling hundreds of miles to see a weekend series.

Much of *College Slugger* involves Marty's love affair with Jean, who keeps him grounded while attending a different college herself. He often needed solid advice during a disappointing junior year, which was spoiled by dissention within the team, involving fraternities. Marty declines to be recruited into a fraternity, not wanting to leave his parents' home (he commutes to college throughout his career at Fordham). But, when he is tempted to talk with Hansen about summer ball (in this series, Marty is not a plaster saint), Hansen quickly turns him down. Marty, not knowing the Yankees have threatened Hansen if he so much as talks with him, becomes puzzled over his future. Fitzgerald effectively portrays Marty's insecurities, including his doubts over what the Yankees really think of him.

As a senior, Marty wins the conference batting title at .383, leading his team to the championship, and hits .415 in the NCAA tournament. Fitzgerald adds a realistic touch: even though Marty hits three homers and a double in two games, the University of California eliminates Fordham, 6–5 and 7–6. But Marty soon learns the Yankees haven't forgotten him and he quickly signs with the team on the final page of the book.

On the plane trip home, McBride tells Marty that "If you can't make it in the majors, quit. Don't hang around the minors. It's a lousy life. You don't make any money and you get so you don't want to work. You have a 50–50 chance or better of turning into a baseball bum. In the majors, it's a career. In the minors, unless you know you're on the way up, it's just an excuse for not working [in a job outside baseball]."

It wasn't necessarily bad advice. In 1950, before the effects of television badly hurt minor league attendance, it was indeed possible to become a "baseball bum," since there were so many minor league teams. It was also an era when a minor league job indeed often paid less than working as a mechanic at a gas station. Even many major leaguers earned only marginally more than people in many professions. Before the advent of free agency in the 1970s and an explosion in the minimum salary for major league players, it wasn't uncommon for a rookie or journeyman to earn less than a veteran newspaper columnist. Today, when even rookies must be paid at least $300,000 per season, players make far more than all but the most stellar people in any media. In an era when the game has gone global and players are much more often signed from Latin America and Asia, most players today are given only a few minor league seasons, at best, to show they are prospects, or they are released to make room for younger players.

The realism of being a "Yankee Rookie"

Yankee Rookie is a fascinating look at baseball life at mid-century in New York, consistently well-written and logically developed without melodrama. The book skips over Marty's first season in the minor leagues, when he hit .315 in 75 games for the Triple-A Kansas City Blues in the American Association, one of three Triple-A leagues at the time. Marty's sincere approach is contrasted to the cockiness of a fellow rookie, Bruce Kellett. Eventually, Marty is sent down to Kansas City, having begun the season with basically home run-or-strikeout batting. Kellett goes down later, perhaps never to return; the reader will never know, since this is the last book of the series.

Marty inadvertently makes an enemy of a fading Yankee slugger, Mike Schultz, when his comments to a reporter are misconstrued. Fitzgerald, with a background of successful Big Apple journalism, writes one of the most telling paragraphs ever published in a sports story: "Forget it [manager Steve Bannon advises Marty]. I know how it is. Just let it be a lesson to you. Don't tell these guys anything you think might offend anybody. They're [writers] not interested in you or your problems. All they care about is making a big fuss and selling a few more papers."

Then Fitzgerald, showing an admirable ability to refuse to portray the melodramatic, black-and-white world seen in so many sports stories, changes course. "That doesn't go for all of them, of course. There are plenty of writers who're more interested in making friends and being decent guys than they are in kicking up a lot of phony excitement. The trouble is, the other kind are in the majority. Take a tip from me, kid. Be friends with all of them but don't tell any of them too much. And if you do have to open up in a weak moment, pick on one of the good guys, like Frankie Graham or Red Smith or Arthur Daley or Tom Meany. They're great. They'll be in your corner from the start. It'll be up to you to keep 'em there." Those four writers, all major figures in the New York media elite and nationally known, must have gotten a kick out of that paragraph, since few novelists ever used the names of real reporters, even though it wasn't uncommon to refer to past or present athletic greats.

In the year after Joe DiMaggio retired from the Yankees following the 1951 season, Fitzgerald has a nervous Marty doing a television interview with The Yankee Clipper, shortly before Marty is informed that he will start in right field on Opening Day. (Fitzgerald knew that on the real Yankee team, Mickey Mantle had center field wrapped up, even though Mantle and other current Yankees are not mentioned, although historical figures are often referenced.) The kidding that Marty gets from teammates, most of whom met him in *The Turning Point*, is hilarious.

Marty hits a team-leading nine home runs in the first couple of weeks, including a home run in his first major league at-bat, followed by hitting into a double play and striking out twice in that game (a nice realistic touch by Fitzgerald). But Marty's batting average is too low and his strikeout totals too high for Bannon's taste, and he is sent back to Kansas City. His demotion, however, does not come soon enough to save him from embarrassment. He is caught in the company of a gorgeous movie starlet at "21," the famed night club, following a buddy pose for the papers earlier in the day with the iconic restaurateur Toots Shor, whose place was ground zero for the celebrities of the New York sports world. It was all perfectly innocent, but the tabloid *New York Daily News* hints of something else: "The gorgeous baseball fan holding hands with the candidate for Rookie of the Year is curvesome Jessie Worth, the Paramount starlet. Marty's traveling in fast company."

Marty's misadventures, along with his inconsistent hitting, convince Bannon to send him down for "seasoning," as the papers so often put it. In 28 games with Kansas City (which didn't become a major league town until the Philadelphia Athletics moved there in 1955), Marty hits .402 with 14 home runs and 41 runs batted in and is called back up by the Yankees. Fitzgerald must have been inspired by Mantle's spectacular success in Kansas City when he was sent down in 1951: a .361 average with 11 homers and 50 RBIs in 40 games. For the Yankees, Mantle struggled in 1951 before and after his Kansas City stint: he batted .267 with 13 homers and 65 RBIs in 96 games, but struck out 74 times in only 341 at-bats. Mantle's well-publicized rookie struggles developed at the perfect time for Fitzgerald. When

The Turning Point was published in 1948, the author probably never had heard of Mantle, who was not yet Yankee property and was playing amateur ball in Oklahoma at age 17.

One of the few unrealistic aspects of *Yankee Rookie* occurs when Marty returns to Yankee Stadium a few moments before a night game following a flight from Kansas City. Bannon, short-handed because of injuries, rushes Marty into the lineup even though he had not warmed up. Marty plays well, but he does not earn Schultz's respect until the rookie ditches his agent while passing up a chance for television appearance money in order to participate in Ethel Merman's charity show with the entire Yankee lineup. The story ends with a mildly improbable but far from impossible finish: Schultz lands "at least four solid blows" on an opposing catcher, who has slugged Marty for legally but aggressively crashing into him while scoring the winning run. The last line, delivered by Schultz, is an appropriate, if ungrammatical, classic: "That's all right, kid. Us Yankees have to stick together."

Somehow, we know Marty Ferris will do just fine.

EIGHT

Duane Decker's
Unique Blue Sox Series

Former sports pulp magazine writer Duane Decker's 13 Blue Sox baseball novels for young adults make up perhaps the toughest series challenge for collectors of post–World War II books. The Blue Sox stories, originally published from 1947 to 1964 and reprinted into the early 1970s, are among the most cherished and best remembered sports books of the baby boom generation.

There literally had been nothing quite like them, although Gilbert Patten's 17-book Big League series (1914–1928) about the Blue Stockings, Wolves and Specters bore similarities. Indeed, author Andy McCue, in *Baseball by the Books*, speculates that "From the similarity of the names, Blue Sox and Blue Stockings, I am tempted to believe Decker read Patten's Big League series as a boy." Patten wrote his series as Burt L. Standish, the name he used to pen his many millions of words about Frank Merriwell.

The sharp focus on the team aspect is why readers have never forgotten the Blue Sox, who were tied together with compelling and varied novels of the struggles of 13 different players. The one constant in the Blue Sox universe was manager Jug Slavin. During the course of the series, the Blue Sox included more than 50 different players and coaches, with at least two or three at every position.

Clair Bee's concurrent Chip Hilton series (1948–66) has long generated probably the most appeal among nostalgia buffs (see chapter seven) if only because the 23 original Grosset and Dunlap books were sold almost entirely to readers, not libraries, for prices ranging from 75 cents to $1.50. But most of the 23 Hilton epics are far more common than the Blue Sox series.

Unlike the far more inexpensive Big League and Chip Hilton series books, libraries purchased the vast majority of the Blue Sox novels, most of which cost $2.50 and more in an era when bookstores seldom offered discounts. Most of the 13 Blue Sox books went into several printings, but they were so frequently checked out of libraries that it remains extremely difficult to find copies with dust jackets in fine condition. True first editions with nice jackets—not ex–library copies—have long been worth well over $100 apiece on the collectors' market. The jackets were all colorful and all unique, and some jackets are seldom seen, especially on the first two books.

The Blue Sox 13 novels range from 185 to 221 pages and I speculate that not a few were also read by adults, especially those who had enjoyed sports in the pulp magazines. By the 1950s, only a handful of sports pulp magazines remained, but that decade was the Golden Age of the young adult sports novel.

Decker released his first novel, *Good Field, No Hit*, through the M.S. Mill Company in 1947, but William Morrow & Company soon swallowed up Mill. The first book introduces combative third baseman Johnny Madigan, whose problems with lack of size and power make for a memorable story. Blue Sox readers loved to guess which players Decker modeled his books around. In this case, Madigan resembles infielder Eddie "The Brat" Stanky, of whom it was often said, to paraphrase, "He can't hit, he can't field, and he can't run; all he can do is win."

The second book, *Starting Pitcher* (1948), details the gritty and challenging conversion of Eddie Lasky from shortstop to pitcher following a leg injury. Major league history is replete with pitchers who became batting stars, such as Babe Ruth and Stan Musial, but the opposite is not as frequently true. Hall of Famer Bob Lemon of the Cleveland Indians, however, originally appeared briefly in the major leagues as a third baseman and outfielder before going on to a stellar career as a starting pitcher, beginning with his first pitch in the majors in 1946. Lemon's .232 career batting average remains one of the best for a pitcher with a long career.

Hit and Run (1949), the third book, tells the familiar story of how a small but speedy slap hitter, Chip Fiske, replaced aging power-hitting legend Augie Marshall in right field. The fittingly named Fiske learns that a chip on his shoulder won't do him any good with the fans. This book is testimony to the enduring popularity of the Blue Sox as it ran through at least 10 printings.

The Catcher from Double-A (1950) shows how young catcher Pete Gibbs overcomes his lack of confidence to become a distinguished club leader. Ultimately, as the series progresses, he becomes a rock of stability in every way. Indeed, Jug Slavin often considers the erudite catcher a manager on the field. Indeed, had the original series continued beyond 1964, Gibbs probably would have become the team's manager.

Decker's fifth book, *Fast Man on a Pivot* (1951), shows how second baseman Bud Walker overcame his lack of flashy skills to become a consummate team player and hustler. One of Decker's constant themes is how important effort and team play are. That helped make the books popular with many of his baseball-playing teen readers, most of whom could identify with players who had to overcome significant deficiencies, both on and off the field.

The Big Stretch (1952) details the unusual mental and physical transformation of one-time Blue Sox batboy Stretch Stookey into a first baseman good enough to beat out aging home-run hero Marty "Beef Trust" Blake, the team's longtime first sacker. Stookey was known as "Buster" when he was a batboy early in the series.

Switch Hitter (1953), the seventh book, is one of the best of the series. Russ Woodward, a center fielder with fabulous natural fielding and batting skills, must learn to become a team player before Jug Slavin and his teammates can learn to accept him. Woodward's skills seem based on those of Mickey Mantle, who came up to the New York Yankees in 1951, but Mantle did not have Woodward's early personality problems.

Decker's eighth Blue Sox book in as many years, *Mister Shortstop* (1954), concludes a remarkable initial run. The story of Andy Pearson's bid to move from utility infielder into the regular shortstop's job ahead of a more flashy competitor is similar to Bud Walker's tale in *Fast Man on a Pivot*. The man Andy must beat out, Slick Hammill, appeared in a non–Blue Sox book two years earlier—*Wrong Way Rookie*. The prolific Decker wrote that volume under the name Richard Wayne, as he did *Clutch Hitter* in 1951.

Four years later, Decker's books were able to run a unique graphic advertisement: a diamond with nine names. The final name in the original lineup was the star of *Long Ball to Left Field* (1958), in which would-be pitcher Mike Jaffe unwillingly is asked to make the transition to the outfield because of his slugging ability. What makes this story unusual is that ever since Babe Ruth went from being one of the best pitchers of his day to being the greatest of all sluggers in the 1920s, most players with great batting ability were more interested in playing every day — if they could. This is another outstanding story.

Third-Base Rookie (1959), the tenth book, appeared 12 years after third baseman Johnny Madigan's story began the Blue Sox saga. The timing was right for Vic Scalzi, a swarthy player with a dark and unsettling past to attempt to replace Madigan, who ultimately became Jug Slavin's trusted third-base coach. Madigan, though, is all too human in this story, in which Scalzi must prove he is not only a good player, but a good guy as well. Juvenile delinquency was much in the news and in pop culture during the 1950s, and Vic

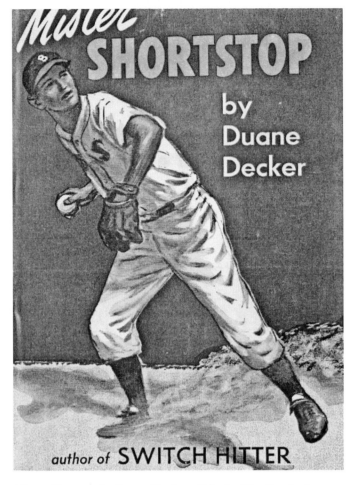

Mister Shortstop by Duane Decker, #8 in the Blue Sox Series (jacket copyright 1954, William Morrow). "Handy Andy" Pearson emerges as the Blue Sox shortstop in one of the best novels of an outstanding series.

Scalzi wasn't the first fictional athlete to run afoul of the law.

Showboat Southpaw (1960), the eleventh book, may not have sold well, because copies seem extremely difficult to find. I was fortunate to locate a volume in a small antique mall in Illinois, and I felt as though I'd found a real treasure, especially for $3! This tale of the humbling troubles of a cocksure left-hander, Sam Sloat, holds up as well as, or better than, any of Decker's books, though all 13 remain highly readable today if one can overlook details of finances. Nothing has changed more in professional sports since these books were written than salaries.

Chip Fiske finally found himself on the way out in the twelfth book, *Rebel in Right Field* (1961), when talented Danny Redd arrives on the Blue Sox scene. Redd is the antithesis of Pete Reiser, the 1940s legend whose stardom with the Brooklyn Dodgers was cut short because he kept challenging outfield walls. Redd must learn that playing it safe in the field or on the bases is an even more certain way out of big-time baseball, especially as Jug Slavin sees it.

After a long, honorable career, Pete Gibbs, the rock of the Blue Jays at catcher, finds himself next in line for retirement in *The Grand-Slam Kid* (1964), the thirteenth and last book. Young backstop Bucky O'Brian literally makes a grand-slam major league debut to win a pennant, but the next season O'Brian must learn the hard way that baseball can be a humbling game no matter how talented a player may be. Pete Gibbs learned that when O'Brian was barely out of diapers.

Decker's books, which can be read and enjoyed by any fan regardless of age, provide a keen insight into a different era of baseball, yet they still seem far fresher from a remove of five or six decades than turn-of-the-century volumes would have seemed in the 1950s. Middle-aged fans today have been known to encourage their baseball (and softball) loving grandchildren to read Decker to gain a better concept of what self-sacrifice and teamwork still mean.

What especially keeps Decker's books timely is crisp dialog that seems only marginally dated. This contrasts with how stilted Frank Merriwell-style dialog must have seemed a half century later in the far more realistic post–World War II literary era for young readers. It helps that the principles of baseball have changed relatively little — at least on the field — from Decker's era. His smooth writing style, devoid of clichés such as "circuit clout" for home run, remains a pleasure to read.

Ironically, and unfortunately, many of the selfish, grasping primary and supporting characters in Decker's books seem even more true-to-life today than they did in his era. There are, of course, no references to hard drugs, much less to the likes of steroids or Benzedrine pills. Much to his credit, Decker consistently avoided cardboard characterizations and wildly unlikely circumstances. His stories usually develop methodically and logically, yet he is never boring.

The last three books

By the time Decker published the final three books in the series during 1960 to 1964, all of the original Blue Sox players in the three 1940s volumes, *Good Field, No Hit, Starting Pitcher* and *Hit and Run*, are either coaching or retired. Decker almost never refers to any of them except, of course, former players Johnny Madigan, Chip Fiske and Bix Hanson, all active as coaches at the end of the series. Such a turnover greatly enhances the realism of the series.

Showboat Southpaw, Rebel in Right Field and *The Grand-Slam Kid* all seem more difficult to find than most of the earlier volumes. This may indicate the ever-growing influence of television on young readers in the 1960s. Nevertheless, characterization in sports novels has seldom been as well-handled as Decker does in these three human-interest novels. All three feature compelling characters who ultimately become likeable when they learn the team always comes before their individual aspirations and fears.

Although cocky left-hander Sam Sloat, the protagonist of *Showboat Southpaw*, is not a major figure in the ensuing two volumes, his story is perhaps the most heartwarming of the series. He is the only one of the 13 featured players who must face a potentially career-ending injury, and how he overcomes his limitations makes for a memorable story.

The plot isn't particularly original, but Decker holds the readers' interest because of the intriguing interaction between Sloat and his team. Sloat, called up to the Blue Sox late in the season before his 20th birthday, is convinced his overpowering fastball is all he needs to succeed. Given a chance to win an important season-ending game, he is allowed to throw fastballs only and thus "throws out" his arm with ligament damage. How Jug Slavin and Pete Gibbs convince Sloat that he still can win by learning how to place his diminished fastballs with curves and changeups is a compelling story.

When his kindly minor-league manager, Pops Medlicott, tells Sloat he has been called up, the cocky hurler responds, "I think it's about time. If Jug Slavin had called me up early in May instead of now the end of September, he might maybe have won himself a pennant." Medlicott responds, "I was twenty-seven before I made it, and I had been in pro ball [the minor leagues] nine years. A miracle has happened to you and all you can say is 'It's about time.'" That sets the tone right away, along with Sloat's retort: "I can throw harder than any pitcher the Sox have got. I know. I saw them all, in spring training."

Decker would occasionally go far over the top, taking extreme literary license in order to define character. That happened before Sloat's first start, made possible because of an injury to number one starter Eddie Lasky. During a team meeting, the young newcomer tells his teammates, "What I want to say is principally to Vic Scalzi on third and Mike Jaffe out there in left. I have noticed that when a right-handed hitter is at bat, especially a power hitter that they both lay very close to the line. That is normal, especially when a left-handed pitcher is throwing." An annoyed Jug Slavin tells him, "Sam, we do not have time for an analysis of things that are obvious to one and all. What if anything, is your point? Please come to it in a hurry." And Sloat continues: "My point is, that with me out there throwing, throwing as fast as I do, I would like it much better if both of them played farther away from the line. Because no right-handed hitter, not even a power hitter like that Mansell or that Bower or that Skanran, is going to pull [the ball] that much on me. That is my point and that is all I have to say."

Such openly verbal cockiness would never be tolerated today, and Slavin and the players don't think much of it, either. Fiske, still a right fielder

Long Ball to Left Field by Duane Decker, #9 in the Blue Sox Series (jacket copyright 1958, William Morrow). Bonus boy Mike Jaffe unwillingly converts from pitcher to outfielder.

at that point makes that very clear: "Skipper, is this teen-age donkey, who is pitching his first game, going to tell us how to play the hitters we all know backwards and forwards?" To which Jug, in typically gruff style, tells everybody, "End of discussion. As usual, the men will position themselves as they know best for each hitter. Any shifting of those positions will come from me."

Clearly, Decker doesn't want the reader to think any more of Sloat's attitude than do the Blue Sox. Over the top or not, this is the type of dialog that draws readers into Decker's stories and doesn't let them go. Likewise, catcher Pete Gibbs shouts, "Busher!" to Sloat when the pitcher throws away a potential game-ending grounder, giving Sloat a chance for a record-tying 17th strikeout. It's never clear that Sloat deliberately makes an error with a 7–1 lead, but the ever-ethical Gibbs has a legitimate beef, especially knowing that Sloat committed the unpardonable sin of asking in mid-game what the strikeout record was. For an athlete to openly ask about his chances to set a record was, and still is, heresy.

The Grand Slam Kid by Duane Decker, #13 and last in the Blue Sox Series (jacket copyright 1964, William Morrow). Charles Geer does an impressionist image of Bucky O'Brian, a rookie catcher who learns how important team play can be.

When spring training begins, and Sloat's arm still seems less than what it once was, Decker slowly turns him into a pitcher instead of a thrower. It is Gibbs, of course, who first asks Sloat point-blank if he has lost his best fastball and obtains a confession. And it is Gibbs who ultimately teaches the young man how to pitch with guile as well as humility. "It suddenly came to Sam," Decker perceptively writes, "that this kind of pitching was more fun than throwing straight fast ones past a hitter. This way you went into a man's mind and outsmarted him. It made you feel like some kind of genius or something. Of course, in this case, the genius was named Gibbs, not Sloat, even if the crowd didn't know that. But in due time [Sam] might get to be that kind of genius himself. A new and different sense of confidence made little soundings somewhere inside him."

Decker obviously kept abreast of all baseball trends, for late in *Showboat Southpaw* the first reference to a statistician appears. It wasn't until the late 1950s and early 1960s that teams began going beyond a combination of ordinary statistics and a manager's gut feelings to analyze a player's chances for success. Younger fans who read the complex box scores of the 21st century would be amazed to see the basic box scores of 1960. Nowhere was there any reference to the seasonal number of home runs or stolen bases, or the number of runners left in scoring position, or the number of pitches made. A box score that now runs six to eight inches in *USA Today* might have been two inches in those days.

One of the charming aspects of Decker's writing is how he spices his conversation with genuine baseball humor. During an exhibition game, Gibbs tells Sloat, "No rush today. The President failed to show up. He is obviously saving his arm for opening day."

Even young readers, however, would be jarred by the few references Decker makes to finances. The great center fielder, Russ Woodward, is said to make forty or fifty thousand dollars — a realistic figure for 1960, when future Hall of Famers such as Willie Mays led all of baseball with incomes in the $100,000 range. Even considering inflation, that's still less than $1 million today   and even most journeyman veterans make more than $1 million. Woodward, though, was still handsomely paid in an era when a nice home could be purchased for $25,000.

The plot of *Rebel in Right Field* may have been told a few dozen times in the pulps, but Decker still manages to contrive plenty of interest in his story of brilliant but brittle Danny Redd. The 20-year-old rookie, with the ability but not the heart to take gritty veteran Chip Fiske's place, fails to impress his team because of Redd's unwillingness to dive for catches, risk collisions with fences, or crash into catchers while trying to score. There are even references to "Pistol Pete" Reiser, whose brilliant real-life career with the Brooklyn Dodgers was cut short in the 1940s by the injuries he suffered with his daredevil style.

The story is contrived right from the start, when Redd's first minor-league manager, Rip Radjecki, benches him after his first game for being weak-willed. Radjecki's own major league career was derailed because he took so many chances and was injured so often, a la Reiser. Radjecki, however, is called to manage another team and Redd figures he'll won't see him again — only to see him show up as the replacement for one of Jug Slavin's retired coaches during Redd's rookie season with the Blue Sox.

Early on, it's a shock for Danny to be replaced by Chip Fiske with one out left in a game. It's true that managers often use defensive replacements, but to be "yanked," as Danny puts it, with one out remaining is beyond embarrassment. Eventually, after a collision lands him on the 30-day disabled list, Danny slowly discovers that true team play involves taking legitimate chances. He also learns about true team spirit when the aging Fiske pulls himself out of a game in favor of the far faster Redd.

The philosophy of Jug Slavin — and thus of the baseball-savvy Decker — is reflected in this comment by the frustrated manager: "There's dissension on this team now. I can smell it from here to the shower stalls. The others have resented it each time you [Redd] didn't go all-out — meaning you let them down. But now...." Redd responds: "Just one thing I want to say, I've helped win more ball games than I've helped lose in the little time I've played." Jug has the perfect answer: "That's not the point! The point is you only help win them when it doesn't cost you anything. And sometimes it's got to cost to win in baseball, like in just about everything else."

Even during a tension-packed period, Gibbs senses that Redd isn't a bad guy. Indeed, Decker reveals this through humor. Gibbs, following a particularly strong throw from Redd, tells him, "With an arm like that, maybe it's too bad it turned out you could hit" [and thus did not become a pitcher]. Retorts Danny, "Someday I'll show you my fuzz ball." Gibbs bites: "Why do you call it that?" "Because it's peachy," Danny responds, ducking a mitt thrown at him by Gibbs.

The Grand-Slam Kid leaves a reader wishing Decker would have continued the series. This story is far less contrived than *Rebel in Right Field*. Bucky O'Brian, a stubby rookie catcher in the Yogi Berra mold, arrives in the last week of the Blue Sox's season not expecting to play in the heat of a pennant race. But the young power hitter, given a chance to pinch hit, slugs a grand slam in his first major league at-bat on the last day of the season and the Blue Sox win the pennant. (Decker never identifies the name of the league in which the Blue Sox play.) Numerous players have hit homers in their first major league at-bats, so this isn't quite as unlikely as it might seem, especially because young hitters with power tend to get more opportunities as rookies than others.

The grand slam, however, convinces O'Brian that he is a great power-hitting prospect, better than he really is. When the next season begins, he suffers mightily through most of the book until he finally realizes both his limitations and the need for team play. Before that, he twice violates Jug Slavin's orders to bunt, resulting not in the likes of Jim Thorpe's legendary home run in that situation, but in game-losing double plays. Jug finally benches him, intending to send him to the minors after another promising young catcher recovers from an injury. Says Jug, "You're not Bucky O'Brian, and you never have been, not one minute since you hit that grand slam. You're a guy you dreamed up, and you didn't dream him up real good, either."

But an injury to Pete Gibbs, who is obviously in his final active season, and the insistence of O'Brian's pitching buddy, the brainy left-hander Oklahoma Crane, lands the embattled young catcher in the lineup one more time. He doesn't come close to hitting a glamorous home run, but he shows the Blue Sox he is what Jug had already told him he is: "You really handle a pitcher. And you're so alert, which is what a catcher — above all — has to be. You know what's going on out there. You could hit maybe .290. You could hit maybe 15 or so home runs. But you're not *great*, Bucky. You're just good, just a pro, like the rest of us. If only you could see that." Dialog like that is what makes these books so memorable.

Decker generally kept the continuity in his books accurate, though once in a while he would slip up, such as calling pitcher Eddie Lasky 36 years old in *Showboat Southpaw*, 39 in *Rebel in Right Field* one year later, and still 39 in *The Grand-Slam Kid* three years after that. In addition, dust jacket artist Charles Geer portrays Bucky O'Brian as a tall, lanky kid, but Decker describes him in much the same words that could have been used to describe Yogi Berra. But those are minor quibbles, indeed. Decker also may have puzzled the teen readers of the mid–1960s with Jug's references to Frank Merriwell, the dime-novel hero of their grandfather's day.

Switch Hitter is a change of pace

At the mid-point of the Blue Sox series, Decker produced a gem: *Switch Hitter*. In some ways, this is the best book of the series, for it delves fairly realistically into the psychology of a troubled potential superstar, rookie center fielder Russ Woodward. Spoiler warning: The ending has a sentimental, pulpish feel, but it's a warm and not entirely unrealistic approach.

Decker wrote almost entirely about players who overcame physical shortcomings to become significant contributors on championship teams. In *Switch Hitter*, he does the opposite: Russ Woodward has more physical talent than anyone on the team, if not the entire league, but his mental approach lands him in one woeful situation after another.

For most of the story, matinee idol-handsome Russ's self-centered nature betrays him. He cares about almost nothing besides home runs and big money; he feuds with manager Jug Slavin and his teammates; he fights with sportswriters and fans. In his mind, his talent is all that really matters. Slavin tries everything to win him over: he plays psychologist, he sends Woodward back to the minor leagues after the rookie punches a critical sportswriter, and he benches him after he has been recalled from the minors but shows he has not learned his lessons about team play.

For Woodward, the final indignity occurs when he is asked to pinch run while the third-string catcher pinch hits. Woodward "jumps the club," as the phrase went in those days, and returns to his hometown. There, he encounters well-meaning but harsh criticism from his mother, his older brother, his high school coach, a local sportswriter friend and even the police chief—an old friend and potential employer. Woodward, who was consistently portrayed as intelligent and essentially honest—even if his honesty constantly lands him in trouble—finally realizes the only enemy he really has is himself.

Always good with the youngsters throughout the book, Woodward signs a ball for a youngster during his sad return to his hometown. He is appalled when the kid returns the ball to him because the boy's father had labeled Woodward a quitter. The most unrealistic aspect of the book follows: Woodward throws the ball as far as he can. Such a throw, without a proper warmup, could seriously damage an arm. Woodward, though, returns to the Blue Sox and the ever-wise Jug Slavin takes him back following a $500 fine (a huge penalty in 1953) for jumping the club. Woodward gets a chance to pinch hit with the bases loaded, realizes he needs to get on base any way he can, and produces a game-winning bloop double with the appropriately measured swing while just trying to meet the ball instead of attempting to hit a home run.

Decker nicely wraps up the story with the sort of true-to-life baseball ribbing that earlier in the story bothered Woodward. "A puny kind of hit for a slugger," shortstop Patsy Bates tells him. "Try to do better next time." "Yeah," adds second baseman Bud Walker, "you'd have looked pretty sick on that one, if [the pitcher] hadn't looked sicker." Chimes in third baseman Johnny Madigan, "Better luck next time, Switch." Decker then applies the perfect finish: for the first time in his career, the humbled and chastened Woodward tips his cap to acknowledge the fans' cheers.

This is a captivating story, truly suitable for both adults and younger readers. Anyone with an inclination toward the selfish—always the ultimate baseball sin in Decker's eyes—could easily relate. Of the thousands of young players who read Decker's books, not a few of them must have found the saga of Russ Woodward a window into their own minds and hearts. This novel truly taught the psychological principles of team play. That's a major reason this story seems to hold up better today than any of Decker's other books, although each remains readable.

Early in *Switch Hitter*, there's a touching scene where Decker contrasts Woodward's lack of humility with a scene involving Jug's reluctant release of washed-up veteran slugger Marty "Beef Trust" Blake. The ever-present clubhouse man Pickles, a constant throughout the series, had always admired Blake. But when he realizes Blake's dilemma and asks him, "Hey, Marty! What's new?" the proud veteran replies, "Not much, Pickles. You know how it is—one day just like another." That wonderfully realistic exchange shows how an "old pro" simply refused to go out whining or even commenting about his fate at all.

Decker's crisp dialog is never better than when Woodward observes that Blake has hit into a game-ending double play, thus costing the team even more than a mistake by Woodward. Retorts Jug, "Shut up. Shut up. You're talking about one of the greatest ballplayers the Blue Sox ever produced. If you wind up half so great, you can feel proud of yourself." Responds Woodward, "I'm sorry." Jug continues: "And I believe you. But why do you like to go around doing and saying things that you have to be sorry for?"

Later, long before the end of Woodward's troubles but following a couple of his contributions, Decker writes, "His biggest day in the team's eyes, Russ was thinking, had turned out to be the first one in which he had failed to get a bailout of the infield."

Good Field, No Hit: The strange story of Johnny Madigan

The antithesis of Russ Woodward, both in physical ability and temperament and on the field, was light-hitting but ever-hustling, ever-serious third baseman Johnny Madigan, the hero of the first book of the series in 1947. The opening paragraph was a masterpiece: "You cannot always tell, from watching a ballplayer take his practice cuts inside the batting cage, whether he will hit .300 over a full season. But with Johnny Madigan you could tell. He definitely would not." What baseball enthusiast wouldn't want to continue reading?

Decker goes a bit over the top to introduce readers to Madigan, who has played full time for six years in the minor leagues without ever hitting a home run. That's a highly unlikely statistic; indeed, since the "lively ball" was introduced following World War I, few, if any, such players are likely to have made it to the major leagues. The idea of playing six years without a home run simply doesn't wash, and it's one of the few times Decker could be faulted for emphasizing a story point without being reasonably true to life. He would have been better to say something that "averaged three home runs a season," or some such, since that would have been far more realistic.

Good Field, No Hit includes only one of the 12 succeeding players who would star in his own book: Eddie Lasky, then a standout young shortstop who played alongside Madigan. It wasn't until the second book, *Starting Pitcher*, that Lasky converted to pitcher following a career-threatening leg injury suffered in a hunting accident. The rest of the players appeared in a few succeeding books: first baseman Marty "Beef Trust" Blake, second baseman Tommy Shore, left fielder Luke Carpenter, center fielder Vic Valenti, right fielder Augie Marshall, No. 1 pitcher Bix Hanson and catcher Bus King. None of those seven regulars in Madigan's rookie year, however, had a full book devoted to him. Even so, Decker manages to squeeze in bits and pieces about their personalities, especially the aging slugger Marshall.

Despite his speed and skill at third base, Madigan is due to be sent to the minors because talented home-run hitter Mike Marnie convinces Jug Slavin he should be the team's third baseman. An injury to the cocky, hot-headed Marnie, however, gives Madigan a reprieve and, ultimately, a chance to show Slavin that he is the man for the job.

The final chapter (spoiler warning) is unexpected. Marnie, as unethical as he was powerful at bat, earlier hired someone to heckle Madigan from the stands following Marnie's injury. A canny sportswriter, Ed Daly, caught wind of the situation and convinced Jug Slavin that he should hire someone to heckle Marnie after he returns to the lineup. That way, Jug would learn whether Marnie's hot-headed nature would cause him to blow up —

it did — so the fans would realize why a player labeled "good field, no hit" would be the right man in the lineup. After Marnie strikes an umpire, he's never heard from again, having been dispatched to literary limbo by both Slavin and Decker. That plot twist, unlike most of the ensuing angles in the Blue Sox series, was pure pulp.

Ed Daly, an often critical and analytical yet entirely ethical figure, continues to appear in several books in the series, providing a good look at a reporter's insights. While his interaction with Jug Slavin might seem unlikely in today's world — in which the print media is often seen as antagonistic to the best interests of the coaches and players — the relationship was by no means entirely unrealistic in 1947. Reporters often ignored off-the-field antics by players, unless they directly affected their play in the field, and sometimes (though not always) had close relationships with the authority figures on baseball teams.

The first book is not entirely focused on Madigan, but instead provides a series of vignettes in which he learns involving teammates, notably eccentric pitcher Harry Diefendorf, who was convinced he was really an outfielder, and Augie Marshall, an outfielder who once cared only about trying to hit home runs. Blue Jays scout Bugs Boff (a wonderful name for a baseball man) takes Madigan under his wing and tells him story after story about his teammates. Many of these stories seem likely to have been based on the plots of pulp stories by Decker, who was sometimes listed in the Blue Sox books as the author of more than 500 magazine pieces of fact and fiction. To the best of this author's knowledge, there has never been a list of Decker's short pieces, but there is no doubt he was prolific.

Tim McCord, the "millionaire owner of the Blue Sox," appears in the Madigan story but soon disappears. Instead, Decker focuses on a series of general managers and another owner later in the series. That, of course, was true to life; baseball teams frequently changed ownership.

"*Hit and Run,* a sports novel for men and boys"

A phrase seldom seen in books targeted for young adults, "sports novel for men and boys," appeared on the inside flap of the dust jacket of *Hit and Run* (1949), which stayed in print for well over two decades through at least ten printings. As such, it may be the most common of the Blue Sox series for collectors to find. Rookie right fielder Chip Fiske's story, in the vernacular of the era it first appeared, "is a pip." In fact, even when the hustling slap-hitter Fiske became a coach late in the series — after Danny Redd replaced him in right field in the penultimate volume, *Rebel in Right Field* — *Hit and Run* remained popular and in print. It may have initially confused readers in the 1960s to have books devoted to different right fielders, but *Hit and Run* was apparently too good to retire.

Morrow's publishing habits can best be described as confusing, if not downright odd. In the tenth printing (1970) of *Hit and Run* the company retained the familiar full-page baseball diamond chart of "Duane Decker's Blue Sox Heroes: The position played by each and the book where he belongs." This chart began appearing in 1958 with the publication of the ninth book, *Long Ball to Left Field,* in which Mike Jaffe completes the lineup following a four-year break in the series. Yet the tenth printing of *Hit and Run* advertises *Rebel in Right Field* on the inside flap of the other side of the dust jacket! In addition, the back of the jacket advertises *Third-Base Rookie,* the first book to feature a player not in the original nine men. Thus, the team's two new stars are not included in the diamond chart, even though their books had been in print for about a decade by 1970.

In retrospect, another aspect of *Hit and Run* seems stranger still. In addition to telling the story of how singles-hitting defensive star Chip Fiske replaces aging fan favorite Augie Marshall, much of the book deals with the saga of Kennie Willard, the only African American player to star in the Blue Sox series and a close buddy of fellow rookie Chip Fiske. Kennie Willard made his literary debut two years after Jackie Robinson broke the "color line" in the major leagues, with the Brooklyn Dodgers in 1947. In temperament if not skills, Willard is obviously modeled on the poised Robinson, who knew he could not aggressively retort to fans' and opponents' taunts except through his excellence on the field. Decker presents Willard in a manner admirably devoid of racism and the social attitudes still prevalent in much of America at the time. Yet to have a book entirely devoted to an African American hero, well before the civil rights era of the 1960s, may have been judged financially risky. One of the few such pre–1960 books the author has located is the 1956 young-adult football novel *Hard to Tackle* by Gilbert Douglas. It may not be a coincidence that *Hard to Tackle* is a difficult book to find.

How Chip Fiske and Kennie Willard interact makes for a compelling story, for Willard's self-control is the opposite of Fiske's combative personality. Fiske — whose answer to criticism is to take it very personally indeed, often with a punch — absorbs a terrible mental beating from fans and sportswriters who still think power-hitting Augie Marshall should be playing right field. Wrote one anonymous reporter following Fiske's first game, "Jughead's new right fielder, this wee kid, Fiske, is an eager beaver, sure. In all fairness, he played a good game — if you like that kind of a game. He beat out a bunt [and] poked a dinky little grounder through an infield hole which got official scoring as a hit. He laid down a fine sacrifice bunt and he walked once. He's an artist on the hit-and-run play. In the field, he made a gem of a catch on a ball which, if he'd played it right, would have been fairly routine. And, he got walked home from third when he rattled Duncan.... [S]ome teams would probably highly prize such stuff. But the Sox team and the Sox fans won't. Not after Augie Marshall. The contrast is too great. The picture for Fiske is hopeless.... [H]is style of play, no matter how good is nothing that will ever be in demand by the Sox fans."

Fiske, though, ultimately prevails, both over his own thin skin and the fans who think he doesn't belong in the lineup. Along the way, there is some amusing writing, especially about a certain breakfast modeled on the iconic Wheaties, "The Breakfast of Champions." Writes Decker, in the comments of a radio announcer: "Don't forget, try Oaties. Give yourself a BREAK instead of a BREAKfast." There is also much insider-type baseball wisdom such as this advice from Jug to Chip regarding his risky sliding habits: "You let your hands drag along the ground when you hit the deck. Always keep your hands in the air when you take that big jump at the base.... When you're on first [base], grab a handful of dirt in each hand and clench it inside your fists. Keep that dirt there all the time you're on base. Then, when you slide into second, your hands will stay in the air all right, because they're clenched over the dirt."

Willard, who arrives as a third baseman but finds his path blocked by Johnny Madigan, temporarily takes over for Fiske in right, aided in no small measure by his increasingly self-aware buddy's tips on how to play the position. But Fiske prevails in the end when Willard is injured. In the only such example of a successful position shift in the series, Willard takes over in left field and enjoys a prosperous career. It would not be until nine years later that the Blue Sox would have a new left fielder, Mike Jaffe in *Long Ball to Left Field*.

Near the end of the book, Jocko Tyler, "the professionally breathless purveyor of play-by-play radio dope on the daily diamond doings of the Blue Sox," as Decker describes him, conducts a hilarious interview with Chip Fiske. While Jocko expounds at great length, Chip's entire verbal output in answer to Jocko's questions is "rough," "yeah," "tough," "yop," "plenty" and "that's about it." Finally, when asked what his favorite breakfast food is, Chip replies with the name of the other advertiser, Black Marvel cigars! "Well! So you like a cigar after breakfast! Well, well, that's a very interesting personality sidelight for the fans. But after a breakfast of what?" to which Chip replies: "Oaties!" Such humor was infrequent in the series, but it provides a most welcome insight into Chip's "strong, silent type" personality.

After Chip finally wins over both fans and teammates following an injury to Willard, he learns of his acceptance on the final page. In a hurry to take a taxi ride to the hospital to see Willard, Marty Blake tells Chip, "Hurry up, small fry." To which Tweet Tillman adds, "Yeah, step on it, cockroach," and Johnny Madigan says, "Get a move on, beetle." Chip, not long before that highly irritated by any reference to his size, finally realizes he belongs. It's a wonderful ending to one of the best baseball novels ever written.

Decker's first three books dealt with distinctly different plots. Third baseman Johnny Madigan must overcome physical limitations with effort and smarts; shortstop Eddie Lasky injures himself to the point that he has no choice but to convert to pitching; and catcher Pete Gibbs is forced to confront his lack of self-confidence at the major league level.

After conquering his self-doubts in *The Catcher from Double-A*, Gibbs becomes a classy role model for all young players throughout the rest of the series, including what was sure to be his last season in the final book, *The Grand-Slam Kid*. He emerged as a distinguished star, sure of himself on and off the field, and a source of stability for his team. He became the obvious choice to succeed Jug Slavin as manager and that doubtless would have made a fascinating book had Decker been able to continue the series.

In contrast, the stars of the fourth and fifth books, second baseman Bud Walker in *Fast Man on a Pivot* and Buster "Stretch" Stookey in *The Big Stretch*, overcame rivals on the field but were never more than supporting characters from then on. They were the epitome of solid but not flashy personalities, the type of players managers love because the only headlines they make are for occasional on-the-field examples of excellence.

Even, there, though, Decker came through with original concepts. Walker, a rock of stability best known for his double-play pivot and knowledge of the game, did not lack for confidence. But the subtle aspects of his game failed to win over the majority of the fans, who preferred the flashy, greedy rookie batting star Joe Devlin, until Devlin's self-serving nature became obvious to everyone.

"Stretch" Stookey overcame an entirely different problem: how to put his history as the team's batboy behind him in order to replace an aging home-run hitting legend, Marty "Beef Trust" Blake, both on the field and in the team's pecking order of respect. Even though Blake did not have his own book in the series, having joined the Blue Sox long before Johnny Madigan's story began the series, he was very much a notable figure in the first four books. In contrast, Stookey began the series as *Buster the Bat Boy*. Batboys in the major leagues in those days tended to be of high school age, in many cases high-school stars in their own right with connections to the team.

Walker's story, however, was perhaps even more compelling, since it was obvious to readers that Blake would be replaced by Stookey. Walker, whose given first name was Harold, represented a legion of Buds in American life and sports: solid citizens without flashy skills. It's likely that more readers could identify with Bud Walker than with any other character in the series; he's the Everyman of baseball. As such, the story is compelling, although the oft-sneering Devlin is such a disreputable if talented character that no reader could root for him. Again, Decker's pulp origins emerge, but in a healthy way.

When the story opens, Bud Walker has arrived at spring training, having bought a junker car for $90. He sells it for $40, meaning he figured out reasonably cheap, convenient travel to the Blue Sox camp in Glensota, Florida. That turns out to be entirely typical of practical Bud, who is 27 years old — old for a rookie — and has spent seven years in the minor leagues. Five years earlier, he seemed to have won the second base job, only to have the Blue Sox trade for all-star Tommy Shore, who was the star second baseman of the first three books. In the days before free agency, that meant Bud was destined to remain in the minors as Shore's unofficial insurance policy. This, unfortunately, was very much true to real baseball in that era. In addition, teams were loathe to trade talented minor leaguers to rivals, because those players might come back to haunt their original club. But as Bud begins spring training, Shore has retired, realizing his skills have slipped too much to continue at his former high level.

Bud, however, soon sees the Blue Sox sign 21-year-old college star Joe Devlin to a $40,000 bonus (big money in those days, equal to close to half a million in buying power today). Devlin's flashy nature and cocky comments contrast vividly with Bud's stability and subtle skills. "The kid, at twenty-one, had already made more money [from baseball], without even putting on a glove, than [Bud] had made after seven years in the minors," Decker writes. "And now Devlin would be the favored one for the job Bud had sweated through those seven years to get, because Devlin represented a big lump of Blue Sox money, invested in a gamble." Decker nailed a major problem of the era; veterans often resented bonus boys, and for good reason, even if they weren't loudmouths like Devlin.

When Devlin is assigned to room with Bud in spring training, after Bud's previous roommate has been sent to the minors, the dislike is instant and visceral. Without even asking, Devlin has taken Bud's bed, which Bud won in a coin flip with his previous roommate. Even worse, in Bud's mind, Devlin says the sport he really loves is golf and he intends to play baseball only long enough to capitalize financially. The traveling secretary soon separates them, but Jug Slavin is distinctly displeased by the squabbling between the two second basemen. Ultimately, because of the nature of baseball politics, it threatens Bud's job.

As usual, Bud finds consolation in perceptive comments from Pete Gibbs. "I began to believe I was nothing but a Double-A catcher," he tells Bud, "the way the sportswriters were claiming. It came to me, finally, that I was sort of a star, too.... I'd never have made the grade without Tweet Tillman's help. He believed in me. I think he was the only man on the team who did. But because of him I quit feeling like a second-rater among stars. I quit feeling awed by everybody else. That's what you've got to do, too.... I think you're a better second baseman than you think you are. I think you'll do the team a lot of good, because that's what the pitchers think. Give this bonus beauty everything you've got in this dogfight. Will you?" Responds Bud, "That's one thing you can count on."

Decker includes a world of inside baseball knowledge throughout the rest of the book, so the reader will fully understand just why the pitchers realize Bud is their best option at second base. So does Jug Slavin, even though he is forced to send Bud to the minor leagues briefly, because of baseball politics. But Bud has a key ally in sportswriter Ed Daly, "the Boswell of the Blue Sox," and Bud's never-quit nature ultimately wins over his teammates.

There is perhaps no more heart-warming development in any of the Blue Sox books than the one that decided Bud Walker's status. (Spoiler warning:) Forced to play shortstop when Patsy Bates is injured, Bud again runs afoul of second baseman Devlin, who has returned to the lineup and apparently deliberately tries to make Bud look bad with Devlin's subtle mistake during a botched double play that leads to a loss. A fistfight in the clubhouse ensues, leading the team's owner, Charlie K. O'Neill, to tell Bud he is through. Bud tells O'Neill, who never played professional baseball, "I know a lot about professional baseball and what makes it tick. So when you tell me Devlin is a better second baseman for this team than I am — well, I don't think it's true and I don't think the team thinks it's true." To which O'Neill responds, "You're a very smug young man, Walker. And a little mixed up about your value to the team." Bud answers: "The next month's record of this team will show just how mixed up I am. Let's leave it that way."

At that point, the Blue Sox arrive at the clubhouse and are shocked to see Bud packing to leave. Eddie Lasky, who knows more than anyone how valuable Walker is, respectfully tells the owner that if Bud is forced out, he will turn in his uniform, too. "You can't break up a team to protect an investment," Lasky says. "We may be pros, but we're still a team of human beings. We're not coupons. You can't clip us." A line quickly forms, and Fiske, Gibbs, Madigan, Bates, Valenti and Blake tell O'Neill he can have their jerseys. The owner has no choice but to back down, and Bud's sacrifice bunt helps win the game that day. "Well, kid, now you've seen everything ... team mutiny! ... Devlin's gone to a farm club. O'Neill is going to peddle him for a fancy price so he'll save face with his stockholders. That means the job is all yours finally. Have a good year, kid." "I will," Bud responds. "It's my year, this year." Perhaps no story in the series leaves the reader more satisfied.

Although it's truly picking a nit, Decker did make one jarring error in the continuity. When Bud is retained on the team to start the season as a utility man and is playing shortstop in the opener in place of Bates, a first-inning fight between Bud and Devlin in the field leads Slavin to send Bud to the bench and the owner to send him to the minors. "Five years the Sox have owned me, and in those five years I've played exactly one half an inning for them. I still think I'm a major-league second baseman." However, the story earlier made clear that Bud had "gotten into a few box scores" during a September call up the previous season. Such errors were uncommon for Decker, who did a commendable job of keeping the facts straight throughout the long series.

Mister Shortstop and *Long Ball to Left Field*: The link and the lesson

The worst baseball sin in Decker's books is the unwillingness to put aside personal goals for the benefit of the team. In the four years between *Mister Shortstop* (1954) and *Long Ball to Left Field* (1958) — the widest gap in the series — he uses flashy but self-centered shortstop Slick Hammill as an effective lesson in both books.

As *Mister Shortstop* opens near the end of Andy Pearson's fourth year in the major leagues, Andy has long since become known throughout the league as "Handy Andy" because he can fill in almost anywhere. The Blue Jays — finding themselves needing a shortstop for September because longtime star Patsy Bates is obviously falling victim to age — acquire Andy for the final month. Andy responds with his best batting showing in the majors, a .327 average. Andy gets the reasonable idea that he just might have a strong shot at establishing himself as a solid starter the next season.

Jug Slavin's philosophy emerges when he meets with Andy and talks about what it means to join a team with the purposeful nature of the Blue Sox even though they won't win this year's pennant: "The [new] man just starts to play harder [with the Blue Sox], that's all. Take you, for instance. You'll find that you will." Andy's retort is appropriate: "I never figured myself for a loafer," to which Jug replies, "Neither did I or you wouldn't be here right now. But second-division ballplayers, nearly all of 'em, don't know what it even means to go all out to win a game. That extra step, that extra jump — my boys learn to get it or they don't last around here. You get the message?" "I get it," Andy says, and indeed he does.

However, when he returns the next spring, he finds that over-confident Slick Hammill's flashy power-hitting and precocious personality have captured the imagination of the fans and reporters, not to mention the Blue Jays' front office. Unlike feisty second baseman Bud Walker three years earlier, Andy isn't involved in as many direct confrontations. He simply feels he has already proved he's a steadier, headier player. When Jug informs Andy that he's going to go with Hammill as his regular shortstop for now, there's an important lesson for young readers in baseball politics.

"I could have sworn I was doing all right," Andy tells Jug after receiving the bad news. "You were," Jug replies. "But I'm getting strong beefs from the front office about how I'm crippling the spirit — so help me that's how they put it — of the finest shortstop prospect to come up in years.... My orders are to give the kid every break, which they think I haven't been doing. Just take it easy." But Hammill, when informed he will start the game and bat eighth because Johnny Madigan is entrenched at leadoff, reveals his lack of team orientation when he mutters, "Eighth! I never hit that far down in my life!"

Andy never quits, though, because politics aren't part of his vision. Instead, he sees much the same way Bud Walker saw in his battle for second base the little things that Hammill fails to do. Decker provides a nifty example along with sound baseball information:

> He [Slick] plucked one deep from the hole to his right, with a pretty, skidding stop, and nailed the runner at first. But he would not have nailed a fast runner on [Hammill's throw], because he had put on the brakes at the exact moment he gloved the ball and so had lost at least a full second, perhaps two, in getting [the throw] over to first. It had been the pitcher who hit it and he was no reindeer going down the base line. But it had been a beautiful play all the same. Only, Andy was thinking, it did not have that last ounce of perfection with which, time and time again, a shortstop wins or loses a ball game for the team. [Andy] did not expect the stands to see such a thing. But he had an idea it did not pass Jug by, unnoticed.

Notwithstanding redundancies such as "wins or loses a ball game for the team," the wisdom of these observations shines throughout Decker's books. Nor does Decker allow his star players to make excuses. For example, in a later sequence, when Andy is filling in at second base while Hammill remains at shortstop, a subtle technical mistake by Hammill is instead charged as an error to Pearson. But he refuses to alibi when Jug asks him what happened. "I did not catch the ball," Andy tells Jug. "I missed it clean." "Well, it probably happened to [Rogers] Hornsby," Jugs says. "And he came back," Andy replies. "Yeah," Jug answers. "He came back." Hornsby, of course, was one of the greatest second basemen of all time.

Slick Hammill ultimately self-destructs near the end of the story while getting into a nasty, unnecessary fight with Marlin, the feisty second-baseman of the Clippers and obviously modeled on combative Billy Martin of the New York Yankees. Andy takes over at shortstop to stay, with even the front office finally convinced that his steady approach is best for the Blue Jays.

Mister Shortstop was the only book in the series in which Decker did not introduce any new players — starters or reserves — for the Blue Jays. The lineup, except for the Pearson-

Hammill situation, is as solid as it ever has been or will be — until four years later in *Long Ball to Left Field*.

As *Long Ball* opens, Kennie Willard, the team-oriented African American left fielder, has retired. Typifying his series-long dignity, Willard has decided he won't hang on since he isn't the player he once was (that was one of Joe DiMaggio's reasons for retiring after the 1951 season). Just as Decker designed Willard's debut to parallel the poise under pressure of Jackie Robinson, so did Decker model Willard's departure after Robinson's retirement following the end of the 1956 season. The Brooklyn Dodgers attempted to trade Robinson to the rival New York Giants, but Robinson would have none of that and called it a career after a decade with the Dodgers.

Unlike any other player in the history of series, Jug Slavin gives the left field job to young power-hitting Mike Jaffe — or tries to give him the job. Jaffe, whose pitching record was 12–14 for the Blue Jays the previous season, is convinced he is a pitcher who can hit, not a hitter who can pitch. Jaffe even accepts a trip to the Triple-A Blues, rather than give up pitching, when he continually encounters difficulty on the pitching mound. And whom should Jaffe meet upon his arrival other than bitter and disillusioned Slick Hammill, playing Triple-A ball, four years after losing out to *Mister Shortstop* Andy Pearson.

Slick, vividly showing the reader why he'll never make it back to the big time, has a serious message for both Jaffe and the reader. Writes Decker, "Hammill, at twenty-six, was just about as bitter on the subject of pro ball as it was possible to be at that age." "You're crazy, of course," Hammill tells Jaffe of his refusal to play left field. "But I admire your kind of craziness," to which Mike replied, "What's crazy about wanting to be what you know you were cut out to be?"

Slick has the answer: "Listen to me, my young friend. If you don't already know that those boys upstairs [the major league front office] are all mixed up, you'll know it soon." Continues Decker, providing an effective description of a mental failure: "Slick was a wiry man with a boy's face on a full-grown body. He had a hard set to his mouth and a belligerent thrust to his sharp chin. Mike knew, from stories he had been told about Slick, that he could hit and field in major-league style, but that he had an ego and an attitude no manager in the league wanted to tangle with. The Sox had offered to sell him to a half-dozen clubs, but there were no takers."

Responds Mike: "I'm not mad at anybody," sensing that Slick was mad at just about everyone. "You will be, you will be," Slick retorts. "When you're twenty-six like me, and still playing in a bush league, like me, and you know you're better than at least half of them up there ... you'll be mad.... They gave me a bum deal; now they give you a bum deal. If you want to quit on yourself—convert [to the outfield] I mean — they'll give you another chance. Otherwise, you're to stay."

"What did they do to you?" asks Mike. Slick, with a sneer, replies, "They didn't want me to convert [to another position]. Just wanted me to change my style of play, change my way of looking at things. And because I stuck to my guns, the way you have so far, I'm still in exile.... I wouldn't put him [Jug Slavin] in charge of a bunch of hamsters."

Jaffe, though, knows Jug is honest and refuses to listen to any more of Hammill's rants. Eventually, Jaffe finally realizes that his late father's pitching dreams for him simply weren't realistic, especially considering what a natural hitter he continues to be. It was a simple story — perhaps the most basic of all the books — but the contrast between Jaffe's stubborn but essentially rational approach and Hammill's bitterness could not have been more striking. The contrast could not have sent a better message to young readers.

The world of the Blue Sox

Duane Decker created a remarkably consistent "baseball universe" for his 13-book Blue Sox series. The major link in all 13 books was manager Jug Slavin, formerly a power-hitting shortstop who was said to have begun his career as a player-manager but was strictly a manager in the novels. Slavin seems to have been modeled along the lines of Joe Cronin, who was inducted into the Baseball Hall of Fame in 1956 after managing for 15 seasons through 1947. Cronin hit 170 home runs, one of the highest totals for a shortstop in his era, during a 20-year career from 1926 to 1945. During the era Decker's books were most popular, many managers had been shortstops.

Eddie Lasky, who was forced by an injury to convert from shortstop to pitcher in the second book, *Starting Pitcher* (1948), was the only featured player to last through all 13 stories. Third baseman Johnny Madigan, the star of the first book in 1947, appeared in every novel, but became a coach for the final three. Otherwise, players debuted with the Blue Jays and never left: right fielder Chip Fiske (a coach in the final book), catcher Pete Gibbs, second baseman Bud Walker, first baseman Buster "Stretch" Stookey, center fielder Russ Woodward, shortstop Andy Pearson, left fielder Mike Jaffe, third baseman Vic Scalzi, pitcher Sam Sloat, right fielder Danny Redd and catcher Bucky O'Brian, who appeared only in the last book. Bix Hanson, first the No. 1 pitcher and later a coach, was the only other character in every book, along with the diehard Pickles, who was never known by any other name and served throughout as the devoted clubhouse man (that's also realistic, since clubhouse men lasted a long time with many teams).

The following list includes most of the names in the series. Most of them appeared more than once, but many appeared only in one book, which created a true-to-life feeling, since every major league baseball team undergoes at least a minor roster turnover every season, especially among the utility and backup players. Free agency did not exist in the "Decker Era" of 1947–64, so teams retained many of their players longer than they do today. Even though Decker's reference to the Blue Sox's primary rivals, the Clippers, was obviously directed at the New York Yankees, the Blue Sox themselves also resemble the Bronx Bombers in many respects.

Characters in the Duane Decker Blue Sox Series

Catchers: Bus King, Tweet Tillman, Pete Gibbs, Sol Feinman, Willie "The Lion" Simms, Frank Palaski, Ray "Zip" Zeitler, Bucky O'Brien.

Pitchers: Eddie Lasky, Bix Hanson, Harry Diefendorf, "Honest Abe" Macklin, Joe Condon, Yank Yoland, Herb Ward, Roger Brentano, Turk Pavone, Ran Douglas, Bernie Glaser, Max Fitelson, Joe Rodriguez, Oklahoma Crane, Phil Doyle, Conrad Hom, Sam Sloat, Bracken O'Neill, Fred Cushing.

First basemen: Marty "Beef Trust" Blake, Buster "Stretch" Stookey.

Second basemen: Tommy Shore, Bud Walker, John "Side Pocket" McNulty, Joe Devlin, Varney.

Shortstops: Eddie Lasky, Patsy Bates, Andy Pearson, Slick Hammill.

Third basemen: Johnny Madigan, Mike Marnie, Vic Scalzi.

Left fielders: Luke Carpenter, Tony Piel, Kennie Willard, Sonny Bellucci, Bob Blossom, Mike Jaffe.

Center fielders: Vic Valenti, Dutch Steinhuber, Russ Woodward.

Right fielders: Augie Marshall, Chip Fiske, Duke Page, Danny Redd.

Pinch hitters/utilitymen: Jack Brinkey, Frank Adams, Milo Burns, Buck Riordan, George Wettling, Dick Martin, Chico Rodriguez, Wild Bill Davidson.

Manager: Jug Slavin.

Coaches: Tammany Jones, John "Side Pocket" McNulty, Pops Medlicott (also a manager of other teams), Tweet Tillman, Fido Murphy, Johnny Madigan, Chip Fiske, Rip Radjecki.

General managers: Stan Davis, Nate Tufts.

Owners/Presidents: Tim McCord, Charlie K. O'Neill.

That's a remarkable "universe" of at least 62 players (this author may have missed a pinch hitter or utilityman along the way), plus at least 13 authority figures.

In *Good Field, No Hit,* Decker uses actual major league teams for most of the opponents of the Blue Sox in his first book. For the most part, however, he uses names like the Clippers — forever managed by the combustible Shanty Milligan — along with Redskins, Chiefs, Grays, Panthers, Robins, Cougars, Westerns, Hawks and Pelicans. No one book contains all of those names, or more than the normal number of teams in a league (eight and, later, ten).

Decker created an endless list of names for opposing players, sometimes using names obviously referring to real stars; he also often referred to any number of real Hall of Famers. He usually used only last names, which was not unusual at the time. Most of the time he especially enjoyed creating names obviously intended to refer to real-life stars with the New York Yankees, who won the American League pennant every year from 1947 to 1964 except 1948 and 1954 (both Cleveland) and 1959 (Chicago). There was Mansell for Mickey Mantle, Marlin for Billy Martin, Blondy Lord (and variations) for Whitey Ford, Bower for Hank Bauer, Colman for Joe Coleman, Skanran for Bill Skowron, Bayer for Clete Boyer, Seebum for Norm Sieburn, Berry (and variations) for Yogi Berra, Palazzo for Phil Rizzuto, Richards for Bobby Richardson, Woodlund for Gene Woodling, and on and on.

For fans of postwar baseball, it's especially fun to spot aspects of each book relating to the real-life scene. Decker, probably more than any other prolific novelist of his period, used contemporary names, personalities, problems and developments to inform his series.

NINE

The Sports Series Also-Rans

Clair Bee's Chip Hilton, Wilfred McCormick's Bronc Burnett and Rocky McCune, and Duane Decker's Blue Sox never had any big-time competition in postwar sports series books, from the standpoint of either quality or quantity. Contemporary "rivals" Win Hadfield and Mel Martin were strictly minor-league in terms of sales, but they were nonetheless noteworthy in their own way.

Win Hadfield was unique in series book history: Six novels, six sports, all published by Simon & Schuster in 1960 in one-dollar hardbacks under the house name Mark Porter. They may have been written by as many as six different authors, although Mel Bolden was credited with all six pictorial dust jackets.

Win Hadfield, whose real name is Winfield, was obviously created to take advantage of the popularity of Chip Hilton, who by 1960 had appeared in 18 of his 24-novel series from series book titan Grosset and Dunlap. By that year, Chip Hilton's books had sold untold thousands of copies, beginning in 1948, first for 75 cents and then for one dollar. Today, the Win Hadfield books are difficult to find, especially in dust jackets, and even more difficult to find in nice condition, since they were printed on cheap pulp paper, similar to the poor-quality paper Grosset and Dunlap was forced to use during World War II. All six of my Win Hadfield books are marked "first edition" and all have pages that must be turned carefully to avoid tears.

When Tempo Books, Grosset and Dunlap's paperback arm, reprinted all six from 1962 to 1966, they apparently weren't good sellers, either, with the possible exception of *Winning Pitcher*, #1 in the hardback series and #6 in the Tempo line. Graham Holroyd's fabulous compilation of collectible paperback series and prices lists the titles of all six, but does not identify the author of four of them! Since Holroy identified thousands of authors in a remarkable work of paperback scholarship, this attests to how scarce these paperbacks are.

Although Andy McCue's *Baseball by the Books* identifies the author of *Winning Pitcher* as the little-known novelist Robert H. Leckie, *A Collector's Guide to Hardcover Boys' Series Books* credits *Winning Pitcher* to Jack Pearl. There followed, in order, *Keeper Play* (football), credited to Leckie; *Overtime Upset* (basketball), credited to John Ott; *Set Point* (tennis), uncredited; *Slashing Blades* (hockey), credited to James Anthony Cox; and *Duel on the Cinders* (track and field), uncredited. Simon & Schuster came late to the series book games and apparently believed in releasing all the stories at once, or at least in close proximity. All six of the publisher's Sandy Steele Adventures by house pseudonym Roger Barlow were released in 1959. *A Collectors Guide* credits them to Ott, Pearl and Leckie along with two uncredited books.

The Win Hadfield books suffer from having different authors, since there is little continuity referenced in any of the books other than the names of the characters. They all take place before Win's senior year at Dixboro High School in Massachusetts, during his junior year (and in the case of the tennis story, in the summer before his senior year). This, apparently, was done to allow for Hadfield's senior-year exploits, but those would never occur. In each story, Win Hadfield must overcome serious problems posed by Dan Slade, Win's highly skilled but often unethical and unsportsmanlike rival. Slade, whose father is a wealthy and influential but not unlikable businessman, always seems to be at least moderately reformed at the end of each story. Yet he always turns up as an unreformed bad sport in the next tale.

Tom Joyce, a devoted bachelor coach and physical education teacher with more than two decades of experience following a stellar college athletic career, is the other central figure in each story, although his role in the tennis tale is limited. Joyce is head coach of the football, basketball, baseball and track teams — an unlikely combination at virtually all American high schools by 1960 except the very smallest — and he also plays a major role in the hockey story. In none of the stories does Joyce have more than one assistant, and that assistant is named only in the football story. By 1960, such a load would have been unheard of in any American school. And while the vast majority of American schools today allow athletes to participate in only three sports seasons, there were (and still are) a few schools that allowed dual spring competition in baseball and track.

Chip Hilton, the most famous three-sport athlete in all of fiction outside of the Merriwell brothers, never competed in track during the spring, much less hockey or tennis at any time. Win Hadfield thus was the most versatile athlete in the history of modern American sports fiction. It will come as a surprise to no one that Win was quarterback of the football team, playmaking guard on the basketball squad, and star pitcher/hitter of the baseball team. In track, he was both a star sprinter on the 880 relay team (an event long since supplanted in real life by the mile relay) and an outstanding half-miler.

Oddly, the tennis story is #4 in the series, even though it apparently takes place in the summer after all the other stories. Even Simon & Schuster, however, could not find a way to cram tennis into the school year. In fact, Dixboro apparently did not field a tennis team — Dixboro is a small town — and there is no reference to interscholastic tennis. The hockey story, which takes place during the winter, features Win and his buddies, plus the devilish Slade, on a club hockey team, fulfilling the Massachusetts boys' not unreasonable dream of playing competitive hockey. There is, however, no mention of basketball, so internal logic is definitely missing here. Since the back of each dust jacket refers to all six books, the publisher definitely intended the reader to seek out each volume.

Even more oddly, the baseball story concludes in June at the end of Win's junior year, even though this apparently comes after the action in the football, basketball and hockey books. On the third page of the track story, it's written that "Win looked around appreciatively at the campus — so familiar now in his third year at Dixboro" (which is always referred to as a school with freshmen). There is, however, no mention of track in the baseball story and vice versa. Yet in the hockey story, there is a reference to Neal Travers, a sportswriter who causes no end of trouble for Hadfield and Joyce in the basketball story during the school year before the hockey story is set. It's all a bit confusing for those who appreciate the logical continuity of the Chip Hilton series, but apparently Simon & Schuster figured the young readers wouldn't be picky about the time elements.

Although McCue lists *Winning Pitcher* as "young adult" in his review in *Baseball by the Books*, the Hadley series seems intended for a younger audience of readers 10 to 14 — readers not yet as old as Win, who is clearly 16 years old in each story. McCue's entire review could serve as a concise plot summary of each book: "Win Hadley pitches well, reforms teammates, does good."

Winning Pitcher gives an extensive origin of the characters in the first chapter, with much more background than any of the other books provide, so this book clearly was intended to be read first. The chapter introduces Win's best friend, fellow three-sport athlete Matt Hughes, who plays the roles typically assigned to sidekicks: offensive lineman, catcher, reserve forward. The reader is told how Win's father, the physician Eldon Hadley, had died 10 years earlier, when Win was 6 years old and his ever-faithful brother Walt was 14. So, like Chip Hilton, Win grows up in the home of a widowed single mother.

The first chapter also introduces another key character, George "Scoop" Slocum, who is such a star school journalist that the local professional paper sometimes pays him for stories. Although Slocum is respected as a loyal supporter of the Dixboro Cougars, he is also the butt of jokes and hijinks, although he plays a couple of heroic roles, as well. Ironically, Slocum may be the most fully realized — and most realistic — character in the series, which otherwise does not portray journalists in a good light.

Every now and then, the Win Hadfield series offers wisdom that young readers would have done well to try to understand. *Winning Pitcher* offers this conversation between Win and Walt after the older brother tells Win that Dan Slade is jealous of him:

> Walt: Everything Dan has was given to him. He never earned anything on his own.... Look, do you remember how you felt when you earned your first couple of dollars on the old paper route? It was different from asking Mom for money, wasn't it? Why? Because you had worked for it and took pride in it.
> Win: Yes, I think I see what you're driving at. Dan is still getting handouts from his father. I can see how he might feel about that. But what's that got to do with sports? Dan works plenty hard at baseball. You should have seen him today. He was terrific. Maybe I'm a little jealous of him.
> Walt: Dan doesn't work hard at playing the game. He works hard at playing the big shot. There's no satisfaction in doing a thing just to feed your ego. The real reward is sharing the fun with the rest of the fellows of a victory won together. You know that, Win.

In the third chapter of *Winning Pitcher*, however, the author goes from the sublime to the ridiculous. He has Dan Slade ordering his teammates to sit around the pitching mound as he strikes out the side in a scrimmage. Tom Joyce, of course, doesn't like this and expresses his distaste, but he doesn't suspend Slade, either, which is hardly realistic, then or now. Then the book quickly returns to the sublime, as Slade tells Win, "You're the kind of kid makes me sorry I don't have a son of my own."

After Win pitches a one-hitter in the championship game, the book oddly finishes with a boxing bout between Win and Dan, even though they seemed to have somewhat patched up their differences. Joyce referees the bout, because, unknown to the two athletes, he plans a boxing team during the next school year, much to the satisfaction of both boys when they find out.

As the story concludes, Win tells Matt, "You know, Dan Slade and I may never be friends, but at least I think we understand and respect each other a little better than before," to which Matt replies, "I know what you mean. I have the feeling that the long war between Dan Slade and the rest of Dixboro High is over. At least the truce looks promising." Obviously, *Winning Pitcher* should have been #5 in the series, not #1.

In the football story *Keeper Play*, Slade learns his lesson in a confrontation with his father, who learns just how sneaky and egotistical his son is. In the climactic game against rival Crawford High, Dan laterals to Win for the game-tying touchdown and Matt Hughes wins the title with his extra point kick. This comes after Walt tells Win a few chapters earlier that: The worst thing a man can do with his troubles, Win, is to keep them to himself. That's something most men don't learn until they go out in the world. But you can save yourself a lot of grief if you learn it now. Now, let's have it."

An otherwise entertaining story — probably the best in the series — is terribly unrealistic in one regard, however, with this line when Win seeks help from Joyce on the sidelines: "Other coaches might be guilty of coaching from the side lines, but not Tom Joyce." Many coaches still let their quarterbacks call the plays in the Win Hadfield era, but precious few would have avoided coaching from the sidelines!

In *Overtime Upset*, the book ends early in the basketball season — in fact, before a big game against Crawford — after Win and his buddies solve the political problems caused by a phony community junior high school coach and a selfish sportswriter. Like *Keeper Play*, this one also had an unusual angle: The real big game was Win's coaching victory while leading his youngsters to an upset over a heavy favorite. If *Keeper Play* isn't the best book in the series, this one is. What mars this book, however, is cardboard characterizations of the self-serving coach and the troublesome writer. Other than Dixboro student journalist "Scoop" Slocum — who is upbraided several times by Joyce several times in the series— reporters in this series are always dunderheads or worse. Other writers also frequently made the press the villain of the piece, which might work well in a story about pro sports but seems overstated in a story about high school athletics. Most reporters who cover high school sports— at least the older ones— actually enjoy giving fair-minded recognition to hardworking youngsters.

Set Point, the tennis story, should have been #6, not #4, unless the reader prefers to believe that *Flashing Blades*, the hockey story, should have been the last book. *Set Point*, in which Win claims the state championship, is the weakest book of the series in many ways, especially since there is a ludicrous 50-page encounter with two bank robbers! This story harkens back to dime novel days

Keeper Play by Mark Porter (a pseudonym), one of six Win Hadley stories, all about a different sport (jacket copyright 1960, Simon & Schuster). Mel Bolden portrays Win Hadfield playing quarterback as the most versatile of all series athletes.

and villains with black mustaches. Even sillier, when the boys beat the baddies, a bandit tells the boys, "Nice going, kids. You did us in, all right, but I got to hand it to you, you done real good." This from a man who threatened the boys with a gun!

Flashing Blades, in contrast, has a more likely if still unrealistic scenario, when Win helps rescue the son of a former professional hockey star from drowning in an ice mishap. The hockey star, fittingly named Buffer Bouchere, is a nicely realized character, perhaps the most realistic in the entire series. He helps Win and his buddies—who form a club team to fulfill their dreams of playing hockey—to develop the skills needed to beat a powerhouse club from Crawford after an earlier embarrassment against the same team.

Duel on the Cinders is a solid track and field story, filled with interesting references to the sport and not a few setbacks for Win. But it has one glaring flaw: There are repeated references to how difficult it would be for Win to compete on both the 880-yard relay and in the 880-yard run. In 1960, the mile—the event Win had to give up to help his team—was the longest distance held in high school meets; the 2-mile was more than a decade in the future, except during cross-country season. But even then, the idea that someone could not run both a 220-yard sprint relay leg and the open half-mile would not have made much sense. Win's big victory in the 880, by the way, was accomplished with a good but far from great time. Today, both high school boys and girls have been known to compete in the 800, 1,600 and 3,200 meters—the equivalent of the half-mile, mile and 2-mile—in the same meet.

All in all, the Win Hadfield series featured more good than bad reading, leaving the reader wondering what would have happened to Win as a senior, or in college. But Win came late to the inexpensive series books, which were generally shunned by libraries during their heyday. Series book publishers abandoned dust jackets in the early 1960s in favor of picture covers and later paperback formats. Series books of all types were pretty much finished as a hardback genre by the end of the 1960s or early 1970s except for the still-prospering Hardy Boys and Nancy Drew.

A few postwar sports series books were obviously intended for readers 12 to 18, and can still be read with enjoyment. These weren't the $1 variety—prices were generally in the $2 range—and this probably explains why they were short-lived. Libraries, however, did carry most of them. The longest series was also the most obscure—the five-book Frenchy Beaumont series from Charles Spain Verral from Thomas Y. Crowell for young readers, covering hockey, basketball and baseball in the 1950s.

Former pulp writer R.G. Emery contributed three books for Macrae Smith about Johnny Hyland, a Major League Baseball player who goes from pitcher to catcher to third baseman. Emery, who wrote as "Lieutenant R.G. Emery" for the pulps, also had two books about Larry Warren, a West Point Cadet. The prolific pulp author Burgess Leonard turned to hardbound books in the 1951–63 period, writing six for Lippincott dealing with Major League Baseball including two about pitcher Clem Gompers and three about shortstop/manager Stretch Bolton. Likewise, another prolific pulpster, Arthur Mann, penned a three-book series about baseball "bonus baby" Bob White in 1952 and 1953 for the David McKay Company, which also published the first editions for Bronc Burnett #12–23 before Grosset and Dunlap endlessly reprinted them.

The only prolific hardbound author who developed a series was John Tunis, often considered the best of all sports fiction writers for young people and the author of 16 hardbound sports stories from 1938 to 1958 (see chapter ten). Tunis, who got his start in the pulps in the 1920s (see chapter one), wrote three books about pitcher/outfielder Roy Tucker:

The Kid from Tomkinsville (1940), *World Series* (1941) and *The Kid Comes Back* (1946). Tucker also appears in the rest of Tunis' baseball novels except for *Buddy and the Old Pro* (1955).

Ed Fitzgerald, a famed sportswriter and for many years editor of *Sport* magazine, turned to fiction with three books about Marty Ferris from 1948 to 1952: *The Turning Point, College Slugger* and *Yankee Rookie* for A.S. Barnes and Co. (see chapter seven). For many years, Barnes was the undisputed king of "how-to" technical nonfiction books about sports.

There were also short series by little-known authors such as Ken Anderson (the three-book, three-sport Tom Huntner series from Christian publisher Zondervan during 1944 to 1947), Robert Wells (the four-book Five-Yard Fuller football series for Putnam from 1964 to 1970) and Isadore S. Young (the three-book, three-sport Carson series for Follett from 1961 to 1969).

The ever-battered batter: Mel Martin

Baseball and mystery mixed with murder became common in novels intended for adults beginning in the 1980s, but sports-connected sleuthing was a rarity for both juvenile readers and their elders when star pitcher/batter Mel Martin hit the scene in 1947. Even though he appeared in only six books, Mel took enough physical abuse from crooks and rivals to fill more than twice that many volumes. These stories, written under the house name John R. Cooper by anonymous authors, owe a lot to Stratemeyer's best-selling Hardy Boys series, which began two decades earlier under the Grosset and Dunlap imprint.

Cupples & Leon, the publisher of numerous series books intended for young people in the 1930s, including the popular Kay Tracey mysteries for girls, published a Stratemeyer Syndicate baseball story, *Mystery at the Ball Park*, in 1947, followed up in the same year by *The Southpaw's Secret*.

"Mel Martin Baseball Stories" was prominent on the dust jackets of the Cupples & Leon books, which indicated the stories were designed for readers 9 to 13 years old. Indeed, they were written in such a basic, albeit breathtaking, style that it's doubtful they would have held the interest of many high-school age readers. The final four volumes — *The Phantom Homer, First Base Jinx, The College League Mystery* and *The Fighting Shortstop* — were first printed by Garden City Books in 1952 and 1953 and reprinted on poor-quality paper by Books, Inc., using the same dust jackets. Both firms also reprinted the first two volumes, with new dust jackets. Fifteen of Kay Tracey's original 18 adventures from Cupples &Leon were rewritten and renumbered for publication by Garden City and Books, Inc., during the same period. The Garden City volumes were priced at 95 cents, but Books, Inc., did not indicate a price anywhere on the book, apparently leaving merchants to supply their own pricing labels.

Reference books all list *The Fighting Shortstop* as fifth in the series, but it's clearly the sixth book, what with references to the outcome of the fifth story. This mistake is understandable since *The Fighting Shortstop* referred to itself as the fifth book! In fact, in the Books, Inc., reprint, *The College League Mystery* is not listed.

I can't possibly improve on Andy McCue's description of the first Mel Martin story in *Baseball by the Books*: "A high school junior, Mel must beat out a senior, discover what's fishy about the new coach, solve a string of robberies, and save the ballpark." That nicely sums up the entire series: all plot, with no complex character development to speak of. Even so, the books are fun to read, if only because they're so outrageously improbable. Although their language is up-to-date and the baseball slang is not too far-fetched, the plots seem to have come out of the Frank Merriwell dime novels of two generations earlier. After suffering the occasional setback in each story, Mel and his buddies always prevail in spectacular form to claim championships at the end of each story, not to mention solving every mystery and making sure the bad guys get theirs.

Unlike the six-book Win Hadfield series in 1960, the Mel Martin stories did have a logical, progressive continuity. In *The Southpaw's Secret*, the boys claim honors in a summer camp league after overcoming much nefarious activity by both youngsters and adults alike. *The Phantom Homer* details Mel's senior season at Westwood High — it's never clearly stated where Westwood is — and *First Base Jinx* covers conquests and crime as Mel & Co. graduate to a summer league town team populated primarily by adults. *The College League Mystery* follows with the way Mel and his buddies win a freshman league championship for Starbuck College and even get promoted to the varsity for the season's final game (which

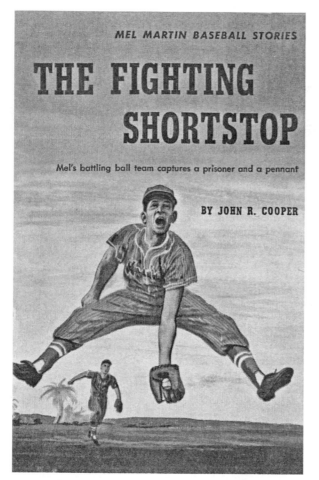

MEL MARTIN BASEBALL STORIES

THE FIGHTING SHORTSTOP

Mel's battling ball team captures a prisoner and a pennant

BY JOHN R. COOPER

The Fighting Shortstop by John R. Cooper (a pseudonym), one of the six Mel Martin baseball stories (jacket copyright 1953, Cupples & Leon). Mel Martin solves a crime and leads Starbuck College to baseball glory.

would have been illegal at the time!). A new character, Cuban shortstop Chico Gomez, plays a major role for Starbuck and then talks Mel into summer adventures in a Cuban league in pre–Castro days in *The Fighting Shortstop*.

The Stratemeyer Syndicate's writer(s) had a propensity to make outrageous puns out of names, such as the nickname of Mel's beloved high school coach: Pop Korn (his real name is Fred). Mel's best friends are the twins Lefty and Righty Wright — that's correct, they throw with different arms — and Hobart "Speed" Ball, who hates his real name but throws so hard from the outfield that everyone calls him Speed. Then there were obvious ne'er-do-wells such as on-field rivals Nick Naston in *The Phantom Homer* and Ray Sharp in *First Base Jinx*. One of the key characters in the series is Mel's kindly and wise uncle, Robbie Smith, described in *First Base Jinx* as "brother of Mel's widowed mother ... a sporting goods salesman ... and a former big leaguer. He had coached Mel since he was a lad."

The most entertaining — and perhaps most unlikely — story is *First Base Jinx*, in which Lefty invents a new type of first baseman's mitt, only to see it stolen and copied. It's a pip of a mystery, and ends with Lefty recovering his mitt and using it to make a leaping, game-ending catch for a championship. The story is written at a breakneck pace, with most of the 25 chapters in the 180-page tale ending with a cliff-hanger paragraph. Here are a few examples:

> A second later, Mel and Lefty were lying flat on the sidewalk — unconscious!
>
> Before Mel could shout a warning, the boy ran near the end of the board, slipped, and cracked his head hard on its edge. Stunned, he went limp, then dropped into the water!
>
> "Hey, fellows, Gere's in jail!"
>
> Mel was in a crushing vise as the truck rolled out of the freight yard!
>
> After that [chloroform attack], there was blackness.
>
> "You've been a hard fellow to track down," the stranger said ominously. "I want to talk to you!" With that he shot his fist into Mel's face.
>
> But it was too late for Geronimo to jam on the air brakes to avoid a crash.
>
> From the Westwood stands, a groan arose as their star pitcher [Mel] toppled forward off the rubber!

All that in one story! The Mel Martin Baseball Stories were clearly not designed for the faint of heart. The series ends with Mel shouting, "And a chance at varsity baseball in the spring!" But, alas, we can only guess about his ensuing heroics at Starbuck College. Mel Martin never took the literary field again, except in the early 1980s with the first four volumes from Simon & Schuster.

TEN

John Tunis:
The Best of the Best

In terms of production, John Tunis was nowhere near the most prolific sports novelist for the young-adult market, even though he wrote 16 outstanding sports novels over a two-decade period (1938–1958), among other books before, during and after this remarkable phase. Even so, Tunis probably sold more nonseries sports novels than any other author of his day, although Clair Bee's Chip Hilton series almost surely holds the overall sports literature record. Tunis' books inevitably won favorable reviews and numerous awards, and every municipal and school library contained his work. They were reprinted endlessly and some have remained in print for many years, albeit as historical curiosities of what the best sports fiction was like. Ask any sports-oriented fellow born from about 1930 through 1960 what sports author he remembers best, and chances are you'll hear "John Tunis," along with series titans Bee and Wilfred McCormick (see chapter seven). Tunis' books were everywhere. Although first editions in jackets are not common, reading copies turn up by the dozens in used-book stores.

Tunis (1889–1975) was a former sportswriter who also contributed a little fiction to pulp magazines, plus much nonfiction, to a wide variety of publications for many years. He was nearly 50 when he reworked one of his pulp stories to produce *The Iron Duke* (1938) and *The Duke Decides* (1939), both stories of ethics, college life and track and field, pretty much in that order. He hit the sports novel jackpot, however, with *The Kid from Tomkinsville* (1940), which is quite likely the best-remembered young-adult sports novel of all, and was followed by an immediate sequel, *World Series*. Millions upon millions of baseball players came to identify with pitcher-turned-outfielder Roy Tucker, The Kid himself, who ultimately appeared in all eight of the author's stories about the Brooklyn Dodgers. Indeed, even though Tunis' novels were still selling well in 1960s reprints, the Dodgers were forever to be located in Brooklyn, long after they began playing in Los Angeles in 1958.

Tunis' stories are not only sheer, unadulterated Americana, but also are generally well ahead of their time. Above all, they stressed character, conscience, effort and teamwork but in ways far ahead of most of their pulp-style brothers. Tunis almost always wrote with original twists seen in no other works about sport. He was the first to write seriously about racial, political and religious issues. His athletes often failed, even though they usually succeeded in the end. They were frequently injured and his descriptions of both physical and mental pain in sports still remain among the most vivid ever consigned to the printed page. You can almost feel the tears, the sweat, and, frequently, the blood staining the pages! To the adult reader, much of his work seems padded with greetings, cheers, and small talk, not to mention some of the game descriptions, but to the middle-school and high-school students who read his work, much of this creates atmosphere and is relatively fresh.

If you want to know what sports, society and both school life and Major League Baseball's environment felt like in the 1940s and 1950s, read Tunis. Other prolific sports novelists of the era, notably Duane Decker and Frank O'Rourke, wrote in a similar vein, but only a few writers could approach Tunis. He occasionally would come up with improbable circumstances to finish the story in a dramatic way; but, on the whole, he was about as "un-pulp" as an author for young-adult readers could be. Many adults read his stories with pleasure, too, and they're still being read today. Ironically, the only movie made from one of his splendid novels was RKO's obscure *Hard, Fast and Beautiful* (1951), very loosely based on *American Girl* (1929) (although the film is often credited to his tennis classic *Champion's Choice* (1940), which was his only young-adult novel about a female athlete (see chapter twelve). Probably not so coincidentally, original editions of the tennis stories are the hardest to find among his output. Indeed, *Champion's Choice* was the only one of his novels to be resold as part of a reprint series in Tunis' lifetime: the 1948 Falcon Sports Books from World Publishing. They were a cheaply produced six-book series, and most people now have to settle for a Falcon edition, complete with disintegrating paper, if they want to read the worthwhile *Champion's Choice*.

Tunis wrote more than half of his output in distinct pairs: the Duke and Kid from Tomkinsville books were followed by the pairings of *Keystone Kids* (1943) and *Rookie of the Year* (1944) — both Dodger epics with Tucker as a background character — then *Highpockets* (1948) and *Young Razzle* (1949), yet more Dodger tales with Tucker in a minor supporting role. The other pair were two of the finest stories ever written about high school basketball and citizenship issues: *Yea! Wildcats!* (1944) and *A City for Lincoln* (1945).

Tunis wrote one football story, *All-American* (1942), and a third Kid from Tomkinsville tale, *The Kid Comes Back* (1946), the first third of which involved Roy Tucker's perilous military duty in the European Theater of World War II. Tunis wrote a third, unrelated basketball story, *Go, Team, Go!* (1954), followed by a brilliant and shockingly unsentimental lesson for grade-school readers, *Buddy and the Old Pro* (1955). His eighth Dodger story was his final sports novel: *Schoolboy Johnson* (1958), something of an alternate-world tale in which the Dodgers never left Brooklyn and Roy Tucker's heretofore unknown daughter played a major role, falling in love with a brash rookie pitcher during Tucker's last season as a player.

Tunis' first ten young-adult sports novels were published by Harcourt Brace, through *A City for Lincoln* in 1945. Morrow published the final six sports novels, usually with a listing of all of the author's work, the publishers and the year each was published. This, in itself, was highly unusual. Most sports novelists of the 1940–1970 period did not update their work, but many tried to write in a timeless fashion. Not so Tunis, whose 1940s books were obviously artifacts by the time I first read them in the early 1960s. That, however, did not detract from my enjoyment of them. Older readers could easily accept the stories as time machines; younger readers might not care.

Tunis' books are also distinguished by original dust jackets, unlike most of the pulp-style book cover art then popular on most sports novels. The Tunis jackets are all impressionistic. I like the realistic style better, but the jackets may not have been a sales issue, since Tunis was probably bought largely by libraries. His books were $2.50 or higher, too expensive for most parents except as special gifts in the 1940s and 1950s.

The Kid and others compete well

Tunis was fortunate to face relatively marginal sports competition for the original editions and early reprints of his books published from 1938 to 1946, although the sports pulps were at their peak during that period (see chapter five). However, the second wave of sports series books, not to mention the exceptional hardcover novel production from most of the prolific sports novelists such as C. Paul Jackson and Joe Archibald, had not yet begun, while most sports authors were still writing primarily for the pulps.

The many sports series hardbound books from the 1900–1930 period — well over 300 volumes — already seemed very much like antiques in the late 1930s when Tunis began his fresh and creative assault on the young-adult market, in large part because of the growth of radio, autos and aviation, along with other societal developments that made heroes like Frank Merriwell, Baseball Joe and Gary Grayson seem archaic indeed, even during the 1940s. There was something else that Baseball Joe, the Merriwells and their several dozen sports series brothers never had to face: serious financial competition from comic books, movie serials and B westerns, all of which really got going in earnest in the mid–1930s. Comic books, albeit usually sold for only a dime apiece, cut into the half-dollars youngsters needed for even the cheapest age-appropriate books. Loud and creative special effects, not to mention the colorful verbiage, of the movie serials and westerns, especially those from Republic Studios, were undreamed-of competition for the Merriwell types at the turn of the century.

Nevertheless, the thousands of librarians who bought Tunis novels were not concerned with series books, movies or comic books. They just wanted what they perceived as good contemporary literature for young adults, and Tunis' stories were ideal.

Notwithstanding the many 1920s and 1930s pulp track and field stories from Olympic medalist Jackson Scholz — who later wrote well and long about several other sports — track novels have never been particularly popular. So Tunis turned from his Duke stories to baseball, always the most popular sport in the literature along with the grittier aspects of boxing, which was out of bounds for Tunis. *The Kid from Tomkinsville*, with one of the most endearing titles of any sports books, became a huge hit, especially when Tunis quickly followed that story with *World Series*. Readers didn't absolutely have to know *The Kid* first, but it helped.

When *The Kid* appeared, the most famous of all baseball success stories was Babe Ruth, then five years retired from a career that reads like fiction. Even though he was one of baseball's most feared pitchers in his early 20s with the Boston Red Sox, Ruth was too powerful at bat to be denied a spot in the everyday lineup. When traded to the New York Yankees before the 1920 season, Ruth exploded with 54 home runs, nearly double his own record of 29 homers for the Red Sox in 1919. He went on to set the career record of 714 home runs — a mark that stood for nearly four decades until Hank Aaron surpassed it in 1974 — and all of these fabulous feats made Tunis' first Roy Tucker story seem less unlikely. The difference is that Tucker became a hitter out of necessity, not design, because of an injury. Not even Tunis could have his hero playing every day plus taking a regular pitching start every four days — nobody in Major League history has ever done that — so Tucker, like Ruth, became a fulltime batter.

It wasn't Ruth, however, who inspired the Tucker switch but rather Johnny Cooney, who spent an unspectacular decade primarily as a pitcher (34–44 record) with the Boston Braves from 1921 to 1930, then returned to the major leagues at age 35 as a regular outfielder and occasional first baseman with the Brooklyn Dodgers in 1936 and 1937 and the Braves from 1938 to 1941. Cooney hung on into 1944. During his six seasons as a regular, he hit a grand total of two home runs, both in 1939, and his career total of those two home runs in 3,372 at-bats is historic testament to his determination. No other major leaguer has ever played regularly in the field from age 35 to 40 after such long duty as a pitcher — not to mention a record for power-hitting frustration. Fortunately for Tunis' version of the Dodgers, Tucker had more pop in his mythical bat. He was such a hustler in the outfield, always willing to challenge the fences, that some readers thought Roy was originally fashioned after Pete Reiser, the Dodgers' ill-fated, fence-busting outfielder of the 1940s. But Reiser did not come up to the majors until 1940 and played only 58 games that year, including just 17 in the outfield. Moreover, he was not a pitcher.

The Kid was bombed in his first spring training appearance with the Dodgers. He soon begins to pitch well, but is fined $50 for his blunder on the bases. Soon, just as he begins to learn under reserve catcher Dave Leonard, a patient, empathetic old-timer, he finds out that the Dodgers plan to release Leonard. In the catcher's last game, the heartbroken Tucker throws a no-hitter, giving Leonard a precious memory. Up and down, up and down, this was Tunis' life-like way of handling his characters. Roy wins 14 games in a row but injures his shoulder when he trips in the shower. His 15th victory is an ominous struggle; when he gets bombed trying for number 16, he realizes he is seriously hurt. Not much later, player/ manager Gus "Gabby" Spencer — a dead ringer for Leo Durocher — dies in an auto accident and the Dodgers bring Dave Leonard back as manager. Under Leonard, who likes Tucker's batting potential, the rookie earns playing time as a productive and hardworking outfielder. By the end of the season, Tucker's 14th-inning catch beats the Giants, whose manager had said, "The Dodgers! Say — is Brooklyn still in the league?" Tunis had fun with a similar jinxed comment by Bill Terry of the Giants, already a legendary response to a writer's question.

World Series is just that — an entire book devoted to how Roy helps the Dodgers win the World Series. The dust jacket of an early reprint of *World Series* markets the volume as *The Kid from Tomkinsville in the World Series*. It's an emotional roller coaster for Roy as the World Series goes the limit and Roy, beaned early in the World Series, quickly recovers and receives the chance to win the seventh game at bat. In typical Tunis fashion, the author has the pitcher walk Roy, only to give up a game-winning three-run homer to a teammate! The entire eight-book Dodger series is like this; the real star is the team. This really was the last game as a player for Leonard, who is pressed into duty as the catcher, not long after forcing Roy to apologize to sportswriter Jim Casey for slugging him. The two make up and Casey eventually becomes one of Roy's biggest boosters. On the last page, Dodgers owner Jack MacManus introduces Roy to a fellow Tunis describes as "a white-haired, elderly man with a prominent jaw. MacManus tells the visitor, 'Here, meet Roy Tucker, our right fielder, who did as much as anyone to win that game today. Shake hands with Judge Landis, Roy.'" Greeting the legendary commissioner of baseball caps a World Series in which Roy meets sportswriter Grantland Rice, baseball comedian Al Schact and Philadelphia A's manager Connie Mack — the royalty of the sports world.

Roy is an easy character to like, an inspiration for his attitude, his effort and his occasionally bumbling humanity, and the reader hungers to know him better. Readers, however, had to wait for 1946 to see a full book devoted to him again, *The Kid Comes Back*, although he plays minor roles in both *Keystone Kids* and *Rookie of the Year*. Somehow, it would have been unimaginable not to see a devoted person such as Roy Tucker serve in

World War II, and he does so admirably as a tail gunner who is shot down over Germany and sustains a career-threatening injury early in *The Kid Comes Back*. More than the first third of the book recounts perilous adventures with the French underground and German military foes, along with the frustrations of trying to recover and be discharged, before Roy makes it back to the Dodgers.

When Roy recovers some measure of health, he visits Ebbets Field and is warmed by conversations with his old teammates. When he and Casey spot each other, the respect is palpable. "To Roy, war correspondents were merely sportswriters in uniform," Tunis writes. "But Casey had seen service. He had been with the 4th Marines at Iwo Jima, had gone back to enter Manila with the 37th Division, had flown over Tokyo more than once. Roy's respect for him increased." The next day, Roy reads Casey's column in the doctor's office:

> Roy Tucker, ace center fielder of the Brooks, is home after four years in the Army, of which 22 months were spent abroad in Africa, Corsica and France. When drafted, back in '41, Roy was sent to Fort Riley to play on the ballteam there, but the unusually good-natured farm boy made such a fuss they had to send him into combat duty overseas. He told them he didn't come into the Army to play baseball, and meant it, too. Finally they sent him across in late '42 as sergeant in the 12th Air force, where he had fifty-six missions over Europe, was brought down, captured, and escaped shortly before D-Day. The Kid from Tomkinsville refused to talk about his Army experiences, although he returned with the Silver Star and other decorations. He looks in first-class shape and is ready to rejoin the club.

Tunis' literary time frame is out of whack, since Roy does appear in the 1943 and 1944 baseball books, but it's understandable storytelling license. After all, the author was writing primarily for young adults and he probably never imagined pop cultural historians would still study and review his work more than 60 years later! Late in the story, Roy helps a rookie, Lester Young, who is trying to take Roy's job. When the rookie thanks him, Roy tells him, "What helps you, helps all. I'll get my cut of the Series dough if we win, whether I'm a regular or not. That's how the boys are; they'll vote it to me, that's the spirit on this here club." In those long ago days, three decades before the advent of free agency and long before high salaries, a winning World Series share could sometimes double a player's salary, and the share was important to everyone.

Roy's attitude helps Young adjust to being shifted to first base, for manager Spike Russell, who was introduced in *Keystone Kids*, wants to find ways to field the strongest lineup, regardless of personal feelings. And, near the end of the season, Tunis surprises the reader when Spike Russell, who is also a lot like Leo Durocher, shifts Roy to third base because he is the best person available to replace the injured regular. Roy is frankly fearful and hesitant to make the change; he has already gone through much agony recovering both his health and his position in the outfield. Then, in the ninth inning of the game the Dodgers must win to claim the pennant, comes this description: "Suddenly there came [to Roy] words he had heard as a youngster, words he had heard men repeat many times before, words he had often read but that had had no real meaning to him. For the first time now they had a meaning. 'The only thing we have to fear is fear itself.' Forget this thing that's holding me back. Forget it. The only thing to fear is fear."

With two outs and last-gasp veteran Fat Stuff Foster on the mound, Roy chases a foul fly as everyone else warns him to "look out!" because he is in danger. Then Tunis writes as only he could, making the reader tingle and sweat with admiration for Roy:

> Then the low rail of the front boxes smashed into his thigh with a terrific blow. Off balance he lunged, jumped forward with a last-second stab, and speared the ball with his gloved hand as he

plunged over the rail and into the box. His shoulder whanged against an iron chair hastily vacated by a frightened customer. His head hit something hard as he tumbled to the concrete floor. His shoulders first, then his body, and then his legs disappeared from sight. But the ball was in his mitt. Someone helped him up, yanked him to his feet, and pulled him onto the field again. He tossed the ball to the grass and staggered ahead until someone put an arm about his shoulder and led him to the dugout. His hip ached where he had fallen, his arm was skinned where he had scraped it on the floor, his head hurt where he had smacked it. But he had held that ball. The game was over.

Soon, Fat Stuff is telling Casey, "Six months ago he couldn't even walk.... [T]he best thing I had out there today was my fielders, and especially that Kid from Tomkinsville." What person who loves baseball, who ever argued with his coach over a change in position or a bad break, wouldn't learn from this story? Tunis was single-handedly responsible for teaching millions of readers the meaning of unselfish teamwork and sportsmanship, over and over and over again.

The Kid Comes Back was Tunis' first book for Morrow; the previous 10 were for Harcourt, Brace. When he completed two more baseball books, *Highpockets* (1948) and *Young Razzle* (1949), that gave him 12 full-length, non-series sports novels in 12 years. While earlier writers like Gilbert Patten, Ralph Henry Barbour, William Heyliger and Harold M. Sherman turned in more stories, Tunis had set the bar far higher for high-caliber sports fiction, and all between the ages of 49 and 60. For that matter, nobody else in America wrote 10 sports novels in the turbulent 1940s, when younger authors were either away on military duty or still toiling for the sports pulps. In fact, in Andy McCue's year-by-year list in *Baseball by the Books*, Tunis has seven of the 26 non-series baseball novels in the 1940s, either adult or young adult. By any standard, it is a remarkable stretch of baseball fiction.

Keystone Kids

Tunis' next two baseball books, *Keystone Kids* (1943) and *Rookie of the Year* (1944), eventually take place in the same season but are quite different thematically. Although ostensibly the story of two North Carolina country boys — shortstop Spike Russell and second baseman Bob Russell, slick-fielding brothers who have long played together through school and the minor leagues — the tale eventually becomes one of Tunis' numerous stories involving social justice.

Ginger Crane, yet another Leo Durocher type, is the new manager of the Dodgers but an unwelcome contrast to the patient, wise Dave Leonard, who has moved on to another team. Ginger, in fact, tries to split the brothers not long after they have joined the Dodgers by sending Bob to the minors, causing much emotional consternation for both. Bob and Spike finally relent, but Bob stays in the big leagues thanks to a teammate's injury. Early in the story, at the end of the 1942 season (which is referred to in *Rookie of the Year*), Tunis has a sportswriter describe them this way: "Spike, the elder, is quiet and conscientious; Bob, the younger [a good editor would have excised those unneeded words], is rowdy and raucous. Besides being Ginger Crane's solution to the infield problem that has been bothering the little manager all season, both boys have the ability to make the tough ones look easy.... These Dodger freshmen may turn out to be one of the finest keystone combinations in baseball."

In the off-season, Spike displays the business acumen and people skills that will soon lead Dodger owner Jack MacManus to promote him to manager. Determined to hold out for what he feels is a fair salary for both brothers, Spike receives an amazing lecture about team finances: "Then we spent $19,856 for railroad fares.... [Y]our uniforms were worth exactly $4,626. We spent $8,111 for baseballs. Your bats alone cost the club $632. I made out a check the other day to the Brooklyn Laundry for $6,789 for cleaning your uniforms, your underwear, and the towels. Away from home your hotel bills amounted to $17,146." That was only the middle of his lecture! So what does Spike do? He reaches into his pocket and tells the owner, "Mr. MacManus, sir, here's a five spot if it'll help you any." A few pages of hemming and hawing later, the owner has given in and awarded the boys even more than they had sought! The idea that any owner could spout off figures like this was ludicrous, of course, but a marvelous tongue-in-cheek touch by Tunis.

When the Dodgers call up Jewish catcher Jocko Klein midway through the book, the story turns and becomes far more intense. Spike soon is made manager of the Dodgers. Hall of Fame shortstop Lou Boudreau became the real-life player-manager of the Cleveland Indians at age 25 in 1942. Telling his teammates he wants to "win ballgames, not arguments," Spike says the team's many rhubarbs are history. "I b'lieve players do better when they keep cool, when they don't lose their heads." He even forces the diva of the Dodgers, flamboyant but outstanding pitcher Razzle Nugent, to take his turn throwing batting practice. Klein is the target of "Jew-boy" barbs from teammates and opponents alike, including Spike's brother Bob. Klein lets it get to him and he slumps badly, much to Spike's frustration. Spike knows Klein is a fine person and a fine ballplayer. Eventually, when Klein tells him "OK, Spike, I'll try. I'll give it everything; gimme a chance and I think I'll pull out of this spin," Spike replies, "Dam [sic] right you will. I'm not giving up on you, Jocko. Don't you give up on yourself." Roy Tucker, not at all to the reader's surprise, is not part of the prejudice.

Nothing is easy for Spike, however, especially when he tells his brother Bob "If you'd only try to understand the guy a little, he might be [a good teammate]. And we might become a team, too." Bob hurts Spike when he responds: "Hey, what is this? A Lonely Hearts club? I always thought it was a bunch of ball players. Be reasonable, Spike. C'mon now, be reasonable. Be a good fellow; be reasonable about this. You got the whole team against you. What can you expect of a Jew-boy? You better trade him, and the sooner the better, I'd say. No wonder he can't take it; he never will with you a-babying him the way you do."

Spike, though, won't give up on Klein and won't let his teammates continue to abuse him. During a clubhouse meeting, Spike bluntly talks to the team:

> He isn't yeller. He's a scrapper. Yessir, he's a fighter. He's a fighter and he's fighting something big. He's fighting, how shall I say it, he's fighting what all of us who aren't Jews have done to all those who are, not just right now, not just right here, but so far back you wouldn't understand. It's what they've had to fight, really, since the start of things. You see, you fellas, this isn't just one kid, here, now. It isn't only Jocko Klein you guys are riding. I wonder can I make you understand? This boy Klein isn't yeller. He's a fighter, only he isn't fighting any of you. He's fighting two thousand years. Now all this has gotta stop. As long as I'm manager, all you boys will make Jocko Klein feel he's one of us.... [W]hat you boys are doing is murder. You heard me, murder. I know he's weak when it comes to a question of his race. [Here, Tunis deliberately points out that even well-meaning people still call the Jews a race.] OK, you guys are using it to destroy his confidence. You're also destroying the team.... [F]rom now on, this Jew-boy stuff is out.

Roy Tucker, clearly on Spike's side in contrast to Bob's negative attitudes, struggles hard to convince Bob that Jocko Klein has the right stuff. Or, as Roy tells Bob of the lesson Dave Leonard taught Roy when he was a troubled rookie, "Only the game fish swim upstream."

Many, many more words of conflict and encouragement follow; Tunis makes it clear that fighting prejudice is a grinding, difficult process, and not something worked over in a day or a speech, however powerful. Coming on the heels of Tunis' exceptional, groundbreaking treatment of racial themes in *All-American* (1942), *Keystone Kids* isn't shocking, but it is surprising in its raw power. Moreover, the story proved phenomenally prophetic in dealing with the mindless hatred Jackie Robinson faced in 1947 from many sides when he broke baseball's color line with the Dodgers. *Keystone Kids* is an emotional milestone in baseball writing and the story became more, not less, pertinent as the years went on. By the end of the story, Bob and Spike shake hands and the Dodgers are on the move as a team, including Klein.

Rookie of the Year, which refers to eccentric young pitcher Bones Hathaway, is nowhere near as profound, but the story does strengthen Spike Russell's credentials as a discipline-oriented yet fair and smart manager. Brother Bob Russell and Jim Casey, the opportunistic but fair sportswriter who appears in most of Tunis' baseball stories, ultimately help expose a complex plan by a jealous old traveling

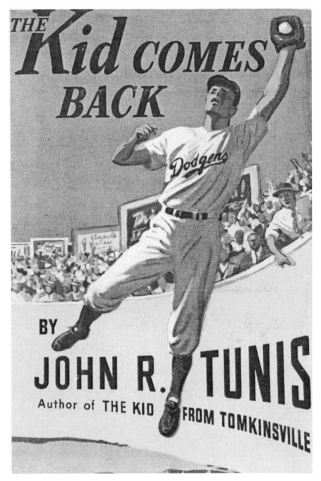

The Kid Comes Back by John R. Tunis, 1946 (jacket copyright, William Morrow). This is the third in the iconic Roy Tucker trilogy, although *The Kid from Tomkinsville* appears in all five of Tunis' other stories about the Dodgers.

secretary, Bill Hanson, who does not like Spike. Hanson tries to undercut Spike's authority and success, and also to frame and ruin Hathaway and another valuable rookie for rules violations. Hanson appeared in the three previous books as a hardworking lover of baseball, prone to nostalgia and a feeling that baseball was better in an earlier era. He was not yet a villain, but his unfairness in *Rookie of the Year* leads to his being fired by team owner MacManus. Spike ultimately plays a hunch and gives the hypercompetitive Hathaway, who is also a good batter, a chance to win the pennant clincher instead of taking him out for a pinch hitter in the climactic game. Hathaway doubles home Bob Russell with the winning run and the Dodgers are headed for the World Series as the story ends.

Leverett T. Smith, Jr., wrote a perceptive essay — one I highly recommend — about the first four Tunis baseball novels, "John R. Tunis' American Epic," which appeared in *The Achievement of American Sport Literature* (1991), edited by Wiley Lee Umphlett. Smith's concluding comment nicely captures the meaning of these connected stories:

My contention is that in light of Tunis' inspirational source [World War II], they constitute a single complex action, epic in scope, one that dramatizes what it means to be a member of a team and what it takes to lead that team. Accordingly, because these novels have no hero, unless it is the Dodger team, the villains are not so much the opposition as they are those who prevent the smooth functioning of the team. That this philosophy might most naturally emerge during a national crisis like World War II is clear. Though Tunis mistrusts the profit motive and opposes authoritarian bureaucracy, he embraces many other values associated with the American business community, above all the primary value ascribed to teamwork ... [and] these four novels reveal him as a keen observer of what it takes to hold a nation together in time of crisis. From this larger perspective, they can be viewed as a bridge between the earlier fantasy element of the sport-fiction tradition and the more realistic and human concerns of later adult fiction that began to proliferate in the late 1950s and 1960s.

In John Dinan's *Sports in the Pulp Magazines*, he accurately says that "While these stories were groundbreaking, Tunis' most popular series (The Kid from Tomkinsville) would

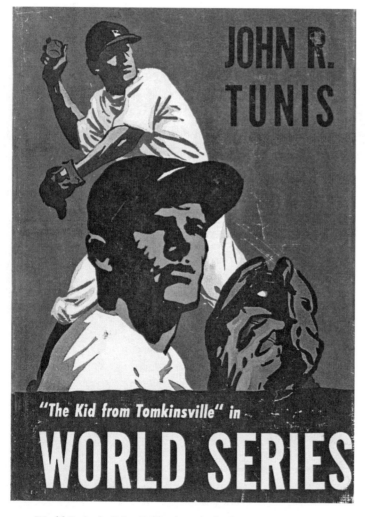

World Series by John R. Tunis, 1941 (jacket copyright, Harcourt, Brace). The second Roy Tucker epic was perhaps the first novel entirely devoted to a World Series.

address what Bobby Knight now tells his team: something to the effect that you're not playing against 'them,' you're playing against yourself. The [Roy Tucker] trilogy is about a boy, growing into manhood, fighting his own demons." Dinan makes one mistake, however, by assuming Tucker in *The Kid Comes Back* is "nearing the age of 40" during his comeback. In reality Tucker is not 40 until *Schoolboy Johnson* (1958), Tunis' last baseball story; and, indeed, Tucker was in his early 20s when he joined the Dodgers in *The Kid from Tomkinsville* (1940). Instead, Tucker is nearing 30 in *The Kid Comes Back*. Dinan, pointing out that "a survey of 50,000 boys in 1949 revealed Tunis as their most popular author," also used a quote from the *New York Times*, which oddly but colorfully said the books had "prose which has the good hard smack of ash against leather." The *Times*, of course, should have said "against horsehide," since that is what balls were made of, along with ash for bats and leather for gloves.

The Tunis classics

When Harcourt Brace Janovich reissued *The Kid from Tomkinsville* in 1987 as part of its Odyssey Classic paperback line for young-adult readers, the publisher included an introduction by Bruce Brooks. In 1987, the world had changed drastically in the near half-century since the book had originally appeared. Yet Brooks' piece pointed out that Tunis' world in 1940 was also far different from that of his youth, when Frank Merriwell reigned supreme and nothing like *The Kid from Tomkinsville* could have been imagined 40 years earlier. "With this book, John R. Tunis rescued the sports novel from the land of fairy tales and put it back where it belonged — between the hard chalk lines of the playing field," Brooks wrote. Later, in writing about the appeal of Roy Tucker, he added, "We also like seeing Roy because, unlike many heroes, he is good without being goody-goody, uplifting without being a heavy-handed example of absolute rectitude. Who needs preachy lessons from a ballplayer? From a ballplayer we need ballplaying.... The Kid from Tomkinsville and other

All-American by John R. Tunis, 1942 (jacket copyright, Harcourt, Brace). Tunis' only high school football novel provides a remarkably farsighted, courageous view for the time concerning the ethics of bigotry.

books in the series give today's readers a rare chance to enter the good old world of pure baseball." True enough. Even so, Tunis also used athletes and athletics to preach citizenship, honor and a stick-to-it determination — whether in pro baseball or high school sports — without being preachy. One can only imagine how many teenagers were influenced for the better by his novels.

Tunis could also, however, just tell a ripping good story, and did so in both *Highpockets* (1948) and *Young Razzle* (1949), which were reprinted in 1991 by Morrow in response to the Odyssey Classic Series. Interestingly, the Odyssey reprints, on a page listing "also by John R. Tunis," listed only the author's 10 books for Harcourt, Brace (1938–1945). Morrow reprinted the rest, beginning with Tunis' first book for Morrow, *The Kid Comes Back*, but nonetheless listed all 16 sports novels along with two non-sports books he wrote in the 1960s (there were other books, but these were long out of print). To explain the player-manager Spike Russell to readers, Morrow included a note: "On baseball teams before 1950, unlike those of today, it was not unusual for the team's manager to also play one of the positions in the field. In this book, Spike Russell is both the Dodgers' manager and its short-stop."

Highpockets and *Young Razzle* are strong stories of the Dodgers, with many familiar names, including Roy Tucker and Spike Russell, but racial and citizenship issues are not part of the stories, even though Jackie Robinson and a few other blacks caused a sensation in 1947 and 1948 when they broke teams' color lines in both the National and American leagues. The stories are instead pure plot, more pulpish in their approach than Tunis' previous five baseball novels.

Yea! Wildcats! by John R. Tunis, 1944 (jacket copyright, Harcourt, Brace). The legendary Indiana High School Tournament was only 33 years old when Tunis' first basketball novel appeared, covering every aspect of the event, on and off the court.

Highpockets tells the tale of Cecil "Highpockets" McDade, a conceited, arrogant, self-absorbed rookie outfielder with plenty of power-hitting talent but few friends, in or out of baseball. Tunis throws in a nifty twist when Cecil, driving a car fans have given him on his "day," injures young stamp collector Dean Kennedy. This changes the lives of both; Cecil picks up an interest in stamps to help the youngster recover, and the boy becomes intrigued by baseball for the first time.

Young Razzle is a stronger story, the account of how the flamboyant old Dodger warhorse, pitcher Razzle Nugent, and his estranged son, second baseman Joe Nugent, come to an understanding that each is a flawed but worthwhile person. It's sad, but somewhat realistic, that it takes virtually the entire story for them to have a genuine conversation, so stubborn, misinformed and confused are both players. Tunis himself gets excited when, with Razzle demoted and Joe promoted to Triple-A, he writes, "For the first time in big-league baseball a father and son were to meet on the diamond." This was a minor-league game!

When Joe hits a home run off his out-of-shape father, his only words to him are "Watch it there, Whale Belly" when his father tries to shake his hand on the diamond. The amazing ins and outs of the rest of the story, following Razzle's recall by the Dodgers and Joe's promotion by the Yankees, result in a World Series climax after both players have slowly come to realize how much the other is worth in his life. When Joe scores the winning run for the Yankees in his father's last game for the Dodgers, he won't let the photographers take his picture until, as he says, "Take me with my old man, boys. You gotta take me right here with my pa." Thus ends possibly Tunis' most entertaining, if not profound, story. It's also the story that is most likely to bring the reader to tears.

Baseball underwent its first geographical upheaval in the lives of most adults with several changes between 1949 and 1958, when Tunis' eighth and final Dodger novel appeared, *Schoolboy Johnson*. There were still only 16 teams in the major leagues, but five had changed cities by the time of the publication of *Schoolboy Johnson*, which was also the author's last sports novel. In the National League, Boston had moved to Milwaukee, New York to San Francisco and Brooklyn to Los Angeles. In the American League, St. Louis had shifted to Baltimore and Philadelphia to Kansas City. Expansion to 10 teams in 1961 in the American League and 1962 in the National League dramatically changed the game, but Tunis' books were reprinted unchanged, still inspiring visions of the game that was when readers' parents grew up. Not a few young readers must have talked with their folks about this.

As *Schoolboy Johnson* opens, veteran pitcher Speedy Mason — who was not part of the previous books — faces his release from the Dodgers, just as the likes of Jocko Klein, Razzle Nugent, Bones Hathaway and others had before him. Roy Tucker soon is cut as the Dodgers pursue a youth movement, and Speedy and Roy wind up on the same Triple-A team. Injuries to others, however, lead to their return to the team, and they then provide help to immature but talented 20-year-old pitcher Schoolboy. Roy gets called back first, and Tunis describes a wrenching appeal from his road roommate, Speedy, for a good word to manager Spike Russell from Roy: "All the strength, all the fortitude of the man, vanished. This proud veteran was begging. Roy had never seen him like this. He was desperate now, throwing away his pride just as he tossed four wide ones to a dangerous hitter. Here in this dingy bedroom, unseen by anyone except a pal, he was just an old ballplayer asking for another crack at it. This tough, hard competitor, who never gave or asked for anything, was pleading for one more chance in the big time."

When Speedy returns and is assigned to room with Schoolboy, the veteran warns Schoolboy against too much nightlife. "OK, Daddy-O, if that's how you feel about," Schoolboy tells Speedy, humoring him. The expression "Daddy-O" is one of Tunis' few concessions to pop culture. Schoolboy soon meets Maxine Tucker, Roy's grown-up daughter, of whom nothing had been written in earlier stories! After a tough day, Roy receives encouragement and when asked what he would give to be 20 years old like Schoolboy, blurts out, "Twenty! What I wouldn't give to be thirty-five again!" What wisdom for the few young readers who were likely to absorb it! Near story's end, Roy tells an angry Schoolboy on the mound, "Quit being sorry for yourself. Act your age. Get in there and pitch like you know how to." And Schoolboy considers the wisdom of Speedy Mason, who had tried to tell him this: "Baseball is a test of character, how you react under pressure."

How many wise parents and coaches, long before and long after this book appeared, have counseled their Little League or high school-age boys and girls: "Baseball (or fastpitch softball) is a game of failure. Along with your hard work, and your God-given abilities, what will be most important is not how you react to your successes, but how you respond to your failures. Everyone is happy after getting a hit or making a fine fielding play, but it takes character to respond to a strikeout or an error, and to accept responsibility while looking ahead to your next opportunity, not back on your tough times." This, as much as anything else, is what Tunis tells his readers, over and over and over, in a way no other author could in his day.

Schoolboy ultimately helps win a pennant. Nearly two decades after Casey's first interview with Roy Tucker, Schoolboy responds to another reporter who asks about an error by the aging Roy: "Brother, any man's done as much as Roy Tucker to win this pennant for us, why, he's entitled to boot one now and then. That error, lemme tell ya something, it put the iron into me, made me bear down all the harder. Roy Tucker is one grand ballplayer; believe me, he's a man to have on your side." When canny reporter Casey, nearly 20 years after he first appears in *The Kid from Tompkinsville*, asks Schoolboy about his pitching mentor, the young pitcher responds: "Speedy taught me that changeup, Casey; there's where I got it. That was the pitch I used to strike out Burke in the fifth. It was Speedy taught it to me, and it sure came in handy this afternoon." So when a batboy tells Schoolboy that "There's a lady waiting for you in Box 56. She said you wasn't to hurry, Schoolie," the series comes full circle. One can only imagine the son of Schoolboy Johnson and Maxine Tucker — Roy Tucker's grandson — playing for the Dodgers; and wouldn't that make a great story?

Buddy and the Old Pro

Tunis' only non–Dodger baseball story, *Buddy and the Old Pro* (1955), is nothing less than brilliant. The short novel was written for baby boom grade schoolers, and it's still just as fresh as anything published today. It's the simple but effective story of how a Little League star, Buddy Reitmeyer, strikes out in his last chance to preserve an unbeaten season for his grade school. The opposing coach, a former big leaguer named McBride who had been one of Buddy's first baseball heroes, has turned into a nasty martinet, a poor example for youngsters, albeit a knowledgeable coach.

Buddy, ashamed at discovering his father had seen him throw his bat following the game-ending strikeout, and frustrated over being spiked during the game, confronts his failures in a frank conversion with his dad.

"It's better to lose, much as it hurts, than to play dirty — than play McBride's kind of baseball. That so?" his father asks. "Well, maybe," Buddy responds. "But isn't it?" His father persists. "Think it over a minute, Buddy. You know, if you want to win badly enough you usually can in any sport." "Ha!" responds Buddy. "Then why doesn't everyone win all the time? Huh?" "That's easy," his father answers. "Because decent people feel the way we do, when they think it over. They'd rather lose than play dirty. Besides, if one team plays that way, it's catching. The other side is mighty apt to do the same thing. Then it's no game! It's just a gang war. Understand?"

His father, telling Buddy he's OK as long as he knows he was wrong, reminds Buddy that "[McBride] took advantage of you because he was older, because he knew tricks you didn't know, because he pulled every fast one in the game. He's a bully. And everyone in town knows it." Then, in typical Tunis fashion, Buddy's father adds a humanizing comment: "What made him [McBride] like that? Remember, he was a poor kid with no home. He had to scrap and fight and scramble the best way he could. No wonder he acts the way he does."

Later, after Buddy has broken down and sobbed away his frustration, he tells his father, "That third strike. It was good." And his father agrees: "I know. I was back of the plate; I saw it catch the corner." Soon, Buddy takes his clippings of the past couple of years, before McBride retired, and burns them as his mother tells his sister not to bother him.

The fact that Buddy comes to realize the strikeout was his own fault — even though McBride had coached an unethical game — and the fact that his father did not criticize the umpire, but agreed with him, makes this little fable one of the best lessons Tunis could have taught. *Buddy and the Old Pro* was written for children, but every parent of an athlete could benefit from reading it as well. It's a remarkable book.

Yea! Wildcats!

Tunis sometimes wrote in almost a stream of consciousness style, reflecting the bits and pieces of thought and conversation that make up so much of everyday life for athletes and everyone else. He frequently uses this style in the four books he wrote about high school athletes and coaches: *All-American* (1942), *Yea! Wildcats!* (1944), *A City for Lincoln* (1945) and *Go, Team, Go!* (1954). They all move remarkably fast, even though they contain relatively few pages of game action.

The first and fourth books are one-off stories, but *Yea! Wildcats!* and *A City for Lincoln* are a pair, telling the compelling tale of young Indiana high school basketball coach Don Henderson. They are the only linked Tunis tales outside his Dodger stories.

Yea! Wildcats! is something of a basketball soap opera stew, about as unlikely a story as was ever written about high school hoops; yet it is one that rings true with regard to each individual issue, however unlikely that so many such developments would take place in the same season or even during the career of a coach. The incredibly fast-moving story — virtually every page crackles with tension, torment and small triumphs — involves small-town politics, parent-child conflicts, the relationships between teammates and with their coach, race relations and social status, ticket gouging and issues involving students and citizens, school administration foibles, and much more. To read this novel requires something of a suspension of disbelief, unlike Tunis' baseball stories; yet the reader is pulled into the time warp that is 1940s Indiana high school basketball. It's likely that nobody has ever done such a story better.

Henderson, a coach about 30 years old with high morals and sporting ethics, leaves a small private school at midseason when Springfield's Wildcats come calling. This is odd, because the ethics of a coach leaving one team for another at midseason are never questioned in the book, and they certainly would be today. When Henderson soon cuts his entire varsity team, all seniors, at Springfield for protesting after he earlier drops a senior standout over disciplinary issues, he finishes the season with the sophomores and juniors who had seldom played. Even more oddly, the coach lets the younger players vote on whether they want the older players back!

The story then moves into Henderson's second season, and the conflict between school-board bigwig and self-made businessman J. Frank Shaw and Henderson, plus between Shaw and his son Tom, who is the coach's best player along with what was still called "a colored fellow," Jackson Piper. The coach also meets a fair local sportswriter, Dick Lewis, and his idealistic editor, Peedad Wilson, who play key roles. The team, hardened by its tough-luck experiences of the season before and then the many conflicts of the current year, drives all the way to the Indiana state championship game. Just before tipoff, Tunis talks about coaching: "This was what made coaching so wonderful, so awful, too. It was giving to kids, giving them everything you had, your experience, your knowledge, your life, yourself. And then sending them out into the world while you sat and looked on and suffered with them and for them."

This was *Hoosiers* four decades before *Hoosiers*. But in typical Tunis fashion, Springfield loses the championship game after pages and pages of wonderful description. Jerry Kates, a player Henderson had developed at his previous school, had transferred to an Evansville school, Bosse, and found success. Kates' steal and layup in the final seconds beats Henderson and his Springfield boys, leaving the reader stunned but not really surprised. Kates, in fact, had been the target of Springfield "recruiters," but Henderson had refused to see him transfer, knowing it wouldn't have been right. (Fourteen years later, Kates comes up again in the 1958 *Schoolboy Johnson*, Tunis' last sports novel, and is referred to as a Major League baseball player whose career was cut short by a beaning.)

The town's know-nothings respond to the defeat with anger and potential racial violence, something not seen in other Tunis stories: "Frank Shaw's right.... [Henderson] should never have let that colored boy play. It all started back then. First thing you know, we'll have a colored team representing this town.... Throwing off one of our good boys for a nigger.... Who is this man, Henderson? Who does he think he is? Thinks he's running this town.... Well, he isn't running this town. Nor the colored folks, neither. They're getting mighty uppity lately, you noticed that. They don't know their places like they usta. Let's us do something about it.... How 'bout that colored boy, the boy who held up two–three women in town last month, snatched their purses, remember? He's out on bail. Ain't no justice in this-man's town.... Let us get the blighter."

Henderson and Peedad, the editor, race to prevent what might have been a lynching:

"Tinhorn sports, cheap sports, that's what you are; all of you!" Henderson tells the mob. "I just came from the Coliseum down there [in Indianapolis]. And from those boys, our boys, our kids who gave everything they had, and a little bit more, every last once and then some, to lose the state by a single point. Out there fighting Bosse, while you were back here slinging bricks at the mayor. Just a bunch of kids with guts; that's all they had — guts ... and you guys ... ganging up on a defenseless colored boy down there in jail. Call yourselves sports! ... Why they feel so bad, these kids, they didn't want to come home. They hated to come back to Springfield tonight. They feel they let you folks down. You, you, cheap sports, you tinhorn gamblers, here you are, taking it out on a colored boy in jail. They lost. So you're quitting on 'em, quitting cold. You're gonna prove the town's not behind 'em. When we win, oh, sure, that's fine. Not when we reach the finals and lose by a single point."

The band, the student body, and the team all join Henderson and the mob breaks up.

When Henderson gets the chance to coach at Yale, and announces he will leave Springfield, Peedad Wilson does his best to discourage him from leaving: "You have the most influence of any man in town; more'n any editor, more'n any preacher, more'n the chief of police, more'n the mayor, even. You saved us from a race riot last Saturday night when the mayor and just about everyone else had failed. Everybody in town knows you and everybody likes you, too. I wish you'd stay, here, with me.... Don, you're the one man we have who can really lead."

Tom Shaw, the son of the town's big shot, finally convinces Don to consider staying when Tom tells his coach about his verbal fight with his father. "What makes the J. Frank Shaws of this world," Don thinks. "Once the old man was like Tom; once he looked this way, felt this way, was fresh, young and keen." The team petitions Don, and he finally relents: "Look, Tom. The way I feel at present, I'm plenty sick of basketball. I hardly know's I'll ever want to coach in a town like this again, even did they all want me. But you're right; if I leave now, I'm quitting. So if you think the kids need me round here, I might make some arrangements."

Henderson does just that and Tom Shaw and Jackson Piper win the state championship in the sequel, *A City for Lincoln*. Henderson, though, never sees the final game; he is so tense he is laid low in the locker room by severe gastric pains. Tunis, in yet another twist, describes only the scene in the locker room, where Henderson is on his back in frustration, rather than the game action. Thus, *A City for Lincoln* is a novel not of sports, but of civics and the lessons the kids learn from Don, and those that Don learns from the community as he first works in the juvenile aid division and the new teen court, then runs for mayor. Aided by a police chief determined not to let unethical voting shenanigans deny Don, Don becomes mayor. The story ends with no clue whether Don will continue to coach, but he definitely will try to make Springfield "a city for Lincoln."

Even though J. Frank Shaw is not portrayed as an overt rabble-rouser, attitudes like his permeate Springfield, much to Henderson's frustration. Early in the story, Shaw tells the doctor who is the coach's friend that "He [Henderson] never would take advice from those who are older [not true, of course], who have forgotten more basketball'n he'll ever know. Nope, you take a colored boy, now; they're fine when things are easy. When a team's on top of the heap. Push 'em around a little, and they just aren't there." Many people then agreed with Shaw, who could say this in the era before baseball's Jackie Robinson and football's Marion Motley began to change minds as well as hearts.

Few, if any, writers before Tunis had a coach say things like Henderson said to Peedad Wilson, the idealistic newspaper editor: "Peedad, I don't really believe there are any bad kids, leastways not many. One or two, one or two perhaps, just a few. There're not many bad kids, Peedad, but there's plenty of bad parents."

When Henderson campaigns for mayor, he talks about who he sees as Americans:

First of all, he's either a foreigner, or the son of a foreigner, or the descendent of one. He thinks, on the whole, this thing we like to call democracy is pretty good. He believes in education for all. He believes in the right of workingmen to organize; in freedom of speech, of religion, of the press. Lastly, he believes in a government of the people, by the people and, most important of all, for the people. Which is exactly what we haven't had in this town lately.... Then there's two more things that can make an American. He won't ever believe a thing can't be done merely because it hasn't been done before. That isn't the way we made this nation. We made the U.S.A. by believing nothing was impossible. Finally, when an American sees something, when he sees injustice, by golly, it hurts, he gets angry. He wants to do something about it.

Near the end of his campaign, he reads to the crowd from the labor organization CIO, showing how *A City for Lincoln* is still relevant for today's reader: "We are for: a job for everyone who wants to work; fair wages for every worker; the protection of the rights of labor; a good home for every family; medical care for all who need it; a chance for everyone to become educated; insurance for the sick, aged, crippled; fair play for all nations; if you are for these things, you are with us.... Folks, what's un–American about that program? If we had all those things here in Springfield, we might have a city good enough for Lincoln."

Call it the Tunis Manifesto, because even though the rest of his sports stories aren't political, the feelings expressed by people like Spike Russell, Roy Tucker and Dave Leonard pretty much mirror these concepts.

All-American

Tunis' only football story is only marginally about football; it's a perceptive novel of character, of morals, and it's far ahead of its time. *All-American* (1942) isn't about an All-American at all, except in the attitudes about human dignity and fellowship that Ronald Perry develops after he transfers from a private school to a public school, Lincoln High (the name was doubtless no coincidence, and there may have been more Lincoln Highs than any other name in America for schools).

Other than the first 10 pages, when Perry unwittingly participates in a tackle that injures the opponent's star, there is no football at all until the last third of the book, and then not much. Instead, the story vividly and at great length describes Perry's frustrations, self-doubts and gradual acceptance at his new Indiana high school, along with the realization that the only good football is clean, fair football. Perry is good, but not of All-American caliber. The player who scores the season's big touchdown, the one who puts Lincoln in a postseason intersectional game in Miami, Florida, is the black pass receiver Ned LeRoy. Illustrator Hans Walleen's drawing of Ned making the big catch may be the first of an African American football player in action in an American sports novel. It's certainly one of the first.

The crackling tension at the end of the story involves the refusal of the players, led by Perry, to play in the Miami game unless Ned is allowed to participate. Tunis gives the reader food for thought when he has the president of the chamber of commerce ask Perry this question: "Do you think it's better to disappoint one colored boy or 40,000 people?" Perry eventually responds with this question for the president: "[D] you guess Abraham Lincoln would like this? Would he say OK leaving a colored boy of your team when we go to Miami?" The point becomes moot when officials in Miami, as would have been true in 1942, refuse to back down, and another team is invited instead of Lincoln High. But LeRoy and Perry and the other two boys who stood up for LeRoy will play again after all. A team from Oak Park, Illinois, invites them to play in a different intersectional game as the story ends. The boys on this Lincoln High team turn out to be All-Americans in ethics.

All-American stayed in print for a good many years, and it may have been in more school libraries than almost any other novel, about sports or otherwise. It's unquestionably one of the finest books ever written for teenagers. One can only guess how many hearts and minds it might have changed for the better.

Go, Team, Go!

This 1954 stand-alone novel, Tunis' last high school sports story, again deals with ethics and the real meaning of sportsmanship, just as Tunis' three previous such stories did. It's another story of Indiana basketball, and how the unwavering coach Hooks Barnum cut a star, and then the other first-stringers returned from a state championship team at Ridgewood High because of rules violations and poor attitudes. Tom Williams, one of the players who is cut and the primary protagonist, eventually realizes the star does not deserve defending, that the coach was correct, and that he can still help his old coach and what has become a young but hardworking team. Williams becomes a student–assistant coach and wins his father's respect for helping the team win sectional and regional titles and a berth in the state semifinals.

In true Tunis fashion, it's left to the reader's imagination to determine how the team fares in the semifinals; there is no hokey championship, since this team has accomplished something of a miracle just to get there. Instead, Tom Williams does win the affection of Mary Jo Berry, a girl who never wavers in her support for doing the right thing, not the expedient thing.

The astonishing Tunis autobiography

Ring Lardner and the ensuing writers of literary sports fiction have been dissected many times, but there are few biographies and autobiographies about the authors of young adult and pulp sports fiction. There was one notable exception, and anyone can guess who it was — the inestimable John R. Tunis. He wrote *A Measure of Independence*, published in 1964 by Atheneum, six years after he wrote the last of his 16 young adult sports novels.

The book is highly readable, even entertaining, with its charming family references and stories of how the author became one of the few to make a good living as a freelance writer for dozens of different magazines and newspapers (hence, he says, the title). Nonetheless, I was astonished by this book, since the greatest sports fiction writer of his era — a prize-winning, highly praised author — mentioned almost nothing about the books that made his name a byword for excellence among librarians and teachers. In fact, he named only one of them —*Iron Duke*, his first — and that was only in passing and only on a second, brief reference to a prestigious honor the book earned.

By 1964, Tunis had long since achieved his objective — to have a series of frequently reprinted novels bring in a comfortable income in the wake of the disappearance of so many of his freelance magazine and newspaper markets, beginning in the late 1930s and early 1940s. Even in 1964, virtually everything he had written for the magazines and newspapers — by his account, more than 2,000 pieces between the two world wars — had been forgotten, most of it never to be reprinted or read except by the most dedicated enthusiasts of the author's work. Yet it's likely that virtually every school library in America still had multiple copies of his novels, many of which remained in print (and were to be reprinted several times again in the 1980s and 1990s).

I read the book hoping to gain insight into how Tunis wrote his sports novels. He did provide a few pages' worth — a trip to spring training in Florida for *The Kid from Tomkinsville* and a trip to the Indiana state basketball tournament for *Yea! Wildcats!*— without even mentioning the books except to call them "my first baseball novel" and "my basketball story" and the like. He surely must have known how important these books were to millions of readers — and still are to many baby boomers and their elder siblings— and yet he dismissed them in favor of long discussions of his love for European and American tennis tournaments. It's true that tennis playing and reporting was his passion, and perhaps he did not anticipate any younger folks reading his autobiography, but I still find it utterly astonishing that he ignored his books this way. There is far more about Tunis' work in *Ball Tales* than he himself ever wrote about his work — anywhere.

I did learn one thing about his books—he considered his first sports novel, the long-forgotten *American Girl* (1929), to be the genesis of the 1951 RKO tennis film *Hard, Fast and Beautiful*, when most sources list his novel *Champion's Choice* (1940), which apparently was something of a rewrite of the first women's tennis story. Tunis was quite taken with the French legend Suzanne Lenglen and the American star Helen Wills Moody and saw them play many times. With his own vast knowledge of tennis, he was probably more qualified than anyone else to write tennis fiction, yet *Champion's Choice* was his last tennis novel, apparently because the market for such fiction on any level was virtually nil.

A Measure of Independence, however, is highly recommended for anyone who aspires to be, or remain, a freelance writer, or even a salaried writer in these perilous days for the print media. "Lucy [his wife] and I were now thirty, the time when most couples were pretty well established. But we seemed to be getting nowhere in particular," Tunis writes of his life in 1920, not long after he returned from military service in World War I: "A writer? Yes, only how does a writer eat?" He spent the rest of the book answering that question.

Writers today, though, can only be jealous of the money he received, even though Tunis himself dismissed it with phrases like "Until the early thirties, [*New Yorker* editor Harold] Ross paid me only $200 for a long profile." That's well over $3,000 in today's dollars, and $200 was fully 5 percent of the $4,000 mortgage Tunis said he negotiated for his home in Connecticut, first occupied in the early 1920s. Today, few magazine writers can come close to commanding $3,000 for anything. Tunis complained of being paid the same $400 by *Collier's* in 1939 that he earned in 1925 — during a period when inflation was minimal — even though $400 in 1939 equates to well over $5,000 now. (He died in 1975 and never lived to see serious inflation.)

Tunis noted a 1962 essay by free-lance author Hartzell Spence in which Spence writes that "A generation or two ago there were at least two thousand highly successful freelance writers. In 1940, Standard Rate and Data's Yearbook listed 529 general magazines open to free-lance contributions.... [In the] 1962 Yearbook, I find only a hundred and four general markets that pay a respectable price.... The situation is even more dire than the statistics imply. The trend is toward the exclusively staff-written issue."

Tunis says that "Mr. Spence estimates that today there are hardly two hundred free-lance writers who earn $15,000 a year." (Nearly $100,000 in today's buying power. In 1962, many perfectly nice American homes still sold for $15,000 or less. My guess is that he overestimates.) "A few sturdy souls survive, but if there are more than a hundred I should be astonished.... In the twenties and thirties there were many magazines, half trade journals, half not, to which any industrious writing gent could easily sell a piece a year. They paid a minimum of $50 up to a maximum of several hundred." Today's freelance writers can only gasp in astonishment, since $50 in the 1920s and 1930s is easily $500 to $1,000 now. And in 1942, Tunis tells of a *Reader's Digest* payment of $2,000!

Tunis writes of arranging a deal with the *New York Post* in 1927 for three pieces a week at $75 for the three, or about $1,500 today! Only the most famous journalists—or those long employed on one of the few remaining papers with high union salaries—could come close to that. Tunis says he "never made less than $5,000 a year" during the Great Depression (well over $50,000 today): "Somehow, although frightened like everyone else by the poverty and the breadlines, the uncertainty added a peculiar zest to life. True, copy was more difficult to sell, some magazines failed, many others cut prices paid to writers, for it is invariably the writing gent who is the first to suffer and the last to profit." Times haven't changed, have they? That sentence, by the way, is somewhat typical of Tunis' stream-of-consciousness style—a type of writing that few editors would allow today, with its run-on sentences and other grammatical problems. "I kept plugging, what choice was there?" Tunis adds.

Tunis tells the entertaining tale of his visit to Kokomo, Indiana, courtesy of a newspaper friend who invited him to see the original March Madness—the Indiana state high school basketball tournament in the early 1940s, little more than three decades before March Madness officially began and long before major college basketball co-opted that phrase. Here's why I wish Tunis had written more than a few pages about his novels: "Suddenly a boy on the floor stole the ball, dodged, feinted, dribbled toward the Kokomo basket. Fever conquered the crowd as he passed the ball, took it back, passed it and received it again. The tension tightened, became taut, unendurable. There was no world but this. Reality was that overheated enclosure below. Time was the electric clock beating out the final seconds of the game. Adroitly the boy swung the ball around, zigzagging under the goal, pivoting. The little grandmother beside me could endure it no longer. She learned out over the railing. 'Get the son of a bitch,' she shrieked. 'Get the son of a bitch.' That was my introduction to Indiana basketball."

Tunis had long been noted for his numerous articles condemning the over-commercialization and over-emphasis on sports in schools and colleges. Near the end of *A Measure of Independence*, he addressed this: "One sacred cow is our sport and leisure-time activities. To raise doubt about the value of big-time sport and the path it has taken in the United States in the last 50 years [which then coincided with Tunis' adult life] is tantamount to spitting on the flag. When you do this you question the American national religion. Proceed at your own risk. It was obvious early to me that speculating about a national religion was a dangerous thing. I began to be called in print—and by persons whose friendship I esteemed and whose judgment I respected—an 'agitator,' 'a grouch,' 'wrong-headed,' 'tiresome' and 'despicable.'"

Later, he expressed astonishment over the Columbia Broadcasting System's $28 million contract to televise National Football League games in 1964; at Ohio State University's $2 million football gate receipts in 1963; at that university's $3 million earnings for fiscal year 1963–1964. "This, mind you, is at a tax-free, government and state supported university. Nobody asks what place tournament basketball has in the physical education program of high schools, or whether its overall effect is disruptive of the educational process. Nobody thinks of this. When $3 million is at stake, there is no time to bother about sportsmanship. General David Sarnoff of R.C.A. put it succinctly: 'Competition brings out the best in products and the worst in men.'"

One can only wish that there was a Tunis alive today, not only to write sterling examples of sports fiction, but also to express indignation over college football coaches being paid four, five or six times (or more) than the president of the United States, much less the presidents of their own institutions!

ELEVEN

The Prolific Sports Fiction Authors

John R. Tunis' 16 sports novels, including 13 dealing with baseball, basketball and football, may have been groundbreaking in their vivid use of realistic circumstances in his 1938–1958 writing period, but they were only a tiny fraction of the market. Throughout the half-century of the 1930s through the 1970s, the vast majority of the hundreds of baseball, football and basketball novels were written for the young-adult or juvenile market. Adult sports fans, however, could and did read young-adult stories with much the same enthusiasm with which they consumed the pulp sports magazines; a few of those magazines lasted into the mid–1950s.

The Golden Age of the young-adult sports novel was the 1940s and 1950s. No fewer than 20 of 21 "prolific authors" began writing baseball, basketball and football novels between 1940 (Tunis' first baseball novel) and 1954 (juvenile-story specialist Matt Christopher's first novel). These writers, almost all of whom honed their writing skills in the pulps, released so many books that it would have been possible to read at least one new hardcover sports novel every week during this two-decade period, and probably in the 1960s as well.

These novels were intended primarily for two markets. The one-dollar young-adult series books starring the likes of Clair Bee's Chip Hilton and Wilfred McCormick's Bronc Burnett were marketed directly to teenagers, often as gifts, in much the same way the Hardy Boys and Nancy Drew books found their millions of fans (see chapter seven). The sports series books, though, were vastly outnumbered by stand-alone or short-series volumes, always priced from two to three dollars. These were sold primarily to public and school libraries, the vast majority of which rejected all types of the one-dollar series books during their heyday.

Most of the sports series books are relatively easy to find nearly a half century or more after their original publication, even though all of them have either long been out of print or produced only in revised, paperback editions. Yet just a small percentage of adults, much less teenagers, could buy large numbers of young-adult books in the two- and three-dollar range. In many homes, these were reserved as gifts for Christmas and birthdays. Enthusiasts thus find many of these volumes difficult to find, even some of the low-value, ex–library copies. It would take a collector much money and several years, even using the Internet, to find fine-condition first editions in dust jackets. Many of these are seldom seen in any condition.

I have purchased genre fiction including sports during visits to more than 500 cities and towns nationwide and have searched through untold thousands of volumes, yet I still have not been able to locate some of these non-series novels, especially at affordable prices. Ironically, because they were often checked out by young adults far more often than other books, libraries discarded many of them on criteria of both condition and age beginning in the 1980s. Many volumes in my collection of more than 600 vintage sports novels came from library sales. A decade into the 21st century, however, most of these books have long since been weeded from library shelves, to be replaced by frankly better stories, such as those from talented contemporary authors such as Carl Deuker and Mike Lupica.

Three prolific sports authors were only a slight bridge of the gap from the 1920s to the 1940s: Ralph Henry Barbour (with books originally written from 1899 to 1945), Harold M. Sherman (1926–37) and William Heyliger (1911–37). Though competently written for their era, these stories seemed dated in the post–World War II era and were out of print by the 1950s. It's a testament to their popularity, however, that some of these books — especially cheap reprint editions — are still more frequently found in used-book stores than are post-war titles, albeit seldom with dust jackets.

The most prolific post–1940 young-adult sports novelist was the versatile Joe Archibald, also a prolific pulp writer, magazine and newspaper cartoonist, and briefly a comic book editor. Archibald produced at least 44 baseball, basketball and football novels from 1947 to 1974, apparently all stand-alone stories without recurring characters. Although juvenile story specialists such as C. Paul Jackson and Matt Christopher have more book credits, Archibald's novels were so detailed and lengthy that the combination of his novels and hundreds of pulp sports stories make him the king of sports fiction writers of his era. Tunis, though, was far better known because of his popularity with children's librarians, and because his books were reprinted many times over until the present era.

Along with Wilfred McCormick, who wrote 48 series-character young-adult novels from 1948 to 1967 (see chapter seven), Archibald's primary competitor was another former pulp story writer. Olympic sprint medalist Jackson Scholz wrote at least 29 baseball, basketball and football novels from 1942 to 1971 after beginning with *Split Seconds* (1927), a collection of his track and field stories. Like Archibald, Scholz used few, if any, series characters.

Another prolific pulp writer, C. Paul Jackson, switched to novels in 1947 and produced at least 68 sports novels, including a few about swimmers, runners and go-kart racers, from 1947 to 1974. These included at least five novels as by Colin Lochlons, four as by Caary Jackson, three as by Jack Paulson and at least seven collaborations with O.B. Jackson, his wife. C. Paul Jackson took an unusual about-face after beginning as a novelist with mainstream young-adult stories such as *All-Conference Tackle* (1947), *Tournament Forward* (1948) and *First Base Rookie* (1950). He produced only a handful of young-adult stories before going on to pen more than 55 juveniles, most of them only about one-third as long as one of his early books. When he began these with *Stretch Makes a Basket* (1949), as by Lochlons — a book about junior high school basketball — he nicely filled a niche. Matt Christopher, who produced more than 80 novels about a wide variety of sports over more than four decades, later came to epitomize this category, but it was wide open when C. Paul Jackson began writing.

Yet another pulp writer with hundreds of story credits devoted to aviation, adventure, heroes and sports went on to rival Archibald and Scholz. He was Robert Sidney Bowen, whose 29 football, basketball and baseball novels were published from 1948 to 1969, including three early novels as by James Rodney Richard. Three others can be numbered among the "prolific authors" as well: Duane Decker, Dick Friendlich and William Heuman, all of whom also wrote for the sports pulps. Decker penned 15 baseball novels from 1947 to 1964, including 13 in the classic Blue Sox series (see chapter eight) plus two books as by Richard

Wayne. Friendlich wrote 18 solidly constructed baseball, basketball and football novels from 1948 to 1967 while working for more than four decades as a highly respected San Francisco sportswriter and columnist. Heuman produced 27 sports novels from 1950 to 1972, including many with a wacky sense of humor and humanity.

These ten prolific authors— Archibald, Bee, Bowen, Decker, Friendlich, Heuman, Jackson, McCormick, Scholz and Tunis— produced the astounding total of at least 329 books of sports fiction from 1938 to 1974, including no fewer than 242 football, basketball and baseball novels in the Golden Era of the three decades from 1940 to 1969.

Four other prolific writers specialized in the juvenile baseball and football market along with Jackson: pulp magazine graduate Curtis Bishop wrote at least 32 books from 1942 to 1968; Matt Christopher penned 27 books from 1954 to 1969 and dozens more beyond; Marion and James Renick did at least 23 from 1941 to 1977, including 16 on the primary three sports; and Bill Knott, writing as by Bill Jo Carol, did at least 25 (including the first under his own name) from 1963 to 1974. Almost all of their books concern the adventures of Little League baseball, Pop Warner football and junior high school and sandlot athletics. The same can be said of C. Paul Jackson, although he also wrote about high school, college and professional athletes in stories from a young reader's viewpoint. That's why Jackson is the most difficult sports novelist to categorize.

Also in the "prolific author" sports category of this era are seven others with at least 10 books apiece, all high-caliber writers: pulpsters William Campbell Gault, William Cox, Burgess Leonard, and R.G. Emery; the remarkable Frank O'Rourke, an accomplished baseball and football writer of novels and short stories for both pulps and slicks along with many westerns and other genre novels; the versatile Philip Harkins, who covered seven sports in at least 14 sports novels; and Hamilton "Tex" Maule, the famed *Sports Illustrated* writer and editor.

These seven authors combined to write at least 63 baseball, football and basketball novels from 1940 to 1969. The total number of such books written in the 1940s, 1950s and 1960s alone by only 21 authors is 442 volumes. That means of the approximately 650 such novels of the three primary sports in those three decades, nearly two-thirds were produced by those 21 authors! I have identified at least 207 other full-length young-adult and juvenile baseball, football and basketball novels by at least 87 other authors during the same period. I have found only one or two sports novels by many others, so a few other stories and authors doubtless remain to be discovered from the lesser publishers.

Gault wrote dozens of pulp stories beginning in the late 1930s before becoming an award-winning mystery novelist for adults in the 1950s. He wrote at least 15 mainstream sports novels, most about football, along with at least 15 motor sports novels, from 1952 to 1980. Gault was the only major sports novelist who continued to produce young-adult and juvenile novels after making it big in stories for adults. Maule produced 10 literate football and baseball novels for young adults from 1961 to 1968. Some still remain on library shelves because they seem fresher than most sports stories written in the 1960s.

Joe Archibald: Personal stories of intensity

Joe Archibald's ability to rattle off sharp, in-depth sports novels was pretty much unparalleled for nearly three decades, from his first books, *Rebel Halfback* (1947) and *Touchdown Glory* (1949) to his last, *Centerfield Rival* (1974). Westminster Press, which was Dick

Friendlich's publisher, produced Archibald's first two books. As far as I know, he wrote the rest for Macrae-Smith, a leading publisher of books for youth during the period. Archibald, like most of the 21 "prolific authors" identified in this chapter, had one primary publisher after honing his skills with hundreds of stories in the pulp magazines.

Archibald's pulp roots often show in his novels, which often involve intense plots dealing with his protagonist's victory over himself, with sometimes unlikely circumstances and coincidences providing opportunities for self-awareness and self-redemption. He was the young-adult sports storyteller's version of a Russian novelist, filling his books with dozens of names and plot shifts, along with flashbacks on occasion. But an Archibald novel is almost always absorbing. His stories can be read with equal enjoyment by teenagers or adults, but it takes a highly accomplished reader younger than 12 or 13 to fully grasp one of his books. They were virtual time capsules of their period, dealing as they do with the coaches, managers, sportswriters and team officials of their era. Archibald (1898–1986) often refers to genuine historic figures, but it's also fun to see how he converts the names of then-current players into similar but definitely different terms, such as the Yankees, for whom he at least once used The Missile for Mickey Mantle and The Mask for Yogi Berra. Archibald's love and knowledge of sports shines in his stories, along with his respect for most of the people involved in sports.

Archibald sometimes has a harder edge in his stories compared to other sports authors, such as in *Catcher's Choice* (1958), the odyssey of a talented but self-deprecating catcher from Little League to the World Series. Eddie Murcheson, having made a game-losing error in the championship Little League game, hears the mayor of his town yell to him, "You won't get to be a bonus kid [in the major leagues] the way you played that ball, Eddie." Eddie's father, Harry, who wants to keep secret a youthful indiscretion that resulted in jail time, tries to discourage him from playing baseball, but Eddie loves the game. His father, however, has sowed the seeds of cynicism in Eddie, and he not only shies away from interviews and any manner of publicity, but also feels, often in error, that everyone is out to use him.

When his minor league manager challenges Eddie to learn every detail he can about the game, and to work harder to fulfill his obvious potential, Eddie tells him, "It sounds like kindergarten." The manager responds: "Exactly. This is the baseball nursery. I'm glad I'm getting under your skin, Eddie. I wish I could see inside your head." Archibald has the manager recalling a Detroit player, Rick Wakeman, who had "a minor league record that was fabulous.... Detroit finally wrote off his seventy-five thousand dollar price tag and made a utility outfielder out of him. Amateur psychologists said he lacked the spark, that necessary incentive and enthusiasm that is often the difference between greatness and mediocrity. Ashton suspected the spark in Eddie had been blown out years ago, and he could only hope that someone or something would come along and fan it to flame again." Archibald's story, of course, is modeled after Dick Wakefield, an outfielder who batted .316 for Detroit with a league-leading 200 hits in 1943, Wakefield's rookie year. He hit .355 in an injury-plagued second season but was never more than a journeyman in five more seasons with the Tigers.

Catcher's Choice turns when Eddie sees a small-town play and becomes enchanted with a young actress, Dawn Mayworth. (And how Hollywood is that name?) How he fulfills his ambition to meet her is pure pulp: When she comes to one of his Class D minor-league baseball games, he hits a foul ball that sends her to the hospital! He brings her flowers and an attraction ensues. But soon, after a celebration of her return to health at the ballpark,

Eddie knows he has fallen in love. Yet he asks himself: "What was she? An over-ambitious pixie who would use anything or anybody to get famous. Even a third-rate ballplayer." Then he wonders how much her press agent got.

Al Trainor, an unselfish old pro who managed Eddie in Little League and ultimately returns to organized baseball as a minor league manager, eventually becomes Eddie's manager in Class B. He openly questions Eddie's desire to fulfill his potential because of lack of ambition: "You're an introvert, Eddie. Almost antisocial, and I'll bet when your mother put the cookies up on the top shelf out of your reach, you never even figured a way to get to 'em. You weren't supposed to go after them and so you didn't. Why don't you want to be better than just good, Eddie?"

Trainor and Eddie ultimately learn the answer after Eddie is promoted from Class B to the St. Louis Redbirds and helps the team rally to win the pennant, even though he is bothered by his acrimonious split with Dawn over her ambition. He faces the Bombers in the World Series and plays well until he is beaned and seriously injured in the fourth game. He is through for the Series, but proves to be the ultimate winner. He listens to the Redbirds win the World Series. He learns his father has come out of his shell and even plans to reorganize the hometown Little League. He learns publicity isn't such a bad thing. And when Dawn comes to visit him with roses, he realizes that she is genuine, however strong her ambition to become a famed actress. Eddie tells the photographers, "Take all the pictures you want. I can stand it. Be sure to get the roses in."

Archibald's *The Easy Out* (1965), about self-sacrificing second baseman Frank Hyatt, is similar and just as absorbing, providing you can look past all the pulp-like circumstances. The author takes us through Hyatt's eight frustrating years in the minor leagues, preceded by his earlier life beginning when he sacrifices Little League baseball so he can help his brother. Archibald provides a variety of situations where Hyatt steps aside as a good role player in favor of someone else's opportunity, including switching positions with a shortstop who has a serious illness (and later dies, helping Hyatt to realize that his time to make an impression in baseball is short). When Hyatt is finally called up to the major leagues, an aggressive "bonus baby" gets playing time ahead of him. The kid, who clearly hasn't paid any dues, is sent into the game instead of Hyatt after Hyatt's major league debut is limited to pinch running duty.

The Easy Out has a satisfying finish for the reader who has become frustrated by Frank's baseball martyrdom. When Frank finally gets a chance for his first time at bat in the major leagues, he is asked to lay down a sacrifice bunt in a critical situation. In a neat twist on the old theme of the selfish player refusing to bunt and hitting a home run, Archibald allows Frank to swing away as the player realizes how self-defeating he has been throughout his life. The pulp influence is felt when Frank hits a home run and his manager rages, "That'll cost you a hundred, Hyatt! [a stiff fine in the 1960s]. Y-You fresh busher! You---!" Frank responds: "If you had hit me for two hundred, Sam, I would have called it money in the bank. Sometime when you have three or four hours to spare, Sam, I'll tell you why I had to tie into that pitch. You've heard it before — a man does only what he has to do." Still furious, the manager tells the proud rookie, "Sure, so when I hand you a pink slip and a bus ticket back to the boondocks, you remember that, Hyatt!" To which Frank replies, "But this time I'll have something to take along with me, Sam." Of course, the reader realizes Frank is too good to be sent to the minor leagues.

The Easy Out has an unusual sequence late in the story where Frank and a sportswriter get into a fight, in large part because the writer is drunk. There were earlier mentions of alcoholism in young-adult novels, but this is one of the most graphic, reflecting the changing mores of society in the mid–1960s. Archibald was one of the first writers to use black characters in his novels, sometimes calling them "dusky" and always reflecting a sense of respect.

Archibald began writing novels in 1947, the year Jackie Robinson broke Major League Baseball's color line, and by 1961 he wrote a novel, *Outfield Orphan*, with a black protagonist, Benjie Sadler. Racism and Sadler's inability to handle adversity — a typical Archibald theme — cause him to fail with his first team, the Boston Pilgrims, before he makes the most of a second chance with a different team in the World Series. It was probably no coincidence that Archibald picked Boston as his unusual protagonist's first team, since the Boston Red Sox were the last team to call up a black player, the infielder Elijah "Pumpsie" Green, in 1959. It's interesting to note that *Outfield Orphan*, written in the final years of Jim Crow laws, is one of the most difficult Archibald novels to find. It could be that the subject hampered sales.

Archibald's novels through the 1950s featured colorful, pulp-style dust jackets. It's my theory that sales were not helped when the dust jackets turned impressionistic, such as the penciled line image by Francis A. Chauncy of a second baseman fielding a ball in *The Easy Out*. It's not that the art is poor — it's actually quite creative — but youngsters were undoubtedly more attracted to more realistic action scenes. Chauncy did many jackets for Archibald.

Archibald's numerous football novels also featured players in need of a personality inventory, such as *West Point Wingback* and its undisciplined hero, Ronald Ellis Burritt, and *Powerback* (1970) and its selfish fullback, Steve Borek. *Go Navy Go* (1956) was another service academy story of a plebe, Jim Dorrance, who is misunderstood by others and takes the entire novel to understand himself amid the pageantry of the annual Army–Navy game.

Jackson Scholz: Stories with an angle

Jackson Scholz, who became the first track and field medalist in three Olympics and won the 1924 gold medal in the 200 meters, was surely the most successful athlete ever to write sports novels, just as Clair Bee, the creator of Chip Hilton, was the most storied coach to become a legitimate novelist. (This doesn't include novels "cowritten" by the likes of Willie Mays and Yogi Berra.) Scholz wrote numerous short stories about track and field, but his novels primarily involved football, basketball and baseball, since he doubtless knew the market for track novels was limited. His first book, *Split Seconds* (1927), a collection of 10 track and field stories, was his only collection.

Scholz infused his novels with both humor and extensive side plots that had little or nothing to do with sports. For example, in *Johnny King, Quarterback* (1950), adventure in a lumber camp played a major role along with the hero's exploits in high school, college and pro football. *Fullback Fever* (1969) dealt with the complications of college student politics and what happens when a football hero runs for campus president. In *A Fighting Chance* (1956) college football coach Jim Carter must cope with finances and politics. *Pigskin Warriors* (1944) takes place partly on the battlefields of World War II (and, like John R. Tunis' wartime story *The Kid Comes Back*, was reprinted many times after the war ended). The baseball novel *Man in a Cage* (1958) features a baseball catcher who is also a circus lion tamer! His hero in *Fielder from Nowhere* (1950) is an ex-convict who was unjustly convicted of a crime.

There was almost never anything straightforward about a Scholz epic. One of his most convoluted—and entertaining—stories is *Bench Boss* (1958), the tale of manager Kerry Flannigan and his anything-to-win tricks. "Flannigan Shenanigans" make up the bulk of the tale about a man who has to learn the hard way about the difference between the letter of baseball law and its spirit. Scholz's plots often reflect his pulp origins, yet his stories are logical and well developed, with only a handful of unlikely coincidences and circumstances. Scholz, however, is pure storyteller: unlike Tunis and Bee, citizenship, civil rights and love of country aren't usually issues in stories by Scholz. Even in a book written well into the hippie and Viet Nam protest era, the 1969 *Fullback Fever*, he only mildly confronts an issue of students who don't want to pay for sports teams and benefits for athletes. He calls the organization SASSOPA, which stands for Student Association to Stop Spread of Pampered Athletes. It's typical Scholz humor.

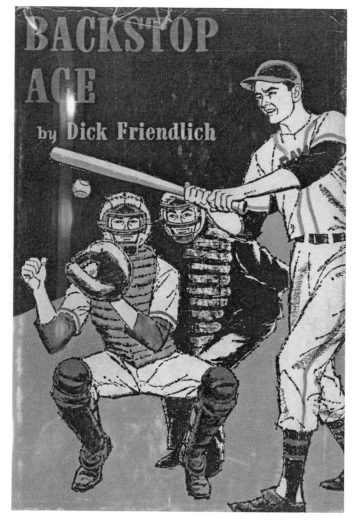

Backstop Ace by Dick Friendlich, 1961 (jacket copyright Westminster Press). Famed San Francisco newspaperman Friendlich wrote 18 realistic and insightful sports novels from the late 1940s to the late 1960s.

One of the reasons the prolific authors could turn out so many sports novels so quickly was the extensive use of game description. Scholz, for example, uses 37 pages to describe Chuck Denny's first game of his controversial and election campaign-plagued junior season, plus a total of 50 pages to describe two later games. That is 87 pages of play-by-play in a 192-page book. Scholz could be pardoned for that, however, since his books were generally targeted for readers a bit younger than those who read Tunis or Archibald, not to mention the adult stories of Frank O'Rourke and Ed Fitzgerald (see chapters four and seven). Younger readers generally loved play-by-play, since they were still dreaming of performing on the high school level and often did not have the opportunity to play as many games as their older brothers and sisters did.

Few, if any, young-adult novelists infused their sports novels with as much wacky humor as did Scholz (1897–1986), who probably was influenced by Ring Lardner's humorous stories as a young adult himself. One of the best examples is *One-Man Team*

(1953), the tale of amiable country boy Elmer Finch and how he learns to take football seriously, if not life. *Dugout Tycoon* (1963) tells the unlikely tale of bonus baby Danny Mercer, who uses his bonus money to become involved in the worlds of high finance and boxing. A bronco named Buttercup is central to the story of the *Backfield Buckaroo* (1967), which combines thrills and laughs in the worlds of rodeo and football at Buckskin University, a name only Scholz could have imagined for this unique story. In *Halfback on His Own* (1962), which combined college football and skin diving (!), a pelican named Mike provides the unique brand of Scholz humor.

When Scholz's career-long publisher, Morrow, posthumously reissued several of his books beginning in 1993, Morrow could be forgiven for this dust jacket exaggeration: "Recognized throughout his forty-four-year career as the preeminent sportswriter for boys." Scholz certainly ranks as one of the best and most important of his era, but Tunis and Bee are still by far the best-remembered writers and Archibald and McCormick were the most prolific. It was also an exaggeration to

Circus Catch by Joe Archibald, 1957 (jacket copyright Macrae Smith). Archibald wrote 44 sports novels after enjoying a prolific career in a wide variety of pulps. Joe Letven did this and many other Archibald jackets.

imply that Scholz wrote novels for 44 years, although his 29-year run was certainly one of the most admirable of any sports novelist.

Morrow could, however, legitimately boast that Scholz "was the only sprinter in history to appear in the finals of three consecutive Olympic games. His performance in the 1924 Olympics is featured prominently in the Oscar-winning 1981 movie *Chariots of Fire.* Scholz also raced in exhibition races around the world, often against the self-proclaimed 'World's Fastest Human,' Charlie Paddock. During the course of his running career, Scholz won twelve of his seven races against Paddock. He was inducted into the National Track and Field Hall of Fame in 1977."

C. Paul Jackson: The youth franchise

Prolific pulp writer C. Paul Jackson—for many years a teacher, coach and referee in Kalamazoo, Michigan—did an abrupt about-face and focused on books for small fry after beginning his novel-writing career with eight lengthy young-adult novels about football, baseball and basketball. Jackson's first sports novel, *All-Conference Tackle* (1947), was followed by *Tournament Forward* (1948), *Rose Bowl All-American* (1949), *Rookie First Baseman* (1950), *Rose Bowl Linebacker* (1951), *Clown at Second Base* (1952) and *Dub, Halfback* (1952), along with *Fourth-Down Pass* (1950) written as by Jack Paulson, one of his three pen names. He also collaborated on at least seven juvenile novels with his wife, Orpha B. Jackson, to whom he touchingly dedicated *Rose Bowl All-American* "for memories of our trip to the coast in that big old car." Crowell published all eight novels except *Fourth-Down Pass*, which appeared from long-established young-adult publisher Winston, a firm that seldom produced sports novels. Winston went on to focus on other genres, most famously the firm's iconic 36-book science fiction series for young adults from 1952 to 1961.

Jackson's eight early young-adult novels are all lengthy, in-depth portrayals of college and professional sports scenes, taking the reader behind the scenes with coaches, broadcasters, sportswriters and everyone else involved in big-time sports along with many, many athletes. His stories are engaging and occasionally humorous portrayals of sports life at mid-century, but they are generally less quirky and melodramatic than books by the other prolific authors. Jackson's coach in *Rose Bowl All-American*, Steve Foster, never says anything stronger than "Confound it!" Yet, as Jackson put it, "he could speak volumes with [Confound it!] in different inflections. And his eyes all but talked." Jackson also used Foster and Michigan in his first book, *All-Conference Tackle*, and in *Rose Bowl Linebacker* among possibly others.

Jackson's protagonist in *Rose Bowl All-American*, fullback Dick Thornley, grows emotionally and athletically throughout the book, overcoming self-doubt and jealousy and sometimes arrogant teammates. There's also a famed sportswriter, Flash Flager, who plays a big role in Thornley's self-effacing life. Thornley avoids publicity because he doesn't want

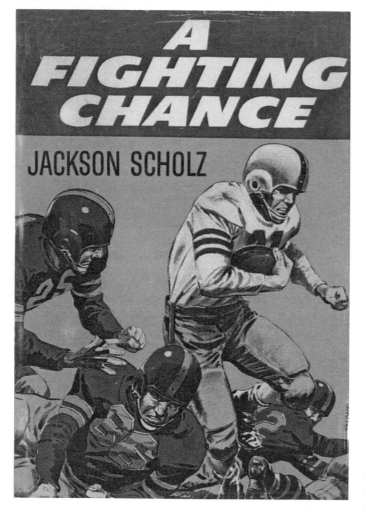

A Fighting Chance by Jackson Scholz, 1956 (jacket copyright William Morrow). The Olympic gold medal sprinter wrote numerous track and field short stories, but he focused on the more commercially viable team sports for more than 30 novels over three decades.

his great-grandmother to learn he is playing football, but it turns out she knew it all the time. Thornley's performance in the Rose Bowl leads Michigan over Southern California 29–0 — no melodrama here.

Jackson also throws in a little citizenship in his books, though nowhere near as much as John R. Tunis and Clair Bee. For example, Thornley stands up for the United Nations and Jews (the Rose Bowl epic was published one year after the creation of Israel in 1948). Thornley speaks his mind to a bigoted Germanic sort named Mueller: "The idea that there is anyone — or two, or three, or four — superior races or religious creeds or what have you is simply archaic." About the only negative aspect of *Rose Bowl All-American* is Jackson's odd spelling of "head coach" as "headcoach." It's jarring to see that spelling repeated countless times.

Jackson ended *Rose Bowl All-American* with the sentence "He felt wonderful," then used the exact same sentence to end his next novel, *Rookie First Baseman*. (Jackson did not end other early novels this way, however, although he became well known for happy endings and satisfied athletes in almost all of his books.) *Rookie First Baseman* is the story of Detroit Tigers rookie Johnny Parr, who has to learn all about selfishness and cockiness the hard way through 266 pages. He turns back attempt after attempt to help him until he ultimately realizes how self-defeating he has been. It's amusing how Jackson often converts a name like Ty Cobb into Hy Corn when Parr hears a baseball story. Jackson's characters are only slightly extreme in their character flaws and they definitely aren't "sports superheroes" in the Merriwell manner.

Jackson, though, plunged into the young-adult novel market in the same postwar period as most of the other prolific writers — the late 1940s. Soon, however, he carved a significant niche for himself, while writing about 60 short juvenile tales, as one of the first novelists to tackle Little League and junior high school sports, along with stories about high school, college and professional athletes written primarily for grade-school readers. Most of Jackson's juvenile books were published by Follett and Hastings House, and libraries bought them by the untold thousands. It's doubtful if there was an elementary school library in the nation without a few Jackson books, not to mention junior high and high school libraries. His novels still stand up fairly well today.

Jackson created one of the few long-running series characters for grade-school readers, Bud Baker, among the prolific writers, since the publishers of Clair Bee and Wilfred McCormick generally targeted their books at readers 12 to 16 years of age. Jackson's series of seven Bud Baker books — which are seldom seen today — began with *Bud Plays Junior High Football* (1957) and ended with *Bud Baker, College Pitcher* (1970). Bud Baker was a four-sport athlete: football, basketball, baseball and swimming. More to the point, he was *Bud Baker, Racing Swimmer* (1967) in an oddly titled book that was apparently meant to distinguish Bud from the run-of-the-mill recreational swimmer.

Jackson's first juvenile books were *Stretch Makes a Basket* (1949) as by Colin Lochlons, and *Shorty Makes First Team* (1950). His last was probably *Beginner Under the Backboard* (1974), a title reminiscent of Jackson's pulp roots in the late 1930s and 1940s.

Jackson's first book, *All-Conference Tackle*, in 1947, established the author's pattern of stressing personal growth and teamwork. Barry Leighton Shane goes from a Boston prep school to the University of Michigan as a halfback, but ultimately makes a shift to the offensive line and learns about humility and teamwork in the process. The book was billed for readers 12 to 16, the typical age range of novels defined as "young adult." The dust jacket quotes Jackson as saying, "I'm quite a character around here now, after twenty years of anonymity," referring to his fellow faculty members at Lincoln Junior High in Kalamazoo, which is described as a town of 55,000 "which song writers and sociologists alike consider one of America's most typical communities." Jackson wrote books into his 70s. The dust jacket acknowledges his 10 years of "various sports and detective stories in magazines," but does not refer to them as pulps, in the manner of the day. As typical for female writers of sports and western stories during this period (see chapter twelve), Jackson's wife published under her initials.

Robert Sidney Bowen

As the various genres of pulp magazines slowly declined and vanished in the 1950s, Joe Archibald and Jackson Scholz were joined in the ranks of the prolific authors by Robert Sidney Bowen (1900–1977), yet another sports novelist with hundreds of pulp stories to his credit since the 1930s. Although always a versatile writer, Bowen specialized in air war heroes before he began the first of his 29 baseball and football novels published from 1948 to 1969, all by Lothrop, Lee and Shepard, including three novels written as by James Rodney Richard during 1950 to 1953.

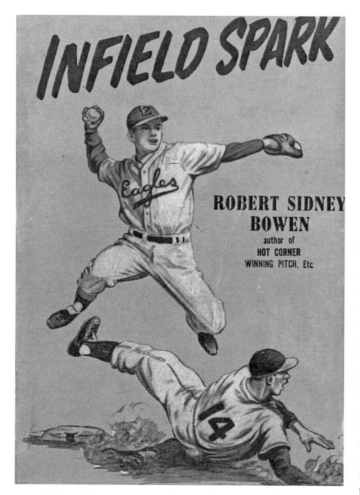

With the end of World War II, and with aviation becoming a less exotic subject for both pulp readers and the young-adult market, Bowen's market for air stories vanished. Bowen created "Dusty Ayres and His Battle Birds," a dozen issues from Popular Publications in 1934 and 1935, and "Captain Danger," 15 adventures that appeared in Air War from Standard Publications from 1940 to 1944, and also wrote several "Lone Eagle" stories for Standard in the late 1930s and early 1940s. Altogether, he is credited in *Bookery's Guide to Pulps* with work in at least 80 different pulp titles! Bowen also wrote the eight Red Randall aviation series books for Grosset & Dunlap (1944–1946).

Infield Spark by Robert Sidney Bowen, 1953 (jacket copyright Lothrop, Lee and Shepard). Like Joe Archibald and Jackson Scholz, Bowen was a prolific pulp writer who turned to a long series of sports novels as the pulp fiction market faded and then vanished.

Like John R. Tunis and Joe Archibald, Bowen did not write his first young-adult sports novel,

Winning Pitch (1948), until he was in his late forties. Like Archibald, Bowen's stories stressed the personal growth and response to adversity of a single protagonist. Bowen, however, did not write basketball novels, apparently feeling that there was a much better market for baseball and football.

As leading pulp historian John Gunnison has said, "a ripping good story" typified much pulp fiction, however unlikely the circumstances needed in the plot. *Infield Spark* (1955) was a typical Bowen sports novel —"a ripping good story" but tied together by so many coincidences that one must suspend one's concept of disbelief. The star of *Infield Spark* is Eagles rookie second baseman Jerry Tate and the theme is tied in with President Franklin D. Roosevelt's famous 1933 observation: "The only thing we have to fear — is fear itself!" It's an unusual psychological exploration of Tate's inability to handle the fear that he might be "yellow," in the baseball vernacular.

An encounter with a cruel foe's "gleaming spikes" and an ensuing performance in which he does, indeed, appear to be "yellow" leads Tate to jump the club. Having been raised in an orphanage, Tate seeks the mysteries to his mind by trying to explore his past in the tiny mythical town of Sayre, Kansas, not far from Wichita. On the flight there, he meets a stewardess, to use the language of the day, named Betty Cole, who is also from Sayre. Observing a semipro game in Sayre, he grabs a fly ball bare-handed and guns a strike to the plate, impressing manager Joey Hoik, who was brave enough to win the Congressional Medal of Honor during his service with the Marines after Hoik's failure during a tryout with the Eagles about two decades earlier.

Tate spends a little time with the semipro club, not realizing he hasn't fooled Hoik as to his identity, and it turns out that Betty Cole is an Eagles fan who also realizes his identity. She's the one who tells him about Roosevelt's speech. She tells him that "It takes courage to face danger, doesn't it? All right, what does it take in a person to have that courage? Faith, I think, Jerry. Faith in oneself. That we will not let our own self down. In other words, that we do have the courage to face danger, but also [to face] a fear that we may be afraid to face it when the time comes." Moments later comes a plot twist right out of either a Nancy Drew story or a pulp novel: a nearby house fire, an elderly resident in mortal danger, and Jerry's plunge into the fire to rescue her, knowing he has no choice but to test himself. "I had to, see?" he tells Hoik. "Not for Mrs. Besson. For me, see? I had to find out I wasn't being yellow."

It turns out that Cy Barlow, a big league writer who had wanted to believe in Jerry in his first stint with the Eagles, tracks him down to Sayre at about the same time as the heroic rescue. And, wonder of wonders, Barlow and Hoik were buddies in the Marines! Barlow talks the Eagles' manager, Buck Holt, into taking Tate back for a trial. On his way back to the big city, Tate and Betty Cole find themselves on the same flight, endangered by a radio failure and bad weather. Cole confesses that as one of five survivors of a plane crash that killed 31 passengers, she's "scared stiff." So they both find themselves afraid — but not of being afraid — and the flight makes it through.

When Jerry greets Holt in the locker room before Tate's first game back, Holt tells the rookie, "Don't thank me for a thing. This is a business with me. You do all right, and I'll love you. You mess it up, and I'll personally give you the boot. Let's have that part straight, too." Then, placing his hand on Tate's arm, the manager turns good kid: "Just give it all you've got. Nobody can give more than that. All right?" As fate and Bowen would have it, the game turns out to be a crucial makeup game with pennant implications against Jug Mullins and the Hawks — the same player and team that led him to jump the Eagles. You can guess the rest: Jerry faces down Mullins' "flashing spikes" and completes a crucial double play. Knowing he now has the young star he knows he needs, Holt ends the story by telling his coach, "I'm going to get my first sleep in the last hundred years. The little old pennant at last!"

It's pure pulp, but it's indeed "a ripping good yam." It just isn't what John R. Tunis or Duane Decker or Dick Friendlich, to name just three stellar contemporary prolific authors with minor pulp backgrounds, would have written.

Lothrop, Lee & Shepard usually gave Bowen's books a buildup on the back of the dust jackets, and the plot descriptions must have tempted many a librarian seeking to find books that would interest sports-minded readers. For *Fourth Down* (1949), the plug went like this: "At the height of Johnny Sloan's football career, a series of suspicious events occurred which put him in disgrace and made him an outcast from the game he loved. But that was only the beginning." For *Touchdown Kid* (1951), who could resist this: "Jerry Benson, a star quarterback at Stoddard University, was a one-man football team. At college, he never gave anybody else a chance to shine, but the professionals taught him a lesson." And for *Ball Hawk* (1950), the attraction was: "When Jerry Harriman was dropped from the training squad of the New York Bears, he realized there was plenty he hadn't learned in college. So he started at the bottom, with the Texas League 'chain gang.'"

Dick Friendlich: a sportswriter who also wrote sports novels

Of all the prolific authors during the 1940–1970 era, San Francisco journalist Dick Friendlich was the only one to take something of a commercial gamble. He was the first of the million-plus word men to make basketball the subject of his first two novels, *Pivot Man* (1949) and *Warrior Forward* (1950). Friendlich, however, wrote only two more basketball novels among his remaining 16 books. Friendlich always loved basketball — he became president of the U.S. Basketball Writers Association in 1965 — but basketball was a definite third behind the Big Two of baseball and football when it came to sports novels in the three decades when the prolific authors dominated the field. Not until the mid and late 1960s, with the likes of UCLA's Lew Alcindor-led basketball teams and the Boston Celtics' NBA dynasty, did any type of basketball begin to approach the glamour that Major League Baseball and college football enjoyed in the 1940s and 1950s, with the NFL beginning to break through in the 1950s as well.

Like most of the prolific authors, Friendlich had one primary publisher. Westminster, a leading purveyor of young-adult literature, produced all but two of his 18 hardcover first editions. Friendlich was a thoroughly professional, not to mention highly versatile, writer of realistic sports fiction, with seven baseball stories (all about the pro game), seven football novels (all but one about the college game), and four college basketball novels. As a young journalist — having joined the *San Francisco Chronicle* in 1935 — he soon began to contribute short stories to the sports pulps, although he had nowhere near the extensive pulp background of Joe Archibald, Jackson Scholz and Robert Sidney Bowen. During his two decades as a sports novelist, Friendlich was a fulltime journalist, serving as reporter, feature writer and columnist. He was a much respected figure in San Francisco and I had the privilege of a few pleasant conversations with him when I was a 20-something journalist in the early 1970s. I only wish I had asked him more questions about his fiction, for he was not the type to boast.

Friendlich had plenty to boast about. He was certainly among the most professional of all sports novelists. His books reflect the pragmatism and no-nonsense approach of the finest journalists. Unlike many other sports authors, he wasn't one to fill space for the sake of filling space, and his efficient writing sparkled without redundancies and hackneyed slang and phrases. A Friendlich book is always easy to follow, yet often profound in what it reveals about the true-to-life personal growth of his protagonists. He did not count on pulpish circumstances to tell a good story; his novels always seemed like they really could have happened. His books were neither manic nor dull; they were the real stuff of the highs and lows of genuine athletics. It's telling that his titles always inform the reader immediately which sport they cover.

His first baseball novel, *Baron of the Bullpen* (1954), dealt with the psychological struggles of fastball-throwing relief pitcher Jim Baron. This was his only novel to use a pun in the title, but, of course, it must have such a natural. It was not surprising he dedicated the book to Bob Stevens, the legendary *Chronicle* baseball writer. It was just like Friendlich to write an innovative story about a reliever, not many years after those players began coming to the fore with the likes of the New York Yankees, Brooklyn Dodgers and Philadelphia Phillies. Like almost all his stories, the baseball lore and lingo are real but relatively low key. Even Jim Baron's conflicts with aging sourpuss slugger Hack Francis are far from melodramatic. At the end, when Francis pays Baron a compliment and issues an apology for dropping a fly ball, one only knows they have accepted each other as teammates, if not necessarily buddies.

Friendlich obviously well understood both the tactics and psychology of sports. For example, when Jim Baron is serving a short stint with a Triple-A team, having signed for a $6,000 bonus and made the long leap from "Stannard University," he receives this pitching advice from his first professional manager: "You're too smooth, too regular. Just like you gotta have a change of pace, you gotta slow up your windup now and then. You throw with the same rhythm every time and you look awful pretty up in the stands, but the smart batters will be studying your motion and setting their clocks in the middle of it. Guys with the herky-jerk deliveries keep a man guessing; they gotta keep looking for that ball."

Baron throws nine consecutive strikes in his first major league inning, including a strikeout of former college teammate Tony Glick in the first big league game for both. Glick, though, later hits a game-winning home run off Baron on the last day of the season, costing the rookie pitcher's team a shot at qualifying for a pennant playoff. Baron eventually recovers his self-confidence, but only after suffering the tortures of the baseball damned in the off-season, spring training and early in the next regular season. Eventually, for better or worse, he realizes he has taken too much advice from too many people and returns to his fastball. As a young reliever, that will be enough for now; the reader gets the impression Baron has plenty of time to develop other pitches later.

It's intriguing to note that Baron works at a service station in the off-season, something that would be inconceivable with today's salaries, when the rookie minimum of $300,000 obviates the need to find work between seasons. It's also noteworthy how Friendlich works in the fact that even though the legendary Fred Merkle cost the Giants the 1908 pennant with a base running blunder, he went on to help win three championships as an outstanding first baseman.

Friendlich's books, which could be read for pleasure by either teenagers or adults, were definitely not aimed at the small fry. He didn't write about high school athletes, either, except in his penultimate book, *Touchdown Maker* (1966), one of two books he did for Doubleday.

In this story, the protagonist, Russ Harkness, sours on football as a transfer student in a small town, following a disaster in the state playoffs for his previous school in a large city. Russ, however, learns that both he and the townspeople have much to offer each other at his new school. It's just another low-key Friendlich gem.

Like Archibald and Bowen, Friendlich focused his stories on the psychological struggles of athletes who needed to become better team players, or switched positions to achieve success, or realized that there is more than one path to success. Friendlich, though, almost never uses melodrama to satisfy the reader. Friendlich's characters have some Merriwellian aspects to their character, but the Merriwell finish is seldom part of his eminently readable formula.

The unusual *Hard to Tackle*

The prolific authors weren't the only writers to tackle issues of social justice in sports stories. In fact, the obscure *Hard to Tackle* by Gilbert Douglas, published in 1956 by Crowell, was the first football novel with in-depth coverage of the civil rights issues that were beginning to roil the nation following *Brown vs. Board of Education* in 1954 and the Rosa Parks bus challenge in 1955. Coming 14 years after John R. Tunis first had white athletes standing up for a black teammate, *Hard to Tackle* was a commercial and social milestone. The book cost $2.75 — not a cheap price in the era of one-dollar series books — and it featured both white and black athletes on the historic dust jacket.

Douglas never reveals the location of Monroe High, but one gets the feeling it's his native Idaho or another northwest state, especially since there's a passing reference to the Washington family's move north from the smog of Los Angeles. Central to the theme of talented "colored"—"African American" had not yet entered the cultural lexicon — end Jeff Washington's struggle for acceptance involved his father's inability to land a job suitable to his college education and the Washington family's struggle to move to a white neighborhood. The book was published in an era where Jim Crow laws still obtained in the south, but occupational and housing options were still restrained in many parts of the West, Northeast and Midwest. Douglas is never maudlin or preachy about the black-white struggle, but he leaves no doubt about where justice lies.

Most of the characters essentially realize what is right and what is wrong in the world of race relations, but most of them, including protagonist Clint Thomas, are far from being civil-rights crusaders. The beauty of this remarkable book, aimed at the young-adult market, is the gradual realization by most of the multitude of characters that Jeff Washington and his family deserve not only the opportunity to gain a better income and a better home, but simple human dignity. Even though Jeff shows up shortly before the big game in the final pages, it's not a Merriwell-style miracle. He merely realizes that his week-long absence from practice — while he and his family coped with the emotional aftermath of likely arson at their new home — has put his own concerns first and the team second. One gets the feeling his father, who had been a football star in his youth but does not play a major role in the story, had a talk with his son in light of how the community had pitched in to repair their damaged home.

Even the big game itself is realistic, a 13–7 victory for Monroe over Norwalk that results in a league co-championship for the teams. Jeff catches touchdown passes of 20 and 65 yards, the latter early in the final quarter, and the team holds on. But Jeff's heroics are not extraordinary, for it had been made clear in pregame talks that standout quarterback Walt Tracy and Jeff were the offensive keys, since Norwalk's rushing defense was fearsome.

The star halfback, Ralph Vanderpool, and his father, a real-estate developer, are the villains of the piece, but they are portrayed as racists, not arsonists. Ralph, having ended his friendship with Clint over the racial issue, is dropped from the team for his confrontational attitude midway through the season, but he eventually comes to realize what a fool he has been. Even his father changes slightly, agreeing to supply new wood for the Washingtons' damaged home. The arsonist, if there was one, is never revealed or punished.

Early in the story, Clint's attitude is reflected when Ralph severely criticizes blacks, especially their desire to integrate a neighborhood, and Clint answers, "I don't know the score about this race problem, and I don't much give a hang. Maybe you're just borrowing trouble," to which Ralph responds, "If that Washington turns out for football, he sure isn't going to get a welcome from

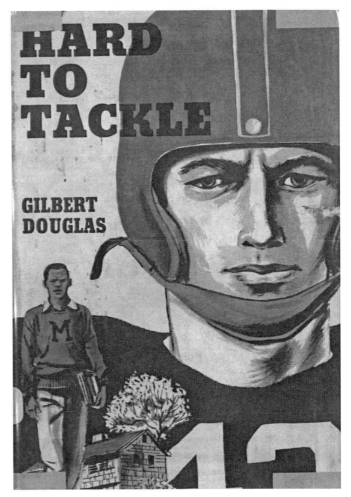

Hard to Tackle by Gilbert Douglas, 1956 (jacket copyright Thomas Y. Crowell). **This scarce novel is one of the first outside of John Tunis and Duane Decker to feature a black protagonist, who is shown approaching on this jacket by Paul Galdone.**

me. If we show those people how we feel maybe they'll stay where they belong." Earlier in the conversation, Ralph says, "If we let a Negro in one of those houses, the price on the others would drop like a rock — if you could sell them at all." In 1956, very few young-adult stories, sports or otherwise, involved such conversations.

Midway through the story, Clint and a teammate, the Eastern European immigrant Paul Slansky, have a conversation that shows just what a remarkable book this is for its time. "I guess I'm edgy [about race issues]," Clint tells Paul. "I'm confused. I've heard it said by people who can quote figures to prove it, that Negroes commit the biggest percentage of crimes in the cities. I've heard some good arguments in favor of keeping the races apart." Paul responds: "When people live in slums, the crime rate is high among whites as well as Negroes. If people think that nobody cares about them, they're not going to care about themselves."

Clint gradually realizes that his girlfriend, the star swimmer Judy Harlin, and her family have the right slant on civil rights. Late in the story, but before the house catches fire, after coach Leon Sullivan has dropped four regulars for their attitudes and divisive nature, the coach tells the team, "Some boys of high-school age aren't quite men enough to handle the prestige and popularity that comes with being a representative of the school on the football field. They get the idea they're indispensable. No one is indispensable. We'll plug the holes and keep on playing. They were good players. Our team may be weakened. But we'll go on trying and playing the game. If I had given in to those [four] boys, the idea of playing the game would have been a mockery."

Jeff, shaken, feels the need to speak out to his teammates for the first time. "Why do they pick me out to ride? Am I dirty or lazy? Am I a criminal? What's the matter with me? It's just because I'm colored, isn't it? Once I heard a white lady say she felt sorry for me because I couldn't help it that I was a Negro. Just like it was something to be ashamed of. Well, let me tell you something. I'm not ashamed of being a Negro and never will be. I guess I should turn in my suit so that you can call those guys back and tell 'em they can play. But I'm not going to. I'm not quittin'. I'm tired of being pushed around."

His coach has this to say to Jeff: "The majority of the fellows are on your side, Jeff. You're one of the few Negro students in our school. You're so much in the minority that it looks as if only white boys are capable of cruelty and prejudice. But deep down, people are pretty much the same everywhere. There are people of your race who have the same faults as some of us. So don't go judging all of us by what a few may do. That's not fair, either."

It's not difficult to see why this is such a remarkable book for its time. Douglas followed it in 1957 with two other Crowell football novels, *The Bulldog Attitude* and *Hard Nose*.

A bonanza for young readers

Until the end of World War II, stories both for and about grade-school student-athletes were uncommon in hardcover form. The Young Readers books from Grosset & Dunlap, billed for children 7 to 11, were a significant challenge for 7- and 8-year-olds in the 1950s, but most 12-year-olds would have moved on to books today listed as "juvenile" or "young adult." However, during the first half of the 20th century, along with the second of the 19th century, grade-school readers were pretty much forced to slog their way through long stories devoted to much older sports heroes, plus all sorts of other characters both real and fictional, such as Frank and Dick Merriwell, Baseball Joe, Fred Fearnot and Buffalo Bill.

Suddenly, though, many options from prolific authors developed for the youngest readers in the 1950s, thanks to C. Paul Jackson, Curtis Bishop and William Heuman, all of whom got their start in the sports pulps of the late 1930s, along with Matt Christopher and Bill J. Carol, the pen name of Bill Knott. All told, these five men produced well over 150 books for grade-school readers in the 1950s and 1960s (and more than 30 years beyond, in the case of Christopher). Bishop switched from pulps to the juvenile market in the early 1950s at about the same time C. Paul Jackson made the shift from both pulps and young-adult novels. Bishop wrote for numerous sports pulps and was a mainstay of the Fiction House line, but by the 1950s making a good living in the pulps was becoming impossible for almost all writers.

Bishop, a University of Texas graduate with a background in journalism, brought his experiences as an outstanding tennis and baseball player to his well-told tales, which were almost entirely about baseball and football with a little basketball thrown in. All told, he wrote at least 32 short novels from 1947 to 1968, and is credited with "some 25 novels" in his 1962 basketball novel, *Rebound* (he had actually written some 22, though he soon caught up to 25). Bishop's publishers, heavily involved in the youth-oriented trade, were the Steck Company of Austin, Texas, and Lippincott. His novel *Banjo Hitter* (1951) — about a star hitter who went from college to the major leagues but was forced to convert to pitching because of poor batting — shows his pulp origins and is similar to Duane Decker's 1948 Blue Sox story *Starting Pitcher* (see chapter eight) about an injured shortstop turned pitcher.

Bishop's two sons got him interested in Little League in the early 1950s. Untold thousands of boys were involved in Little League during the baby boomer 1950s and 1960s (in the era before girls were allowed), following the establishment of the Little League World Series in 1947, so Bishop had a ready-made market for Little League stories. He wrote 14 of them, from *Larry of the Little League* (1953) to *Little League Little Brother* (1968). Like Jackson, Bishop stressed character, personal growth and teamwork.

Much in the mold of Jackson and Bishop, New York State high school teacher and coach Bill Knott came along more than a decade later with his first sports book, the young-adult novel *Junk Pitcher* (1963). This book, originally published by Follett, was reprinted by Signet in 1967, well after Knott began his short but prolific career writing for grade-school readers. He used his background as a baseball player to follow *Junk Pitcher* with at least two dozen more short novels of baseball, football and basketball as by Bill J. Carol for Steck from 1963 to 1974. As the colorful pulp-style dust jacket — unusual for its era — of *Squeeze Play* (1971) indicates, the Carol novels were marketed for readers 9 to 12 years old. Like the other prolific authors, Knott stressed sportsmanship and personal growth over raw heroics and sports glory.

Matt Christopher broke all records for juvenile short novels, with more than 80 in a wide variety of sports over more than four decades. His fame increased exponentially in the post–1975 period, when other young-adult sports novelists had gone out of print and he dominated the genre and the market, in large part because he branched out to more different sports than anyone dreamed of writing about in the pre–1970 era. Christopher — whose longtime publisher was Little, Brown — broke in with *The Lucky Baseball Bat* in 1954. His stories focused on youngsters who overcome a barrier to their success. Like Jackson, Bishop and Knott, Christopher's tales immensely benefited young readers who gained a perspective — a sense of self and life lessons less available to the readers' parents and grandparents. Beginning in the 1970s, Christopher was the first prolific author to see his readers benefit from reading the books that their parents had read. The parents of the young followers of the multitude of first editions from Jackson, Bishop and Carol did not have books like Bishop's *Larry of the Little League*, which was published one year after Jackson's *Little Leaguer's First Uniform* (1952).

William Heuman, yet another of the prolific authors, wrote hundreds of stories for the pulps and slicks in several genres and appeared in most of the sports pulps at one time or another over two decades, until the market dried up. He first turned to young-adult novels with *The Fighting Five* (1950), a basketball story, and *Wonder Boy* (1951), a baseball epic that appeared not long before Bernard Malamud gave Roy Hobbs' bat that name in the distinguished adult novel *The Natural* (1952). But it wasn't long before Heuman was competing with Bishop and Jackson for grade-school readers. He wrote *Little League Champs* (1953), an original story of a highly diverse team winning the Little League World Series, when the event was only six years old. In 1953, the event was not yet shown on television and did not include overseas teams such as the Asian squads that would come to dominate it two decades later.

Heuman wrote at least 27 sports novels from 1950 to 1972 about basketball, baseball and football, many of them with bizarre humorous slants such as his three Horace Higby short novels, along with the likes of *The Horse That Played the Outfield* (1964) and *Hillbilly Hurler* (1966). Heuman's sports books often bridged the gap from readers 10 or 12 years old to teenagers, but in general he wrote for grade-school and middle-school readers. When he wrote his first sports book in 1950, Morrow Junior Books pegged *The Fighting Five* for readers 12 to 16. Heuman showed his sense of humor and irony right from the start, creating a garbage collector who coached basketball at a tiny college. Heuman displayed his pulp roots by involving gamblers and by writing about how a college without a gym wins a national title! *Gridiron Stranger* (1970), billed for readers 10 to 14, is the story of a drop-kicker in pro football.

The dust jackets on Heuman's later books revealed the secret of his success: "He writes on a schedule, nine to noon and three to five, punctually, exactly, five or six days a week."

Stephen Meader's odd basketball story

Stephen Meader was among the most prolific, widely read and most respected of all American authors for the young adult and juvenile markets, primarily from the 1930s through the 1960s, with more than 40 novels. One of his short-story collections, *The Will to Win* (1936), is among the earliest of its type. He wrote two sports novels, the basketball story *Sparkplug of the Hornets* (1953) and the football tale *The Lonesome End* (1968), both directed at the market somewhere between juvenile and full-fledged young adult.

His primary publisher — Harcourt, Brace & World — listed 12 and up as the intended audience for *Sparkplug of the Hornets*, but this story could have been enjoyed by any literate 10-year-old. When Harcourt, Brace began the 75-cent Voyager paperback reprint line in the early 1960s, *Sparkplug of the Hornets* was one of only two sports novels included among the first 56 books. The other was C.H. Frick's *The Comeback Guy* (1961).

Sparkplug of the Hornets is an odd book, indeed, with very little drama outside of how Meader connects play-by-play descriptions of about a dozen basketball games as tiny Hackersville High wins the high school championship of an unnamed state in the East. Compared with the contemporary books of John R. Tunis, Joe Archibald or Duane Decker, Meader's basketball story is short on plot but very long on action. There is almost nothing of the pulp sensibility in the story of how Gregory "Peewee" Carson, a 5-foot, 3-inch, 14-year-old freshman, becomes the team's sparkplug off the bench after his family moves to Hackersville, which has only 96 boys in the entire high school student body.

The team's youthful coach, the always-ethical and considerate Elmer Brent, dates Peewee's wholesome sister Jane and ultimately becomes engaged to her, while turning down opportunities to move up in the coaching ranks. "I'm going to refuse those bids," he says at the team's awards dinner, "That's because I know I was lucky this year, with a veteran team to build on. Three of those regulars are graduating in June. If I left now I'd never be sure how much I'd been able to contribute to the championship. We may not have as good a record next year [only two losses], but I'd like to prove to Hackersville and myself that we can win games with the material that's left. So I'm staying here at least one more season."

That sense of idealism and honor permeates the entire story. Peewee proudly announces at the celebration that he has grown to "five, four and three-quarters in my sox!" and has become great friends with another transfer player, Thornton Sedgley. Sedgley's parents are among the richest in town, and he isn't used to the rag-tag uniforms at tiny Thornton, but he soon learns how to fit in and his "California one-handed jump shot" helps the team plenty. Other than Peewee and Thornton, the only player with extensive characterization is Joe Pulaski, a crude-spoken, rough-and-tumble reserve player who has a hard time dealing with teammates and weaknesses. Meader does do a good job of characterizing Peewee through his actions, such as his refusing a 90-cent tip for 10 cents worth of newspapers.

Clem Johnson, described as "a tall Negro center," integrates the story but nothing is made of his race, at a time when other leading authors made racial issues central to several plots. Like the other players, except occasionally Pulaski, Clem is an enthusiastic team player, easily the most talented on the squad. Meader writes basketball action well, but he has an odd sense of the game, such as when tiny Peewee is used at forward instead of guard. Today, of course, such a tactic would be described as a "three-guard offense" or "the short lineup." At the time, though, Meader may have been the only basketball novelist ever to have a high-scoring 5-foot-3 forward.

When Meader describes the team's scoring averages for the regular season going into the state tournament, the averages amount to numbers well over the final scores of the games he describes so thoroughly. In one tournament game, Clem Johnson must oppose a 6-foot-9, 220-pound center who is known to be 20 years old. (Perhaps at the time Meader wrote this there were states that would allow a 20-year-old competitor in high school sports, but even in the 1950s the vast majority of the states would not allow 20-year-olds to play. Today, most states say a player can't turn 19 until after the start of his senior year, with occasional exceptions or exemptions.) When a fluke forces both the state semifinal and final games on the same day, Brent decides to play his entire squad in the first game, including seldom-used reserves — something that truly seems highly unlikely in real life, two games or none. The plan works, and Peewee's steal in the final seconds of the title game sets up his pass to Clem Johnson for the game-winning basket at the buzzer.

If anything, *Sparkplug of the Hornets* is a polemic against what the author apparently perceived as the excesses of sports journalism, although there are no overtly unethical journalists, such as Clair Bee sometimes used in the famed coach's Chip Hilton series. When Joe Pulaski threatens to quit the team during the playoffs because "You hot-shots that do all the playin' an' get the write-ups in the papers can practice if you want to. Me — I'm quittin'." As he says that, Brent walks in with "tight lines around his mouth and they could feel the anger in him. ... 'All right, Joe,' he said quietly. 'I heard what you said, and I can't say I blame you. I'd like to burn every sports page that comes into this town before anybody has a chance to read it. I've told all of you before, and I'm saying it again now — there are no stars on this squad. We've been winning games because we were a team.'"

Meader soon says that "Following Brent's orders, they avoided reading the sports pages that week. Peewee's father reveled in the columns of type that were devoted to the [final] four teams that were in the state championships, but the boy refused to listen to his comments. "The coach says those guys make up half of what they write," Peewee says. "They do more harm than good, building up stars. What he wants us to do is go after one game at a time, just like we have all season, and forget about the wonder boys on the other team." Yet, despite all this vitriol directed at the press, Meader oddly has the coach letting photographers and reporters from the local newspaper interrupt a practice! Very few coaches would ever allow that, even those with the best of relations with the media.

All in all, *Sparkplug of the Hornets* is a good book, but it also shows what can happen when an otherwise experienced author tackles a sports novel for the first time.

TWELVE

Making Sports History:
The Girls of Central High

The first series devoted entirely to books about sports and other extra-curricular activities for girls was *The Girls of Central High* by Gertrude Morrison. The author penned no other series books, but nonetheless left her mark with a historic but now obscure seven-volume series nearly 100 years old. I have not found any earlier volumes devoted in such depth to girls' sports, other than stories where athletics, especially a team sport like basketball, are considered minor activities for girls, at best.

Grosset & Dunlap published the first five volumes in 1914, including the earliest books I have found that go into any depth at all regarding basketball, *The Girls of Central High at Basketball, or The Great Gymnasium Mystery* and track and field, *The Girls of Central High on Track & Field, or The Champions of the School League*. These are not short stories; they are every bit as long as the earliest Nancy Drew mysteries of the 1930s. But they were as affordable as hardbound books came in that era. My first edition of the track and field book lists the price in an ad as 40 cents (albeit in an era when some jobs paid about 10 cents an hour).

It's telling that Morrison's other volumes are more into recreational activities: *The Girls of Central High, or Rivals for All Honors* (the founding of the Girls Athletic Association involving five schools, and obtaining money for an athletic field and gymnasium); *The Girls of Central High on Lake Luna, or The Crew That Won* (rowing); *The Girls of Central High on the Stage, or The Play That Took the Prize* (theatre); *The Girls of Central High in Camp, or The Old Professor's Secret* (camping on an island); and *The Girls of Central High Aiding the Red Cross, or Amateur Theatricals for a Worthy Cause* (more theatre). The latter two books were published in 1915 and 1921, respectively.

These books must have proven popular, even though Grosset surrendered the rights for reasons lost in the mists of time. Three reprint houses, Goldsmith, Saalfield and the World Syndicate, republished the series, apparently into the 1930s, because there was enough plot, conflict, character development, action and humor to stand the test of time. Despite dated language, the books actually still hold up fairly well and can be read with enjoyment, as readers learn what school life was like in their grandmother's and great-grandmother's days. While reading about the girls of Central High, I couldn't help smiling, wondering if my grandparents, who graduated from high school in 1913, lived this way.

All five high schools in the girls' league, including three in Centerport and one in Lumberport and Keyport, are near Lake Luna, a large, inland body of water, situated in a forested area such as upstate New York. Like the settings in many series books, the exact geographical location is left to the reader's imagination. Just the fact the officials form a girls' interscholastic league, complete with championship competition, was remarkable in 1914 — well over half a century before the advent of Title IX and widespread girls' leagues throughout the United States.

Morrison does a commendable job of characterizing the girls, who include the bright, witty leader, Laura Belding, nicknamed Mother Wit; Clara (Bobby) Hargrew, an extroverted, highly athletic girl without a mother; identical twins Dora and Dorothy Lockwood; Nellie Agnew, the highly intelligent and team-oriented daughter of a wise physician, along with a half dozen or more other names in every story.

One of the primary characters of *The Girls of Central High at Basketball* is Hester Grimes, a highly athletic yet selfish and temperamental girl who is the antithesis of the team player. She is prone to frequent fouling, leading to the intense displeasure of the sportsmanlike coach, physical education instructor Mrs. Case. In an era when schools often listed teachers only by their last names and left students to ask their first names — if they dared — her first name is not mentioned. Hester has a weak-willed friend, Lily Pendleton, who remains on the team after Hester is dropped for her lack of sportsmanship. Other girls, all in good standing, who make up the starting nine-girl (!) lineup include Josephine Morse and Evangeline Sitz, a student from Switzerland, plus Roberta Fish, who eventually takes Hester's place.

When this groundbreaking basketball story first appeared in 1914, basketball was only 22 years old, following the posting of rules of its inventor, physical education instructor Dr. James Naismith. "A New Game" was the headline in the January 1992 school paper of the YMCA Training College in Springfield, Massachusetts, where Naismith's rules first appeared. A few women quickly adopted the game. *Annals of American Sport* by John Allen Krout, published by Yale University Press in 1929 as part of the Pageant of America series, noted that women's basketball was played at Smith College "as early as 1892." For several decades, however, the game was not played by unified rules — teams ranged from the five-player men's game to as many as 10 players, stationed in three distinct zones on either indoor or outdoor courts. *Annals of American Sport* notes that a 1928 survey by the American Physical Education Association "disclosed that only one in fifteen teams used the [five-player] rules for boys in their [girls] interclass and interscholastic competition."

Games in *The Girls of Central High at Basketball* are played with nine-girl lineups, using three zones and defensive tactics in every zone. These tactics almost always involved specific girl-to-girl "guarding," as defense was consistently called. The story makes clear that for a defender to go from one girl to another was frowned upon as overly aggressive. Clearly, it was a much slower game, stressing passing instead of dribbling: Central High wins the championship game over Keyport at the climax of the story by 4 to 2! In fact, the word "dribbling" does not appear in the book! As girls became more skilled, and as acceptance of their physical abilities grew, most girls' games in the four decades before Title IX were played with six girls — three on each side of the court.

By 1929, as *Annals of American Sport* pointed out, "Within recent years there has been a significant growth in intramural basket ball without a corresponding increase in contests scheduled between schools. Those responsible for the development of women's athletics have discouraged any attempt to place the emphasis upon the staging of a spectacle for the audience and have stressed the benefit to be derived from the outdoor as well as the indoor game." The Central High girls, in contrast, play before cheering crowds and the boys in the student body clearly support their efforts without seriously insulting them (although kidding is a big part of the often witty repartee).

The Girls of Central High at Basketball introduces aspects of the game, a kindness to the many readers who may not have been familiar with basketball. "You are breaking another rule of the game by directly addressing the referee," Mrs. Case tells Hester on the first page! In the opening chapter, it is revealed that girls involved in basketball "exercised for from fifteen to thirty minutes at basketball" in five-minute intervals! After explaining that girls' basketball had come under some criticism in recent years, the narrative goes on to say (correctly) that "basketball is the first, or one of the first, vigorous team games to become popular among women and girls in this country, and under proper supervision will long remain a favorite pastime." Morrison proved prophetic about the nationwide popularity of girls' basketball.

High school life is realistically portrayed, if with a wholesome slant, and numerous boys are brought into the narrative. One of them, "Prettyman" Sweet (!), wears only the finest fashions and speaks in much the lisping style that Elmer Fudd—"wealy" and "pwior" are spelled that way here—would express himself in cartoons in battle with "that Wascally Wabbit" Bugs Bunny three decades hence. Sexuality is not part of the narrative, but one can imagine "Prettyman" Sweet is one of the first gay characters in children's literature.

Dr. Agnew, Nellie's father, expresses a fascinating bit of period-piece philosophy in the second chapter: "Do you know what seems to me to be the kernel in the nut of these school athletics, Nell? ... Loyalty. That's the kernel—loyalty. If your athletics and games don't teach you that, you might as well give 'em up—all of you girls. The feminine sex is not naturally loyal; now, don't get mad! It is not a natural virtue—if any virtue is humanly natural—of the [female] sex. It's only the impulsive, spitfire girls who are naturally loyal—the kind who will fight for another girl. Among boys it is different. Now, I am not praising boys, or putting them an iota higher than girls. Only, long generations of working and fighting together has made the normal male loyal to his kind. It is an instinct—and even our friends who call themselves suffragettes have still to acquire it." After women gained the vote in 1920, "suffragettes" remained in the text!

The girls are not permitted to play tie games, and Morrison never reveals the score, writing only that Central was four points behind or two points ahead, etc. Likewise, win-loss records are never mentioned, only where a team stands in the league—"second," "third," etc. There is much melodrama—vandalism in the gym, shady characters, Hester's rescue of a toddler from drowning—to go with vivid game descriptions. There are also racist references to Laura Belding's family servant, Mammy, who speaks like this: "Dese yere literary folk is suah a trouble. Leabin' books, an' papers, an' pen an' ink eroun' fo' odder folks to pick up." And when Mammy is asked, "Is Laura literary, Mammy?" the servant replies, "Suah is. Littahs t'ings all ober de house!"

Near the end of the story—as Hester learns the meaning of teamwork and the other girls learn "there is good stuff inside her," as the doctor says—is inserted this bit of wisdom espoused by coaches ever since: "Hester was learning what really paid in life—especially in the life of school and athletics. A good temper, a tongue without a barb to it, and thoughtful for the comfort of others. Those attributes won out among the girls of Central High—as they are bound to win out in every walk of life."

Before Hester helps win the league trophy in the final game against Keyport, this astonishing 1914 description in a 1930s Saalfield reprint makes it difficult to believe the story had not been updated: "From the first toss-up the girls played with a snap and vigor that amazed and delighted even their instructors. Trained as they had been all the fall, there were few fouls to record, and very little retarding of the game. The signals were passed silently and the girls indulged in little talking. Unnecessary talking and laughter mars basketball. It was a pleasure to watch the lithe, vigorous young girls. They were untrammeled by any foolish fashions, or demands of dress. Their bodily movements were as free as Nature intended them to be. They jumped, and ran, and threw, with a confidence that none but the well trained athlete possesses." (Talk about misplaced modifiers! One can only laugh at the thought of fouls being trained.) The frontispiece illustration showed girls in bloomers, the typical basketball attire of the period. "Foolish fashions, or demands of dress" doubtless refers to the likes of corsets or girdles.

Not surprisingly, the Central High girls win the championship in Frank Merriwell fashion. Hester, having learned to devote herself to unselfish defense after being taken back on the team, makes the key defensive play: "There were but a few moments of play left. It is not good basketball to oppose other than one's immediate opponent; but for once, Hester went out of her field to stop the ball. A side swipe, and the ball was hurtled directly into Laura's hands. She turned and threw it swiftly, making the signal for the famous massed play which was the strongest point in the game as played by Central High. Down the field the ball shot, from one to the other. Hester's quick break in the Keyport plan had rattled the latter team for a moment. And before the visitors recovered, the ball was hurtling through the air straight for the basket. The whistle blew. But the ball sped ON. [An amazing connection! As though the reader might not have understood that the whistle could not stop the ball.] It struck the edge of the basket; but the next breath it slid in and — the game was won! Central High had outstripped its strongest opponent ... and the beautiful cup would remain in the possession of Central High."

Hester's reward is tears of joy: "They all had something nice to say to her; Hester couldn't reply. She stood for a moment or two in the middle of the room, listening to them; then she turned away and sought her own locker, for there were tears in her eyes."

The last lines of the book still ring as true as ever with regard to girls' love of sport: Says spunky Bobby Hargrew, "It's all right to say that school takes up all our time; but it's the fun we get out of school that makes Latin, and French, and mathematics, and — and — Gee Gee [an ill-humored teacher] bearable! My! Suppose we didn't have any athletics at all?" "That would certainly be a state of existence perfectly unbearable — for you, Bobby," Nellie Agnew says gravely. "You'd burst, wouldn't you?" Bobby responds: "Into flinders! Athletics is the 'scape-valve for me — and I guess it is for some of the rest of you. Now, tell the truth! And her friends had to admit the truth of her declaration."

Jane Allen: The "basketball series" that wasn't really about basketball

Basketball was ostensibly the innovative attraction of the first three volumes of the five-book Jane Allen series. Instead, the series became a telling indictment of early 20th century society's feelings about the real importance of basketball for female athletes, or at least for two of the most commercially successful publishers of the period.

College life was an exotic subject for young females in the quarter century from 1917 to the early 1940s, the period of the effective commercial life for the original five-book Cupples and Leon series (1917–1922 and possibly second editions) and the ensuing cheap-paper Saalfield reprints circulated into the early 1940s, many of which literally crumbled away in heat and humidity. Only a small fraction of girls in the United States attended college at the time, and college life was often seen primarily as a haven for girls of means, at that.

Even though basketball was featured in the titles of *Jane Allen of the Sub-Team* (1917), *Jane Allen, Right Guard* (1918) and *Jane Allen, Center* (1920), there were only a handful of pages in the three books actually devoted to the sport, first popularized only a few years earlier in Grosset & Dunlap's *The Girls of Central High at Basketball*. The Jane Allen series was credited to Edith Bancroft (possibly a pseudonym), who was credited with no other series books. The entire Jane Allen series, which finished with *Jane Allen, Junior* (1921) and *Jane Allen, Senior* (1922), included only the briefest descriptions of game action or strategy, leading one to suspect that the author knew very little about the game. Instead, the stories are full of descriptions of social life, the complexity involving relationships between the girls at Wellington College, fashions, parties, and vivid accounts of the constant schemes of the nasty female rivals who were dedicated to ruining Jane and her friends.

The style of third book, which ignored most of Jane's friends and teammates in the first two books, was significantly different from the first two volumes. That led series book expert Kate Emburg — in the 1995 edition of her privately printed Girls Series Book Companion by the Society of Phantom Friends, a group of expert collectors — to speculate about different authors.

When Saalfield reprinted the first three books, the early dust jacket (used on each book) was dull: The jacket showed Jane strolling down a tree-covered path on an autumn day, books in hand, with several girls at play on the grass in the background. It's understandable that Saalfield would want a more compelling jacket, but what the publisher did was astonishing. For the final printings of all three volumes released sometime in the 1930s, the jacket featured a giant symbolic megaphone behind a tall, proud Jane Allen. She is heroically walking toward the reader, with shorts several inches above her knees and a striped blouse — both the latest fashions — and a basketball cradled in her right arm. Seldom in any sports book for girls has an athlete been portrayed exuding such confidence. One can only wonder at the disappointment basketball-loving readers must have felt when their sport turned out to be only a minor backdrop for each story.

In the first two books, Jane's first two teams — the Wellington College freshman and sophomore squads — face only each other. They conduct a series of three games played weeks apart. It isn't until Jane is a junior that Wellington faces another college, and then only one outside school. Practice throughout much of the winter and spring is referenced, but basketball is treated more like a physical education activity than a serious team sport. Nor are the Saalfield reprints the least bit updated; in *Jane Allen, Center* she is referred to as member of the class of 1920! There are numerous references to World War I.

In *Jane Allen of the Sub-Team*, Jane has been raised by her well-to-do, widowed father on a picturesque ranch in Montana. She loves her horse, Firefly, so much that her father sends the steed to be stabled near Wellington in the East Coast locale of Chesterford! Jane clearly doesn't understand the other students at Wellington, a girls' school, and spends the entire book growing in social and physical maturity. Marian Seaton, a mean-spirited social snob on the freshman basketball team, spends much time working at cross purposes to Jane, whom Marian quickly grows to hate.

Jane turns out late for basketball — she didn't think she wanted to play — and plays well with the team of substitutes. The first-string freshman girls eventually realize she should be promoted, even though Marian works against that. The girls, except for Marian, tell school officials they will leave the team if Jane is not treated fairly, and Jane replaces an inferior, injured player. In the last chapter, "The Great Game," Jane's feelings are portrayed this way just before the game begins: "To Jane Allen, as she stood ready for action, it was the supreme moment of her life. The gay decorations, the clamoring audience, the opening ceremony of introduction by the mascots, thrilled her to the core. Most wonderful of all, she was at last a part of that which she had so often vainly dreamed."

Jane leads the freshmen to their first victory over the sophomores, 18–10, a typical score of the era. She caps her performance with "the star play of the afternoon: a long over hand throw to [the] basket." But the author's description of the big day —cheers, mascots, music, and the crowd that so thrills Jane—takes up so much space that there are less than two pages of game action. "She was in her glory," Jane is described in the second half, "and her

clever footwork, lithe movements and quick, catlike springs won for her that day a lasting reputation as a star player." The story ends with warmhearted Jane and her teammates bringing festive greetings to Alicia, the girl Jane replaced.

Each Saalfield reprint was 308 pages; these were long, involved tales, notwithstanding the lack of genuine basketball tactics and action. In *Jane Allen, Right Guard*, basketball isn't mentioned until the sophomore team tryouts on page 167! However, there is one possible groundbreaking basketball portion: chapter 19, "Rank Injustice," may be the first in-depth reference to the politics of female sport. In this chapter, Judith Steams, Jane's close friend and roommate, is denied a place on the sophomore team in favor of Marian Seaton. Two of the three senior managers make that decision because of favors Marian has granted them. Eventually, justice and Jane win out for Judith, after a long, convoluted series of moves and countermoves involving school officials and the players. Marian is aided by freshman Elsie Noble, dubbed the "ignoble Noble" by Jane's friends, until Elsie sees the light.

Jane Allen, Right Guard by **Edith Bancroft, Saalfield reprint of 1918 novel (jacket copyright Saalfield). This dust jacket from the late 1920s or early 1930s is one of the first, if not the first, to portray a female basketball player in uniform. However, there wasn't much basketball in the five-book series.**

Uniforms described in detail

Late in the story, more lines are given to describing the players' uniforms than to how Jane's sophomores, led by Jane's "dash and skill," beat the freshmen in their first matchup of the school year:

> The sophomores won, though the freshmen gave them a hard tussle, the score standing 22–18 in favor of the sophomores when the hotly contested game ended. [Note the poor writing; all the words following the score are extraneous. Though the plot is interesting, probably twice as many words as needed are used to tell this story.] Both teams made a fine appearance on the floor. Neither team had adhered to class colors that year in choosing their basket-ball suits. The freshmen wore suits of navy blue, decorated with an old rose "F" on the front of the blouse. A wide rolling sailor collar of the same color further added to the effect. The sophomores had elected to be patriotic, and wore khaki-colored suits, unrelieved by a contrasting color. It was a decided innovation of its kind and they liked it.

Today, this kind of writing in either a novel or a newspaper story would be considered silly and incomplete at best and sexist at worst, since men's uniforms are rarely described (and, indeed, were seldom portrayed even in Jane Allen's day).

The second game merited only passing mention on page 277 and is noted only as a two-point victory; the third game was not covered at all. Late in the story, when Marian's sidekick, Maizie Gilbert, realizes how wrong she has been about Jane and how unprincipled Marian really is, Maizie tells Jane, "You're a real Right Guard. Not only on the team, but in everything else. I'm sorry it took me so long to find it out."

In *Jane Allen, Center,* basketball again takes a backseat to intrigue and Marian's skull-duggery. Basketball doesn't show up until well into the second half of the book, which doesn't even begin the girls' junior year until page 115, with much of the early story taking place in Montana. It's just amazing how shameless the Saalfield firm could be to try to sell the book with such a dynamic dust jacket portrayal of Jane and yet feature so little basket-ball. In the final tryout game — on page 209, two-thirds of the way through the book — Jane plays so well at center, in order to help her team, that she earns the job. The first game against Breslin receives three convoluted pages of description on pages 252–254, meaning the reader had to wait almost to the end of the book to read about a real game — the first in any of the three volumes.

Here's the description of Jane's game-winning heroics: "[W]ith an astonishing fumble [by an opponent], the ball slipped and rolled to Jane's feet. Quick as a flash Jane was after it. Then the dribble, and Jane took one bounce, and with one toss of the ball to her [unnamed] forward under the basket, the ball went home for a goal! And the goal was made for Wellington! ... The cyclone broke. That strategy on Jane's part won a victory for which she would have been more content to have had any other [member] of the team than herself, strike the decisive blow." The author ignores the obvious; someone else scored the basket on Jane's pass.

Ironically, then, these three volumes are most noteworthy for the best illustration to date of a female basketball player to go with the sketchiest possible writing about the sport.

Amelia Elizabeth Walden's noteworthy *A Girl Called Hank*

Probably the best novel about girls' basketball in the era before Title IX changed the game so drastically in the 1970s was *A Girl Called Hank* (1951) by Amelia Elizabeth Walden.

It's a charming coming-of-age story that nicely mixes generous details about the mental, physical and tactical sides of the six-girl game. Notwithstanding that Hank scores 29 points in the second half of the league championship game to lead her Brighthaven team to a one-point victory in the final chapter, it's a realistic look at the game and the girls who play it, thankfully minus bizarre melodrama or cardboard characterizations. This is an ideal story for those who would like to see how the girls' game had evolved by mid-century.

The author, who wrote numerous young-adult novels for girls, explains on her acknowledgement page that she was permitted to closely follow and travel with her local high school girls' team in Connecticut. That explains how someone outside the playing and coaching realm could capture the feel of the game so well. "While this book is pure fiction as to its events and characters," she wrote, "I hope it shows something of what our democratic schools are accomplishing by way of good fellowship and character development." Morrow Junior Books, the outfit that published most of Duane Decker's outstanding Blue Sox series, published *A Girl Called Hank*.

The story opens shortly before the senior season for Henrietta "Hank" Baxter, a tall shooting forward who learned her basketball style from her four older brothers, all of whom played the game. Growing up as a tomboy, everyone in a small New England town got to know her by the nickname the family gave her. When a beloved and respected coach at Brighthaven High leaves before Hank's senior year, she must cope not only with a rigid new coach, former tennis star Maggie Dorn, but also with Francie Weller, a glamorous senior teammate who is jealous of Hank's ability to shoot. Because of that jealousy, Francie and Hank, once as close as sisters as young girls, had steadily grown apart by the time the story starts.

Walden cleverly uses the limitations of the six-girl game to provide Francie, an outstanding athlete, with a logical first-string spot on the defensive end of the court. The author also brings in a fellow senior, Gregory Sutherland, who is not an athlete. Instead, he is involved in the school's theatrical programs and corresponds for the local paper, with the goal of becoming a writer. Hank is willing to be interviewed and photographed, but in typically headstrong fashion she evaluates Greg this way: "'The kids say he wants to be a writer when he finishes college. Imagine anyone being so dumb' she added in disgust. 'Writers,' she said with an air of final superiority, 'writers starve!'"

It's obvious that Hank and Greg are headed for Hank's first romance, though nothing more than light kisses take place in a chaste story until a hint of a possible marriage shows up at the finish. Greg, who meets Hank on an interview assignment in the first chapter, ultimately helps to provide the maturity and stability Hank still lacks, especially when Hank and her new coach clash. Where Walden excels is in her portrayal of both star and coach as women who have significantly different personal styles of communication, yet ultimately prove to be people with ethics and an innate decency. Hank's limitation is her stubborn nature and inability to communicate verbally; Maggie's chief drawback is her bitterness over the two crippled fingers that ended her high-level tennis career. At the end of the story, Maggie teaches Hank what being competitive really means, after the coach decides to stop feeling sorry for herself and resigns, effective at the end of the season. She intends to return to high-level tennis while she is still young enough to cope with her physical problems.

Long before Maggie makes that decision, she reinstates Hank as captain of the team because she feels it gives the team its best chance to win. This is one of the first times a female coach has spoken like this: "I want you girls to win this afternoon. I'd like to see you win every game and keep that championship. I hate people who can't win. If you can't win, you shouldn't play. That's why I'm putting you back in as captain, Henrietta, because I can't stand a team that doesn't win." Whether Maggie really meant that last sentence, or whether she implied "a team that doesn't try to win," is a distinction left for the reader to make because it's never clarified. Maggie, indeed, is a ferocious competitor throughout the story.

The catch toward the finish is Francie's plot to discredit Hank when one of Hank's friends jokes that her father, a member of the school board, played the key role in seeing that Maggie Dorn resigned. Francie's plot doesn't make a lot of sense, since Hank is a senior and the season is almost over, but Francie sees that a nearby town's scandal sheet writes up the situation as though the joke were serious. Walden also adds a nice touch when she has Francie apologize at the finish, when she is too guilt-ridden to play in the championship game, yet doesn't make clear whether the girls will resume their once-close friendship. Nor is there any hint that Hank will continue to play basketball in college;

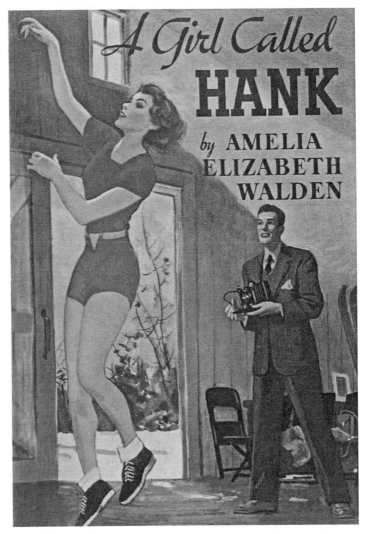

A Girl Called Hank by Amelia Elizabeth Walden, 1951 (copyright William Morrow). Walden wrote several solid sports-themed novels with female protagonists, including this scarce and little-known early basketball story. The twist on the jacket is that she is the athlete and the man she loves is a budding journalist.

her goal is to eventually run the family's lumber company, since none of her four older brothers want to. Instead, Walden uses basketball as a road to maturity for Hank.

Not many American high schools played interscholastic basketball when this book was written, and there are some distinct oddities that startle the basketball-oriented reader from a remove of more than half a century. Greenport, a team with a reputation for overly aggressive basketball and foul-mouthed fans, is Brighthaven's foe for the final two games, with Brighthaven needing a sweep to claim the title. In the penultimate contest at Greenport, Hank is an emotional basket case after the newspaper article linking her father with her coach's resignation. Hank fouls out in the first half as the fans and Greenport players shower her with verbal abuse. She then leaves the scene with Greg — an action that today would almost certainly result in a player's suspension — as her team rallies to win without her in the second half. Yet there is no hint that this action is out of the ordinary!

Maggie Dorn, though, meets with Hank and tells her the gossip and Francie's role in it have been clarified with the school administration. Maggie tells Hank about her real reason for leaving, which is to resume playing tennis in California (which, in those days, seemed like another planet to girls from New England). Hank and Maggie seem to have reached a new understanding, after a talk that Hank never expected. Yet when Brighthaven plays host to Greenport with the title on the line — both teams now have one loss in the eight game league season — the coach ignores Hank in the first half. When Hank's substitute who had played so well in her place in the previous game finds herself struggling against Greenport's tactics, Hank is astonished that Maggie Dorn seems oblivious. At halftime, though, the coach asks, "Are you ready to go in there now and play the game, Hank? ... Are you ready to forget Hank Baxter [meaning her ego] and everything the spectators might yell at her? Are you ready to ignore the crowd and go in there and play the game?"

"Yes, I'll play the game," Hank responds, startled but pleased that the coach has finally begun to call her by the name she answers to, instead of Henrietta or Miss Baxter. The coach adds, "Now forget the vicious heckling and go out and shoot! Just go out and shoot, Hank. That's all you have to do!" And that she does, having just enough time to score all 29 points in the second half when her teammates see how driven she is, despite the physically punishing tactics of Greenport's defender. Hank makes the winning basket with a shot at the buzzer, and then there's another astonishing oddity.

When the crowd closes around Hank in a wild celebration "all she wanted to do was get out of here and go home. Greg and Sam Taylor [Hank's friend] and Russ [one of her brothers] grabbed her and pushed and shoved their way through the crowd at the door." And Greg takes her home! Again, even though it's the end of the season, to leave the team at this happy point — aside from being a severe violation of the rules — is something a player would be severely criticized for today. There is a certain degree of internal logic, since Hank had played herself to exhaustion, but the implication is that all these heroics, following the previous game's embarrassments, were too much for a girl to handle.

When Hank returns home, Greg kisses her and her beloved grandfather greets her with "You won, lass. I can tell by your face." (It's astonishing that he doesn't come to the game that means so much to her, nor is there any mention of her loving, affectionate parents.) But Francie is also waiting at Hank's home, with an apology for starting the lie. Before the game, Hank had decided to forgive Francie, and told her mother she was sorry Francie couldn't play. There followed this mental flashback: "Hank looked at Francie. This time she did not see a swollen, pale face. She saw a girl with blond curls and a pink pinafore, racing down the street to meet her. Hank saw herself put out her hands to clasp Francie's, and heard Francie say, 'We haven't any sisters of our own, Hank, so let's be each other's sisters.'" Walden concludes, "She went over to Francie and put her arm around her. Francie sobbed softly, as if she really meant it when she said she was sorry."

Though there are more basketball practice, tactics and game action in this story than in any other to this point, there is also a marvelous chapter about a shopping adventure Hank takes with her stylish sister-in-law. Most girls must have enjoyed this chapter, too; it clearly shows the book is written entirely with a girl's sensibilities in mind. There's a telling line after Hank returns home from her big day: "No basketball game had ever tired her as much as today's gallivanting."

Early in the story, Hank tells Greg, "I don't know how much you know about girls. I mean in athletics. They take their sports differently." When Greg responds, "Even when they play a man's game like you?" Hank replies, "Even so. It's the little things that go on in a girl's mind that make her game good or bad. Girls worry more. About home and their families and their grades and their boy friends. It shows up in their game."

Still early in the story, in reference to how Hank analyzes the schedule, Walden refers to Greenport as "more experienced than any other team in the county, because they were trained by men at recreation centers. Most of them played basketball every night in the season. It was a special feather in Hank's cap that since she had been on the team, and only since she had been on it, Brighthaven had won the championship from Greenport." It's this observation that dates the story, as any of the thousands of highly competitive women coaches would attest today.

Walden later wrote *Three Loves Has Sandy* (1955), a young adult novel featuring Sandy's three loves: horses, a boy named Bill and softball, in which she pitches. This is one of the earliest books involving softball, though the sport doesn't play as large a role in the protagonist's life that basketball does for Hank Baxter. Walden followed in 1972 with *Play Ball, McGill*, a softball story set in Ginger McGill's senior high school season. *Play Ball, McGill* came from Westminster Press, a leading publisher of young adult books and the outfit that printed most of Dick Friendlich's outstanding sports novels for boys in the 1949–1968 period.

Sink the Basket

While sports novels for boys exploded with well over 300 books in the three decades following World War II, there were only a handful of sports novels marketed for girls during that period. On the other hand, there were many more mystery and adventure stories for girls, notwithstanding the Hardy Boys, which many girls also not so secretly enjoyed.

Sink the Basket, an inspiring 1953 novel by Sally Knapp, a well-known author of books, short stories and articles for youngsters, is one of the few sports stories with female protagonists. Even more unusual for the period, the story includes African American and Chinese athletes, perhaps the first such non-stereotypical portrayals in a sports novel for girls. Libraries snapped up *Sink the Basket* but few parents could afford the $2.50 price tag (Nancy Drew books were $1 at the time). The book also benefits from handsome illustrations by Dorothy Bayley Morse, although her impressionistic dust jacket seems like something out of the 1930s.

Sink the Basket was published by Crowell and selected by the Junior Literary Guild. In its descriptions of basketball, the story is far more sophisticated than the pre–1920 Girls of Central High and Jane Allen series, both of which featured characterization over game descriptions. The plot of *Sink the Basket* is also unusual, dealing with the mental frustrations of a high school basketball player who takes on the challenge of coaching middle-school girls.

As the story opens, Briardale's Kay Nelson wins the Westchester County championship with a shot at the buzzer, then goes into a funk when she realizes her basketball days may be over. Kay dreams of playing basketball at Smith, but basketball scholarships were not then an option for girls, and college would have been a financial burden for Kay and her kindly mother. As Knapp writes, Kay and her teammate and best friend, Debby, "both looked like what they were: girls who had had endless time and considerable money already spent on making them proper members of society." The story clearly has an East Coast social slant, but Kay is not snobbish. Far from it, in fact. Much like many lead characters in boys' series books, her father has died and she lives with her loving, concerned mother.

When Kay arrives home following her heroics, her mother asks her, "How was the game? Did you win the championship?" It's difficult to imagine that her mother, a homemaker, could not have found time to attend the game, but such was the importance, or lack of it, attached to girls' athletics in that era, other than in a few states such as Iowa; where girls' basketball sometimes outdrew the boys' tournaments.

Telling her mother she has decided college is not for her, Kay makes a statement very much in evidence in mid-century thought: "It's foolish for me to go to Smith or any place else right now. I'd be a square peg. There's nothing I want at college except maybe a chance to play basketball again and that hardly seems enough to justify spending so much time and money. After all, Dad left me enough in my trust fund to live on. I don't need a career. Careers are foolish unless you have a talent or need the income."

Sink the Basket by Sally Knapp, 1953 (jacket copyright Thomas Y. Crowell). Dorothy Bayley Morse penned the jacket and illustrations for this scarce early basketball story by a frequent contributor to girls' magazines.

Kay, though, becomes friendly with the slightly older Steve Brooks, who had been a basketball star at the same school. Working as a recreation center leader, he offers her the chance to coach an intriguing team of eager 12- and 13-year-olds, including Maria (Italian), Rose (Chinese), Helen (African American) and Red (apparently the self-assured tomboy of the group). There is also a big blonde girl named Erva, who plays the role of temperamental talent that Hester Grimes filled in *The Girls of Central High* nearly four decades earlier. Erva plays her way off the team and is replaced by the lesser talented but far more team-oriented Peggy along with an unselfish girl named Irene.

Kay's first impression of the girls is nice writing: "'Oh no!'" Kay cringed in mock horror. "'It can't be. It looks more like bargain day in a department store basement.'" That sets the stage for Kay's many joys and frustrations. Erva's wealthy all-business, stuffy uncle complicates the situation, offering the girls, called the Thayer team, a new facility if they can become good enough to beat Carlton, a first-rate rival. "A bargain's a bargain" he likes to say, but he is eventually so impressed with Kay's social work with Erva that he becomes more philanthropic without demands. There's yet another Merriwell finish, of course: Erva, having learned sportsmanship, passes the ball to the open Red instead of taking an awkward potential game-winning shot in the final seconds. Red is fouled while shooting at the buzzer and "sinks the basket" twice to win before a large crowd at Carlton, which had earlier beat Kay's team.

It's noteworthy that when the crucial foul is called, "a shout of jubilation starting from five [Thayer] throats was quickly muffled. The girls were learning to be good sports." How much the game has changed in little more than half a century! Now fans at either a boys' or girls' game would be going nuts, players would loudly exult and the opponent's fans would shout at the tops of their lungs, trying to rattle the free throw shooter. In this story, however, "A hush settled over the gym; it was so quiet that a throat-clearing by one of the spectators seemed to crackle through the silence." As though this wasn't enough sportsmanship, Carlton, the host team, served refreshments to all, and Erva's once cold uncle announces a plan to get their girls their new recreation center.

Kay accepts the opportunity to work with Steve at the new center, with both indicating the possibility of college plans. The only hint of romance comes in the final line: "She looked up into Steve's eyes, and Kay liked the future she saw stretching out before her — a future in which Steve would very definitely have a part."

The contrived last-second heroics notwithstanding — after all, such histrionics occurred in real life many times each season — this is a top-notch story of emotional growth for both a young woman and her middle-school players. Any girl would have benefited from reading it.

It's interesting to note, however, that at no place in the story do any of the girls complain about not playing both offense and defense, the ways the boys had been doing since the invention of the game six decades earlier. Six-girl teams and half-court zones were taken for granted and accepted as the right way to play. By the end of the 20th century, however, the six-girl game had been abandoned everywhere, beginning in the 1970s in many states. Middle school girls routinely play basketball, and the best of them play dozens of games a year in AAU competition on select travel teams. Adults can still appreciate *Sink the Basket* for its ethical and inspirational qualities, but a current 12-year-old girl who loves basketball would see the book as an antiquarian example of the game in its Paleolithic age.

A milestone for girls in sports

Only two years before *Sink the Basket* advanced the literary cause of girls' athletics, a story in a 1951 anthology for readers 7 to 12 years old, *Young Readers' Stories of the Diamond* by Charles Coombs, included two tales involving girls in baseball.

The Young Readers series of more than two dozen anthologies included several devoted to athletics (see chapter thirteen), though the sports stories clearly were aimed primarily at boys. That's what makes *You Just Never Know* so interesting. Andy McCue, the editor of the groundbreaking *Baseball by the Books* (1991), was perhaps the first to point out the importance of this story. "The young woman in the background [of a drawing by Charles

Geer] is Sally Morgan. Sally is, I believe, the first girl or woman to be accorded a major on-the-field role in baseball fiction as she is named the coach of a town team [for Little League age boys] after proving her knowledge of the game."

There's a catch (pardon the pun). After giving the boys tips they use to win a big game, Sally tells them, "You can't live around baseball players all your life, without picking up a few pointers, whether you want to or not. And it doesn't matter whether you're a girl or a boy." Sally's brother, Bobo Morgan, pitches for the Philadelphia Phillies. Sally, however, declines the boys' offer to become a regular coach at "the tempting salary of one ice cream soda a week. "Oh, I'm not good enough to be a coach," she blushed modestly. "You see, baseball is just sort of a hobby with me."

In the same anthology, a story entitled "Diamond Double Trouble" features a right fielder named Ruth Cooper, who gets the chance to play for a boys' team due to a lack of players. Ruth's brother Ned is having trouble batting and Ruth can't seem to catch the ball in the outfield, discouraging both players. The twist is that Ned goes to work pitching hay and Ruth works with countless eggs, and they develop the strength and skill both need to succeed. Ned hits a home run and Ruth makes a game-winning catch. Both realize that important work on the farm has paid dividends, after all. "They looked at each other, but neither said a word. They were much too happy to go delving into deep problems like that."

Both of these stories probably startled the young boys who read them, for to have girls play or participate as a coach in a game would have been rare, indeed, except in pickup contests around the neighborhood. Even at that, how many "women of a certain age" remember being picked last by a grudging boy who had to take a girl to field a full team?

The first girl takes her cuts on a dust jacket

One of the joys of collecting obscure sports fiction is making discoveries like *The Dooleys Play Ball*, a seldom-seen 1949 juvenile novel by Marion Renick, who wrote numerous stories for grade-school children. At $2.25, this was an expensive juvenile book in 1949, and probably was purchased almost entirely by libraries. After examining hundreds of books about baseball and softball, along with other sports, this is the first book I can find where a girl is shown on the dust jacket playing in a team sport with boys. In this case, the girl is Linda Dooley, the cousin of a family of boys (and men) who are all avid softball players. Linda, who is about 10 years old, is shown stepping up to bat with a boy catching.

This charming story — a genuine piece of Americana — features many pages of tips about how to play and understand softball, including a 13-page section at the end of the book. It's recommended for readers 9 to 11 years old, and would make a perfect introduction to softball players of that age. There's also a charming side plot about Linda's pet, a duck named Mortimer, plus lots of other details that would appeal to girls of Linda's age.

Linda doesn't get to actually play in games until the final 10 pages of the story, and there is a description of only the championship game. But it turns out she's better at shortstop than any of the boys, and wins the big game when she pulls off a game-clinching double play. There's a cute angle: She didn't know a double play was allowed! She is chosen Most Outstanding Player of the tournament.

This is not as unlikely as it might seem, because many modern Little League parents have seen girls perform in an outstanding fashion since girls were first officially allowed in 1974. Top-notch prepubescent female athletes aren't that much different in ability than boys (and indeed, girls usually reach puberty earlier). Sometimes, like Linda, females can be the best player on a team of 10- or 12-year-olds. By the time athletes reach the high school varsity level, however, it's a rare girl who can keep up with the best boys.

Linda, by the way, is dismayed in the story to learn that girls have not been allowed to play American Legion baseball on any level, ever since an Indiana girl, Margaret Gisolo, played on a Junior Legion team in 1928, when she was not quite 14 years old. (Margaret's story is well told in Barbara Gregorich in *Women at Play* (1993), a history of females in baseball.)

An even earlier softball milestone

In the 11 sports anthologies in the Teen-Library from Lantern Press/Grosset & Dunlap in 1947–1950 (see chapter thirteen), only one of the 117 stories concerning team sports involves female athletes. This story, *Double Play* by Thelma Knoles, was part of the first anthology in the

The Dooleys Play Ball by Marion Renick, 1949 (jacket copyright Scribners). This jacket by Dwight Logan seems to be the first ever to portray a girl batting on the cover of a novel. It's a cute story for elementary school readers.

series, *Teen-Age Sports Stories* (1947) edited by Frank Owen. This story, which originally appeared in a 1945 issue of *American Girl* magazine, is one of the earliest accounts of girls' softball to appear in a hardback book.

Double Play is nicely written and features a twist ending, when the unselfish substitute, 15-year-old sophomore Caro Kennedy, receives a coveted opportunity to serve as a copy girl at the *Spriggsville Sun*. It turns out the editor, Miss Gail Clarke, is a baseball fun and is impressed by Caro's team-oriented approach, even though Caro had to fight temptation to try to be a more overt heroine in a big game. Before Miss Clarke makes the big announcement, Caro herself reacts this way when the team's star congratulates her: "Nuts! I just followed your orders."

"Do you know," Miss Clarke tells Caro, "I like to think of the newspaper staff as a team. A team working together for one purpose. To gather and publish the news of the world. Anyone new, coming into such work must be the kind who will fit in, who will obey orders, and be willing to sacrifice personal glory if necessary. Many a story has been ruined, Carolyn, by some reporter selfishly trying to scoop everyone else. Watching you play ball this afternoon I could see you had the qualities of cooperation that are needed in the newspaper business—even a copy girl."

It's interesting to note (in true adult fashion of the time) nobody calls Caro by her real name, Carolyn, except for the only adult featured in the tale. This story appeared more than a decade before a girl named Caroline Kennedy would achieve worldwide fame as the daughter of a president.

A rare pulp female sports cover

I have not seen the covers of all 1,530 sports pulp magazines, published from 1923 to 1957, but I have seen well over 900, including the nearly 800 that I own. The only cover I've seen with female sports competition portrayed was a little masterpiece by Modest Stein, a

noted illustrator, on the first March 1939 number of the twice-a-month *Sport Story* magazine from Street & Smith.

The cover, illustrating *Six Girls & A Basket* by Handley Cross, shows a jump ball between two leggy, full-breasted women, apparently of college age, wearing shorts, sneakers and socks, plus shirts neatly tucked into their pants. Nowhere on their "uniforms" is there any team identification! "If you think girls' basketball is a sissy game, go to see one," says the blurb on the title page, identifying the piece as "feature article" instead of fiction. "You have to see it to believe the brand of fast, highly-skilled hard-fighting basketball that is being played by the up-to-date women's teams of today," reads the blurb before the illustration that begins the article. The article begins with a description of a 1937 AAU national tournament semifinal round game between the Wichita Thurstons and the Little Rock Flyers. Lucile Thurman scores the winning basket for Little Rock in sudden-death overtime (the rule following first, scoreless overtime)—and then faints!

In talking about the history

Five Against the Odds by C.H. Frick (pseudonym for Constance H. Irwin), 1955 (jacket copyright Harcourt, Brace). This well-told story of Indiana high school basketball is one of the few — and one of the best — written for the boys' book market by a female author.

of the women's game, the author says, "The girls' rules made the game easier for the girls, but they made it hard for the spectators. I don't think that any male who, twenty-five years or so ago, was lured to one of those pitty-pat contests between teams composed of young women weighed down by heavy flannel bloomers, middy blouses and thick stockings ever went back to see another. I know I didn't." He adds that in AAU competition, "Bright-colored and much-abbreviated silk basketball suits have replaced the cumbersome bloomers and flapping middy blouses. A girl who wore stockings on the court would be suspected of trying to attract attention, and the game itself has been pepped up and streamlined as much as have the playing costumes.... Six girls and a basket — or rather, twelve girls and two baskets— provide a game that is chock-full of interest and thrills." There follows an explanation of AAU rules, including the ability of one player to cross the center line and join either offense or defense, along with a history of outstanding Canadian and AAU teams.

The article ends this way:

Sport Story, March 1, 1939 (copyright Street & Smith). One of the few pulp sports magazines with female athletes on the cover: Modest Stein's illustration for the fact-based article "Six Girls and a Basket" by Handley Cross.

"When I was first offered the job of coaching the Flyers," says [Little Rock] coach Bill Dunaway, "I didn't want it. I had played fourteen seasons of basketball, and had done some coaching, but I was only twenty-seven, and had never had anything to do with girls' teams; in fact, I'd seen few girls' games. I'd heard a lot of talk about feminine temperament and hair pulling in the dressing room. When I finally accepted the offer I felt sure that I was drifting into certain trouble. But the girls fooled me. They weren't any different to coach than any other basketball players. Of course, I have to take a lot of ribbing from my friends because I'm 'involved' with a lot of good-looking girls whose average age is twenty-two. But, so far as I'm concerned, they're just a bunch of basketball players— and darned good ones!"

Dunaway, though, wasn't about to compare women favorably with men. Earlier in the article, Cross writes this: "'The greatest girls' team that ever played,'" he [Dunaway] contends, with more frankness than gallantry, "'couldn't beat a fair-to-middlin' boys' team. Girls just aren't up to men's par in athletics, no matter how classy they may look while they are playing among themselves.'"

But Cross brings Phog Allen, the famed University of Kansas basketball coach and the last word on the subject in his day, to the rescue while talking of the famous Edmonton Grads, the greatest women's team of the era: "I have seen college teams composed of men who would have to hustle to take their measure. The Grads are the greatest team, male or female, that it has ever been my pleasure to see in action." Allen was referring to the relative merits of team play.

Everygirls Sports Stories

Grosset & Dunlap not only produced more series books for both girls and boys than any other publisher from the 1920s through the 1970s, but also more anthologies. Beginning in the late 1940s, the firm released well over 50 reprint anthologies, all for readers ranging from 7 to 18 years old, most of them in an arrangement with Lantern Press, the publisher of the original, more expensive volumes. These books drew on the talents of prolific short-story specialist Charles Coombs, who began his career with pulp magazines, along with dozens of authors published in magazines for youth such as *Calling All Girls*, *Boys' Life*, *American Girl*, *Scholastic*, and the like.

Beginning in the mid–1950s, Grosset tried a series called the Everygirls Library, in which the publisher invented a term, and an ungrammatical word at that, anticipating a media and branding trend that would accelerate three decades later. (One wonders how many budding members of the comma police, now elderly women, noticed the term should have been Every Girl's, referring in this case to individual readers.) There were Everygirls Romance Stories, Career Stories, Mystery Stories, Horse Stories, Adventure Stories and so on, meant primarily for girls from 10 to 14.

It's telling that in 1956, when *Everygirls Sports Stories* was released, edited by anthologist A.L. Furman, not a single team sport was portrayed on the Grosset dust jacket, even though there were four basketball stories and a softball tale among the 15 short stories selected. Instead, there were images of the sports generally "approved" for girls in pre–Title IX days—bowling, skating, swimming and diving, skiing and sailing. The other 10 stories covered all of these individual sports plus tennis. In those days, few women pursued track and field.

Since the 1972 Title IX federal funding law began creating ever-growing interscholastic and intercollegiate athletic opportunities for females, four team sports are played throughout most of the United States—basketball, soccer, volleyball and softball. In some areas, girls also can play lacrosse, rugby, field hockey and ice hockey, on either high school or club teams, along with the occasional girl who participates on boys' teams in football (most often as a place kicker) and baseball.

Basketball, though, was the first team sport in which girls widely participated, if only mostly on intramural and Girls Athletic Association intraschool teams in most of the country. Several states, most famously Iowa, played interscholastic high school hoops long before Title IX. So it's no surprise to see four basketball stories in *Everygirls Sports Stories*, although one of them, "Score!" by Adrien Stoutenberg, from *Calling All Girls*, involved girls only as spectators. It's telling that all four stories are focused on high school basketball; not only was intercollegiate play uncommon at this point, but readers 10 to 14 identified more with high school girls.

"Score!" tells the tale of a hero-worshiping clarinet-playing band member named Marlis (no last name) and how she roots for Don Bailey to set a scoring record for the Wood

City Foresters while her lanky friend Ted Ritter warms the bench despite his constant practicing and attempts to mold his style after Don. Marlis' band hat drifts onto the court and into Don's eyes, causing her mortification and making her worry that he won't get the points he needs to break a five-year-old record. Don, though, is forced to the bench by an injury. Ted, finally deciding to take advantage of his height instead of "a turning, twisting run in Don's style," takes his place and scores the winning basket. It turns out that Ted earlier retrieved Marlis' hat and, when she went back to the gym to claim it, he took the opportunity to approach her. "Imagine! Me, a hero. At this rate I'm even apt to get my letter." Don then tells Ted to grab his date for the postgame celebration — and Ted grabs Marlis, much to her delight. It's a cute bit of fluffy Americana, with no indication that Marlis or her friends could ever hear basketball cheers themselves.

In "Swede," by Vadonna Jean Hughes, a self-centered but talented scoring standout, Christine Jorleson, learns the meaning of teamwork at Dunford High, as taught by a male coach and Christine's mother, herself a former player who loves the game. "I've talked to you so much about basketball," her mother says, "You have the same love for it I had. That love is good, Chris, but for it to help you, you must feel it, dear. It's your love of the game for yourself [that is the problem], not as a team." A benching then stuns Christine. Near story's end, Hughes writes, "'It was always me,' Christine told herself with a sickening sense of self-realization. 'I wanted to star. I hogged the ball! I didn't play — together!'" Sent into a game in the fourth quarter, she helps the team rally with team-oriented play — then uses her superior ability to drive for the winning basket when the opportunity develops. "The glimpse of her mother's face, as Christine passed to the locker room, was wonderful," Hughes writes at the end of a realistic, inspirational story.

"Basket Bantam" by Eleanor Evans is likewise inspirational, showing how Brookside benchwarmer Peggy Sellers, all 5-feet, 1-inch of her, develops self-confidence. Her teammates, seeing the talent she has developed in practice, ask their coach, Miss Proctor, to send her into a game where they need a fast, not tall, player, because they are playing five-girl basketball instead of the regulation six-girl game because of a small gym. Peggy scores the winning basket but says, "I was just playing way over my head today. Really, I can't imagine what happened." Miss Proctor wisely replies, "You can't? Why, Peggy, it was really quite simple. I, and I suppose some of the girls, have been hoping for it all season. Peggy, they wanted you all the time. But, well, you were so worried about your size that your game just didn't get a chance to come forward.... Peggy, today you found your confidence. Of course, the girls might have helped when they asked that you play but, after all, real self-confidence is one of those things that comes only from within." And off Peggy goes, having also scored a long-sought invitation from her teammates for one of those Sweet Shop malts. Stories like this, stripped of melodrama and silliness, showed girls how boys weren't the only ones who could benefit from unselfish teamwork, and self-confidence gained through hard practice.

On the other hand, *Nets Are for Fish* by Jay Worthington harkens back to many of the somewhat unrealistic pulp epics. Even though Hamilton High needs to beat an opponent it earlier defeated easily, or Hamilton's season would end, Coach Joe Kezell insists that the girls feed the ball to Betta Carr so she can score the 24 points she needs to break the district's season record. "I want all of you to feed Betta today," the coach says. "I don't like to ask a team to play that type of game, but I know you'll agree that this is an exceptional case. You can help Betta put Hamilton High on the map. That's why I'm asking you to feed her the ball until she's scored those 24 points." It's difficult to imagine many coaches cooking up such a plan, especially in a vital game and especially without telling the team until the day of the game. Even in this improbable setting, however, Betta's character shines through when she asks to play defense in the final quarter, after she has scored 22 points, because that's where she can help the team most. In this case, the six-girl game — in which defenders don't score and must pass the ball over the center line — provides the basis for a heroic finish. "I'd want to kick myself, if I weren't so proud of having you on my team, Bet," the coach tells her. "It was a shame about that record, Bet," a teammate tells her. "I wish you could have netted those last two points, instead of me." To which Betta ends the story with this line: "Nets are for fish."

Eleanor Evans also has a high school softball story, *Diamond Dilemma*, in which Helen, a pitcher with a "smokeball" learns the meaning of teamwork and friendship, and asks former pitcher Jill to replace her in a big game. "It wasn't the ball game so much, was it?" Jill asks at the finish. "No," Helen cried, "It wasn't the ball game. O Jill, let's be...." "Friends?" Jill asks. "Friends!" Helen replies. "It's a deal," Jill smiles happily. Adds Evans, "And, looking every bit as happy as a couple of bees in a clover patch, they turned and raced side by side to the locker room."

It's interesting to note that in *Calling All Girls*, a 1959 Grosset anthology with reprints of 24 stories from the 1955 to 1959 issues of the magazine, the only sports story involves golf. In *Stories to Live By*, a 1960 anthology from Platt & Monk consisting of 30 inspirational stories from *American Girl*, the national Girl Scouts magazine, there is only one story involving sports. "Champions Walk Alone" by J. Myron Christy tells the tale of Gina Mack, a high school student whose photograph shows an illegal 12-man formation during the winning play in a state championship football game. The photograph and negative disappear, ultimately revealed as having been snatched by the team's star, who then fesses up because he has learned to admire Gina for her ethics. State officials declare the team will not have to forfeit, since the winning kick was not affected by the formation, and in any event rules dictate such calls must be made on the field by the officials.

It's revealing that in *Stories to Live By*, edited by Marjorie Vetter, all manner of concerns commonly held by adolescent girls are covered by the 30 stories, but none involve athletics. The stories are well-written, definitely stories any parent would approve of, yet in this anthology sports are just not an issue for girls. In the modern era, when at least one in every three or four girls participates in athletics in most high schools — and even more girls participate in sports when they are younger — how the world has changed!

Calling All Girls — but not to team sports

During the "Golden Age of Comics" in the 1940s, the publisher of *Parents* magazine produced several successful comic book titles, including *Calling All Girls*, the first comic book designed specifically for teen-age girls.

From issue #1 (September 1941) through #89 (September 1949), *Calling All Girls* was an entertaining mishmash of comic strips, illustrated text stories, rotogravure photography, wartime information and articles about everything of interest to teen-age girls, including fashion, school, cooking, dating, movies, books and dozens of other topics, including the occasional article or story about individual girls in sports — everything, that is, but team sports.

Calling All Girls was published in comic book size through #51 (July 1946), when it became a full-sized magazine similar to *Seventeen* and other such publications, loaded with dozens of advertisements directed at teenage girls. When *Parents* magazine dropped its entire comic book line in 1949, *Calling All Girls* briefly morphed into a magazine titled *Senior Prom*, then in the 1950s became a digest-size magazine with the original title. Issues can be difficult to find but my survey of all but eight of the first 51 issues was indeed telling.

The survey included every issue from #15 (February 1943) through #51, except #27 (March 1944) and #47 (March 1946). That coincided with the first three seasons of the historic All-American Girls' Baseball League (1943–1945), yet there was no coverage of the league in *Calling All Girls*. In fact, in the 43 issues surveyed, there was exactly one article or story about any team sport—a how to-play softball article in #49 (May 1946) entitled "Girls Get on the Softball" by Arthur D. Morse. He's identified as the editor of "Sports Stars," a fact-based comic book from *Parents* magazine. That title, which focused on sports for boys and men, lasted only four issues in 1946.

There were, however, no less than 18 articles, biographies or stories covering individual sports for teen girls, everything from tennis and roller skating to skiing, swimming and even pigeon racing. There was simply no encouragement, fact or fiction, for girls interested in any team sports. But then, in those pre–Title IX days, few high schools and colleges offered extensive interscholastic or intercollegiate team competition for females.

In the first issue of *Calling All Girls*, one of the feature articles was "Girls in Sports" by John R. Tunis, who in 1941 was three years into his two-decade career as one of America's finest sports novelists. (Tunis wrote two tennis books with a female protagonist, *American Girl* (1929) and *Champion's Choice*.) In this article, the noted writer covers tennis, golf, archery, fencing, swimming, skating, badminton and bobsledding, but no girls' team sports. Since the article appeared in the first issue, the publishers may have sought out Tunis, or perhaps used a manuscript he intended for the highly successful "True Comics," which first appeared with an issue dated April 1941. At any rate, Tunis can't be faulted for not including team sports, since there was virtually nothing on the market at the time about that topic.

Team sports and girls simply did not mix from the standpoint of the *Parents* magazine publishers. For example, on the cover of #33 (October 1944), the only sports-related cover in my survey, a well-bundled girl is shown with a signed football (!) with the pennants of numerous college football teams in the background. A story on roller skating in #8 (July 1942) is entitled "Dancing on Wheels." In #52 (August 1946), the first magazine-sized issue, the only item involving athletics is a two-page photo spread on movie stars in sports. *Calling All Girls* #60 (April 1947) features an advertisement for the first issue of *Varsity*, billed as "For Young Men of All Ages." *Varsity*, of course, features a large image of a baseball star on the cover.

When *Calling All Girls* became a magazine, the publisher replaced the comic book version with *Sweet Sixteen*, which ran from #1 (August-September 1946) through #13 (January 1948). A survey of all 13 issues shows one fiction story involving sports, "Net Result" by Jerry Tax, a tale of tennis, but nothing involving girls in team sports. In fact, in the humorous "Dirinda" comic strip in #11 (November 1947), our heroine acquires knowledge about football and baseball solely to impress boys at a dance! And when *Sweet Sixteen* carried an ad for the new *Varsity* magazine, it was directed to girls as "A wonderful new magazine for big brother."

Parents magazine also published a comic book for grade-school girls, "Polly Pigtails," which ran 43 issues from 1946 to 1949. "Polly Pigtails," too, covered sports only in the most tangential ways. A similar publication today would likely be loaded with articles and stories about soccer, gymnastics, basketball and the like. Perhaps an issue of one of the comic books from *Parents* magazine mentioned Babe Didrickson, the most renowned of all female athletes and an inspiration to millions of girls, but I haven't seen such a mention.

Indeed, only a tiny fraction of comic books carried any sports themes (see chapter six). The only such publication in the entire history of comics to run beyond 14 issues was Street & Smith's fact-based "True Sport Picture Stories," with a 50-issue run from 1940 to 1949 (the first four issues were entitled "Sport Comics"). Like *Parents* magazine, Street & Smith dropped all its comic books in 1949 (along with all of its pulp magazines) in order to focus on its more profitable magazine ventures.

Like other sports-based comic books, "True Sport Picture Stories" almost entirely ignored females; not a single one of the 50 covers featured a female athlete. Even during the explosion of noncorporate, independent comic books in the 1980s and 1990s, when a few series featured sports themes, absolutely nothing was directed to girls. The only sports fiction in comic books featuring girls were occasional stories in the romance comics, which were almost entirely published from 1947 to 1977. Even then, the stories tended to focus on sensationalistic themes, such as the conflicts and rivalries involved in roller derby, or on tomboys who sought to play with the guys and had to be taught the error of their ways — by a man, of course.

Women who wrote fiction marketed to boys

Of the well over 1,200 baseball, football and basketball novels targeted for the young-adult "boys' book" market through the 1960s, fewer than two dozen were written by women. All the women wrote either with initials or obviously male pseudonyms. That is the extent of female participation, along with numerous juveniles about several sports by Marion Renick (some cowritten with her husband, James Renick) and five juvenile baseball novels by M.G. (Mary) Bonner from 1947 to 1959 dealing with grade-school sandlot players.

The obscure Penn Publishing Company produced a four-book series, The School Athletic Series, from 1908 to 1911 about the baseball, football and outdoor adventures of prep school boys as one of more than 60 sports-related series published through the 1920s and usually selling for 40 or 50 cents per volume. Beth Bradford Gilchrist wrote as John Prescott Earl for the four-book series (a fifth was advertised, but never published) and was, as far as I can determine from collectors' guidebooks, the only female author who wrote for boys. (A small number of girls read sports books, too, as indicated by the female fan letters in the weekly Frank Merriwell nickel magazines.)

One of the last of the old-style books, very much in the mode of Frank Merriwell and Baseball Joe, was *On the Forty Yard Line* written by Elsie Wright as by Jack Wright in 1932 and issued on cheap paper by the World Syndicate Publishing Company, complete with a primitively drawn dust jacket. Wright followed with *Champions on Ice* (1940), a hockey story, and both were reprinted in the six-book Falcon Sports Series from World in the late 1940s. Wright's football story was good of its kind in 1932, but it surely was among the most dated of all sports tales available in 1948, considering how drastically John R. Tunis and Jackson Scholz had already changed the tone of young-adult sports fiction.

Jim Davis, one of three buddies who are the college-life heroes of *On the Forty Yard*

Line, is disgraced, kidnapped by racketeers, rescued and ultimately vindicated. In order to play in the final quarter of the big game, he parachutes into the stadium! (this in an era when most people had never been in an airplane, much less used a parachute). He throws a game-winning touchdown pass—from the forty yard line, of course—to buddy Bob Clarke. At the end, the two football stars and a third buddy, student journalist Chub Garver, win coveted invitations to a secret society.

Beatrice Joy Chute, the author of hundreds of young-adult and juvenile short stories as B.J. Chute (see chapter thirteen), wrote one sports novel, the literate football story *Blocking Back*. The original edition was published by MacMillan in 1938 and the author revised the novel in 1966 for Dutton. While exploring a used-book store in Illinois, I found a copy inscribed "for my dear Chute cousins, with the author's love." This additional note from the author was paper-clipped to this 1966 edition: "This is a re-issue by Dutton's of my first book which was originally published by MacMillan. I have done some re-writing and brought all the football up to date, and I thought the boys might enjoy it. Love to you all, Joy." A treasure!

The plot of *Blocking Back* involves the struggles of standout Washburn Prep running back Mike Blair and his roommate, student journalist and bon vivant Ducky Wilson, to accept the arrogant but highly talented transfer student Jerry Le Van. With an overflow of students at Washburn, the new guy is crowded into their dorm room and also sets out to take over Mike's starring role on the football team. What makes this book so unusual is the sparkling, witty dialog, some of the finest in any young-adult sports novel of the era. Chute's sense of humor is revealed by the page on which she describes coach "Irish" McBride as "an expert golfer and skater, taught a class in geology, collected stamps and was an enthusiastic amateur ornithologist. The result of this last was that the school soon learned that only a football player had right of way over a crested flycatcher." How many other football coaches have ever been described as bird-watchers?

In the 1966 volume, Chute still has the coach directing a single-wing offense—which was popular in 1938—at a time when only a handful of schools in America still ran that offense. (However, it was done with great effectiveness in a few cases. Coach Joe Marvin of Sequoia High School in Redwood City, California, won 33 consecutive games from 1958 to 1962 with the single wing, and Al Smith coached an undefeated and top-ranked team in 1967 at the same school with that offense, in an era before California installed sectional playoffs.) Otherwise, the novel is a sterling example of what can be done with a realistic plot, marvelous dialog and amusing characterization.

Chute either willingly enters or falls into the trap not a few of the old pulp writers succumbed to when she has a sports reporter tell the coach after both boys perform heroically, "How about 'Touchdown Twins Tally Four Times' for a headline?" But it's all in fun, for the reporter wonders why it couldn't be even more poetic with an alliterative word to replace "four." Reporters, of course, did not in 1966, and still do not, write their own headlines except on the smallest papers, even though even today it seems as though the vast majority of the population doesn't realize the copy desk tackles that task.

In the end, of course, the by-now humbled, and humbler, Jerry realizes he must lateral the football to Mike, and then Jerry makes the key block, so Washburn can score the winning touchdown on the last play of the big game. "Of all the nutty plays I ever saw," their coach tells them, "that last was the nuttiest. You fellows ought to go in for adagio dancing or something. Bright idea, Mike. By the way, that was a beautiful block of yours, Jerry."

The best of the women's fiction

Indiana native Constance H. Irwin, writing as C.H. Frick, turned out two of the best of all young-adult sports novels, *Tourney Team* (1954) and *Five Against the Odds* (1955), both from Harcourt, Brace. It's too bad these two tales of Hoosier March Madness, high school style, have faded into obscurity, for they are brilliantly written and thoroughly original, especially considering how well John R. Tunis took on the same subject in *Yea! Wildcats!* in 1944 (see chapter ten). Irwin also turned out *Patch* in 1957 and *The Comeback Guy* in 1961.

Tourney Team is centered on the social, emotional and athletic struggles of Rocky Ryan, an outstanding sophomore basketball player who is booted off the Hillcrest High basketball team shortly before tournament time. Rocky deliberately fouls an opponent in a vicious way, causing his coach to release him even though he is important to the team's tournament chances. Rocky, having fallen in with some shady friends, sees one of his buddies try to frame one of the basketball players but the coach doesn't fall for the tricks. However, he thinks Rocky is responsible and won't listen to his pleas to rejoin the team. As Rocky gradually begins to realize he has been his own worst enemy, he becomes, of all things, a student sportswriter and chronicles the team's successes in the tournament sectionals, regionals, semifinals and finals.

Although the writer weaves considerable lore about the legendary Indiana state tournament into both *Tourney Team* and *Five Against the Odds*, she leaves it to the reader to comprehend the event's unusual one-loss-and-out structure. The tournament, founded in 1911, allowed every one of the more than 750 Indiana high school teams to enter one of 64 sectionals, from which 16 four-team regionals emerged. The word "semifinals" means the Sweet 16 regional champions, which are whittled to eight and then four on the same day. The word "finals" indicates the Final Four, the winners of which must play a second game on the same Saturday! Throughout most of America, high school athletic associations have long tried their best to avoid having teams playing twice on the same day. But then, most states do not allow all the teams to participate in the first round of postseason play; they must finish high enough in their league standings to qualify.

There's an intriguing subtext of social responsibility in *Tourney Team*. When Rocky is called for his dirty play as the story opens, he tells the official, "Listen, you! That jig cut in front of me." Near the end of the story, after the coach has taken Rocky back on the team for the Final Four when the coach realizes how much Rocky has grown, Rocky responds to an insult about "jigs" with, "Anybody who calls those guys jigs, I'll sock 'em!"

Rocky plays as a substitute in both Final Four games, but his Hillcrest team loses the championship game to Muncie Central 60–58 in the final seconds. Yet the senior captain — the boy the coach thought Rocky tried to frame — says he would be honored to have Rocky wear his number the next two years. It's an appropriate finish to a compelling, realistic story.

In some ways, *Five Against the Odds* is even more compelling. It's the story of twin brothers Jim and Tom Moore, both basketball stars along with younger brother Denny, being reared by their grandparents in Indiana. Their grandfather played in the first Indiana state tournament in 1911 for tiny Catonga High; he lost a leg in World War I six years later. In 1955, the very year Dr. Jonas Salk first distributed the polio vaccine, Tom Moore contracts polio after starring as a sophomore as Catonga drove to the state title game before losing. Tom is forced to undergo an agonizing period of rehabilitation but soon realizes he will not play the following season, if ever again. But his coach, realizing how much Tom can still help the team during the tournament, asks him to scout opponents, to help on the bench, to help both his younger brother mature and his twin to grow as people and players. Tiny Catonga wins the state championship as Jim scores the game-winner m the final seconds. Tim earlier solves the mystery of an arson, helping one of Catonga's key players to achieve the mental peace he needs when his father is absolved of blame. It's all a bit pulpish, but seems real enough, in large part because Irwin conveys such vivid and genuine emotions. For example, the author describes Tim's trip home from the hospital this way: "Of course, he [Tim] wanted to get out and stretch ... stupid question. But when your rear is crushed to pulp, when your back and legs are numb from aching, and your feet are chunks of lead, you don't leap out of the car and turn handsprings. You sit. You sit and curse at each bump in the road as it tears through your muscles, and there's no satisfaction in it, this silent blasphemy. You sit and feel sorry for yourself. And then for diversion, you count the telephone poles as they waver past, and look for familiar landmarks through a haze of aching weariness, sweat, and frustration."

Tim's grandfather doesn't entirely understand polio—"I think it's all in the mind. Make up your mind to play, and you'll play!" he tells Tim — but he does realize that Tim's self-pity is self-defeating. Grandfather is a man of few words, but Irwin has him speak magnificently:

> I can talk where the others can't, and they've shushed me long enough. I left my leg in France in 'seventeen, and sure I minded. But I learned to do without it. I won't say I never miss it, and it itches me still and there's no place to scratch. But after you've lived long enough you'll find out that nobody has what he wants. You just get along with whatever you've got, and you teach yourself to like it.... Maybe our handicaps show more, but everyone's got 'em. Every last man alive has something he isn't proud of, something he finds humiliating. What if the whole world stayed in their room and brooded about it.... When you're ranklin' inside, you rankle the people around you. You do it with satisfaction. And when you've made them rankle inside like you do, they're no better off than you and that makes everything equal. But not one smidgen better! ... While you're sitting there cogitating, remember one thing I learned the hard way. Thinking about yourself all the time — so easy for people like us — just rubs a festering sore on your disposition. Only one way you can heal it. Change the subject!

Has any better essay about self-pity ever been written in a young-adult sports novel? *Five Against the Odds* also reminds us how much more generous society was in the 1950s. There's reference to a $2,000 academic scholarship contest, the equal today of more than $15,000. How many $15,000 academic scholarships have you heard about recently for high school students?

Another woman who wrote sports stories, Helen D. Francis, was the wife of John Francis, then a coach at what is now Fort Hays State University in Kansas. Writing as H.D. Francis, she focused on the short-novel juvenile market and produced four books: *Double Reverse* (1958), *Football Flash* (1961), *Basketball Bones* (1962) and *Big Swat* (1963), a football story reprinted in 1967 as a Signet Key paperback for young adults.

Orpha B. Jackson, the wife of the prolific C. Paul Jackson (see chapter eleven), collaborated with her husband on several juvenile short novels. As O.B. Jackson, she is also credited with writing *Basketball Comes to North Island* (1963) and *Southpaw in the Mighty Mite League* (1965).

"Love Hits a Home Run" in an obscure 1955 comic book

One of the oddest of all sports stories appeared in an obscure 1955 comic book from the tiny publisher Premier. Here is how I described this bizarre story in my McFarland book *Love on the Racks: A History of American Romance Comics* (2008):

Though there was never a comic book entitled *True Love* until independent publisher Eclipse produced two issues of that title in 1986, reprinting stories from Standard Comics, one of the final small publishers of the mid–1950s period came close. Premier Comics, which was affiliated with the Story/Master/Merit folks, published 11 bi-monthly issues of *True Love Confessions* from #1 (May 1954) through #11 (Jan. 1956). Premier's circular logo was similar to the much better-known EC Comics. The covers after #1 were highly unusual in that they featured several panels centered around one large scene, all from the featured story. During the 1954–56 period, no other comics consistently featured romance cover styles of this type.

Kurt Schaffenberger, best known for his hugely popular work on Fawcett's "Captain Marvel Junior," National's "Lois Lane" and "Superboy" and ACG's science fiction and fantasy stories, was largely in between work with those companies when he contributed 6-page stories to "True Love Confessions" #4 and 5 and covers for #9, 10 and 11. These romance comics are so obscure that the massive "Schaffography" in his biography, *Hero Gets Girl!* (2003) by Mark Voger, listed only the covers for #9 (a wonderful baseball scene) and 10. The biography warned, however, that his body of work was so large that it couldn't be complete.

"True Love Confessions" was generic. One of the stories, though, was remarkable for its improbability. Whoever wrote the six-page "Love Hits a Home Run" in #9 (September 1955) penned one of the most whimsical and far-fetched baseball stories of all time, not to mention using one of the strangest metaphors.

As the story opens, Marion has brought her 17-year-old sister, Debbie, along with her girlfriends to ogle the dashing Duke Haley, the star of a team never named in a league not identified. His home run lands in Debbie's lap and, as Debbie narrates, "There was Duke, smiling at me!" Duke comes over — as though this would ever happen during a real game! — to tell her, "Good catch, little girl! Come around after the game and I'll autograph it for you!" Marion insists on getting the autograph, but Duke gives Debbie a pass for Saturday's game.

"And when game time came," Debbie narrates, "I secretly borrowed Sister's high heels and clothes and makeup!" Naturally, she catches another ball. Duke later invites her to dinner and autographs it after again talking with her right after the catch: "You should really catch for our team, Debbie!" A few dates and kisses later, Debbie's mother forbids her to date Duke because she shows him a newspaper showing he's engaged to someone else. But it turns out that it was "last year's newspaper" — a mean-spirited trick by Marion. Debbie races to the next game, catches yet a third ball hit by Duke, and accepts his invitation for another autograph. "It's the marriage license I'm going to autograph, Darling," he tells her, having been informed of the truth by Marion. But what are the odds of one girl catching home runs — by the same player, no less — in three consecutive games?

The Ruth Marini fantasy

By 1983, a handful of women known to grandparents and great-grandparents of that era as "bloomer girls" had been playing baseball since the late 19th and early 20th centuries, as described in depth a decade later by Barbara Gregorich in *Women at Play: The Story of Women in Baseball* (1993). This was one of several books on women's baseball history released in conjunction with the 50th anniversary of the founding of the All-American Girls Baseball League and the release of the landmark film *A League of Their Own*.

Yet by 1983 no women had yet played college or Organized Ball — indeed, there were still many formal rules against it — and, indeed, virtually none had "played" the game at that level in fiction, either. A handful of softball stories were published in the 1940s and 1950s, as detailed earlier in this chapter, but the only pre–1983 women's baseball books listed in Andy McCue's *Baseball by the Books* (1991) were the adult paperback *A Grand Slam* (1973) by Ray Puechner; the adult hardbound novel *The Sensuous Southpaw* (1976) by Paul Rothweiler; and the young-adult paperback romance *The Girl on First Base* (1981) by Ralph Michaels. These were all fantasies, considering the rules in force at the time. Indeed, it wasn't until 1974 that Little League officials relented under pressure and allowed girls to play. In 1987, Gregorich's *She's on First* and Michael Bowen's *Can't Miss* became the first significant attempts at exploring what it would be like for a woman in the major leagues.

All five of those books were one-and-done novels, however, by authors who did not normally write sports fiction. It took another author who had written no other baseball novels, Mel Cebulash, to come up with the first series about a woman in professional baseball. The short young-adult novels *Ruth Marini of the Dodgers* and *Ruth Marini, Dodger Ace* were released in 1983 and *Ruth Marini, World Series Star* in 1985. Given the nature of the titles, all with an $8.95 price tag, the Lerner Publications Company in Minneapolis obviously wanted readers to know this was a series. The vast majority of copies that come up for sale are ex library copies; the price in 1983 was stiff for parents and extremely difficult for the 10- to 14-year-olds these books seemed aimed at. The total page count for the three books was only 402 pages, making the trilogy about 120,000 words.

Although the story arc is sheer fantasy — and remained so in the quarter century following the end of the series — there is much stinging repartee, lively conversation and serious psychological reality. The dialog is by far the best thing about the books, ranging from Ruth's frequent bite-her-lip comments to her managers and teammates to the fans' sardonic and sometimes cruel comments. There is much to recommend this series regarding psychological reality, but where it fails badly is in providing an explanation of Ruth's unheard-of prowess. After all, if a female really could run up a 13–3 regular-season rookie record and pitch a complete-game victory in the World Series, she would have been found and probably even accepted by now. For that matter, if any female was capable of dominating a college league on any level, it's difficult to imagine win-hungry coaches and teammates rejecting her, at least from a remove of a quarter century since the extremely improbable exploits of Ruth Marini.

As the series opens, the reader may be ready and willing to accept Ruth's high school success in New Jersey, even though those feats, too, are still almost unheard of outside the level of the smallest schools. Far more realistic is the relationship between Ruth and her catcher, Mike Garcia, who starts out as her friend in high school and becomes her romantic interest through the rest of the series, which cover's Ruth first two years in professional baseball, including her rookie season at age 20 for the Dodgers. Considering that only a handful of rookies have played regularly at 20 in the major leagues, much less started a Major League All-Star Game, the fantasy elements are just that. Though there is much hemming and hawing between Ruth and Mike, not to mention a realistic insecurity about being apart so much of the time, what really would have been fascinating would have been for the author to explore the intense psychological pain any baseball-loving boy would feel at seeing his girlfriend succeed in professional baseball — when he wasn't even given a chance.

As the story starts, statements from Ruth's high school coach that she was the best pitcher in his 25 years on the job add credibility to her credentials for immediate success, but also tell the reader that this, indeed, is a fantasy. No such high school pitcher had ever existed to that point, or there would have been a plethora of books and articles about her, just as the first couple of women to play small-college baseball attracted national attention in the years following the Marini series. Cebulash goes out of his way to strongly hint that Ruth is entirely straight — she frequently kisses Mike and she loves a new dress now and then — but there is no indication whatsoever of how Ruth achieved the extraordinary physical development necessary for baseball success. It is, however, certain that drugs and artificial male hormones are not involved. Ruth is just presented as a female who can pitch better than just about any male her age in the world.

There are numerous comparisons to the historic way Jackie Robinson broke Major League Baseball's color line in 1947 with the Brooklyn Dodgers. To her credit, Ruth tends to ignore this apples and oranges stuff, other than to appreciate that Robinson probably took even more abuse from fans than she does. After all, considering the obvious talent of the top players in the old Negro Leagues, integration was inevitable, as was the arrival of outstanding Asian talent long after Robinson played, plus the explosion of Latin players in professional baseball beginning in the 1950s. Many readers of the Marini series may not have realized that Japan's Masanori Murakami, who pitched for the San Francisco Giants in 1964 and 1965 and was 5–1 in 54 games at ages 20 and 21, was the first native of Asia to play in the Major Leagues. Many of the Giants' fans then were men who fought in the Pacific Theater in World War II.

Early in the first book, Mike is guilty of tortured logic when he tells Ruth, "You were one of the best pitchers in New Jersey high schools for two years. If baseball were as popular as football in colleges, you probably would have had hundreds of scouts trying to enroll you in college." On the contrary, "draft-and-follow" practices were a common college/pro connection by 1980, and genuine baseball stars gained every bit as much exposure regarding their potential as did football stars— perhaps more so, since National Football League scouts did not attend high school games the way professional baseball scouts had been flocking to them for many years. NFL scouts needed to see college games, since only a tiny fraction of high school boys had developed the physical maturity needed to jump to pro football, in contrast to the many players who signed minor league contracts right out of high school.

On the other hand, there are insightful delights, such as this headline: "DODGERS SIGN A BABE—NAMED RUTH." One can just imagine that gem on a New York tabloid! Ruth makes a witty retort to an opponent who gives her a bad time while calling her "girlie": "Girlie's going to strike you out, hotshot." And she did just that. In contrast, the grammar is often sloppy, with the incorrect "Dodger's" and the correct "Dodgers'" used pretty much interchangeably. Ruth finally gets a chance to pitch in spring training halfway through her first book; all three books are written in a low-key, methodical style. By the end of the initial volume, Ruth has made a successful jump to Triple-A Albuquerque and is 6–1 and leading the Pacific Coast League in strikeouts.

Ruth Marini, Dodger Ace picks up the tale when Ruth meets Sal Surino on an airplane and talks openly about teammates who dislike the idea of a woman in baseball. Surino turns out to be a reporter and he writes about the conversation, but does not reappear until the third book, when he turns out to be a decent sort who has learned to respect both Ruth's competitive approach along with her ability. This episode, however, is disturbing, as teenage readers get the impression that media members are thoroughly unethical (Ruth plays peacemaker, aided by her no-nonsense manager). Most newspapers would fire or censure a reporter who did not identify himself as such with regard to the use of quotes from an athlete, especially someone as high-profile as Ruth. (Even worse, the *Los Angeles Times* has this thoroughly unprofessional headline in the third book: "Our Guys Beat the Yankees.") Not long after the Surino story breaks, a fan tells Ruth early in spring training, "Hey, girl, don't get any lipstick on the ball!"

Ruth makes the Dodger roster, then wins the season opener in her first regular-season game. She wins 11 of her first 13 decisions, leading the National League in victories at the All-Star Game break. As fantastic as her feats are, some are portrayed in a nifty way, such as when she strikes out Phillies star Pete Thorn (!) to end a game.

When Ruth is selected to the National League All-Stars, she is chosen to start the game. There is no end to unlikely circumstances in this series. But in the first inning, as she faces the American League's leading hitter, his bat snaps and whirls toward her, breaking her leg. Having had an encounter with her long-absent father, who abandoned the family when Ruth was a baby, she receives a card from him. There is no way the reader can abandon the series now.

In the third volume, Ruth returns successfully late in the season. She even hits a wind-blown home run, the first of her life, after coming in with a .198 batting average (actually pretty good for a pitcher). She starts the seventh game of the World Series and beats the Yankees 2–1 with a complete game on the last page of the trilogy. The last lines are oddly flat, but in tune with the style of the series: "Laughing and crying at the same time, Ruth tried to spot Mike in the crowd, but there was too much commotion. She knew she'd be seeing him later. The season, Ruth's first, was over." Mike may have seen Ruth later, but the reader never does.

The difficulty of accurate information about women in baseball

While reading an intriguing and informative essay by Leslie Heaphy in *Baseball and Philosophy* (2004) about women in baseball and softball, I was reminded again how difficult it can be to make sure information is 100 percent accurate about obscure subjects. While including a three-paragraph section on "The Courageous Ila Borders," Heaphy got the dates mixed up with regard to Borders' college and pro career. The reason I realized this so quickly was that my son Ray played against Borders in 1997 in the Southern California Intercollegiate Athletic Conference. Borders spent three seasons at NAIA Southern California College, then transferred to Whittier College and played her senior season there in 1997, more than a decade after the final Ruth Marini book appeared. She went 4–5 with a 5.22 earned-run average in 81 innings as a regular starter, as indicated in the outstanding book *Slouching Toward Fargo* (1999) by Neal Karlen. He quoted several of Borders' diary entries and Karlen thus produced far and away the best material ever written about a female playing baseball in a men's pro league. Borders, who looked very much like a competitive pitcher on the mound, showed a sometimes effective array of off-speed pitches to go with a fastball just quick enough to be useful when batters were sometimes befuddled by what might be coming next. That enabled her to pitch primarily as a middle reliever for three teams in the independent Northern League over three seasons, and she became the first woman to gain a victory in a minor league game.

Players often batted in fear against the 5-foot-10, 150-pound Borders, frightened that this clever, athletic woman would embarrass them with the occasional strikeouts she would achieve. Quite often, players would merely try to meet the ball instead of taking a chance on a strikeout. But, of course, that was their problem, not hers, and she was savvy and highly competitive enough to take advantage of it. However, the essay in *Baseball and Philosophy* placed her with her first pro team, the St. Paul Saints, in 1996 instead of the correct 1997, when she was 22 years old. Very few 22-year-olds, especially pitchers, get the chance to sign with any pro team out of a small college. She played only briefly for St. Paul — seven games, six innings— until quickly being traded to the Duluth Dukes, for whom she gained her historic victory in 1998.

While Ila Borders did not fulfill her dream of pitching in the major leagues, much less her ambition of pitching outside the independent Class A Northern League, she doubtless inspired lots of debate about whether any woman could ever pitch well enough to reach Double-A, Triple-A or even the major leagues. She certainly was courageous.

THIRTEEN

Sports Short Stories
for Young and Old

The 1920–1960 period was the Golden Age of short sports fiction in a wide variety of magazines for both younger and older readers along with those in-between. Sadly, most of those stories have been effectively lost, with availability limited almost entirely to a handful of collectors and to libraries.

Not even counting the pre–1920 dime novels of the Merriwell era (see chapter one), it's likely that well over 15,000 sports short stories and novelettes appeared over this four-decade period in American publications. There were sports stories in magazines before 1920 and after 1960, of course. For the most part, however, the dime novels (actually mostly novelettes in length) dominated the pre–1920 period and novels made up the vast majority of post–1960 sports stories, since almost all of the most reliable pulp and slick markets had disappeared.

In addition to the estimated 12,000-plus stories that appeared in the 1,530 or so sports pulps, plus sports stories in the general-interest pulps such as *Argosy* and *Bluebook* (see chapter five), several thousand stories of athletics appeared in periodicals as diverse as the *Saturday Evening Post*, *Collier's* and *Liberty* to *American Boy*, *Boys' Life*, *Open Road for Boys*, *Calling All Girls*, *Senior Scholastic*, and *American Girl*, plus the post-pulp "slick" versions of *Argosy* and other men's magazines, along with comic books. For a sports fiction collector, it's always a joy to look through such ostensibly non-sports magazines in search of sports-themed stories.

When television became dominant in the 1950s and supreme in the 1960s, the short story market largely disappeared other than for literary fiction. Sports novels for all ages are still being published to this day, of course, although nowhere near as frequently as they were produced in the three decades following World War II, but there are few outlets for short stories involving sports.

Sadly, fewer than 500 short stories and novelettes from the 1920–1960 era involving sports have been preserved in anthologies and collections of single authors. Many of these appeared in the second half of that period. Fewer than 100 sports-themed anthologies and collections appeared before 1970, with much of that during a brief boom in the postwar years. Most of these books were aimed toward the school library and gift markets—and stories from the pulp magazines were seldom included. Many stories were culled from early collections, such as those by Charles Van Loan and Ring Lardner, along with stories advertised to parents as "wholesome" and "clean-cut" because they came from magazines aimed at teenagers. There also developed a trend, beginning in the 1950s, to include excerpts from "literary" sports novels in anthologies, such as "The Southpaw" by Mark Harris, taking away space that might otherwise have been devoted to little-known but still-worthy works. This trend continues today.

Reprints of fantastic pulp heroes, such as the novels of The Shadow, The Spider and Doc Savage, along with westerns by Max Brand and a multitude of other types of novels, have been produced in great numbers (and continue to be) in mass-market paperback, trade paperback and hardback formats, both from corporate and private publishers. Many other anthologies of short stories, including hundreds featuring the science fiction and fantasy genres, have continued to appear since the 1940s in the same three formats. All told, well over 3,000 such pulp-reprint volumes have been printed, preserving thousands of the best pulp mystery, science fiction, fantasy, western and horror stories.

Pulp sports and romance ignored by anthologists

Two genres, however, have been almost totally ignored by both corporate and private reprint houses: the romance and sports pulps. It's generally thought that both fan and commercial markets would be far too small. It's no coincidence that far fewer collectors seek romance and sports pulps, both set in "real-world" scenarios, than the fantastic adventures featured in the exotic genres, including the cowboys, spacemen, superheroes and detectives. The likes of *The Black Lizard Big Book of the Pulps*, a magnificent 2007 compendium of 1,150 pages preserving mystery and detective stories, are highly unlikely ever to be accompanied by any sister volume covering either sports or romance stories. Even the private (noncorporate) publishers avoid romance and sports reprint projects like the plague.

Ironically, the only three anthologies I know of taken entirely from the pulps appeared late in the heyday of the fiction magazines. Leo Margulies, for two decades editor of pulps from the Ned Pines Thrilling empire (see chapter five), edited *Baseball Roundup* (ten stories) in 1948 and *All American Football Stories* (nine stories) in 1949, both for Cupples & Leon and consisting entirely of reprints from the Pines sports pulps near the end of Margulies' reign as editor. David C. Cooke, an anthologist and aviation writer, also contributed to the sports pulps and selected seven of his stories from 1948–1950 for *While the Crowd Cheers!* published in 1953 by Dutton. This scarce volume is plugged on the dust jacket as "All-American Sports Stories for All-American Boys." Likewise, the two Margulies anthologies were marketed to boys 10 to 14, as indicated on the dust jacket of the football book.

In contrast, the wonderful *The Argosy Book of Sports Stories* (1953), edited by *Argosy* editor Rogers Terrill, is definitely aimed at adults (and perhaps young adults), as indicated by the modestly pulpish dust jacket showing a boxer trying to avoid being counted out as a gorgeous woman urges him to get up. This compendium of 20 stories, released by the noted sports publisher A.S. Barnes, includes only postwar stories written well after *Argosy* emerged from its pulp roots to become a men's "slick" magazine in 1943, similar to the likes of *True* and *Saga*. None of the dozens of sports stories printed in the 1920s and 1930s *Argosy* pulps were selected, even though some were worthy of anthology status (see chapter two). *Argosy*, one of the most avidly collected pulps today, featured a wide variety of adventure-oriented stories, set in locales all over the world, but many issues included a sports story. In many respects, *The Argosy Book of Sports Stories* may be the best of all sports anthologies, especially since it does not include any excerpts from novels.

The historic American Boy Sports Stories

In 1929, perhaps to celebrate the 30th anniversary of the once-iconic magazine *American Boy*, the publishers released several handsome anthologies through the respected firm of Doubleday, Doran & Company, Inc. This includes one of the earliest sports anthologies, *American Boy Sports Stories*, featuring two stories by the noted sports novelist William Heyliger and three by prolific short story writer Franklin M. Reck.

This 366-page volume can be enjoyed equally by young adults and older readers. The 14 stories, all from the 1923–1929 period, are generally excellent, especially the poorly titled but compelling 53-page novelette *The Shouting Violet* by Heyliger. The awkward title refers to the boastful nature of Grandon College freshman Trimble Roberts. He gains the nickname "The Blond Comet" because *Grandon Times* sports editor Horsey Mott, realizing how good Roberts can be when he spies him performing for the reserve squad, encourages him to play without a helmet to distinguish himself (of course, this would not be allowed today).

In this remarkable story, veteran coach Gene Bancker is shown to care primarily about the character he is trying to inculcate in his players. Bancker, however, is anything but a loser; he is the consummate team-oriented coach and is known for getting results. Sports editor Mott is the villain of the piece and several times deliberately distorts the conflicts between Roberts and his coach. "Boy, when I go after a man, that man is as good as done," the nefarious journalist tells Roberts of his plans to try to get Bancker fired after the coach has dropped The Blond Comet from the roster. Roberts had been the key to winning the first three games, but with a self-aggrandizing style that appalls his teammates. In his third game, he tries a difficult field goal in the third game to make up for his earlier ineffectiveness, instead of going for a more logical play called by the team captain. He makes the kick but his selfish call leads Bancker to drop him from the football program entirely. Eventually, Roberts realizes how cruel and unfair Mott is and sets out to square matters with Bancker.

The coach reinstates Roberts, but keeps him on the bench until the last game, testing The Comet to see if he is truly willing put his ego aside. When Roberts proves to Bancker's satisfaction that he is worthy of playing time, Heyliger adds an ironic twist to the drama of the game-winning touchdown. When Grandon reaches the 3-yard line with a minute remaining, Roberts is truly willing to let the senior team captain, identified throughout merely as Goodwin, try for the winning touchdown because he has never scored in his three years on the varsity. Goodwin, though, astonishes Roberts by ordering him to carry the ball, and Roberts plows over the goal line to win the game. As the story ends, Roberts asks Goodwin why he gave up his chance for a precious memory and the captain replies, "It wasn't the play.... I was tired. I might have fumbled. You were fresh. You were the best bet." Heyliger's final line is a masterpiece of understatement as Roberts turns to his coach with tears in his eyes: "I've just discovered what you've been trying to teach me all season."

What also makes this story so unusual is that the reader is left hanging regarding the nasty Mott's fate. He is not part of the story after Roberts reforms himself, so the reader can only hope that Mott's schemes will continue to backfire until he is fired. It is sad, however, that Heyliger casts sports journalism in a bad light, as reporters were so often vilified in sports fiction. Dozens of reporters, both male and female, played heroic roles in pulp detective stories of the period, but they were portrayed far less often as sympathetic in sports stories. Part of this plays to the stereotype of the reporter as an outsider, primarily interested in selling papers. While most real-life print reporters are decent people, real-life athletes often feel they don't understand what athletes go through to achieve their goals.

Setting a pattern for sports stories

American Boy Sports Stories set a pattern for most general-interest anthologies by using eight stories about football (three), baseball (three) and basketball (two) and only six about other sports, including hockey, tennis, swimming/diving, crew, hunting and track and field. The book included a three-paragraph introduction by University of Illinois football coach Robert C. Zuppke, one of the iconic coaching names during the Roaring Twenties. "In every university, college and school the mass athletics movement has gone booming and rolling along, until we have become pretty much a nation interested in athletics," writes Zuppke, who a few years earlier coached Red Grange, "The Galloping Ghost" himself. He calls the anthology "a book for everybody, for in the twentieth century everybody is interested in athletics!"

Everybody, however, wasn't especially interested in anthologies until about two decades later — in the late 1940s. Perhaps part of the reason was the easy availability of short stories in the pulps, which cost only a fraction of the price of hardbound books. Two or three pulps would easily equal one book in reading value. And, of course, the Great Depression and World War II both interfered with the economics of book publishing. Until the postwar period, reprinted short stories were primarily limited to collections by one author, and even then mostly about baseball.

The eminent Charles Van Loan published four collections of baseball stories between 1911 and 1919 — *The Big League* (1911), *The $10,000 Arm and Other Tales of the Big League* (1912), *The Lucky Seventh* (1913) and *Score by Innings* (1919). Andy McCue, in *Baseball by the Books*, says, "However, undoubtedly his greatest contribution to baseball literature was to persuade the editor of the Saturday Evening Post to print Ring Lardner's Jack Keefe stories, which the editor had rejected previously."

The Red-Headed Outfield and Other Stories, an often-reprinted collection of 11 baseball stories by Zane Grey, was first published in 1915. The great western writer, also highly respected for his fishing books, already had established his diamond chops with *The Shortstop* (1909) and *The Young Pitcher* (1911). Lardner's *You Know Me Al* followed in 1916, with three more baseball-related collections to follow, along with two similar books by H.C. Witwer.

William Heyliger, one of the most prolific sports authors of all time, produced two collections (McCue notes that only two stories in each are about baseball): *Bean-Ball Bill and Other Stories* (1920) and *The Spirit of the Leader* (1923). These scarce volumes are among the earliest true sports anthologies, albeit with stories by the same author. A lesser-known writer named Gerald Beaumont published a now-scarce adult collection of his Lardner-like baseball stories in 1921, *Hearts and the Diamond*.

Harold M. Sherman, one of the few pulp authors who frequently showed up in sports collections for young readers, was a prolific novelist but also released the anthology *Double Play and Other Baseball Stories* in 1932, along with other like-themed books. Other collections included *The Will to Win* by Stephen Meader (1936); *Varsity Letter* by Franklin Reck (1942) and *Shift to the Right* by B.J. Chute (1944), all of which were about a variety of sports. Along the same lines, later followed two little-known collections, *Tall Baseball Stories* (1948) by Jiggs Amarant and *Dunk O'Malley Sports Stories* (1949) by Harold Sandberg to close out the 1940s. There followed one of the few 1950s single-author collections for young readers, *The Kid Who Beat the Dodgers and Other Stories* (1954) by Earl Schenk Miers, a versatile and prolific writer who appeared in dozens of publications. Interestingly, McCue notes that only the title story of Miers' collection is about baseball. That mean's Cooke's aforementioned *While the Crowd Cheers* must be scarce, indeed, since McCue was amazingly thorough in his *Baseball by the Books* yet did not list Cooke's compilation, even though Cooke included three baseball stories along with single tales of football, basketball, auto racing and airplane racing.

A scarcity of adult anthologies

The vast majority of sports anthologies and collections were intended for school-age readers in the postwar period, but there were a few tentative stabs at collecting adult fiction. The first such was *The "Saturday Evening Post" Sports Stories* (1949), an anthology of 22 widely varied stories from the 1932–1946 period. Red Smith was the credited editor for A.S. Barnes, which must have felt this collection fit nicely into its burgeoning line of novels for adults.

Smith, the eminent and pleasingly literate New York sports columnist, touched on the historic nature of his anthology at the end of his introduction. After noting how few sports journalists also turned out fiction, Smith writes:

> The other point that impresses the prospector in this field has to do with the published books of sports fiction. Practically all of them, from the days of Frank Merriwell and Ralph Henry Barbour to the present, were written, printed and peddled as juvenile entertainment. Yet the great majority of those who read the sports pages daily are not juveniles. And although many of us were reared on "The Saturday Evening Post," that isn't a children's magazine. The stories in this book were written by adults for adults. If this is the first book of mature sports fiction to be produced for mature readers, then maybe we've stumbled on something. If so, there'll be more of the same.

It was just like the remarkable Smith — who along with Jim Murray was the best wordsmith in the history of American sportswriting — to use the word "prospector" to refer to the duties of an anthologist. As such, in his introduction he cannily noted a story about the Boston Marathon, *See How They Run*, by George Harmon Coxe, who spent four decades writing best-selling mystery novels. There quickly followed from A.S. Barnes, the most prolific sports publisher, a special book. Ralph Graber edited *The Baseball Reader* in 1951, which included work by numerous adult authors such as Thomas Wolfe, Paul Gallico, Robert Benchley, and Damon Runyon. Pulp fiction this was not.

Red Smith lauds Frank O'Rourke

Of equal quality were adult baseball collections by novelist Frank O'Rourke: *The Greatest Victory and Other Baseball Stories* (1950) and *The Heavenly World Series* (1952), both for A.S. Barnes. O'Rourke published in the pulps, but primarily in the slicks. He earned this tribute from Red Smith in his *Post* anthology:

> Here's a fellow named Frank O'Rourke, too. Never heard of him before the end of World War II, but since then he has come up with a raft of sports fiction that is marked by a special, endearing

quality. That is his ability to capture the authentic flavor of the dugout or the diamond or the press box or the locker room, places which comparatively few people get to visit but which the reader comes to know first-hand through O'Rourke's words. First time I read a baseball story by him, I wondered whether he could be the Frank O'Rourke I knew twenty years ago as a third baseman on the St. Louis Browns. That's how strong the impression was that the guy must have lived in the dugout. Turned out he wasn't the same fellow at all.

Smith included O'Rourke's "The Greatest Victory" in his collection, along with two Ring Lardner stories and Stanley Frank's intensely compelling 1942 baseball masterpiece, "The Name of the Game."

Charles Einstein, the noted journalist, novelist and baseball biographer, and the versatile Herbert S. Zim incorporated sports fiction into what at first glance appear to be nonfiction books — Einstein's magnificent *The Fireside Book of Baseball* (1956) and *The Second Fireside Book of Baseball* (1958) (there were later two more), plus Zim's *Sports Alive!* (1960). Neither of these distinguished editors chose any fiction from pulps, instead focusing on excerpts from novels and stories in high-caliber publications.

Einstein's two 1950s volumes — "must-haves" for all fans of vintage baseball history — included an amazing variety of history from all manner of sources. But Einstein also included 29 fictional pieces in the two books combined. He called on many familiar names — among them Mark Harris, James T. Farrell, Tom Wolfe, Zane Grey, Owen Johnson, Ring Lardner, P.G. Wodehouse, James Thurber, Robert Penn Warren and Bernard Malamud. But Einstein also included work otherwise "lost," such as Einstein's own 1954 *Blue Book* story "The Sleeper" and — for those who missed it in Red Smith's anthology — Stanley Frank's "The Name of the Game."

The little-known *Sports Alive!* — enjoyable for adults and youth alike — contains a mixture of 23 short stories along with dozens of factual pieces to accompany the fiction. This is one of the least-known of anthologies; it appeared only in a textbook-like hardbound edition. Baseball, football and basketball dominated with 11 stories, but sports such as horse racing, tennis, track, golf, boxing, lacrosse, swimming and diving and rodeo were also included.

I came across *Sports Alive!* with no prior hint of its existence. Likewise, later in the decade of the 1960s, Scholastic Book Services printed two now-obscure anthologies, *Hit Parade of Sports Stories* (1966), edited by prolific sports novelist and journalist Dick Friendlich, and *"The Crooked Arm" and Other Baseball Stories* (1968), edited by Tony Simon. "The Crooked Arm" was from Stephen Meader's collection *The Will to Win* (1936). The other eight stories included several for the adult market, including a story from an unlikely source — "Lay It Down, Ziggy!" by Larry Siegel from a 1949 issue of *American Legion* magazine. It just goes to show that sports fiction can show up in the most unexpected places.

Friendlich topped that by plucking stories from a 1954 issue of *Farm Journal*, a 1961 issue of *Ladies Home Journal* and a 1963 issue of *Co-Ed*. I discovered his *Hit Parade of Sports Stories* in my senior year of high school at a school "bookstore," and I recall being impressed by Friendlich's ability to pick off-beat sports stories, including one of the few I've seen about a star girl swimmer.

The Lantern Press/Grosset anthology boom

In the wake of the groundbreaking *American Boy Sports Stories* in 1929, anthologies of sports stories for young readers were just as uncommon in pre–World War II days as were anthologies for adults. In 1947, however, Lantern Press came up with *Teen-Age Sports Stories*, a groundbreaking collection of 14 stories, edited by Frank Owen. Five stories were plucked from *Boys' Life*, two from the *Saturday Evening Post*, and one each from *American Girl* and *Liberty*, plus five tales with origins other than magazines.

From 1948 through 1950, Lantern Press published 10 more *Teen-Age* sports anthologies, plus eventually adding about 20 more anthologies in categories such as mystery and aviation. Grosset & Dunlap reprinted all 11 sports anthologies, and this was how they received their greatest circulation. Today, Lantern Press editions are scarce but Grossets are frequently found. As I gradually completed this series in their handsome dust jackets, all 11 copies I found were Grosset reprints. They must have sold well for Grosset, for the firm kept them in print into the 1960s and gradually raised the Grosset price from $1 to $1.25 to $1.50. Some bookstores sold them for as much as $2, since their 5-by-8 format simply looked more expensive than the hundreds of best-selling Grosset series books featuring Nancy Drew, Chip Hilton and the like.

Grosset's reprints were so well received that all remained in print into the early 1960s. However, when Grosset phased out dust jackets for its series books in the 1961–1963 period in favor of pictorial covers, the *Teen-Age* series retained dust jackets and did not go to pictorial covers, perhaps because librarians in those days often saw non-series books with dust jackets as somehow superior to books with pictorial covers. One of the last Lantern/Grosset anthologies, *Teen-Age Stories of Super Science* (1957), lists all but *Teen-Age Winter Sports Stories* in the advertisement on the back of the dust jacket. They are still often found in used-book stores, although often sans dust jacket.

The 11 *Teen-Age* sports volumes say a lot about how athletics for high school and middle school students has changed dramatically since the 1940s. There were 161 stories in the 11 anthologies; to the best of my knowledge, they were never updated. The stories were mostly from the 1940s, with a few from the 1930s. The vast majority came from youth-oriented publications such as *Boys' Life*, *Open Road for Boys* and *Senior Scholastic*, along with work without specific adult content from the *Saturday Evening Post*, *Collier's*, *Liberty* and the like.

Six of the anthologies were general, including *Teen-Age Treasure Chest of Sports Stories* (1948) and *Teen-Age Champion Sports Stories* (1950), both by the prolific Charles Coombs, and *Teen-Age Sports Parade* (1949), by the equally prolific B.J. Chute, who was one of the few female writers of sports stories marketed to boys, though the stories were doubtless read by a good many girls, as well. Like the famed western novelist B.M. (Bertha Muzzy) Bower of the previous generation, Chute used initials. In the pre-women's liberation era, book and magazine publishers generally believed that female writers of pretty much anything but romance and occasionally science fiction stories needed to use initials or male pseudonyms, in the belief that female writers would not sell to the market for boys and men.

In addition to *Teen-Age Sports Stories*, the other two general anthologies were *Teen-Age Winter Sports Stories* (1949) and *Teen-Age Victory Parade* (1950), both edited by Owen. Anthologies devoted to the most popular school sports were *Teen-Age Baseball Stories* (1948), edited by Owen; *Teen-Age Stories of the Diamond* (1950), edited by David Thomas; *Teen-Age Football Stories* (1948), edited by Owen; *Teen-Age Gridiron Stories* (1950), edited by Josh Furman; and *Teen-Age Basketball Stories* (1949), edited by Furman.

Team sports represented nearly three-fourths of all stories, 117 of 161. There were 42 about football and 33 apiece for baseball and basketball, plus six about hockey and one each covering girls' softball, boys' volleyball and boys' lacrosse. In retrospect, it's stunning but not shocking that only three of the 161 stories involved female protagonists: the softball story in *Teen-Age Sports Stories*, and the skiing and tennis stories in *Teen-Age Champion Sports Stories*. The editors doubtless felt the vast majority of readers were boys, and, in those pre–Title IX days, interscholastic girls' sports were uncommon except for hotbeds such as Iowa girls' basketball.

There were 14 stories about track and field, which in those days was one of the "big four" interscholastic sports. Boxing, one of the biggest sports of adult interest through the 1950s and somewhat beyond, was not sanctioned by high school athletic associations, although exhibitions of high school boxing, similar to Gold Gloves competition, were often held. There were five tennis stories, three covering swimming and diving and one involving golf, all sports then played at some (though far from all) high schools.

The rest of the stories involved skiing (six), fishing (three), rodeo (three), boating (two), crew (two), and one each about camping, model airplanes, soaring, pigeon racing, bobsledding, and gliding. Although material from the pulp sports magazines was not used in these anthologies— perhaps in large part because the various editors did not see or care about them, aside from adult considerations— the pattern of heavy use of the "big three" team sports held true (see chapter five).

What is stunning, in retrospect, is not only how few girls' stories were selected for use, but also how many now-popular sports were completely ignored. Soccer, not yet popularized in America, was not represented by a single story. Today, it's one of the most popular school and club sports for both boys and girls. There were also no wrestling stories; the mat sport is now immensely popular among boys and, increasingly, girls— but in the period of the *Teen-Age* anthologies, few states held wrestling tournaments. Likewise, cross-country is not represented, nor is girls' volleyball, which is another sport in which state tournaments have become hugely popular all over America. Nor is there any represen-

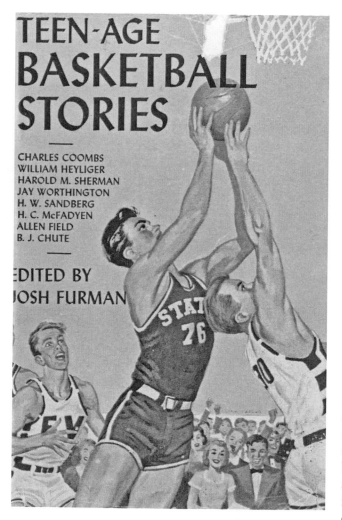

Teen-Age Basketball Stories, edited by Josh Furman, 1949 (jacket copyright Lantern Press and Grosset & Dunlap). Although single-author basketball collections had been published earlier, this is probably the first basketball anthology.

tation for regionally popular high school sports such as water polo, badminton, girls' field hockey, rugby and bowling.

The *Teen-Age* anthologies bear striking witness to how diversified sport has become for both sexes and how today girls' participation has mushroomed to approximately the same as boys' participation, now mandated by both law and, increasingly, social custom.

In the first of the anthologies, *Teen-Age Sports Stories*, editor Frank Owen wrote this introduction, apparently to reassure parents: "As in all Teen-Age Library books, 'Sports Stories' has been prepared especially for those young readers who have put away the books of their childhood, but are not yet prepared for adult fiction. All the stories meet the rigid standards of the Teen-Age Library: they are clean and wholesome, they are interesting and they mirror some phase of the lives and problems of teen-agers. It is to be hoped that they will in great measure be of aid in the process of good character building."

In his foreword to *Teen-Age Treasure Chest of Sports Stories*, author Charles Coombs, talking about the joy of competition, wraps up his two-page essay with this:

> Play clean? Coach needn't worry about that. A healthy mind plus a healthy body automatically takes care of playing clean. A "dirty" player never got any place, not for long. Don't worry, Coach. The game will be hard and clean. Win or lose. And that, I hope, is what you will find about the "heroes" in the stories of this book. Maybe they're a little clumsy at times, even as you and I. But they play hard. They play clean. Sometimes they are tempted to quit — even, perhaps, as you and I. But they don't for they have the stuff of which winners are made. And you know and I know that a quitter never wins — and a winner never quits. Okay, gang, let's go out there and play the game!

Countless coaches have used that phrase in the 60 years since Coombs wrote it, most often turning it around to say, "A winner never quits, and a quitter never wins." Perhaps no other phrase has decorated locker rooms more than that one!

The prolific B.J. Chute

In addition to the 11 stories in her anthology *Teen-Age Sports Parade*, B.J. Chute had 12 other stories selected for the series, for a total of 23. Only Coombs appeared more often. Chute seldom wrote about baseball, but she had eight football stories and four basketball stories anthologized, plus four dealing with track and field, three with tennis, two with skiing and one each about sailing and camping. None of the stories, however, has a female protagonist.

Chute's work was selected for several other anthologies, including *The "Boys' Life" Book of Football Stories* (1963) and *The "Boys' Life" Book of Baseball Stories* (1964), each with 10 stories. The tales were originally published from 1943 to 1961, and several were included in the *Teen-Age* anthologies. Chute had a story in each volume, including "Dumb Bunny," one of her few baseball stories, which originally appeared in *Boys' Life* in 1943 and was first anthologized in Chute's collection *Shift to the Right* in 1944.

"Dumb Bunny" was earlier anthologized in *Crack of the Bat* (1952), a Knopf anthology of eight stories and two nonfiction pieces edited by Phyllis Fenner, a frequently published anthologist. "Dumb Bunny," the tale of a poor player who accidentally hits two home runs in a game with his doting but delusional father watching, is famed for the humanity and humor of the piece without any indication of knowledge about baseball. In fact, when Charles Batty, Jr., hits the first of those two home runs, he is so dazed he runs the bases backward and is called out. At the time, however, there was no official rule against it, as shown by the same stunt pulled by Jimmy Piersall in 1963 when he was with the New York Mets. Piersall deliberately ran the bases backward when he hit the 100th home run of his career, leading to a change in the rules. Because of Piersall, the story had the rule right when it was reprinted in 1964.

Chute, however, was a first-rate writer (see chapter twelve). She is credited with hundreds of stories of all types for *Boys' Life*, the official magazine of the Boy Scouts of America. She wrote several adult novels and many adult stories for the slicks, including *Good Housekeeping, Saturday Evening Post, Redbook* and *McCall's*, all of which published much fiction from the 1930s through the 1960s, when Chute was most active. She became one of the few novelists with enough ambition to rewrite a sports novel for young adults, *Blocking Back*, originally published in 1938 and revised in 1966. When I stumbled across the revision in a used-book store, I discovered not only an inscription to "my dear Chute cousins," but also a personal note clipped to the book: "This is a re-issue by Dutton of my first book which was originally published by MacMillan. I have done some re-writing and brought all the football up to date, and I thought the boys might enjoy it. Love to you all, Joy." It's amazing what treasures show up when you dig through used-book stores and antique malls!

One of the few anthologies with a genuine pulp story was *Player's Choice* (1969), an obscure Whitman anthology of seven football stories purportedly selected by four current National Football League stars. The story honored is "All-American Washout" by William Campbell Gault, who originally published the tale as "Tinsel Tailback" in Popular Publications' *Fifteen Sports Stories* for September, 1950. The title change alone reveals a lot; not only had pulp-style alliteration lost its cache two decades later, but "Tinsel Tailback" was not a title that young readers would have understand.

The historic "Young Readers" anthologies

The Lantern Press/Grosset & Dunlap anthology "team" came up with a concept unique in the late 1940s and early 1950s: Young Readers anthologies, many of them about sports, specifically designed for readers 7 to 12. In fact, the Young Readers Bookshelf Grosset logo appeared on all the dust jackets of the reprints, with "for ages 7–12" prominent in the logo. Whether by concept or design, this new concept was a significant commercial success, especially for the horde of baby boomers that first came along in 1946. The print was large— pages averaged only about 100 words—and book size was about what series books looked like, with some variations.

Coombs wrote all, or almost all, of the stories in the sports series, and quite a few other books, too. Most, if not all, of the stories in the one dollar Young Readers series were original. The sports-themed books included (all with Young Readers above the title) Sports Stories, Baseball Stories, Football Stories, Basketball Stories, Water Sport Stories, Indoor Sports Stories, Outdoor Sports Stories, Stories of the Diamond and Sports Treasury.

Coombs also filled two books with full-length "novels": *Baseball Mystery* (1959, a reprint of the 1955 *Sleuth at Shortstop*) and the highly significant *Young Infield Rookie* (1954). The latter was part of the Young Heroes Library, and was one of the first books devoted to Little League, which was founded in 1939 and famously gained massive publicity with the introduction of the Little League World Series in 1947.

In *Young Infield Rookie*, published seven years after Jackie Robinson broke the color line with the Brooklyn Dodgers, Coombs was one of the first authors to feature an African-

American player as a major protagonist. Amos Jackson, who is talked into playing Little League by his friend Ken Douglas, is described this way when introduced: "Amos was dressed in patched jeans. He wore a white T-shirt that made his skin seem even blacker than ever. As usual, Amos was smiling. And, as usual, Ken found himself wishing he had teeth as white as the colored boy had." Amos' father is described as "a hardworking janitor around town" and lauded as the highly responsible father of 11 children. Amos is never referred to as a Negro, but instead as "colored," in the manner of the era.

Ken's father, praising his son for making the Little League team, tells Ken that in his day, "A lot of boys who should have been playing never got the chance." Ken responds, "It's not that way in Little League, Dad. Everyone gets the same chance. It doesn't matter what his race, religion, or color is, either." Ken's father adds, "That's the way it should be. I see by the paper that Amos Jackson made the Red Sox team."

Ken tells his father how well Amos plays and what a "swell kid" he is. "Maybe his family is kind of poor. Maybe there are more children than his father can keep dressed in new clothes and shoes, and plenty of food, and, and—" His father interjects: "They [the Jackson children] are always neat and clean, and they are not getting into mischief." For the period, this is practically a liberal manifesto. Amos is an exemplary figure the rest of the way, helping the kids' mentor, "Lefty" Gregory, realize that his major league pitching career is not over even though he seriously "beaned" a player, named Johnny Logan (the name of an actual major league shortstop when the book was written). The kids win the league championship and Lefty decides to return to professional baseball, prompting this exchange: "You are all real champions. I hope to see you at the World Series." When a player asks him which—"Little League or major league"—Lefty says, "Both." And the kids finished with an ice cream celebration.

Amos Jackson, however, was not featured on the dust jacket (Charles Geer's illustration was of a sliding player and a middle infielder, both white) or in the plot recap on the dust jacket flap, which mentioned three white players. Nor were there any African American characters in the stories or illustrations in Coombs' *Young Readers Basketball Stories* (1951). The commercial, national nature of publishing—just as it did in the pulp magazines and comic books—made featuring fictional African-American characters a financial risk in the pre–civil rights era.

Until the 1960s, as indicated by a list in Andy McCue's *Baseball by the Books*, only *Young Infield Rookie* and *Skid*, a racially sensitive 1948 novel for young readers by Florence Hayes—well ahead of its time—dealt with African-American protagonists in books for young readers. McCue says that Skid is "the first baseball juvenile to deal with integration. Skid, the captain of his school team in Georgia, moves to Connecticut, where he's the only black kid in school. He eventually wins friends and begins to form a baseball team there. Games are described in early and late chapters."

FOURTEEN

The Departure of Drama in Sports Films

As obscure as the vast majority of sports films were in the two decades before World War II, the fact that more than 80 were made involving baseball or football coincides with the end of the Merriwell dime novel era and the beginning of pulp-style sports fiction, both in the magazines and in the many novels intended for the young-adult and juvenile market.

From 1942 to 1970, however, drama in sports films — other than in numerous movies about boxing — virtually disappeared. Not only were there only 34 films about baseball, football and basketball made by the remaining Hollywood studios, just 14 could be called dramas in any sense of the word. The rest were comedies, musicals, fantasies, or a mixture of all three genres, such as *Damn Yankees* (1958). Sports novels, primarily those for the young adult and juvenile markets, numbered well over 500 during those three decades (see chapter eleven) but sports were, as *Sports Illustrated* once famously called them in a 1969 essay by Robert Cantwell, "Box-Office Poison."

From the standpoint of genre fiction, sports thus had plenty to offer Hollywood screenwriters in the 1940s, 1950s and 1960s. But Hollywood wasn't yet ready during those three decades for adult treatment of sports themes, such as the admirable film based on Frank Deford's classic football novel *Everybody's All-American* (1981) or the instant movie baseball classics *The Natural* (1984), taken from Bernard Malamud's 1952 novel; the pathos-packed *Bang the Drum Slowly* (1973), created from Mark Harris' 1956 novel; and the sexed-up and wildly funny *Bull Durham* (1989), an original story by former minor league player Ron Shelton. At the same time, the many-times-told "hero conquers problem, also wins Big Game" plot was flatly rejected by Hollywood in the 1942–1970 period, even in the era of escapist entertainment following World War II. Genre films proliferated by the hundreds — mysteries, noir or not; westerns, both the "A" and "B" types; and science fiction, fantasy and horror.

Many of the best of the genre writers prolific in the 1940s and 1950s — people like western/mystery master Frank Gruber and hard-boiled novelists Raymond Chandler, Mickey Spillane and Steve Fisher — saw story after story after story adapted by Hollywood. The powers-that-were in films, however, ignored even the finest specialists in sports fiction, even though the likes of John R. Tunis, Jackson Scholz and Frank O'Rourke wrote stories that could be enjoyed by readers (and potentially filmgoers) of all ages.

Francis Wallace, a prolific writer of well-done football serials (which became novels) and stories for "slicks" such as the *Saturday Evening Post* and *Collier's*, was the only sports novelist who had any real luck with Hollywood through the 1960s. Wallace saw five of his 1930s stories adapted for films, and only two of those movies were filmed post–1941— *That's My Boy* (1951), a Dean Martin and Jerry Lewis comedy, and *The Rose Bowl Story* (1952), one of the few sports dramas of its era. The others were *The Big Game* (1936), *Huddle* (1932) and *Touchdown* (1931), based on Wallace's novel *Stadium*.

Otherwise, the only even remotely well-known sports pulp writer to see a film emerge from his work was George Bruce, whose *Navy Blue and Gold* was filmed in 1937, during a decade when films about both military academies and aviation (Bruce's specialty) were all the rage. The number of sports novelists who had stories turned into films is conspicuous by their total absence from the excellent compilation of source material in *Sports Movies: A Review of Nearly 500 Films* from Cinebooks in 1989. (Just the fact that books about sports in film were virtually nonexistent until the 1980s is telling enough.)

Hard, Fast and Beautiful

Ironically, *Sports Movies* somehow missed the one 1942–1970 sports film that was adapted from a story by a mainstream sports novelist — the obscure but effectively downbeat tennis tale *Hard, Fast and Beautiful* from RKO in 1951 and directed by actress Ida Lupino. Many sources have said this story, significantly altered for the film, was partly taken from an upbeat young-adult novel by Tunis, *Champion's Choice* (1940). This was the only one of the much-respected author's 16 young adult sports novels, all written from 1938 through 1958, to feature a female athlete. Tunis, however, said in *A Measure of Independence* that the film was taken from an earlier tennis tale: his 1929 adult novel *American Girl*.

Ask any devoted film buff — or any old-timer who likes athletics — to recall a sports film of the 1940s, 1950s or 1960s, and the answer will invariably be either the amusing box-office winner *Damn Yankees* or the Frank Sinatra/Gene Kelly musical *Take Me Out to the Ball Game* (1949). Go ahead — take the test. Even film fans with fabulous memories will be hard-pressed to name others. They all know *Pride of the Yankees* (1942), of course, but that is a biopic based on Lou Gehrig's life story.

Drama? Forget it. Not a single sports drama made in those three decades is well remembered today. How many of these have you seen? Baseball: *It Happened in Flatbush* (1942) with Lloyd Nolan; *The Kid from Cleveland* (1949) with George Brent; and *The Big Leaguer* (1953) with Edgar G. Robinson.

Basketball? *Tall Story* (1960), with Jane Fonda and Anthony Perkins, is a comedy worth seeing for the sheer spoof of it all, but it is a comedy. Who recalls *The Big Fix* (1947) from Poverty Row studio Producers Releasing Corporation, or *Basketball Fix* (1951) from Realart, one of the last of the Poverty Row production outfits? Those films were made to capitalize on newspaper headlines.

Football? Perhaps the best of the gridiron dramas was the realistic *Saturday's Hero* (1951), with John Derek and Donna Reed based on Millard Lampell's admirable 1949 literary novel *The Hero* (see chapter four), which was among the few adult sports novels produced until the 1970s began a multi-decade explosion of them. *Trouble Along the Way* (1953), with John Wayne and Donna Reed, shortly before she began to achieve television fame, is also a decent drama, albeit a story with a whole lot of unlikely twists. Notwithstanding star power, not many people recall those two worthwhile films.

Along with the aforementioned *Rose Bowl Story*, other football drama include *The All-*

American (1953) with a 27-year-old Tony Curtis; *Easy Living* (1949) with Victor Mature, Lucille Ball and the vastly under-rated Lizabeth Scott; the potboiler *King of the Gamblers* (1948); *Number One* (1969) with Charlton Heston and a chilling antihero's fate; *The Spirit of Stanford* (1942), which is actually one of the last movies of the 1930s, in spirit anyway, and is a fictionalized biography of quarterback Frankie Albert; and *Triple Threat* (1948), in which the biggest name in the credits is Hall of Fame quarterback Sammy Baugh, who did a cameo and was still a productive player late in his career.

Think of the paucity of baseball, football and basketball sports drama of the 1942–70 era this way: If you could find all 14 films, you could watch them all easily in a three-or four-day period! The same couldn't be said of boxing films, the fictional examples of which number well over 100 from 1930 to 1990.

As 1980s fans who flocked to see *The Natural* discovered, baseball and whimsical fantasy and comedy go nicely together, and not just in *Damn Yankees* and *Take Me Out to the Ball Game*. Of the 13 non-biopic baseball-themed films made from 1942 to 1970, 10 were whimsical, by far the best of which was the Ray Milland classic *It Happens Every Spring* (1949). The others include *Angels in the Outfield* (1951); *The Great American Pastime* (1956); *The Kid from Left Field* (1953), *Kill the Umpire* (1950), *Rhubarb* (1951), *Roogie's Bump* (1954) and *Safe at Home* (1962).

While basketball comedies didn't come into vogue until the 1970s and 1980s—when racial themes could be handled with a wink, a nudge and a lot of laughs—there were a handful of football comedies, some of which had precious little football: *Father Was a Fullback* (1949); *The Fortune Cookie* (1966); *Good News* (1947, a remake); *The Guy Who Came Back* (1951); *High School Hero* (1946); *Hold That Line* (1952); *John Goldfarb, Please Come Home* (1964) and *Peggy* (1950).

Father Was a Fullback is well worth seeing for Fred MacMurray and Maureen O'Hara in the lead roles, although for some reason the critics have a hard time with this amusing trifle. *High School Hero* is noteworthy for an energetic lead role by Noel Neill, who was 25 when this was filmed yet was such a hardworking and talented actress she actually seems like a high school girl. Noel Neill, of course, went on to immense popularity and lasting fame as the screen's original Lois Lane, first in Columbia's 1948 and 1950 Superman serials and then in 78 of the 104 episodes of television's *The Adventures of Superman* in the 1950s.

It doesn't happen very often

By far my favorite fictional sports film of the pre–1970 period is the 1949 20th Century–Fox gem *It Happens Every Spring*, a comedy in which the marvelously versatile Ray Milland plays baseball-loving college chemistry professor Vernon Simpson. He accidentally creates a liquid that prevents a ball from making contact with wood, thus enabling the mild-mannered instructor to pitch under the name King Kelly for St. Louis in the major leagues. Club nicknames weren't used in the movie, so it's never specified if it's the Cardinals or the Browns, who were still five years away from moving to Baltimore.

The film has established something of a cult status, since when people see it for the first time, they fall in love with it. Valentine Davies, coming off his fabulous success with the far better known *Miracle on 34th Street* (1947)—also one of my favorite films—wrote the screenplay based on a story by University of Michigan official Shirley W. Smith (who, along with the famed sportswriter Shirley Povich, was one of the few male Shirleys). As Davies explains in the introduction to his novel, Smith published the story in the 1946 University of Michigan Alumni Quarterly Magazine, which is surely one of the most unlikely locations for a sports story in the history of the genre. This has led to much confusion about the origins of the story.

"Being a man of learning and not a vendor of fiction, Mr. Smith told Vernon's tale only for the amusement of friends and associates," Davies writes in his introduction to his novel *It Happens Every Spring*. "It was not until 1946 that he was prevailed upon to allow his story to be printed in the Alumni Quarterly Magazine.... Vernon and his adventures instantly intrigued me, especially as the basis of a story for the screen. With Mr. Smith's kind permission, I went to work and developed it as such." That led Davies to take the then-unusual step of producing a novel, sans the stills of the many "photoplay editions" in vogue in the 1920s and 1930s, to take advantage of the summer success of the film in 1949. Some historians state the novel was the basis for the film, but that wasn't the case. Other historians, though, say the film was based on an unpublished novel. That wasn't the case, either, since Smith's original story was

It Happens Every Spring by Valentine Davies, 1949 (copyright Farrar, Straus). Davies wrote this expanded version of Shirley W. Smith's novelette in response to the success of the film. Richard M. Powers illustrated the rare dust jacket and was shortly destined to become one of the preeminent science fiction cover illustrators.

nowhere near long enough for a novel. Davies, who won the Academy Award for best original screenplay in 1947 for *Miracle on 34th Street*, received a nomination for the same honor in 1949, along with Smith.

At the bottom of the fly leaf on the dust jacket of the first edition of *It Happens Every Spring*, from Farrar, Straus and Company — not exactly a hotbed of sports fiction!— the truth comes out: "This book is not a motion picture edition, but is based on the 20th Century–Fox Production, 'It Happens Every Spring,' starring Ray Milland, Jean Peters and Paul Douglas." This is, indeed, an unusual book, not to mention a scarce edition in a dust jacket. The jacket, one of the first by famed illustrator Richard Powers, is so scarce it is not listed among the hundreds of book covers listed in *The Art of Richard Powers* (2001) by Jane Frank, his daughter. Powers, whose daughter notes he was an outstanding baseball player in his youth — much like contemporary book illustrator Frank Frazetta — was 28 when he drew the jacket.

As good as the 44-year-old Milland is in the film — and he is a comedic genius at times — 42-year-old Paul Douglas is just as effective and actually had a better role as Monk Lanigan, the veteran St. Louis catcher who tried to cope with Vernon's weird, wacky pitches.

It Happens Every Spring video box illustration, 1994 (copyright Fox Video and Twentieth Century–Fox Film Corporation). Ray Milland, Jean Peters and Paul Douglas star in one of the best of all baseball films, now a cult favorite.

Douglas, in effect, was Yogi Berra before Yogi Berra became Yogi Berra (the Yankees' Hall of Fame catcher and syntax mangler was only in his third full season in 1949). Douglas' scene-stealing and good-hearted nature were so effective that he was called to act in *The Guy Who Came Back*, *Angels in the Outfield* and *Rhubarb*, all sports comedies of 1951. Few actors, before or since, have appeared in four sports films.

Since Vernon was pitching in part to earn money so he could marry Peters' character, he continued to pitch in the World Series even when his manager accidentally spilled the last battle of his mysterious compound, thinking it only a hair tonic. Vernon had to pitch on guts alone, and proved he had what it took to win the deciding game in the World Series, 8–7. Vernon leaps to snag a game-ending line shot bare-handed and is severely injured, ending his pitching career with 41 victories in his only season — including three in the World Series — but not ending his love life with Debbie Greenleaf, the college president's daughter. It turns out that everyone back at the university finally learned just what King Kelly was up to, and the folks were rooting madly for him, including Debbie's family.

The really touching aspect of this film is how mild-mannered Vernon Simpson realizes he has courage, after all. There's also a fabulous scene near the end of the film, when Monk Lanigan and King Kelly are going their separate ways yet try to thank each other. "Leave us not try," says Monk, more or less summing up the way men have often dealt with overwhelming emotions, feeling their experiences as teammates said everything that needed to be said. For those wishing to know more about this fabulous film, read the perceptive essay in Hal Erickson's *The Baseball Filmography*.

There was one serious problem with the movie's internal logic, however lighthearted the film may have been. Even more improbable than Vernon Simpson's accidentally produced formula was the idea newspaper photographers would actually honor his request for no photographs after he pitches a no-hitter, since at the time he didn't want people back at his university to know what he was up to. A formula that repels baseballs? Maybe. Photographers willing to let the sensation of the baseball ages go uncovered? No way!

The Kid from Cleveland

Republic Studios produced the vast majority of the best serials, thanks to its crack stuntmen and special-effects crew, and the finest of the "B" westerns, bolstered by the likes of Roy Rogers and Rocky Lane. Republic, though, was known in Hollywood for the uneven nature of its other films, and critics often use *The Kid from Cleveland* (1949) as a good example. I, however, like the film for its period-piece feel.

The drama *The Kid from Cleveland* was made to take advantage of the 1948 Indians' American League pennant and World Series championship (one of only three years the New York Yankees did not win pennants from 1947 through 1964 as the most dominant long-term franchise in history; the others were Cleveland in 1954 and the Chicago White Sox in 1959). The 1948 Indians featured several of the most colorful players of all time: pitchers Bob Feller, Bob Lemon and Satchel Paige, player/manager Lou Boudreau; outfielder Larry Doby; and second baseman Joe "Flash" Gordon, among others. Doby was the first black player in the American League, coming up from the minors in 1947 after Jackie Robinson broke the color line with the Brooklyn Dodgers that season.

The stars of the Indians were all in the movie, along with future television acting star John Beradino, who spent 11 seasons in the major leagues and was a utility infielder for the Indians in 1948 and 1949. He had a regular role in the film, his first. George Brent, who had the lead as a sportscaster trying to reform a potential juvenile delinquent, was a long way from his seven important roles as part of the Warner Brothers scenery Bette Davis chewed so well for so long.

Brent's character, Mike Jackson, helps the eponymous kid, played by Rusty Tamblyn, to get a job as the team's batboy. He reforms and winds up happy with his mother and stepfather; the Indians, however, finished a disappointing third a few weeks after the film was released. Hal Erickson describes the film as "nine reels' worth of sentimental drivel and fatuous psychobabble" in *The Baseball Filmography*, and on that score, it's hard to argue. Republic wasn't exactly known for the tender sensitivities of its screenwriters. Erickson's astute review accurately points out that the Indians' flamboyant owner, Bill Veeck, gave the best performance in the film (as himself). Erickson, however, points out that Boudreau once said of the film, "I would like to buy every print of it and burn it."

When the Brooklyn Dodgers—"Dem Bums"—for so many years in the minds of the media and fans, won the pennant in 1941 under fiery Leo Durocher's guidance, 20th Century-

Fox decided a rare baseball drama was in order. The now seldom-seen *It Happened in Flatbush* (1942) was, in fact, the first genuine baseball-themed film since Warner Brothers' *Alibi Ike* comedy in 1935 (see chapter three). Sports fiction buffs have sometimes gotten the idea that *Flatbush* was inspired by John R. Tunis' first two baseball novels, *The Kid from Tomkinsville* (1940) and *World Series* (1941), but such is not the case, even though Tunis wrote all but one of his nine baseball novels about the Dodgers.

The 80-minute programmer is pure pulp: Lloyd Nolan plays a hard-charging manager, à la Durocher, who romances the new club owner, played by Carole Landis. He lashes his team with his leadership and shows faith in a rookie pitcher — a break he never received as a player. It's too bad this film is so seldom shown; it seems like a marvelous period piece and one of the few really decent, if predictable, sports dramas filmed in the first five decades of sound films. It's the one apparently good baseball film I've never been able to screen. Sadly, the film is so obscure that it isn't listed among Leonard Maltin's more than 20,000 entries in his series of film guides! Nor does it rate a listing in *Halliwell's Guide*, more's the pity. A 20th Century–Fox filmography calls it "an excellent baseball picture."

Edward G. Robinson in *The Big Leaguer*

Just as World War II sidelined the majority of major and minor-league baseball players for a few seasons, there were no more baseball film fictions released until well after the war, in 1949. After *The Kid from Cleveland*, the next drama was the 73-minute bottom-of-the-bill *Big Leaguer* in 1953, giving Edward G. Robinson a role he needed, given how much difficulty he was having for allegedly being too left-leaning in the witch-hunt mood of the fifties. Even though Robinson plays real-life manager/scout Hans Lobert, the film is not a biopic, because it's loaded with the stereotypical blend of ensemble-film personalities in the young players Lobert is trying to train. What I like best about this film is how gritty it is. Erickson points out a great line about parental pressure from Lobert: "This camp is lousy with fathers." In that regard, the picture is years ahead of its time, at least with regard to fictional films. Former New York Giants pitching great Carl Hubbell appears as himself. Erickson is also dead-on when he talks about the film's biggest drawback, what he calls "obtrusive, golly-gee" voiceover narration by Paul Langton: "That narration is so grating it makes you want to give up on an otherwise worthwhile period piece for baseball buffs."

Just as *Big Leaguer* did not receive wide initial distribution, in part because theater managers purportedly thought its appeal would be too limited for general audiences, so was *Safe at Home!* hard to find in theaters when Columbia released the film at the beginning of baseball season in 1962. I tried hard to locate a theater showing this Columbia film, but had no luck and didn't see it until a couple of decades later! The story of a Little Leaguer and his buddies befriended by Mickey Mantle and Roger Maris, it's more comedy than drama and about as hokey as baseball movies come. The film was a shameless attempt to take advantage of the New Yankee slugging duo's success in 1961, when Maris broke Babe Ruth's record with 61 home runs and Mantle hit 54 (sans steroids, it must be noted). Erickson wrote one of the funniest lines I've ever seen in a book on film with this cutline below a picture of Maris in his batting stance: "Roger Maris demonstrates his acting range as he tackles the role of a baseball player in Safe at Home!"

As far as I've been able to determine, *Safe at Home!* was the only fictional baseball movie produced in the 1960s. Likewise, the theaters were just about as barren of football and bas-

ketball themes. I thought *Tall Story* was funny when I first saw this college basketball bur-
lesque as an adult, but I never heard of it when Warner Brothers released it in 1960. But
then, nobody had ever heard of 23-year-old Jane Fonda then, either; it was her film debut,
and she was pretty funny. Ray Walston, of *My Favorite Martian* television fame, stole the
show as a sports-supportive professor.

In football, the comedies *The Fortune Cookie* (1966) and *John Goldfarb* (1964) are good
of their comedic, satiric kind, if you like non-football football films. *Number One* (1969),
which is really a 1970s film in football drag, features a gritty, grasping performance by
Charlton Heston as a quarterback who doesn't know when to quit; but the deadly, downbeat ending would have astonished and appalled Frank Merriwell fans (and a whole lot of
others). In fact, one can only imagine a 60- or 70-year-old sports fiction fan seeing this
grim film and thinking back to how Merriwell would have handled it half a century or more
earlier.

The football dramas *Easy Living* (1949) and *The All-American* (1953) are still watchable, especially if you like hunks like Victor Mature and Tony Curtis, who aren't hard to
imagine as football players. *Easy Living* benefits from solid direction by a real pro, Jacques
Tourneur, and a cool performance by the sultry-voiced Lizabeth Scott — who was then
sometimes compared at her best to the queen of cool, Lauren Bacall — as the gold-digging
wife of a halfback on his way out. Ball, still four years away from becoming Lucy on television, displays her range as a sympathetic club secretary. This is one of the most under-
rated of all sports films, although younger fans would see it as badly dated.

The All-American isn't as profound as *Easy Living*, but it's an easy story to like, dealing in reasonable fashion with the mental maturing of a great college quarterback whose
parents are killed on the way to see him play. Universal rarely made films with sports themes,
but this one is fun, especially because Curtis seems to enjoy the role. There's lots of unfa-
miliar faces, including bad girl Mamie Van Doren (doesn't every football star have to fend
off a Mamie type?), good girl Lori Nelson and former star halfbacks Frank Gifford (then a
young pro football player) and Tom Harmon. Nelson was one of the women ogled by the
gill monster in Universal's mid–1950s three-picture *Creature from the Black Lagoon* series.

The Spirit of Stanford (1942) is another one of the few sports films I've never had the
privilege to see. The 74-minute programmer is listed as a fictionalized biography of quarterback Frankie Albert, but it seems more like a true story. At any rate, Columbia's production values were good enough in those days — nothing like MGM or Warners, but not
Poverty Row, either — that it's probably a worthwhile period piece.

Although crooks of all types have threatened football and baseball players since the
days of the Merriwells, because of the college basketball scandals of the late 1940s and early
1950s the hoop sport has been more connected with skullduggery than any other team sport
in the public's mind. It's also far easier to "point shave" in basketball than to fix a game in
football or baseball, since that would be more obvious, notwithstanding the Black Sox scandal involving eight members of the 1919 Chicago White Sox. Two of the few basketball dramas filmed in the 1942–70 era — there may be others more obscure — were *The Big Fix*
(1947) and *The Basketball Fix* (1951), both obviously influenced by events of the period.
Both films are from obscure studios and neither is listed in Maltin.

It was no coincidence sports fiction on film reached a 20th-century nadir in the 1960s,
even though professional sports made steady gains, resulting in the first Super Bowl, the
first Major League Baseball expansion, and the ever-increasing popularity of pro basketball and hockey. Real life sports heroics had captivated the public's interest, especially with

the influence of television. Chip Hilton and Bronc Burnett pretty much disappeared from retailers' bookshelves by the late 1960s; so did Duane Decker's Blue Sox series. The sports pulps already were long gone, available only in second-hand bookstores, since pulp conventions were a few years away. John Tunis had said all he wanted to say in sports fiction by the end of the 1950s. Most of the other prolific sports fiction authors finished their primary work in the 1960s. High school girls and college women had to wait one more decade until the Title IX law began to create athletic opportunities for them in the 1970s.

By the late 1960s, most team sports enthusiasts had to find their athletic thrills either by visiting the diamond, gridiron or hardwood, or by watching on TV. Though many marvelous sports movies were still to be made well into the future, and though adult sports novels and sports mysteries would eventually proliferate late in the 20th century, nothing like the thousands of stories told in the first 70 years of sports fiction would ever be seen again.

Appendix A:
Sports Pulp Magazines

The first sports pulp magazine, *Sport Story* from Street & Smith, appeared in 1923, and the last, *Super Sports* from Columbia Publications, was published in 1957.

Much of the previous information published on this topic has been wildly inaccurate. I have consulted with most of the leading pulp specialists and collectors while spending more than two decades compiling this list. Since there has never been a complete index of all sports pulps, unlike the science fiction, hero, detective magazines and weird fantasy pulps, a few questions remain and a few issues may remain to be discovered. The Columbia pulps, in particular, have not been extensively collected, and research and discovery continues.

Ace Sports (Ace)—Jan. 1936 (Vol. 1 #1) through Nov. 1943 (Vol. 15 #4) breaks to Nov. 1947 (Vol. 15 #5) through Vol. 17 #4 (Jan. 1949); 68 issues. Four issues to a volume; there is no Vol. 16 #1. An error produced Vol. 15 #5 and the next issue is Jan. 1948 (Vol. 16 #2).

All-American Football Stories (Fiction House)—Fall 1938 (Vol. 1 #1) through Vol. 2 #12 (Fall 1953), 24 issues. Single issues in years 1938 to 1941 and 1950 to 1953; two issues from 1942 to 1949.

All-American Sports (Columbia)—Dec. 1940 (Vol. 1 #1) through Feb. 1941 (Vol. 1 #2). 2 issues.

All-American Sports (All-America Publishers)—Dec. 1933 through Sept. 1938; 45 issues.

All Baseball Stories (Goodman)—Oct. 1947 (Vol. 1 #1); one-shot.

All Basketball Stories (Goodman)—Winter 1947-48 (Vol. 1 #1); one-shot.

All Football Stories (Goodman)—Dec. 1947 (Vol. 1 #1); one-shot.

All Sports (Columbia)—Oct. 1939 (Vol. 1 #1) through Winter 1944-1945 (Vol. 4 #2); Nov. 1948 (Vol. 4 #3(?)); Feb. 1949 (Vol. 4 #4) through Sept. 1951 (Vol. 7 #1). There may be 21 issues, not 20, in the first run, since there were two Vol. 2 # 3 issues (March and May 1942); apparently there are 17 issues in the second run.

Athlete (Street & Smith)—Aug. 1939 (Vol. 1 #1) through April 1940 (Vol. 2 #3); nine issues. Some issues are about half fact, part fiction.

Baseball Stories (Fiction House)—Spring 1938 (Vol. 1 #1) through Vol. 3 #9 (Spring 1954); 33 issues.

Basketball Stories (Fiction House)—Winter 1937-1938 (Vol. 1 #1); one-shot.

Best Football Novels (Standard/Thrilling)—Dec. 1942 (Vol. 1 #1); one-shot.

Best Sports (Goodman)—Jan. 1937 (Vol. 1 #1) through Vol. 2 #4 (June 1939); Vol. 2 #1 (Oct. 1947) through Vol. 2 #4 (Sept. 1948); Vol. 2 #5 (Feb. 1950) through Vol. 2 #10 (Dec. 1951); 10 issues in the first four issues in the second run; six issues in the third run. When the series resumed in 1947, the numbering went back to Vol. 2 #1.

Big Baseball (Goodman)—May 1948 (Vol. 1 #1) through Nov. 1948 (Vol. 1. #3); 3 issues.

Big Book Sports (Goodman)—Nov. 1947 (Vol. 1 #1) through Winter 1947-1948 (Vol. 1 #2); 2 issues.

Big Sports (Goodman)—May 1948 (Vol. 1 #1) through Nov. 1948 (Vol. 1. #3); 4 issues. Sept. 1948 and Nov. 1948 are both listed Vol. 1 #3.

Blue Ribbon Sports (Columbia)—Dec. 1937 (Vol. 1 #1) through April 1940 (Vol. 2 #6); Oct. 1940 (Vol. 3 #1(?)); apparently 13 issues.

First issue has been listed incorrectly as April 1937.

Bulls-Eye Sports (Fiction House) — Winter 1938-39 (Vol. 1 #1) through Fall 1939 (Vol. 1 #3); 3 issues. No issue for Summer 1939.

Complete Sports (Goodman) — March 1937 (Vol. 1 #1) through Jan. 1943 (Vol. 4 #4); April 1943 reported (Vol. 4 #5(?)); March 1946 reported (Vol. 4 #6(?)); Sept.-Oct. 1946 (Vol. 5 #1) through Oct. 1955 (Vol. 10 #1). Apparently there are 24 issues in the first run and 38 issues in the second fun. June 1937 and Sept. 1937 are both Vol. 1 #2; June 1947 and Sept. 1947 are both Vol. 5 #4, with no Vol. 5 #5; Volume 7 has 12 issues.

Champion Sports (Ace) — March 1937 (Vol. 1 #1) through May 1939 (Vol. 4 #1); 13 issues, but possibly 14 issues, since Nov. 1937 has been reported (Vol. 1 #5(?) or a second Vol. 1 #4(?)). Jan. 1938 is Vol. 2 #1.

Dime Sports (Popular) — July 1935 (Vol. 1 #1) through June 1944 (Vol. 14 #3); 81 issues. Resumed in 1947 as New Sports, selling for 15 cents.

Exciting Baseball (Standard/Thrilling) — Spring 1949 (Vol. 1 #1) through undated 1951 issue (Vol. 1 #4); Spring 1953 (Vol. 2 #1); 5 issues.

Exciting Football (Standard/Thrilling) — Winter 1941-42 (Vol. 1 # 1) through Fall 1951 (Vol. 5#1); 11 issues. The series jumps from Vol. 1 #1 to Vol. 2 #1.

Exciting Sports (Standard/Thrilling) — Winter 1940-41 (Vol. 1 #1) through Summer 1950 (Vol. 13 #2); 38 issues. This becomes *Five Sports Classics.*

Fifteen Sports Stories (Popular) — Feb. 1948 (Vol. 1 #1) through April 1952 (Vol. 8 #2); 30 issues.

Five Sports Classics (Standard/Thrilling) — Fall 1950 (Vol. 13 #3) through Summer 1951 (Vol. 14 #3); 4 issues. All issues have credited reprints; this is formerly *Exciting Sports.*

Football Action (Fiction House) — Fall 1939 (Vol. 1 #1) through Fall 1953 (Vol. 3 #1); 23 issues. There is no Vol. 2 #1 or Vol. 2 #2; title jumps from Fall 1946 (Vol. 1 #12) to Second Fall 1946 (Vol. 2 #3). Single issues 1939–1941 and 1950–1953; two issues 1942–1949.

Football Stories (Fiction House) — Fall 1937 (Vol. 1 #1) through Fall 1953 (Vol. 3 #1); 25 issues. Single issues 1937–1941 and 1950–1953; two issues 1942–1949. Since the First Fall Issue of Football Stories in 1946 is accurately

numbered Vol. 2 #2, that may have caused the error that led to the Second Fall 1946 of *Football Action* to be incorrectly numbered Vol. 2 #3.

New Sports (Popular) — Jan. 1947 (Vol. 1 #1) through July 1951 (Vol. 9 #2); 34 issues. This is the resumption of *Dime Sports*, but since it cost 15 cents, the title was changed.

Popular Baseball (Standard/Thrilling) — Spring 1949 (Vol. 1 #1) through Spring 1951 (Vol. 1 #3); 4 issues. Both Summer 1950 and Spring 1951 are Vol. 1 #3. Issues listed in some pulp guides for Spring 1942, 1943 and 1944 may have been copyrighted, but have not been seen.

Popular Football (Standard/Thrilling) — Winter 1940/1941 (Vol. 1 #1) through Fall 1951 (Vol. 6 #3); 12 issues. Volumes 1, 2 and 3 contain only one issue each.

Popular Sports (Standard/Thrilling) July 1937 (Vol. 1 #1) through Spring 1951 (Vol. 22 #2); 63 issues. Feb. and April 1939 are both Vol. 4 #2; Volume 16 does not exist; Summer 1947 is Vol. 15 #3; Fall 1947 is Vol. 17 #1.

Real Sports (Goodman) — Jan. 1938 (Does this exist? Vol. 1 #1(?)); Feb. 1938 (Vol. 1 #2) through April 1939 (Vol. 1 #6); Oct. 1947 (Vol. 1 #7) through Nov. 1948 (Vol. 1 #12); 11 issues, possibly 12.

Sport Story (Street & Smith) — Sept. 1923 (Vol. 1 #1) through July 1943 (volume # uncertain). Company listed 429 issues, mostly twice a month.

Sport Story Annual (Street & Smith) — 1942; 1 issue.

Sports Action (Goodman) — Dec. 1937 (Vol. 1 #1) through Oct. 1942 (Vol. 3 #5); Aug. 1947 (Vol. 4 #1) through Vol. 4 #5 (Dec. 1948); 17 issues in the first run. Is there an 18th issue? 5 issues in the second run, including reported Dec. 1948 issue.

Sports Fiction (Columbia) — April 1938 (Vol. 1 #1) through Summer 1944 (Vol. 5 #2); June 1947 (Vol. 5 #3(?)) through Sept. 1951 (Vol. 8 # 4); apparently 23 issues in first series and 20 issues in second series.

Sports Leaders (Goodman) — April 1948 (Vol. 1 #1) through Oct. 1948 (Vol. 1 #3); 3 issues.

Sports Novels (Popular) — April-May 1937 (Vol. 1 #1) through Vol. 11 #1 (July 1944); breaks to Feb. 1946 (Vol. 11 #2) through April 1952 (Vol. 22 #1); 85 issues.

Sports Short Stories (Goodman) — Dec. 1947 (Vol. 1 #1) through Nov. 1948 (Vol. 1 # 4); 4 issues.

Sports Winners (Columbia)—Feb. 1938 (Vol. 1 #1) through Spring 1944 (Vol. 4 #6); Oct. 1950 (Vol. 5 #1(?)) through April 1952 (Vol. 6 #1). First series apparently 24 issues; second series apparently 7 issues. Becomes *Ten Story Sports.*

Star Sports (Goodman)—Oct. 1936 (Vol. 1 #1) through Nov. 1938 (Vol. 2#4); 10 issues.

Super Sports (Columbia)—Sept. 1938 (Vol. 2 #1) through April 1944 (Vol. 5 #3(?)); July 1946 (Vol. 5 #4) through Sept. 1954 (Vol. 11 #1); a second September issue (Vol. 11 #2) has been reported; annuals in 1955, 1956 and 1957; apparently 21 issues in first series and possibly 42 issues on second run. Vol. 1 does not exist. June 1947 and Sept. 1947 are both Vol. 6 # 3.

Ten Story Sports (Columbia)—July 1937 (volume and # uncertain) through Dec. 1937 (Vol. 5 #2) and on to June 1941 (Vol. 7 #5), then breaks to July 1952 (Vol. 6 #2) (formerly *Sports Winners* Vol. 6 #1) through Jan. 1957 (Vol. 9 #2); apparently 18 issues in first series and 19 issues in second series. Sept. 1938 indicia error lists Vol. 6 #5 instead of correct Vol. 5 #6.

Thrilling Baseball (Standard/Thrilling)— Summer 1949 (Vol. 1 #1) through Spring 1951 (Vol. 1 #3); 3 issues.

Thrilling Football (Standard/Thrilling)— 1939 undated (Vol. 1. #1) through Fall 1952 (Vol. 7 #2); 14 issues. Volumes 1, 2 and 3 have only one issue each.

Thrilling Sports (Standard/Thrilling)— Sept. 1936 (Vol. 1 #1) through Spring 1951 (Vol. 24 #3); Summer 1951 (Vol. 25 #4); Vol. 25 #1, 2, 3 do not exist; Summer 1951 is numbered Vol. 25 #4 in error. Fall 1951 reported; is this Vol. 26#1(?) 74 issues.

Twelve Sports Aces (Ace)—Dec. 1938 (Vol. 1# 2), formerly *Variety Sports*; through Dec. 1943 (Vol. 8 #2); 29 issues.

Variety Sports (Ace)—Sept. 1938; one-shot, becomes *Twelve Sports Aces.*

Additions and corrections are welcomed.

With thanks to pulp experts John Gunnison, Doug Ellis, John Locke, John DeWalt, Tim Cottrill, Al Tonik, Will Murray, Randy Vanderbeek, David Saunders, Frank Robinson, Mark Leonard, Brian Earl Brown, Bob Carter, Richard Hall, Rusty Hevelin and Ed Hulse.

Appendix B: Sports Heroes in Comic Books, 1939–1967

When modern comic books first appeared in the mid–1930s, they were almost all filled with popular syndicated newspaper reprint strips. With the coming of original costume heroes and other genre characters in the late 1930s and early 1940s, a few sports heroes began to appear. Most of what few sports comics began to appear in the 1940s were nonfiction, however. The following list includes only fictional characters involved in baseball, football or basketball through the 1960s, although they weren't necessarily involved in team sports in every appearance. Each character's name is followed by the titles in which the character appeared:

Babe, Darling of the Hills (female baseball player; humor/satire): "Babe" #1 (June-July 1948) to #11 (April-May 1950); Feature Publications.

Bart Bradley, Teen Athlete: "Wonder Comics" #8 (October 1946) to #10 (February 1947); "America's Best Comics" #30 (April 1949) to #31 (July 1949); Standard (Pines) Comics.

The Champ: Champ Comics #2 (December 1939) to #24 (Dec. 1942); title changes to Champion Comics with # 11; Harvey Comics.

Chat Chatfield of Rock Ridge High (coach): "Chat Chatfield of Rock Ridge High" #1 (October 1967), one-shot; Charlton Publications.

Cotton Woods: Dell Four Color Series #837 (September 1957), one-shot; Dell Comics.

Dan Duffy, College Athlete: "Thrilling Comics" #8 (September 1940) to #29 (August 1942), except not in #26; Standard (Pines) Comics.

Dick Cole, Wonder Boy: "Blue Bolt Comics" #1 (June 1940) to Vol. 10, #2 (#101), September-October 1949; "Four Most Comics"

#1 (Winter 1941-1942) to Vol. 7, #6 (#30); "Dick Cole" #1 (December 1948-January 1949) to #10 (June-July 1950), reprints; Novelty Press/Star Publications; "Sports Thrills" #11 (November 1950) to #15 (November 1951), reprints; (Dick Cole became Sports Thrills); Star Publications.

Frank Merriwell: "Shadow Comics" #1 (undated 1940 issue) to #4 (June 1940); Street & Smith Publications; "Frank Merriwell at Yale" #1 (June 1955) to #4 (January 1956); Charlton Publications.

Gil Thorp (coach): "Gil Thorp" #1 (May-July 1963), one-shot; Dell Comics.

Hardy of Hillsdale High: "Cannonball Comics" #1 (February 1945) to #2 (March 1945); Rural Home Publications.

Iron Vic: Singles Series #22 (undated 1940), one-shot; United Features Syndicate; "Comics Revue" #3 (August 1947); St. John.

Jody and the Flaming Dipper Ball (humor/satire): "Smash-Hit Sports Comics" #1 (January 1949), one-shot; Essankay Publications.

Lefty Flynn: "Doc Savage Comics" #4 (May 1941); Street & Smith Publications.

Ozark Ike: "Dell Four Color Series" #180 (February 1948); #11 (November 1948) to #25 (September 1952); Standard Comics.

Rip Rory: "Target Comics" #1 (February 1940) to #4 (May 1940); Novelty Press; "Dick Cole" #9 (April-May 1950) to #10 (June-July 1950), reprints from Target; Star Publications.

Rube Rooky: "Baseball Comics" #1 (Spring 1949), one shot; Will Eisner Publications.

Speed Spaulding, College Athlete: "Sparkling Stars Comics" #2 (July 1944) to #21 (January 1947) except not in #7 and #20; Holyoke Publications.

Speed Taylor of Clayton College: "Speed Comics" #12 (March 1941) to #25 (February 1943); becomes Marine strip; Harvey Comics.

"Sports Action Comics" (anthology with no continuing characters): #10 (January 1952) to #14 (September 1952); first nine issues were nonfiction; Marvel.

"Strange Sports Stories" (science fiction anthology): "Brave and the Bold" #45 (December 1962–January 1963) to #49 (August-September 1963); DC Comics. (Reprints appeared in the 1970s.)

Swat Malone: "Swat Malone Comics" #1 (September 1955), one-shot; Swat Malone Enterprises.

Vic Verity: "Vic Verity Comics" #1 (undated 1945 issue) to #7 (September 1946); Fawcett Publications.

Note: Characters such as Archie and Superboy sometimes played baseball, but this list includes only characters designed as athletes.

Bibliography

Books

Alexander, David T., and Robert Crestohl. *The Baseball and Sports Publications Price Guide: Listings from 1860 to 1997*. Tampa: Century of Sports, 1997.

American Boy Sports Stories. New York: Doubleday, Doran, 1929.

Archibald, Joe. *Catcher's Choice*. Philadelphia: Macrae-Smith, 1958.

_____. *The Easy Out*. Philadelphia: Macrae-Smith, 1965.

_____. *Go, Navy, Go*. Philadelphia: Macrae-Smith, 1956.

_____. *Outfield Orphan*. Philadelphia: Macrae-Smith, 1961.

_____. *Powerback*. Philadelphia: Macrae-Smith, 1970.

_____. *West Point Wingback*. Philadelphia: Macrae-Smith, 1965.

Armstrong, Richard B., and Mary Willems Armstrong. *The Movie List Book: A Reference Guide to Film Themes, Settings and Series*. Jefferson, NC: McFarland, 1990.

Asinof, Elliot, *Man on Spikes*. New York: McGraw-Hill, 1955.

Axe, John. *All About Collecting Boys' Series Books*. Grantsville, MD: Hobby House, 2002.

Barbour, Ralph Henry. *For the Honor of the School*. New York: Appleton, 1900.

Bancroft, Edith. *Jane Allen, Center*. New York: Cupples & Leon 1920.

_____. *Jane Allen, Right Guard*. New York: Cupples & Leon, 1918.

_____. *Jane Allen of the Sub Team*. New York: Cupples & Leon, 1917.

Becker, Stephen. *Comic Art in America*. New York: Simon and Schuster, 1959.

Bee, Clair. (Chip Hilton series). *Backboard Fever*. New York: Grosset & Dunlap, 1953.

_____. *Backcourt Ace*. New York: Grosset & Dunlap, 1961.

_____. *Buzzer Basket*. New York: Grosset & Dunlap, 1962.

_____. *Championship Ball*, New York: Grosset & Dunlap, 1949.

_____. *Comeback Cagers*. New York: Grosset & Dunlap, 1963.

_____. *Clutch Hitter!* New York: Grosset & Dunlap, 1949.

_____. *Dugout Jinx*. New York: Grosset & Dunlap, 1952.

_____. *Fence Busters*. New York: Grosset & Dunlap, 1953.

_____. *Fourth Down Showdown*. New York: Grosset & Dunlap, 1957.

_____. *Freshman Quarterback*. New York: Grosset & Dunlap, 1952.

_____. *Hardcourt Upset*. New York: Grosset & Dunlap, 1957.

_____. *Home Run Feud*. New York: Grosset & Dunlap, 1964.

_____. *Hoop Crazy*. New York: Grosset & Dunlap, 1950.

_____. *Hungry Hurler*. New York: Grosset & Dunlap, 1966.

_____. *No-Hitter*. New York: Grosset & Dunlap, 1959.

_____. *A Pass and a Prayer*. New York: Grosset & Dunlap, 1951.

_____. *Payoff Pitch*. New York: Grosset & Dunlap, 1958.

_____. *Pitchers' Duel*. New York: Grosset & Dunlap, 1950.

_____. *Strike Three!* New York: Grosset & Dunlap, 1949.

_____. *Ten Seconds to Play!* New York: Grosset & Dunlap, 1955.

_____. *Touchdown Pass*. New York: Grosset & Dunlap, 1948.

_____. *Tournament Crisis*. New York: Grosset & Dunlap, 1957.

_____. *Triple Threat Trouble*. New York: Grosset & Dunlap, 1960.

Berrill, Jack. *Gil Thorp Silver Anniversary Yearbook: 1958–1959 to 1983–1984*. Arlington Heights, IL: Take Five Productions, 1984.

Billman, Carol. *The Secret of the Stratemeyer Syndicate: Nancy Drew, the Hardy Boys and the Million Dollar Fiction Factory. New York: Ungar, 1986.

Bishop, Curtis. *Banjo Hitter*. Austin, Texas: Steck, 1951.

_____. *Rebound*. Philadelphia: Lippincott, 1962.

Bowen, Robert Sidney. *Ball Hawk*. New York: Lothrop, Lee & Shepard, 1950.

_____. *Fourth Down*. New York: Lothrop, Lee & Shepard, 1949.

_____. *Infield Spark*. New York: Lothrop, Lee & Shepard, 1955.

_____. *Touchdown Kid*. New York: Lothrop, Lee & Shepard, 1951.

_____. *Winning Pitch*. New York: Lothrop, Lee & Shepard, 1948.

Bragin, Charles. *Dime Novels: Bibliography 1860–1928*. Brooklyn: Charles Bragin, 1938.

Bronson, Eric. *Baseball and Philosophy: Thinking Outside the Batter's Box*. Chicago: Open Court, 2004.

Bruce, George. *Navy Blue and Gold: A Story of the Naval Academy*. New York: Grosset & Dunlap, 1936.

Burns, Grant. *The Sports Pages: A Critical Bibliography of Twentieth-Century American Novels and Stories Featuring Baseball, Basketball, Football and Other Athletic Pursuits*. Metuchen, NJ: Scarecrow Press, 1987.

Carol, Bill J. (pseudonym for Bill Knott). *Squeeze Play*. Austin, TX: Steck-Vaughn, 1971.

Cebulash, Mel, *Ruth Marini, Dodger Ace*. Minneapolis: Lerner, 1983.

_____. *Ruth Marini, World Series Star*. Minneapolis: Lerner, 1985.

_____. *Ruth Marini of the Dodgers*. Minneapolis: Lerner, 1983.

Clear, Richard E. *Old Magazines: Identification and Value Guide*. 2nd ed. Paducah, KY: Collector Books, 2006.

Christopher, Matt. *Baseball Pals*. Boston: Little, Brown, 1956.

_____. *The Lucky Baseball Bat*. Boston: Little, Brown, 1954.

Chute, B.J. *Blocking Back*. New York: MacMillan, 1938; New York: Dutton, 1966 (revised edition).

_____. *Teen-age Sport Parade*. New York: Lantern Press, 1949.

Cooke, David. *While the Crowd Cheers*. New York: Dutton, 1953.

Coombs, Charles. *Teen-Age Treasure Chest of Sports Stories*. New York: Lantern Press, 1948.

_____. *Young Infield Rookie*. New York: Lantern Press, 1954.

_____. *Young Readers' Basketball Stories*. New York: Lantern Press, 1951.

_____. *Young Readers' Stories of the Diamond*. New York: Lantern Press, 1951.

Cooper, John R. (Stratemeyer Syndicate pseudonym). (Mel Martin series.) *The College League Mystery*. New York: Cupples & Leon, 1953.

_____. *The Fighting Shortstop*. New York: Cupples & Leon, 1953.

_____. *First Base Jinx*. New York: Cupples & Leon, 1952.

_____. *Mystery at the Ball Park*. New York: Cupples & Leon, 1947.

_____. *The Phantom Homer*. New York Cupples & Leon, 1952.

_____. *The Southpaw's Secret*. New York: Cupples & Leon, 1952.

Cottrill, Tim. *Bookery's Guide to Pulps and Related Magazines*. 2nd ed. Fairborn, OH: Bookery Press, 2005.

Cox, William R. *Five Were Chosen*. New York: Dodd, Mead, 1956.

Davies, Valentine. *It Happens Every Spring*. New York: Farrar, Straus, 1949.

Dawson, Elmer. *Gary Grayson's Hill Street Eleven*. New York: Grosset & Dunlap, 1926.

Decker, Duane (Blue Sox Series). *The Big Stretch*. New York: Morrow, 1952.

_____. *The Catcher from Double-A*. New York: Morrow, 1950.

_____. *Fast Man on a Pivot*. New York: Morrow, 1951.

_____. *Good Field, No Hit*. New York: Mill, 1947.

_____. *The Grand Slam Kid*. New York: Morrow, 1964.

_____. *Hit and Run*. New York: Mil and Morrow, 1949.

_____. *Long Ball to Left Field*. New York: Morrow, 1958.

_____. *Mister Shortstop*. New York: Morrow, 1954.

_____. *Rebel in Right Field*. New York: Morrow, 1961.

_____. *Showboat Southpaw*. New York: Morrow, 1960.

_____. *Starting Pitcher*. New York: Mill and Morrow, 1948.

_____. *Switch Hitter*. New York: Morrow, 1953.

_____. *Third Base Rookie*. New York: Morrow, 1959.

Dinan, John. *Sports in the Pulp Magazines*. Jefferson, NC: McFarland, 1998.

Douglas, Gilbert. *Hard to Tackle*. New York: Crowell, 1956.

Duin, Steve, and Mike Richardson. *Comics Between the Panels*. Milwaukie, OR: Dark Horse Comics, 1998.

Dunning, John. *Tune In Yesterday: The Ultimate Encyclopedia of Old-Time Radio 1925–1976*. Englewood Cliffs. NJ: Prentice-Hall, 1976.

Edelman, Rob. *Great Baseball Films*. New York: Citadel, 1994.

Einstein, Charles, ed. *The Fireside Book of Baseball*. New York: Simon & Schuster, 1956.

_____. *The Fireside Book of Baseball.* 2nd ed. New York: Simon & Schuster, 1958.

_____. *The Only Game in Town.* New York: Dell, 1955.

_____. *Win — Or Else!* (as D.J. Michael). New York: Lion Books, 1954.

Ellis, Doug, John Locke, and John Gunnison. *The Adventure House Guide to the Pulps.* Silver Spring, MD: Adventure House, 2000.

Emburg, Kate. *The Girls' Series Companion.* 1995 ed. N. Highlands, CA: Society of Phantom Friends, 1995.

Erickson, Hal. *The Baseball Filmography, 1915 Through 2001.* 2nd ed. Jefferson, NC: McFarland, 2002.

Fenner, Phyllis, ed. *Crack of the Bat.* New York: Knopf, 1952.

Fitzgerald, Edward. *College Slugger.* New York: Barnes, 1950..

_____. *The Turning Point.* New York: Barnes, 1948

_____. *Yankee Rookie.* New York: Barnes, 1952.

Fitzsimmons, Courtland. *Death on the Diamond.* New York: McBride, 1941, and New York: Grosset & Dunlap, 1932.

_____. *70,000 Witnesses.* New York: Stokes, 1934, and New York: Grosset & Dunlap, 1935.

Fletcher, Flora. *The Hot-Shot.* New York: Avon Books, 1956.

Frank, Jane. *The Art of Richard Powers.* London: Paper Tiger, 2001.

Frick, C.H. (pseudonym for Constance H. Irwin). *Five Against the Odds.* New York: Harcourt, Brace, 1955.

_____. *Tourney Team.* New York: Harcourt, Brace, 1954.

Friendlich, Dick. *Baron of the Bullpen.* Philadelphia: Westminster, 1954.

_____. *Pivot Man.* Philadelphia: Westminster, 1949.

_____. *Touchdown Maker.* Garden City, NY: Doubleday, 1966.

_____. *Warrior Forward.* Philadelphia: Westminster, 1950.

Furman, A.L., ed. *Everygirls Sports Stories.* New York: Grosset & Dunlap, 1956.

Gault, William Campbell. *Backfield Challenge.* New York: Dutton, 1967.

_____. *Mr. Fullback,* New York: Dutton, 1954.

Gehring, Wes D. *Mr. Deeds Goes to Yankee Stadium: Baseball Films in the Capra Tradition.* Jefferson, NC: McFarland, 2004.

Gerber, Ernst, and Mary Gerber. *The Photo Journal Guide to Comic Books.* 2 vols. Minden, NV: Gerber, 1989–1990.

Gipson, Morrell, ed. *Calling All Girls.* New York: Grosset & Dunlap, 1959.

Goodstone, Tony, ed. *The Pulps.* New York: Chelsea House, 1970.

Gotto, Ray. Introduction by Max Allan Collins.

Cotton Woods. Princeton, WI: Kitchen Sink, 1991.

Goulart, Ron, ed. *The Encyclopedia of American Comics from 1897 to the Present.* New York: Facts on File, 1990.

Gregorich, Barbara. *Women at Play: The Story of Women in Baseball.* San Diego, Harvest, 1993.

Grey, Zane. *The Red-Headed Outfield and other Baseball Stories.* New York: Grosset & Dunlap, 1915.

_____. *The Short-Stop.* Chicago: McClurg, 1909, and various Grosset & Dunlap reprints.

_____. *The Young Pitcher.* New York: Harper, 1911, and various Grosset & Dunlap reprints.

Haining, Peter. *Cheap Thrills.* New Rochelle, NY: Arlington House, 1972.

_____. *The Classic Era of American Pulp Magazines.* Chicago: Chicago Review Press, 2000.

Hano, Arnold. *A Day in the Bleachers.* New York: DeCapo, 1982 (reprint of 1955 edition).

Hersey, Harold. *The New Pulpwood Editor Illustrated: The Fabulous World of Thriller Magazines Revealed by a Veteran Editor and Publisher.* Silver Spring, MD: Adventure House, 2002 (reprint of 1937 original).

Holroyd, Graham. *Paperback Prices and Checklist.* Chattanooga, TN: Guide Media, 2003.

Homme, Joseph, and Cheryl Homme. *Storybook Culture: The Art of Popular Children's Books.* Portland, OR: Collectors, 2002.

Jones, Diane McClure, and Rosemary Jones. *Boys' and Girls' Book Series: Real World Adventures.* Paducah, KY: Collector, 2002.

Karlen, Neal. *Slouching Toward Fargo.* New York: Avon, 1999.

Keltner, Howard. *Golden Age Comic Books Index.* Gainesville, TX: Keltner, 1998.

Krout, John Allen. *Annals of American Sport.* New Haven, CT: Yale University Press, 1929.

Lesser, Robert. *Pulp Art: Original Cover Paintings for the Great American Pulp Magazines.* New York: Gramercy, 1997.

Libby, Bill. *Charlie O. and the Angry A's.* Garden City, NY: Doubleday, 1975.

Locke, John, ed. *Pulp Fictioneers: Adventures in the Storytelling Business.* Silver Spring, MD: Adventure House, 2004.

_____. *Pulpwood Days: Editors You Want to Know.* Elkhorn, CA: Off-Trail, 2007.

Lyles, William H. *Dell Paperbacks 1942 to Mid-1962.* Westport, CT: Greenwood, 1983.

Manchel, Frank. *Great Sports Movies.* New York: Franklin Watts, 1980.

Mattson, E. Christian, and Thomas B. Davis. *A Collector's Guide to Hardcover Boys' Series Books, 1872–1993.* Newark, DE: MAD Book, 1997.

McCue, Andy. *Baseball by the Books.* Dubuque, IA: William C. Brown, 1991.

Miller, Don. *"B" Movies*. New York: Curtis, 1973.

Miller, John Jackson, Maggie Thompson, Peter Bickford, and Brent Frankenhoff. *Comics Buyers Guide Standard Catalog of Comic Books*. 4th ed. Iola, WI: KP, 2005.

Most, Marshall, and Robert Rudd. *Stars, Stripes and Diamonds: American Culture and the Baseball Film*. Jefferson, NC: McFarland, 2006.

Nevins, Jess. *Pulp Magazine Holdings Directory: Library Collections in North America and Europe*. Jefferson, NC: McFarland, 2007.

Nolan, Michelle. *Covering the Boys of Summer in "The Baseball and Sports Publications Price Guide: Listings from 1860 to 1997."* Tampa: Century of Sports, 1997.

_____. *Love on the Racks: A History of American Romance Comics*. Jefferson, NC: McFarland, 2008.

Nye, Russel. *The Unembarrassed Muse: The Popular Arts in America*. New York: Dial, 1970.

Oriard, Michael. *Dreaming of Heroes: American Sports Fiction, 1868–1980*. Chicago: Nelson-Hall, 1982.

_____. *King Football*. Chapel Hill: University of North Carolina Press, 2000.

_____. *Reading Football: How the Popular Press Created an American Spectacle*. Chapel Hill: University of North Carolina Press, 1993.

O'Rourke, Frank. *Bonus Rookie*. New York: Barnes, 1950.

_____. *The Catcher, and The Manager*. New York: Barnes, 1953.

_____. *The Football Gravy Train*. New York: Barnes, 1951.

_____. *The Greatest Victory and Other Baseball Stories*. New York: Barnes, 1952.

_____. *The Heavenly World Series and Other Baseball Stories*. New York: Barnes, 1952.

_____. *Never Come Back*. New York: Barnes, 1952.

_____. *Nine Good Men*. New York: Barnes, 1952.

_____. *The Team*. New York: Barnes, 1950.

Overstreet, Robert. *The Official Overstreet Comic Book Price Guide*. 38th ed. New York: House of Collectibles, and Timonium, MD: Gemstone, 2008.

Owen, Frank, ed. *Teen-Age Sports Stories*. New York: Lantern Press, 1947.

Patten, Gilbert. *Frank Merriwell's "Father."* Norman: University of Oklahoma Press, 1964.

Plowright, Frank, ed. *The Slings & Arrows Comic Guide*. 2nd ed. Great Britain: Slings & Arrows, 2003.

Porter, Mark (pseudonym for Robert Leckie and others) (Win Hadfield series). *Duel on the Cinders*. New York: Simon & Schuster, 1960.

_____. *Keeper Play*. New York: Simon & Schuster, 1960.

_____. *Overtime Upset*. New York: Simon & Schuster, 1960.

_____. *Set Point*. New York: Simon & Schuster, 1960.

_____. *Slashing Blades*. New York: Simon & Schuster, 1960.

_____. *The Winning Pitcher*. New York: Simon & Schuster, 1960

Reichler, Joseph, ed. *The Baseball Encyclopedia*. 7th ed. New York: Macmillan, 1988.

Reilly, John M., ed. *Twentieth-Century Crime and Mystery Writers*. 2nd ed. New York: St. Martin's, 1985.

Renick, Marion. *The Dooleys Play Ball*. New York: Scribner's, 1949.

Reynolds, Quentin. *The Fiction Factory: From Pulp Row to Quality Street*. New York: Random House, 1955.

Robbins, Trina. *From Girls to Grrrlz: A History of Girls' Comics from Teens to Zines*. San Francisco: Chronicle, 1999.

Robinson, Frank, and Lawrence Davidson. *Pulp Culture: The Art of Fiction Magazines*. Portland, OR: Collectors, 1998.

Robinson, Jerry. *The Comics: An Illustrated History of Comic Strip Art*. New York: G.P. Putnam's Sons, 1974.

Scholz, Jackson V. *Backfield Buccaroo*. New York: Morrow, 1967.

_____. *Bench Boss*. New York: Morrow, 1958.

_____. *Dugout Tycoon*. New York: Morrow, 1963.

_____. *Fielder from Nowhere*. New York: Morrow, 1950.

_____. *A Fighting Chance*. New York: Morrow, 1956.

_____. *Fullback Fever*. New York: Morrow, 1969.

_____. *Halfback on His Own*. New York: Morrow, 1962.

_____. *Johnny King, Quarterback* New York: Morrow, 1944.

_____. *One-Man Team*. New York: Morrow, 1953.

_____. *Pigskin Warriors*. New York: Morrow, 1944.

Server, Lee. *Encyclopedia of Pulp Fiction Writers*. New York: Checkmark Books, 2002.

Sheed, Wilfrid. *Baseball and Lesser Sports*. New York: HarperCollins, 1991.

Sherman, Harold. *Hold That Line!* New York: Grosset & Dunlap, 1930.

_____. *Touchdown!* New York: Grosset & Dunlap, 1927.

Smith, Red, ed. *The Saturday Evening Post Sports Stories*. New York: Barnes, 1949.

Stratemeyer, Edward. *Baseball Joe Series*. New York: Grosset & Dunlap, 1912–1928.

Terrill, Rogers, ed. *The Argosy Book of Sports Stories*. New York: Barnes, 1953.

Tunis, John. *All-American*. New York: Harcourt, Brace, 1942.

_____. *Buddy and the Old Pro*. New York: Harcourt, Brace, 1955.

_____. *Champion's Choice*. New York: Harcourt, Brace, 1940.

_____. *A City for Lincoln*. New York: Harcourt, Brace, 1945.

_____. *The Duke Decides*. New York: Harcourt, Brace, 1939.

_____. *Go, Team, Go!* New York: Harcourt, Brace, 1954.

_____. *Highpockets*. New York: Harcourt, Brace, 1948.

_____. *The Iron Duke*. New York: Harcourt, Brace, 1938.

_____. *Keystone Kids*. New York: Harcourt, Brace, 1943.

_____. *A Kid Comes Back*. New York: Harcourt, Brace, 1946.

_____. *The Kid from Tomkinsville*. New York: Harcourt, Brace, 1940.

_____. *A Measure of Independence*. New York: Atheneum, 1964.

_____. *Rookie of the Year*. New York: Harcourt, Brace, 1944.

_____. *Schoolboy Johnson*. New York: Harcourt, Brace, 1958.

_____. *World Series*. New York: Harcourt, Brace, 1941.

_____. *Yea! Wildcats!* New York: Harcourt, Brace, 1944.

_____. *Young Razzle*. New York: Harcourt, Brace, 1949.

Umphlett, Wiley Lee, ed. *The Achievement of American Sport Literature: A Critical Appraisal*. Teaneck, NJ: Fairleigh Dickenson University Press, 1991.

Vetter, Marjorie, ed. *Stories to Live By: A Treasury of Fiction from The American Girl*. New York: Platt & Munk, 1960.

Voger, Mark. *Hero Gets Girl! The Life and Art of Kurt Schaffenberger*. Raleigh, NC: TwoMorrows, 2003.

Walden, Amelia Elizabeth. *A Girl Called Hank*. New York: Morrow, 1951.

Walker, Donald E., and B. Lee Cooper. *Baseball and American Culture: A Thematic Bibliography of Over 4,500 Works*. Jefferson, NC: McFarland, 1995.

Wallace, Francis. *Big Game*. Boston: Little, Brown, 1936.

_____. *Big League Rookie*. Philadelphia: Westminister Press, 1950.

Wallenfeldt, Jeffrey H., ed. *Sports Movies: A Guide to Nearly 500 Films Focusing on Sports*. Evanston, IL: CineBooks, 1989.

Waugh, Colton. *The Comics*. New York: Macmillan, 1947.

Weiss, Ken, and Ed Goodgold, eds. *To Be Continued...: 231 Serials*. Crown, 1972.

White, David Manning, and Robert H. Abel, eds. *The Funnies: An American Idiom*. London, Collier-Macmillan, 1963.

Wood, Stephen C., and J. Davis Pincus. *Reel Baseball*. Jefferson, NC: McFarland, 2003.

Wright, Jack (pseudonym for Elsie Wright). *On the Forty Yard Line*. Cleveland: World Syndicate Publishing Co., 1932.

Zim, Herbert S., ed. *Sports Alive! Fact and Fiction*. Chicago: Spencer, 1960.

Magazines

Beaumont, Charles. "The Bloody Pulps." *Playboy*, September 1962.

Bergen, Philip. "Roy Tucker, Not Roy Hobbs: The Baseball Novels of John R. Tunis." *SABR Review of Books*, Premiere Issue, 1986.

Cantwell, Robert. "A Sneering Laugh with the Bases Loaded." *Sports Illustrated*, April 23, 1962.

Cantwell, Robert. "Sports Was Box-Office Poison." *Sports Illustrated*, September 15, 1969.

Hagerty, Sheward. "The Hero." [Frank Merriwell]. *Yale Alumni Review*, November 1970

Kavanaugh, Jack. "Baseball Joe Matson: The Greatest Player Who Never Was." *SABR Review of Books*, Premiere Issue, 1986.

Lynn, Arthur. "Love in the Funny Papers." *Varsity*, January-February 1949.

McCallum, Jack. "A Hero for All Times." *Sports Illustrated*, January 7, 1980.

Nolan, Michelle. "Dan Duffy, College Athlete." *Comics Buyer's Guide* (#1609), October 2005.

_____. "Dick Cole." *Comics Buyer's Guide* (#1637), January 2008.

_____. "Frank Merriwell: Playing Around in the Ivy League." *Comics Buyer's Guide* (#1612), January 2006.

_____. "Hit the Diamond with Grand Slam Films." *Big Reel* (#399), July-August 2008.

_____. "Ozark Ike." *Comics Buyer's Guide* (#1639), March 2008.

_____. "Setting the Standard for Prolific Production" [Ned Pines]. *Comic Book Marketplace* (#96), November 2002.

Smith, Leverette T. "Baseball Juveniles: Where We All Started." *SABR Review of Books*, Premiere Issue, 1986.

Index